Anonymous

Official Record of the Proceedings and Debates of the Australasian Federation Conference,

1890, held in the Parliament House, Melbourne

Anonymous

Official Record of the Proceedings and Debates of the Australasian Federation Conference, *1890, held in the Parliament House, Melbourne*

ISBN/EAN: 9783337152970

Printed in Europe, USA, Canada, Australia, Japan

Cover: Foto ©Suzi / pixelio.de

More available books at **www.hansebooks.com**

OF THE

PROCEEDINGS AND DEBATES

OF THE

AUSTRALASIAN

FEDERATION CONFERENCE, 1890,

HELD IN

THE PARLIAMENT HOUSE, MELBOURNE.

By Authority:
ROBERT S. BRAIN, GOVERNMENT PRINTER, MELBOURNE.
[REPRINTED BY CHARLES POTTER, GOVERNMENT PRINTER, SYDNEY.]

1890.

THE Proceedings of the Federation Conference, held in Melbourne in February, 1890, were carefully reported by the Official Shorthand Writers of the Victorian Parliamentary Staff, and this Volume contains a reprint of their admirable reports.

CONTENTS.

	Page.
Address	3, 29, 279, 281
Election of President	6
Appointment of Secretary	7
Rules of Procedure	7
Members of the Conference	8
Admission of the Press	8
Notices of Motion	15
Days and Hours of Meeting	15
Business for Meeting	15
Reporting the Proceedings of the Conference	16
Adjournments	16, 18, 20, 22, 24, 32, 286
Federation of the Colonies	19, 21, 23, 25, 33, 96, 146, 202
Admission of the remoter Australasian Colonies	26
National Australasian Convention	27, 246
Constitution of the Convention	27
Extension of Powers of Federal Council	28, 263
Signing and forwarding Address	31
Forwarding Proceedings and Debates to Secretary of State	31
Forwarding Proceedings and Debates to other Colonies	31
Official Record of Proceedings to be Signed	31, 283
Communications addressed to the Conference	31
Convener of the Convention	32, 284
Vote of thanks to the President	32, 284
Vote of thanks to the Secretary	32, 285
Debates of the Conference	33
Extracts from the British Press	289

a

NOTICES OF MOTION MOVED IN DEBATES.

                                                                                                 Page.

MOVED by the Hon. Sir HENRY PARKES; seconded by the Hon. A. DEAKIN,—

    "That, in the opinion of this Conference, the best interests and the present and future prosperity of the 'Australasian' Colonies will be promoted by an early union under the Crown, and, while fully recognising the valuable services of the Members of the Convention of 1883 in founding the Federal Council, it declares its opinion that the seven years which have since elapsed have developed the national life of 'Australasia' in population, in wealth, in the discovery of resources, and in self-governing capacity, to an extent which justifies the higher act, at all times contemplated, of the union of these colonies, under one legislative and executive Government, on principles just to the several colonies" 33

    NOTE.—On mover's motion amended by the substitution of the words "Australian" and "Australia" for the words "Australasian" and "Australasia," and adopted 245

Moved by the Hon. Captain RUSSELL; seconded by the Hon. Sir J. HALL,—

    "That to the Union of the Australian Colonies contemplated by the foregoing resolution, the remoter Australasian Colonies shall be entitled to admission at such times and on such conditions as may be hereafter agreed upon."... 245

Moved by the Hon. A. DEAKIN; seconded by the Hon. Sir J. HALL,—

    "That the members of the Conference should take such steps as may be necessary to induce the Legislatures of their respective colonies to appoint 'delegates' to a National Australasian Convention, empowered to consider and report upon an adequate scheme for a Federal Constitution" 246

    NOTE.—On motion of the Hon. A. I. CLARK, the words "during the present year" inserted before the word "delegates," and adopted 259, 261

Moved by the Hon. A. DEAKIN; seconded by the Hon. WILLIAM MCMILLAN,—

"That the Convention should consist of seven members from each of the self-governing colonies, and four members from each of the Crown colonies" 261

NOTE.—On mover's motion amended by the addition of the words "not more than" before the words "seven" and "four," and adopted 261, 263

Moved by the Hon. A. DEAKIN; seconded by the Hon. J. A. COCKBURN,—

"That as some time must elapse before a Federal Constitution can be adopted, and as it is desirable that the colonies should at once take united action to provide for military defence, and for effective co-operation in other matters of common concern, it is advisable that the Federal Council should be employed for such purposes so far as its powers will permit, and with such an extension of its powers as may be decided upon, and that all the colonies should be represented on the Council" 263

NOTE.—Motion withdrawn 278

Moved by the Hon. Sir J. HALL; seconded by the Hon. J. A. COCKBURN,—

"TO THE QUEEN'S MOST EXCELLENT MAJESTY.
"MAY IT PLEASE YOUR MAJESTY,—

"We, Your Majesty's loyal and dutiful subjects, the Members of the Conference assembled in Melbourne to consider the question of creating for Australasia one Federal Government, and representing the Australasian Colonies, desire to approach Your Most Gracious Majesty with renewed expressions of our devoted attachment to your Majesty's throne and person.

"On behalf of Your Majesty's subjects throughout Australasia, we beg to express the fervent hope that Your Majesty's life may be long spared to reign over a prosperous and happy people.

"We most respectfully inform Your Majesty, that, after mature deliberation, we have unanimously agreed to the following resolutions:—

"1. That, in the opinion of this Conference, the best interests and the present and future prosperity of the Australian Colonies will be promoted by an early union under the Crown, and, while fully recognising the valuable services of the Members of the Convention of 1883 in founding the

Page.

Federal Council, it declares its opinion that the seven years which have since elapsed have developed the national life of Australia in population, in wealth, in the discovery of resources, and in self-governing capacity, to an extent which justifies the higher act, at all times contemplated, of the union of these colonies, under one Legislative and Executive Government, on principles just to the several colonies.

" 2. That to the union of the Australian Colonies contemplated by the foregoing resolution, the remoter Australasian Colonies shall be entitled to admission at such times and on such conditions as may be hereafter agreed upon.

" 3. That the members of the Conference shall take such steps as may be necessary to induce the Legislatures of their respective colonies to appoint, during the present year, delegates to a National Australasian Convention, empowered to consider and report upon an adequate scheme for a Federal Constitution.

" 4. That the Convention should consist of not more than seven members from each of the self-governing colonies, and not more than four members from each of the Crown Colonies"   281

Moved by the Hon. Sir J. HALL; seconded by the Hon. J. A. COCKBURN,—

" That the President do sign the foregoing address on behalf of the Conference, and present the same to His Excellency the Governor of Victoria, with a respectful request that he will be pleased to transmit such address to Her Majesty's Principal Secretary of State for the Colonies, for presentation to Her Most Gracious Majesty" 283

Moved by the Hon. Sir S. W. GRIFFITH ; seconded by the Hon. A. DEAKIN,—

" That the President forward copies of the Report of the Proceedings and Debates of the Conference to His Excellency the Governor of Victoria for transmission to the Right Honorable the Principal Secretary of State for the Colonies" 283

Moved by the Hon. A. DEAKIN; seconded by the Hon. T. PLAYFORD,—

" That the President forward copies of the Report of the Proceedings and Debates of the Conference to the representatives of the colonies at this Conference, for presentation to their respective Parliaments, and for general distribution" 283

Page.

Moved by the Hon. A. I. CLARK; seconded by the Hon. T. PLAYFORD,—

"That the Premier of Victoria be requested to act as Convener of the National Australasian Convention of Delegates to be appointed by the several Legislatures of the Australasian Colonies, and to arrange, upon consultation with the Premiers of the other colonies, the time and place of the meeting of the Convention" 284

Moved by the Hon. Sir HENRY PARKES; seconded by the Hon. J. M. MACROSSAN,—

"That the thanks of the Conference be given to the Honorable Duncan Gillies for the services rendered by him as President of the Conference" 284

Moved by the Hon. J. A. COCKBURN; seconded by the Hon. Sir J. G. L. STEERE,—

"That the thanks of the Conference be given to Mr. George Henry Jenkins for the services rendered by him as Secretary to the Conference" 285

List of Speakers in Debates.

Page

NEW SOUTH WALES—

The Honorable Sir HENRY PARKES, G.C.M.G., Premier, and
Member of the Legislative Assembly 33, 68, 70, 71, 134
197, 201, 202, 233, 245, 255
257, 276, 278, 279, 280, 284

The Honorable WILLIAM MCMILLAN, Colonial Treasurer, and
Member of the Legislative Assembly 102, 117, 146, 257
261, 263, 272

NEW ZEALAND—

The Honorable Captain WILLIAM RUSSELL RUSSELL, Colonial
Secretary, and Member of the House of Representatives...123, 245
273

The Honorable Sir JOHN HALL, K.C.M.G., Member of the
House of Representatives............................. 174, 245, 253, 256
257, 261, 281, 283

QUEENSLAND—

The Honorable Sir SAMUEL WALKER GRIFFITH, K.C.M.G.,
Member of the Legislative Assembly 49, 102, 198, 258
259, 262, 280, 283

The Honorable JOHN MURTAGH MACROSSAN, Colonial
Secretary, and Member of the Legislative Assembly 184, 274

SOUTH AUSTRALIA—

The Honorable JOHN ALEXANDER COCKBURN, M.D., London,
Premier, and Member of the Legislative Assembly 129, 272
282, 285

The Honorable THOMAS PLAYFORD, Member of the Legislative
Assembly............ 60, 68, 76, 77, 90, 96, 97, 98, 102, 104, 105, 117
118, 120, 180, 181, 188, 196, 197
199, 244, 251, 257, 258, 259, 280

TASMANIA—

The Honorable ANDREW INGLIS CLARK, Attorney-General,
and Member of the House of Assembly............ 96, 121, 134, 135
188, 259, 275, 284

The Honorable BOLTON STAFFORD BIRD, Treasurer, and Member of the House of Assembly...................... 118, 158, 187, 256

VICTORIA—

The Honorable DUNCAN GILLIES, Premier and Member of the
Legislative Assembly 68, 232, 257, 259, 278, 279, 284, 286

The Honorable ALFRED DEAKIN, Chief Secretary, and Member
of the Legislative Assembly 48, 70, 74, 118, 134, 246, 261
262, 263, 276
278, 283, 286

WESTERN AUSTRALIA—

The Honorable Sir JAMES GEORGE LEE STEERE, Speaker of
the Legislative Council, and Member of the Executive
Council 114, 157, 188, 285

Extracts from the British Press.

	PAGE.		PAGE.
Birmingham Post	289, 305	Chronicle	369, 411, 432, 434
Glasgow Mail	289, 311, 386	Inquirer	371
Manchester Courier	292	Telegraph	371
Daily Chronicle	295, 313	Globe and Traveller	378
St. James' Gazette	295, 324, 341	Reynolds' Newspaper	380, 438
Pall Mall Gazette	296, 341, 359	Observer	381
Economist	297	Edinburgh Scottish	
Daily News	301, 359	Leader	384
Leeds Mercury	304, 387	Leeds Yorkshire Post	389
Birmingham Gazette	309, 367	Bristol Times	393
Bradford Observer	316	Bristol Western Daily	
Nottingham Guardian	318, 403	Press	394
Ipswich Times	319	Newcastle Journal	395
Leicester Post	319, 398	Nottingham Express	401, 441
Daily Graphic	320, 367, 413	Dundee Advertiser	404
Times	321, 347, 454	Aberdeen Free Press	405
Echo	325	Cork Constitution	408
Liverpool Post	326	Dundee Courier	410
Liverpool Mercury	302, 327, 381	Weekly Budget	413
Manchester Guardian	329	Manchester Examiner	383, 414
Evening News	331	Edinburgh Scotsman	415
Advertiser	331, 375	Commonwealth	419
Belfast News Letter	335	Guardian	419
Dumfries Standard	338	Brighton Gazette	420
Globe	339, 446, 463	John Bull	422
Evening News Post	340	Richmond Herald	425
Glasgow Herald	342	Tablet	426
Newcastle Leader	345	Edinburgh Scots Observer	430
Standard	349	Spectator	434
Saturday Review	353	Scottish Leader	440
Post	360	Home News	443
Statist	362, 427	Railway Journal	444
Investors' Guardian	365	Manchester Guardian	449, 456
Star	366	The Speaker	459

[*The following Address was agreed to by the Australasian Federation Conference, on the 14th February, 1890.*]

TO THE QUEEN'S MOST EXCELLENT MAJESTY.

MAY IT PLEASE YOUR MAJESTY,—

We, Your Majesty's loyal and dutiful subjects, the Members of the Conference assembled in Melbourne to consider the question of creating for Australasia one Federal Government, and representing the Australasian Colonies, desire to approach Your Most Gracious Majesty with renewed expressions of our devoted attachment to Your Majesty's Throne and Person.

On behalf of Your Majesty's subjects throughout Australasia we beg to express the fervent hope that Your Majesty's life may be long spared to reign over a prosperous and happy people.

We most respectfully inform Your Majesty that, after mature deliberation, we have unanimously agreed to the following resolutions:—

> 1. That, in the opinion of this Conference, the best interests and the present and future prosperity of the Australian Colonies will be promoted by an early union under the Crown; and, while fully recognising the valuable services of the Members of the Convention of 1883 in founding the Federal Council, it declares its opinion that the seven years which have since elapsed have developed the national life of Australia in population, in wealth, in the discovery of resources, and in self-governing capacity to an extent which justifies the higher act, at all times contemplated, of the union of these Colonies, under one legislative and executive Government, on principles just to the several Colonies.

2. That to the union of the Australian Colonies contemplated by the foregoing resolution, the remoter Australasian Colonies shall be entitled to admission at such times and on such conditions as may be hereafter agreed upon.

3. That the Members of the Conference should take such steps as may be necessary to induce the Legislatures of their respective Colonies to appoint, during the present year, Delegates to a National Australasian Convention, empowered to consider and report upon an adequate scheme for a Federal Constitution.

4. That the Convention should consist of not more than seven Members from each of the self-governing Colonies, and not more than four Members from each of the Crown Colonies.

D. GILLIES,
President.

Parliament House,
   Melbourne.

THE PROCEEDINGS

OF THE

FEDERATION CONFERENCE, 1890.

HELD IN THE PARLIAMENT HOUSE, MELBOURNE.

No. 1.

THURSDAY, 6TH FEBRUARY, 1890.

Present:

New South Wales
- The Honorable Sir HENRY PARKES, G.C.M.G., Premier, and Member of the Legislative Assembly.
- The Honorable WILLIAM MCMILLAN, Colonial Treasurer, and Member of the Legislative Assembly.

New Zealand
- The Honorable Captain WILLIAM RUSSELL RUSSELL, Colonial Secretary, and Member of the House of Representatives.
- The Honorable Sir JOHN HALL, K.C.M.G., Member of the House of Representatives.

Queensland
- The Honorable Sir SAMUEL WALKER GRIFFITH, K.C.M.G., Member of the Legislative Assembly.
- The Honorable JOHN MURTAGH MACROSSAN, Colonial Secretary, and Member of the Legislative Assembly.

South Australia
- The Honorable JOHN ALEXANDER COCKBURN, M.D., Lond., Premier, and Member of the Legislative Assembly.
- The Honorable THOMAS PLAYFORD, Member of the Legislative Assembly.

Tasmania
- The Honorable ANDREW INGLIS CLARK, Attorney-General, and Member of the House of Assembly.
- The Honorable BOLTON STAFFORD BIRD, Treasurer, and Member of the House of Assembly.

Victoria	The Honorable Duncan Gillies, Premier, and Member of the Legislative Assembly. The Honorable Alfred Deakin, Chief Secretary, and Member of the Legislative Assembly.
Western Australia	The Honorable Sir James George Lee Steere, Speaker of the Legislative Council, and Member of the Executive Council.

Election of President.

Sir Henry Parkes.—I beg to propose, and I have much pleasure in proposing, that the Honorable Duncan Gillies do take the chair as President of this Conference. Mr. Gillies is not only the Premier of one of the largest colonies, but he has held that distinguished position with the assent of the inhabitants for a number of years. He is not only that, but one of the oldest and most deservedly respected public men in Australia, and, seeing that this Conference assembles in the capital of the colony which he so well represents in the councils of this country, I think it is not only an act becoming in ourselves but an honor, and it is really a great honor, which is his just due. I am sure I need say nothing more to commend my motion to your acceptance.

Dr. Cockburn.—I beg to second the motion. I feel that not only is the honor of presiding over such a Conference due to Mr. Gillies, as the Premier of the colony in which the Conference is held, but also owing to the very important part he has hitherto played in the momentous question of the Federation of the Australian Colonies. As far as the general question is concerned, and as far as federating in every possible matter of detail, from the first Mr. Gillies has taken a most prominent position, and I feel that this Conference is doing no more than is due to place him in the chair.

Sir Henry Parkes put the question which was carried unanimously.

The Honorable D. Gillies took the chair.

The President.—In taking the chair I can only say I thank you very much indeed for the honor you have done me in placing me in this position, and I thank Sir Henry Parkes and Dr. Cockburn for the agreeable way in which they have proposed that I should take this position. I am sure the duties of the position will be very simple, and I can only trust that during my presidency we will be in a position to arrive at conclusions, not only satisfactory to ourselves but for the advancement and prosperity of the whole of the Colonies of Australasia.

Sir HENRY PARKES.—It seems a step consequent on the course I have taken that the President of the Conference have the same rights and privileges, both as to expressing his opinions and voting, as other members of the Conference, and in any case of equality of votes that he have in addition a casting vote. I therefore move to that effect.

Dr. COCKBURN.—I second the motion. I think it is a very proper resolution, and that the conclusions of the Conference will be advanced by the President having a voice in the deliberations as well as in the decisions.

The PRESIDENT.—Of course I should have anticipated, under any circumstances, the President would have some little allowance, somewhat different from what is usually allowed in a Legislative Chamber. In this case we are met to do very important work, and no gentleman would like to occupy the chair unless he had more latitude than that usually allowed in the chair.

The question was put and carried.

APPOINTMENT OF SECRETARY.

Mr. DEAKIN moved,—That Mr. George Henry Jenkins be appointed Secretary to the Conference.

Mr. PLAYFORD seconded the motion.

The question was put and carried.

RULES OF PROCEDURE.

The PRESIDENT suggested that a little more latitude than usual in the Legislative Chamber should be permitted to the members of the Conference in dealing with the matters before it. He suggested the ordinary latitude in committee for gentlemen to speak several times should be permitted without any formal question being put.

Members of the Conference.

Sir Henry Parkes.—Might I say I think there should be entered on our Record of the Proceedings the names and the representative character of the several gentlemen who represent the respective colonies. I think it would be a mistake if our proceedings were silent on that point. I should imagine it will be sufficient if those gentlemen present themselves and say they are duly authorized to represent their colonies, without presenting any particular Commission.

The President read the names of the representatives present, who thereupon rose and announced that they were duly accredited to attend this Conference by their respective Governments.

Admission of the Press.

Sir Henry Parkes.—Mr. President : Under ordinary circumstances I should be indisposed to depart from what has usually been the practice of not admitting the public to the proceedings of a body of this kind. But this is unlike any other Conference that has assembled in these colonies. All Conferences—and I believe I am correct in so speaking—have assembled under very general powers, and they have, in point of fact, actually transacted a variety of matters of business. This Conference, however, has assembled through unusual circumstances to consider one question alone, and that is a question which more directly interests the inhabitants of all the colonies than most questions considered by bodies of this kind. Independently of all that, I think the Conference must partake of a character unlike that of other bodies. Most of the Conferences, speaking from some personal experiences, have been more of a consultative character than of a deliberative one. That is, in their proceedings men have said things which naturally enough they have desired to modify, entirely alter, or withdraw. They have spoken sometimes under a misapprehension, which they have to correct, and altogether the proceedings have been, to a large extent, of a conversational character, and exercised by those influences which enter into a private conversation ; but this Conference, if I understand the object of its assembling, will have to fully consider—which we can only do by debating—questions submitted in stated resolutions, and considering that it will be to a large extent a deliberative body to debate questions rather than enter into minute consultation as to the particular form which matters are to take, and also considering the vast importance to the populations of these colonies which the proceedings will present, I should think that the circumstances would be met if we came to the conclusion that for some time at the opening of every sitting we should be considered as in committee, while any matter of a disputatious character, admitting of new views and explanations, and all that kind of thing which arises in committee, should be considered with closed doors; but when the business of which the Conference was seized by a stated resolution from the chair, that the public should be admitted. That is the view of the case which seems to meet, I believe, the general desire of the public, and would give this body confidence in transacting its real consultative business in the ordinary way of a private committee.

I therefore move,—

1. That whenever the Conference is in committee the public be not admitted.
2. That when the Conference is engaged in debating matters formally submitted by resolution the public be admitted.

Dr. COCKBURN.—I think the question depends on what the proceedings of the Conference are to be. If the proceedings are to be more of a deliberative character, and to touch the question more in the general bearings than in the details, then I can very freely second the resolution. If, however, the Conference intends to go into details, I think the resolution might act to the detriment of the business of the Conference. If the intention is that we should deal with the question generally, without attempting to enter into the closest details, then I think there can be no objection, but, on the contrary, there would be every advantage in having the Press present.

Sir JAMES LEE STEERE.—A resolution might be submitted when we are not in committee.

The President.—Of course in that case notice would have been given, and the members would have an opportunity of discussing it, but if it were thought desirable before concluding the matter to consider it in committee, that might be done, and then we could have an opportunity of free discussion while the Press was not present.

Sir Samuel Griffith.—I apprehend we are met here principally for the purpose of exchange of ideas amongst ourselves, as representing the public opinions of the different colonies, as to how far Federation is practicable at the present time, and to that extent we should be witnesses giving our own opinion as to the state of public opinion. We shall be exchanging ideas. Some members of the Conference believe that a perfect Federation is possible now, others that it is not practicable, and they may feel it their duty to point out the difficulties. And those difficulties will have to be met. We cannot shut our eyes to them, and they will be the real difficulties that will meet us when we go to our respective Parliaments, and the doubt I entertain is how far it is desirable those objections should be stated and combated in public. We might possibly give handles to our opponents, or, on the other hand, furnish excellent answers to their objections, but that is the great part of what we shall do. We cannot arrive at any definite resolutions as to a definite form of Federation. On the whole, I come to the conclusion that the greater advantage will be in allowing the public to be present when discussing the general questions.

Mr. Playford.—Without disapproving of the admission of the Press, we have no precedent for it in Conferences, either in the colonies or in America. The Americans never admitted the Press when they made their Constitution; the Canadians at Quebec did not admit the Press; and you cannot point out, I believe, one single precedent for admitting the Press to deliberations of this sort. At the same time, I am willing that the Press should be admitted, and that we should state our case, so that the public may thoroughly understand the grounds on which we have come to certain conclusions. It is utterly impossible that the question of detail can be kept absolutely in the background—the whole subject is based on detail. The Conference we are asked to attend, according to the Commission drawn out by the Governor, and signed by the Acting Administrator of the Government, is that we are met here for the purpose of considering whether an additional forward step with regard to Federation is possible at the present time or not, and in the very nature of things we ought to be able to go back to our Parliament and say that we considered this question along with the other representatives from the other colonies, and we are prepared to say to what extent the Federation shall go. If we just pass a bald resolution to the effect that we are ripe for Federation, one may think that by Federation we will be going on the lines of the United States, another that we are going on the lines of the Dominion of Canada, another the Swiss Republic, another on the lines of the States of Holland. Nobody would know what we meant. We should talk a lot of platitudes, and the people throughout the colonies would not understand what we were driving at. We must consider this point: Is the time ripe for the further extension of Federation? If so, to what extent? And unless you answer those two questions, we shall fail in our duty to those who have appointed us and sent us here. I speak for the two Houses of Parliament in South Australia. It will be impossible to discuss these questions without going in some cases into very close details, and giving reasons why we want the extension or limitation of powers and so on. I shall be quite prepared to do my part publicly, and prepared that the Press should take it down, and that the people of the Australian Colonies should know my views on the matter. We are not met for the purpose of building a Constitution, or drafting a Bill for the approval of the Legislatures, and to go on to the Imperial Parliament; but I contend that the people of these colonies expect us to do more than pass a bald resolution. We must show the limits within which we can go in regard to Federation.

Mr. McMillan.—The remarks of the last speaker lead me to ask what is really the intention of this Conference, and I think we should understand that at the very onset. It seems to me if there is one thing we have not to discuss it is details. It seems to me that the Conference has met together to frame certain resolutions, the outcome of which will be a Convention under the sanction of the different Parliaments. We are here because we believe that a large wave of public opinion has gone over the Australasian Colonies, and no man can judge absolutely to what extent that wave has permeated the masses. No man can say that in his colony there is a large and overwhelming majority in favour of Federation. He cannot say it with certainty. Now the whole object of all our controversy here will be to decide as to the form of that Convention. We are here not to say what particular kind of Federation shall take place in the future, but what is the limit of that Federation, but we are here to decide whether there is such a wave of public opinion throughout these colonies that it has removed the question from the mere sentimental airiness in which it has existed for some years past and has brought it into the region of practical politics; therefore our resolutions, I take it, will, to a great extent, declare that the time is ripe when this matter should be discussed by all the different colonies, and the outcome of this, I should hope, would be that all the delegates here will decide that the colonies should be asked through their Parliaments to send representative men, absolutely untrammelled, to a Convention to discuss the whole of this great question in all its bearings, both generally and in detail. But it seems to me that for us to enter into details in a discussion of this question in this Conference will lead to a great deal of difficulty, insuperable difficulty among ourselves, and great difficulties when we meet our Parliaments when we come into session again. The great reason for admitting the Press is that the discussion is to be, on broad and public lines, on the question whether public opinion has advanced so far that we proceed to the formation of a Convention.

Sir JOHN HALL.—I think it is premature to discuss now how far we should go into detail. The proper time for that will be when the resolutions are before us. The only question now is how far our proceedings should be open to the public, and I submit that Sir Henry Parkes' proposition is a very practical one. If honorable members look at it they will see that it is very elastic. Whenever, either at the commencement of or during our sittings, the time arrives when we think the Press should be excluded, we can declare ourselves in committee. If we wish to discuss details giving rise to differences of opinion which it may not be wise to give to the world, we have only to do so in committee. On the other hand, if we are giving reasons why an earnest attempt should be made to form a grand Federation of the colonies, which reasons it is desirable that the public should know, then the Press will be admitted. I support the resolution, and leave for consideration hereafter how far we shall go into detail.

Sir JAMES LEE STEERE.—I agree that we should be departing from the question before the Conference in saying what shall be our future deliberations. The question is whether the Press shall be admitted; I am entirely in favour of it. Mr. Playford says it is without precedent. I think one of the great reasons why these Conventions have to a certain extent failed has been because the Press has not been present. They have not received the support in the colonies and been so successful as they would if the Press had been admitted. I think the balance is all in favour of the proceedings being public; I shall therefore support the motion.

Mr. BIRD.—It appears to me that we can hardly compare ourselves in this Conference with the Conventions that were appointed and that met to draft a Constitution, either for Canada or for the United States, both of which Conventions, as we well know, met in secret, and all their deliberations were kept secret, unless it was our intention to frame a Constitution here, as was done by those bodies, for recommendation to the several Parliaments of the States or Provinces. It appears to me that the case with us is very different from theirs. I am certainly in favour of the Conference being open to the public when we are discussing those broad questions of a general character which do not, if I may use the term, descend to detail; but it appears to me that, before we shall be prepared to discuss generally such leading resolutions as we are prepared to discuss in public, it will be almost necessary to spend a considerable time in discussion in committee, and those discussions must necessarily involve a good deal of talk about the details which at times must be considered before the resolutions of a general character can be properly debated. I am in doubt whether the resolution submitted exactly and fully meets what is desired, for, according to the second portion of this resolution, it would be open to any member of this Conference to submit a resolution which would involve a considerable amount of detail, and yet as the resolution stands, being submitted as a resolution at the Conference, it must be discussed in the presence of the public or the Press. I think, instead of this, we should have something which would help us when a question which involves very debatable details is introduced by a resolution—there should be a power of referring that to a committee, otherwise, according to this, any member might insist on the discussion being carried on before the public, even though the resolution as submitted formally was of a character involving many details which we would all like to have discussed in private. I suggest a little alteration in that direction, in order to make the Conference open to the public in regard to the more general resolutions, and exclude the public on those occasions when we want to go into details, arranging that those should be discussed in committee, and not take place in connection with the discussion of the resolutions to be formally submitted when the Press is present.

Sir SAMUEL GRIFFITH.—Suppose any member of the Conference proposes a resolution with details in, that can be referred to the committee at once for discussion.

Sir HENRY PARKES.—If any notice whatever is given, the Conference, before it proceeds to its business in its own possession, can discuss that motion, whether it is a motion that should be proceeded with in committee. I apprehend the Conference will be in committee when it first meets every day; and no resolution could be proceeded with until there is an opportunity of deciding it in committee. Suppose I give notice of a resolution full of details as to how a Federal Constitution should be constructed, I could not, by any possibility, proceed with that until the Conference had had an opportunity of considering it in committee.

The question was put and carried.

Notices of Motion.

It was agreed, on the suggestion of the President, that all notices of motion must be given on the day preceding the next meeting, or that if any honorable member desired to bring on suddenly any important motion it must be with the leave of the whole of the members of the Conference present.

Days and Hours of Meeting.

The Conference agreed to sit from day to day as the Conference might determine. It was agreed that the hour of meeting each day should be eleven o'clock.

Business for Next Meeting.

The PRESIDENT asked if members of the Conference desired to give any notices of motion for the next day of meeting.

Sir HENRY PARKES said he desired to give notice of the following motion, to test what he thought must be tested, viz., as to the feeling of the Conference as to the time being ripe for Federation :—

> That, in the opinion of this Conference, the best interests and the present and future prosperity of the Australasian Colonies will be promoted by an early union under the Crown, and, while fully recognising the valuable services of the Members of the Convention of 1883 in founding the Federal Council, it declares its opinion that the seven years which have since elapsed have developed the national life of Australasia in population, in wealth, in the discovery of resources, and in self-governing capacity, to an extent which justifies the higher act, at all times contemplated, of the union of these Colonies, under one legislative and executive Government on principles just to the several Colonies.

Mr. DEAKIN.—I will not give notice of the following resolutions to-day, desiring that they first be considered in committee. As the framing of these resolutions is a matter of some importance, I now only suggest in the rough what seems to me to be the necessary supplement of the resolution to be moved by Sir Henry Parkes:—

1. That the members of the Conference should take such steps as may be necessary to induce the Legislatures of their respective colonies to appoint delegates to a National Convention, empowered to consider and report upon an adequate scheme for a Federal Constitution.

2. The Convention should consist of seven members from each of the self-governing colonies and four members from each of the Crown Colonies.

3. As some time must elapse before a Federal Constitution can be adopted, and as it is desirable that the colonies should at once take united action to provide for military defence and for effective co-operation in other matters of common concern, it is advisable that the Federal Council should be employed for such purposes so far as its powers will permit, and with such an extension of its powers as may be decided upon, and that all the colonies should be represented on the Council.

REPORTING THE PROCEEDINGS OF THE CONFERENCE.

On the suggestion of Mr. DEAKIN, it was agreed that the Conference should from time to time give directions when the Conference was open to the press and public, and that *Hansard* should give the usual full report.

ADJOURNMENT.

Mr. DEAKIN moved,—That the Conference do now adjourn until to-morrow.

The question was put and carried.

And then the Conference, at twenty minutes past four o'clock, adjourned.

D. GILLIES,
President.

GEORGE H. JENKINS,
Secretary to the Federation Conference.

THE PROCEEDINGS

OF THE

FEDERATION CONFERENCE, 1890.

HELD IN THE PARLIAMENT HOUSE, MELBOURNE.

No. 2.
FRIDAY, 7th FEBRUARY, 1890.

Present:

New South Wales ... The Honorable WILLIAM McMILLAN.

New Zealand ... { The Honorable Captain WILLIAM RUSSELL RUSSELL.
The Honorable Sir JOHN HALL, K.C.M.G.

Queensland ... { The Honorable Sir SAMUEL WALKER GRIFFITH, K.C.M.G.
The Honorable JOHN MURTAGH MACROSSAN.

South Australia ... { The Honorable JOHN ALEXANDER COCKBURN, M.D.
The Honorable THOMAS PLAYFORD.

Tasmania ... { The Honorable ANDREW INGLIS CLARK.
The Honorable BOLTON STAFFORD BIRD.

Victoria ... { The Honorable DUNCAN GILLIES.
The Honorable ALFRED DEAKIN.

Western Australia { The Honorable Sir JAMES GEORGE LEE STEERE.

The PRESIDENT took the Chair.

The PRESIDENT expressed his regret that Sir Henry Parkes was not well enough to be present, and it was agreed that the Conference should adjourn until two o'clock.

On the PRESIDENT taking the Chair at two o'clock, Mr. McMillan announced that the indisposition of his colleague still continued, and that Sir Henry Parkes asked the favour of an adjournment till Monday next, when he hoped to be able to attend.

ADJOURNMENT.

Mr. DEAKIN moved,—That the Conference do now adjourn until Monday next.

The question was put and carried.

And then the Conference, at fifteen minutes past two o'clock, adjourned.

D. GILLIES,
President.

GEORGE H. JENKINS,
Secretary to the Federation Conference.

THE PROCEEDINGS

OF THE

FEDERATION CONFERENCE, 1890.

HELD IN THE PARLIAMENT HOUSE, MELBOURNE.

No. 3.
MONDAY, 10TH FEBRUARY, 1890.

Present:

New South Wales — The Honorable Sir HENRY PARKES, G.C.M.G.
The Honorable WILLIAM MCMILLAN.

New Zealand ... — The Honorable Captain WILLIAM RUSSELL RUSSELL.
The Honorable Sir JOHN HALL, K.C.M.G.

Queensland ... — The Honorable Sir SAMUEL WALKER GRIFFITH, K.C.M.G.
The Honorable JOHN MURTAGH MACROSSAN.

South Australia ... — The Honorable JOHN ALEXANDER COCKBURN, M.D.
The Honorable THOMAS PLAYFORD.

Tasmania... ... — The Honorable ANDREW INGLIS CLARK.
The Honorable BOLTON STAFFORD BIRD.

Victoria ... ... — The Honorable DUNCAN GILLIES.
The Honorable ALFRED DEAKIN.

Western Australia — The Honorable Sir JAMES GEORGE LEE STEERE.

The PRESIDENT took the Chair.

FEDERATION OF THE COLONIES.

Sir HENRY PARKES moved,—That, in the opinion of this Conference, the best interests and the present and future prosperity of the Australasian Colonies will be promoted by an early union under the Crown, and, while fully recognizing the valuable services of the Members of the Convention of 1883 in founding the Federal Council, it declares its opinion that the seven years which have since elapsed have developed the national life of Australasia in population, in wealth, in the discovery of resources, and in self-governing capacity to an extent which justifies the higher act, at all times contemplated, of the union of these Colonies, under one legislative and executive Government, on principles just to the several Colonies.

Mr. DEAKIN seconded the motion.

Sir SAMUEL GRIFFITH addressed the Conference.

Mr. PLAYFORD addressed the Conference.

Mr. DEAKIN addressed the Conference.

Mr. CLARK moved, That the debate be now adjourned.

The question was put and carried.

ADJOURNMENT.

Mr. DEAKIN moved,—That the Conference do now adjourn until to-morrow.

The question was put and carried.

And then the Conference, at forty-five minutes past five o'clock, adjourned.

D. GILLIES,
President.

GEORGE H. JENKINS,
Secretary to the Federation Conference.

THE PROCEEDINGS

OF THE

FEDERATION CONFERENCE, 1890.

HELD IN THE PARLIAMENT HOUSE, MELBOURNE.

No. 4.

TUESDAY, 11TH FEBRUARY, 1890.

Present:

New South Wales
{ The Honorable Sir HENRY PARKES, G.C.M.G.
{ The Honorable WILLIAM MCMILLAN.

New Zealand ...
{ The Honorable Captain WILLIAM RUSSELL RUSSELL.
{ The Honorable Sir JOHN HALL, K.C.M.G.

Queensland ...
{ The Honorable Sir SAMUEL WALKER GRIFFITH, K.C.M.G.
{ The Honorable JOHN MURTAGH MACROSSAN.

South Australia ...
{ The Honorable JOHN ALEXANDER COCKBURN, M.D.
{ The Honorable THOMAS PLAYFORD.

Tasmania...
{ The Honorable ANDREW INGLIS CLARK.
{ The Honorable BOLTON STAFFORD BIRD.

Victoria ...
{ The Honorable DUNCAN GILLIES.
{ The Honorable ALFRED DEAKIN.

Western Australia
{ The Honorable Sir JAMES GEORGE LEE STEERE.

The PRESIDENT took the Chair.

FEDERATION OF THE COLONIES.

The debate was resumed on the question,—That, in the opinion of this Conference, the best interests and the present and future prosperity of the Australasian Colonies will be promoted by an early union under the Crown, and, while fully recognizing the valuable services of the Members of the Convention of 1883 in founding the Federal Council, it declares its opinion that the seven years which have since elapsed have developed the national life of Australasia in population, in wealth, in the discovery of resources, and in self-governing capacity to an extent which justifies the higher act, at all times contemplated, of the union of these colonies under one legislative and executive Government, on principles just to the several colonies.

Mr. CLARK addressed the Conference.

Sir JAMES LEE STEERE addressed the Conference.

Captain RUSSELL addressed the Conference.

Dr. COCKBURN addressed the Conference.

Mr. McMILLAN moved, That the debate be now adjourned.

The question was put and carried.

ADJOURNMENT.

Mr. DEAKIN moved,—That the Conference do now adjourn until to-morrow.

The question was put and carried.

And then the Conference, at twenty minutes past four o'clock, adjourned.

D. GILLIES,
President.

GEORGE H. JENKINS,
Secretary to the Federation Conference.

THE PROCEEDINGS

OF THE

FEDERATION CONFERENCE, 1890.

HELD IN THE PARLIAMENT HOUSE, MELBOURNE.

No. 5.
WEDNESDAY, 12th FEBRUARY, 1890.
Present:

New South Wales
- The Honorable Sir HENRY PARKES, G.C.M.G.
- The Honorable WILLIAM MCMILLAN.

New Zealand
- The Honorable Captain WILLIAM RUSSELL RUSSELL.
- The Honorable Sir JOHN HALL, K.C.M.G.

Queensland
- The Honorable Sir SAMUEL WALKER GRIFFITH, K.C.M.G.
- The Honorable JOHN MURTAGH MACROSSAN.

South Australia
- The Honorable JOHN ALEXANDER COCKBURN, M.D.
- The Honorable THOMAS PLAYFORD.

Tasmania
- The Honorable ANDREW INGLIS CLARK.
- The Honorable BOLTON STAFFORD BIRD.

Victoria
- The Honorable DUNCAN GILLIES.
- The Honorable ALFRED DEAKIN.

Western Australia
- The Honorable Sir JAMES GEORGE LEE STEERE.

The President took the Chair.

FEDERATION OF THE COLONIES.

The debate was resumed on the question,—That, in the opinion of this Conference, the best interests and the present and future prosperity of the Australasian Colonies will be promoted by an early union under the Crown, and, while fully recognizing the valuable services of the Members of the Convention of 1883 in founding the Federal Council, it declares its opinion that the seven years which have since elapsed have developed the national life of Australasia in population, in wealth, in the discovery of resources, and in self-governing capacity to an extent which justifies the higher act, at all times contemplated, of the union of these colonies, under one legislative and executive Government, on principles just to the several colonies.

Mr. McMILLAN addressed the Conference.

Mr. BIRD addressed the Conference.

Sir JOHN HALL addressed the Conference.

Mr. MACROSSAN addressed the Conference.

Sir HENRY PARKES moved, That the debate be now adjourned.

The question was put and carried.

ADJOURNMENT.

Mr. DEAKIN moved,—That the Conference do now adjourn until to-morrow.

The question was put and carried.

And then the Conference, at twenty minutes past four o'clock, adjourned.

D. GILLIES,
President.

GEORGE H. JENKINS,
Secretary to the Federation Conference.

THE PROCEEDINGS
OF THE
FEDERATION CONFERENCE, 1890.

HELD IN THE PARLIAMENT HOUSE, MELBOURNE.

No. 6.
THURSDAY, 13TH FEBRUARY, 1890.

Present:

New South Wales
- The Honorable Sir HENRY PARKES, G.C.M.G.
- The Honorable WILLIAM MCMILLAN.

New Zealand
- The Honorable Captain WILLIAM RUSSELL RUSSELL.
- The Honorable Sir JOHN HALL, K.C.M.G.

Queensland
- The Honorable Sir SAMUEL WALKER GRIFFITH, K.C.M.G.
- The Honorable JOHN MURTAGH MACROSSAN.

South Australia
- The Honorable JOHN ALEXANDER COCKBURN, M.D.
- The Honorable THOMAS PLAYFORD.

Tasmania
- The Honorable ANDREW INGLIS CLARK.
- The Honorable BOLTON STAFFORD BIRD.

Victoria
- The Honorable DUNCAN GILLIES.
- The Honorable ALFRED DEAKIN.

Western Australia
- The Honorable Sir JAMES GEORGE LEE STEERE.

The PRESIDENT took the Chair.

FEDERATION OF THE COLONIES.

The debate was resumed on the question,—That, in the opinion of this Conference, the best interests and the present and future prosperity of the Australasian Colonies will be promoted by an early union under the Crown, and, while fully recognising the valuable services of the Members of the Convention of 1883 in founding the Federal Council, it declares its opinion that the seven years which have since elapsed have developed the national life of Australasia in population, in wealth, in the discovery of resources, and in self-governing capacity to an extent which justifies the higher act, at all times contemplated, of the union of these colonies, under one legislative and executive Government, on principles just to the several colonies.

Sir HENRY PARKES again addressed the Conference.

The PRESIDENT addressed the Conference.

On the motion of Sir HENRY PARKES, the question was amended by omitting the word "Australasian" in the second line, and inserting in place thereof the word "Australian;" and by omitting the word "Australasia" in the sixth line, and inserting in place thereof the word "Australia."

The PRESIDENT then put the question,—That, in the opinion of this Conference, the best interests and the present and future prosperity of the Australian Colonies will be promoted by an early union under the Crown, and while fully recognising the valuable services of the Members of the Convention of 1883 in founding the Federal Council, it declares its opinion that the seven years which have since elapsed have developed the national life of Australia in population, in wealth, in the discovery of resources, and in self-governing capacity to an extent which justifies the higher act, at all times contemplated, of the union of these colonies, under one legislative and executive Government, on principles just to the several colonies—which was carried unanimously.

ADMISSION OF THE REMOTER AUSTRALASIAN COLONIES.

Captain RUSSELL moved,—That to the Union of the Australian Colonies contemplated by the foregoing resolution, the remoter Australasian Colonies shall be entitled to admission at such times and on such conditions as may be hereafter agreed upon.

Sir JOHN HALL seconded the motion.

The question was put and carried unanimously.

NATIONAL AUSTRALASIAN CONVENTION.

Mr. DEAKIN moved,—That the members of the Conference should take such steps as may be necessary to induce the Legislatures of their respective colonies to appoint delegates to a National Australasian Convention, empowered to consider and report upon an adequate scheme for a Federal Constitution.

Sir JOHN HALL seconded the motion, and addressed the Conference.

Mr. PLAYFORD addressed the Conference, and moved, as an amendment, that the words " to meet in Hobart some time early in 1891 " be added after the word " Constitution."

Mr. BIRD seconded the amendment, and addressed the Conference.

Sir JOHN HALL addressed the Conference.

Sir HENRY PARKES addressed the Conference.

Sir SAMUEL GRIFFITH addressed the Conference.

The PRESIDENT addressed the Conference.

Mr. CLARK addressed the Conference.

Mr. PLAYFORD, by leave, withdrew the amendment.

Mr. CLARK moved, as an amendment,—That the words "during the present year" be inserted after the word "appoint."

The amendment was put and carried.

The PRESIDENT then put the question,—That the members of the Conference should take such steps as may be necessary to induce the Legislatures of their respective colonies to appoint, during the present year, delegates to a National Australasian Convention, empowered to consider and report upon an adequate scheme for a Federal Constitution,—which was carried unanimously.

CONSTITUTION OF THE CONVENTION.

Mr. DEAKIN moved,—That the Convention should consist of not more than seven members from each of the self-governing colonies, and not more than four members from each of the Crown colonies.

Mr. MCMILLAN seconded the motion.

Sir JOHN HALL addressed the Conference.

Sir SAMUEL GRIFFITH addressed the Conference.

The question was put and carried unanimously.

EXTENSION OF POWERS OF FEDERAL COUNCIL.

Mr. DEAKIN moved,—That as some time must elapse before a Federal Constitution can be adopted, and as it is desirable that the colonies should at once take united action to provide for military defence and for effective co-operation in other matters of common concern, it is advisable that the Federal Council should be employed for such purposes so far as its powers will permit, and with such an extension of its powers as may be decided upon, and that all the colonies should be represented on the Council.

Dr. COCKBURN seconded the motion.

Mr. McMILLAN addressed the Conference.

Captain RUSSELL addressed the Conference.

Mr. MACROSSAN addressed the Conference.

Mr. CLARK addressed the Conference.

Sir HENRY PARKES addressed the Conference.

Mr. DEAKIN, by leave, withdrew the motion.

ADJOURNMENT.

Mr. DEAKIN moved,—That the Conference do now adjourn until to-morrow.

The question was put and carried.

And then the Conference, at forty minutes past five o'clock, adjourned.

D. GILLIES,
President.

GEORGE H. JENKINS,
Secretary to the Federation Conference.

THE PROCEEDINGS

OF THE

FEDERATION CONFERENCE, 1890.

HELD IN THE PARLIAMENT HOUSE, MELBOURNE

No. 7.
FRIDAY, 14TH FEBRUARY, 1890.

Present:

New South Wales
- The Honorable Sir HENRY PARKES, G.C.M.G.
- The Honorable WILLIAM MCMILLAN.

New Zealand
- The Honorable Captain WILLIAM RUSSELL RUSSELL.
- The Honorable Sir JOHN HALL, K.C.M.G.

Queensland
- The Honorable Sir SAMUEL WALKER GRIFFITH, K.C.M.G.
- The Honorable JOHN MURTAGH MACROSSAN.

South Australia
- The Honorable JOHN ALEXANDER COCKBURN, M.D.
- The Honorable THOMAS PLAYFORD.

Tasmania
- The Honorable ANDREW INGLIS CLARK.
- The Honorable BOLTON STAFFORD BIRD.

Victoria
- The Honorable DUNCAN GILLIES.
- The Honorable ALFRED DEAKIN.

Western Australia
- The Honorable Sir JAMES GEORGE LEE STEERE.

The PRESIDENT took the Chair.

ADDRESS TO THE QUEEN.

Sir JOHN HALL moved,—That the following Address to Her Majesty the Queen be agreed to by the Conference:—

To the Queen's Most Excellent Majesty.

MAY IT PLEASE YOUR MAJESTY—

We, Your Majesty's loyal and dutiful subjects, the Members of the Conference assembled in Melbourne to consider the question of creating for Australasia one Federal Government and representing the Australasian Colonies, desire to approach Your Most Gracious Majesty with renewed expressions of our devoted attachment to Your Majesty's Throne and Person.

On behalf of Your Majesty's subjects throughout Australasia, we beg to express the fervent hope that Your Majesty's life may be long spared to reign over a prosperous and happy people.

We most respectfully inform Your Majesty that, after mature deliberation, we have unanimously agreed to the following resolutions:—

1. That, in the opinion of this Conference, the best interests and the present and future prosperity of the Australian Colonies will be promoted by an early union under the Crown, and, while fully recognizing the valuable services of the Members of the Convention of 1883 in founding the Federal Council, it declares its opinion that the seven years which have since elapsed have developed the national life of Australia in population, in wealth, in the discovery of resources, and in self-governing capacity to an extent which justifies the higher act, at all times contemplated, of the union of these colonies, under one legislative and executive Government, on principles just to the several colonies.
2. That to the union of the Australian Colonies contemplated by the foregoing resolution, the remoter Australasian Colonies shall be entitled to admission at such times and on such conditions as may be hereafter agreed upon.
3. That the members of the Conference should take such steps as may be necessary to induce the Legislatures of their respective colonies to appoint, during the present year, delegates to a National Australasian Convention, empowered to consider and report upon an adequate scheme for a Federal Constitution.
4. That the Convention should consist of not more than seven members from each of the self-governing colonies, and not more than four members from each of the Crown colonies.

Dr. COCKBURN seconded the motion, and addressed the Conference.

The question was put and carried unanimously.

SIGNING AND FORWARDING ADDRESS.

Sir JOHN HALL moved,—That the President do sign the foregoing Address on behalf of the Conference, and present the same to His Excellency the Governor of Victoria, with a respectful request that he will be pleased to transmit such Address to Her Majesty's Principal Secretary of State for the Colonies for presentation to Her Most Gracious Majesty.

Dr. COCKBURN seconded the motion.

The question was put and carried unanimously.

FORWARDING PROCEEDINGS AND DEBATES TO SECRETARY OF STATE.

Sir SAMUEL GRIFFITH moved,—That the President forward copies of the Report of the Proceedings and Debates of the Conference to His Excellency the Governor of Victoria for transmission to the Right Honorable the Principal Secretary of State for the Colonies.

Mr. DEAKIN seconded the motion.

The question was put and carried unanimously.

FORWARDING PROCEEDINGS AND DEBATES TO OTHER COLONIES.

Mr. DEAKIN moved,—That the President forward copies of the Report of the Proceedings and Debates of the Conference to the Representatives of the Colonies at this Conference, for presentation to their respective Parliaments, and for general distribution.

Mr. PLAYFORD seconded the motion.

The question was put and carried unanimously.

OFFICIAL RECORD OF PROCEEDINGS TO BE SIGNED.

The Conference directed that the Official Record of its Proceedings should be signed by the President and the Secretary to the Conference.

COMMUNICATIONS ADDRESSED TO THE CONFERENCE.

The PRESIDENT announced that he had received communications from various persons and public bodies addressed to the Conference.

After deliberation, it was resolved that, as the Conference could not deal with these communications, the Secretary return them to the persons or public bodies who had forwarded them.

CONVENER OF THE CONVENTION.

Mr. CLARK moved,—That the Premier of Victoria be requested to act as Convener of the National Australasian Convention of Delegates to be appointed by the several Legislatures of the Australasian Colonies, and to arrange, upon consultation with the Premiers of the other Colonies, the time and place of the meeting of the Convention.

Mr. PLAYFORD seconded the motion.

The question was put and carried unanimously.

VOTE OF THANKS TO PRESIDENT.

Sir HENRY PARKES moved,—That the thanks of the Conference be given to the Honorable Duncan Gillies for the services rendered by him as President of the Conference.

Mr. MACROSSAN seconded the motion.

The PRESIDENT addressed the Conference.

The question was put and carried unanimously.

VOTE OF THANKS TO SECRETARY.

Dr. COCKBURN moved,—That the thanks of the Conference be given to Mr. George Henry Jenkins for the services rendered by him as Secretary to the Conference.

Sir JAMES LEE STEERE seconded the motion, and addressed the Conference.

The question was put and carried unanimously.

The PRESIDENT thanked the members of the Conference on behalf of Mr. Jenkins.

ADJOURNMENT.

Mr. DEAKIN moved,—That the Conference do now adjourn.

The question was put and carried.

And then the Conference, at thirty-five minutes past twelve o'clock, adjourned.

D. GILLIES,
President.

GEORGE H. JENKINS,
Secretary to the Federation Conference.

DEBATES OF THE CONFERENCE.
(OFFICIAL RECORD.)

MONDAY, FEBRUARY 10, 1890.

The Public were admitted to the Conference Chamber at a quarter to Noon, the PRESIDENT (Mr. D. GILLIES) being in the Chair.

UNION OF THE COLONIES.

Sir HENRY PARKES moved—

"That, in the opinion of this Conference, the best interests and the present and future prosperity of the Australasian Colonies will be promoted by an early union under the Crown, and, while fully recognising the valuable services of the Members of the Convention of 1883 in founding the Federal Council, it declares its opinion that the seven years which have since elapsed have developed the national life of Australasia in population, in wealth, in the discovery of resources, and in self-governing capacity, to an extent which justifies the higher act, at all times contemplated, of the union of these colonies, under one legislative and executive Government, on principles just to the several colonies."

He said,—Mr. President, I have to tender my deep regret that I have been the unwilling cause of any delay in the proceedings of this Conference. I am very sensible, indeed, of the goodness and consideration of yourself and my other co-representatives in so readily excusing me on Friday last, and I beg you to feel assured that no cause of my absence which I could have removed would have allowed me to be away on so important an occasion. In submitting the motion which I have just proposed, I will endeavour to steer clear of what may be called sectional politics. I will strive to avoid any reference, or any epithet, that could possibly give offence to any of the colonies represented here. I will try to put my case before the Conference as

c

quietly, as clearly, and as forcibly as my powers will permit, trusting to avoid any half speech, or any holding back of the sentiments of the colony I represent. The first thing that occurs to me is that most of us have little thought how old a question this subject of Federation really is amongst us. I have been really surprised myself, in going back to the earlier records, to find that it was the child—the fondled child—of the greatest men we ever had in any of the colonies. In my own colony I find it had the favour of Mr. Wentworth, who certainly ranked second to none. It also had the support of other statesmen of considerable power and influence in the very early days of parliamentary Government here in Victoria. For instance, I read this morning a report of a select committee of the Legislative Assembly of Victoria, appointed within a year of the advent of Responsible Government, in which all that we are now met to consider is forcibly put forth, and, to my mind, supported by very conclusive argument. I will refer for a short time to one or two of these early records, some of which, in my busy life, I never read until I had occasion to use them. This report of the select committee of the Victorian Legislative Assembly is dated September 8, 1857, that is to say, little more than a year after the introduction of Responsible Government, and is a document showing so much ability and supporting so strongly what I am asking you to consider to-day, that it is well worth very serious perusal. I may mention that it was first reported to the world in 1860, by Mr. William Nicholson, who was at the time Chief Secretary of this colony. I have not hit upon the names of the gentlemen forming the committee, but I think Sir Charles Gavan Duffy was one of them. I am personally aware that, from his first landing here, he took a very wide and warm interest in the subject of Federation. I will only detain the Conference by reading three or four short passages from this report. It says:—

"On the ultimate necessity of a federal union there is but one opinion. Your committee is unanimous in believing that the interest and honour of these growing States would be promoted by the establishment of a system of mutual action and co-operation among them. Their interest suffers, and must continue to suffer, while competing tariffs, naturalization laws, and land systems, rival schemes of immigration and of ocean postage, a clumsy and an inefficient method of communicating with each other and with the home Government on public business, and a distant and expensive system of judicial appeal exist."

This was written thirty-three years ago.

" And the honour and importance which constitute so essential an element of national prosperity"—

I must read these words again, because without this sentiment of honour intermingled with importance attaching to the subject there can never be any Federation. If we proceed on any inferior plans of action—on that of personal interest, for example, which I cannot believe will enter the mind of any member of the Conference—or if we take any less elevated ground than that of public honour, as well as of importance, we can never hope for the next hundred years to give birth to a nation in this part of the world :—

" And the honour and importance which constitute so essential an element of national prosperity, and the absence of which invites aggression from foreign enemies, cannot perhaps, in this generation, belong to any single Colony in this southern group, but may, and we are persuaded would, be speedily attained by an Australian Federation representing the entire."

Then the report utters a sentence which in itself is a chapter of sound political philosophy :—

" Neighbouring States of the second order inevitably become confederates or enemies."

Who can doubt, Mr. President, that, if the colonies had acted upon this report of your legislature thirty-three years ago, many things savouring of enmity, at all events of something more than rivalry, would have been avoided :—

" Neightouring States of the second order inevitably become confederates or enemies."

We have proved it, unhappily, to be too true :—

" By becoming confederates so early in their career, the Australian Colonies would, we believe, immensely economize their strength and resources. They would substitute a common national interest for local and conflicting interests, and waste no more time in barren rivalry. They would enhance the national credit, and attain much earlier the power of undertaking works of serious cost and importance. They would not only save time and money, but attain increased vigour and accuracy, by treating the larger questions of public policy at one time and place, and in an Assembly, which it may be presumed would consist of the wisest and most experienced statesmen of the colonial legislatures, they would set up a safeguard against violence or disorder, holding it in check by the common sense and common force of the Federation. They would possess the power of more promptly calling new States into existence throughout their immense territory, as the spread of population required it, and of enabling each of the existing States to apply itself without conflict or jealousy to the special industry which its position and resources render most profitable. The time for accomplishing such a Federation is naturally a point upon which there are a variety of opinions, but we are unanimous in believing that it is not too soon to invite a mutual understanding on the subject throughout the colonies. Most of us conceive that the time for union is come."

So we see, Mr. President, that all that I can say now was said by this duly organised body of your Parliament, a year after the introduction of Responsible Government into this colony. Passing from that, time does not permit me to refer to the many other similar enunciations of opinion in those early days, both here and elsewhere—that is to say, in this colony, in New South Wales, in South Australia, and in New Zealand. If any one will take the trouble to examine these records he will find, without drawing invidious comparisons, or without indulging in that species of delusion which always imagines that giants lived in some earlier time—without any excessive imagination of that kind—he will find that these views, in the very first years of our freedom, had the support of the ablest men that have ever adorned the councils of any of the colonies. I pass rapidly on now to the Convention of 1883, to which I shall make only a slight allusion. But I have been much struck by the fact that, in the correspondence which is before me here and which I have no doubt is before you all, Mr. James Service, who was the principal mover in bringing that Convention together, had unquestionably in view precisely what I trust we all have in contemplation now—the establishment of a Federal Parliament. This earlier record to which I have alluded speaks of establishing a Legislative Federal Union, not a union without the power of making federal laws, but it is particular in announcing a desire for a legislative union. Mr. Service, beyond all doubt, entertained exactly the same views. Some of his letters were only read by me for the first time this morning, and I felt surprised to see that at the time he was trying to get the other colonies to enter into the Convention of 1883 he never appeared to have dreamt of the limited body which came into existence. I have not time, Mr. President, to read any of the passages from Mr. Service's letters; but of course they are known to you, and must be known to many other gentlemen here—to all who took part in that Convention. With regard to the Federal Council, we must not lose sight of the fact that that development, that that doctrine of development of which we have heard so much, has been going on through the instrumentality of that Council. Through the action of the Federal Council public opinion has more rapidly, more definitely, and, I do not doubt, more clearly, formed itself on this large subject. And the process of development does not necessarily mean that there shall be a kind of sliding scale of our laws, but it means that the action of a body, of a group of individuals, of a community, or even of a single individual, can develop a question, so that it is more and more understood by the general mass whom it concerns. That development has most assuredly been going on from then until now. But something more has been going on. All the elements of national life have been going on amongst us with an increased speed. There is not one of these important colonies which has not felt the wonderful stimulus given to industry, to every kind of enterprise, to education, to refinement in social manners, and in the estimates of moral life which have been going on, until we are now in a condition that we may be contrasted favourably with some of the wealthiest States in the world, not only in respect of our enterprise, our skill, and our industrial vigour, but also in the higher walks of life. The extent to which books are bought and read, the extent to which the vehicles of thought find encouragement and nurture in these colonies, is something not frequently estimated, but incomparably creditable to us. I doubt not for a moment but that, if an investigation could be made, there are more readers of the higher publications issued through the London press—the monthly reviews, the higher order of newspapers, such as the *Spectator*—I do not for a moment doubt that there are more readers out of a given number, say more in every thousand of the population, here than in similar sections of the population of Great Britain. We have now reached a stage of life when we are not behind any nation in the world, either in the vigour, the industry, the enterprise, the foresight, or the creative skill of our working populations, in which I include the directors of labour, and we are not behind in all the higher refinements of civilized society. And if all that is so, let us for a moment pause to consider what this society is made of. According to the best calculations that I have been able to have made—I mean by our own Government Statist—we have a united population of 3,834,200 souls. It is worth noting in passing, though I attach no special importance to it, that of these numbers 2,656,000 are in the three Colonies of New South Wales, Victoria, and Queensland. This fact is of interest to me, because there was a time when those three colonies only represented one colony, and that time was not so long ago. I, myself, had the privilege of voting for the separation of Queensland, and I remember the separation of Victoria. And these three colonies, which occupy the space that formed the one Colony of New South Wales when I arrived in Australia, contain 2,656,000 of the entire population. That, as I have just said, is worth noting in passing; it is of interest to me, and I think it will be of interest to others, but I still prefer to look at the sum total of our people, and that sum total measures our capacity for asserting our claim to national life. Don't let us be mistaken—it is not likely that any man here will be mistaken on that point, but let none be mistaken—population is the one great basis for the growth of nations either here or anywhere else. But pause for a minute to see what this population has done. I have here an estimate of the value of the annual industrial productions of this united population. What I mean is, the value of what is produced from the elements we possess—produced from the land, produced by the power of industry from

the rude elements of nature, and I find that the sum total for a
single year is no less than £95,042,000. Then if we take the
private wealth of this people—I do not mean, and I wish to be
very distinctly understood as not meaning the public wealth,
such as the railways or the lands of the several colonies, but the
private wealth and the income of the free citizens of Australasia—
the result is equally remarkable. We shall best test the private
wealth of the people by comparing it with that of the people of
other countries, and I have selected out of many before me in
the tables with which I have been supplied, four great nations
other than Australasia. I will give you the average private
wealth per inhabitant. In Austria, it amounts to £16 6s.; in
Germany, to £18 14s.; in France, to £25 14s.; in the United
Kingdom, to £35 4s.; in the United States, to £39; and in
Australasia, to £48. Therefore, in reality, we stand at the head
of the nations of the world in the distribution of wealth—
that is, of wealth in its grandest form, because a country
cannot really be said to be in a prosperous condition with a
few colossal fortunes—a few families rolling in luxury, and the
mass of the people in poverty-stricken homes. The real standard
in civilization is the wide diffusion of wealth over the population
to be governed; and, judged by that test, Australasia stands at
the head of the nations of the world; not only so, but a long
way at the head. The private wealth of the United States is
£39 per inhabitant, and the wealth of Australasia £48 per
inhabitant, showing that for each living creature, from the
richest to the poorest, we possess, if our wealth be distributed in
equal proportions, £9 more for the purchase of the good things
of this world than the United States, or than any other country
on the face of the earth. Well, we have done much in all the
chief provinces of government. All the gentlemen who are
listening to me know what wonderful progress we have made
during the last generation, and I need not advert to the subject
in detail. But let us see what this peace-loving people—and we
are a peace-loving people, and I pray to God that we may ever
remain a peace-loving people—have done in rational provision

for the defence of the bounteous lands we possess. We have a united army of 31,795 men; and to show that this army has been constituted with a due regard to the most valuable arms of military service, let me point out that of the total number we have 15,913 infantry, we have 7,226 men in rifle companies—and these rifle companies are in their very infancy—and we have 3,954 artillery. If an army not one-third so great in numbers as that we now possess justified the able men who have gone before us, in contemplating the course we now propose to adopt, have not we arrived at a stage of numbers which amply justifies us in thinking of building ourselves into a nation? We have wealth—and it would be impossible for that wealth to exist if it were not for the well-directed energies of mind and physical strength in creating it—which places us before all the great peoples of the world. There is not one so wealthy as we; not one with the same command of the natural comforts of life which wealth ought to be employed in procuring as we. We have brought into existence systems of education, which, in a very short time, have been followed, and to a large extent copied, by old, powerful, and renowned nations. But what is of more importance to us is this, that we have brought into existence systems of education which practically embrace the children of all the families which live under our forms of government. We have constructed means of communication—we have carried them in all directions where they were most needed—to an extent which, if we had not done so much, would be a marvel to ourselves; and in all the other true provinces of free government we have, making allowance for the infirmities, the mistakes, and the misdirected energies of all human communities, made such progress as has excited the admiration of the best of other countries. If, then, we were fit in the year 1857 to enter into a Federation, how much more fit are we now? And if we are not fit now, with the elements of strength which I have very cursorily pointed out, when shall we be fit? I asked the other night—and I know no better way of putting the case—that if there are any persons who object to complete Federation at the present time, they should point out when we shall be fit for it. That seems to me to be an obligation that is thrown upon them. If they say that we are not ripe for complete Federation now, then when shall we be ripe? Will it be to-morrow, or this day twelve months, or this day five years, or this day ten years? In what degree shall we be better off then than we are now? The other night a gentleman, the most striking feature of whose character is his practical common sense, told us that there was a lion in the path, and that this Conference must either kill the lion or be killed by it. Well, the fabled lion is most frequently presented to us as a foreign monster, as a thing directly opposed to the person who is pursuing the path—that has the most opposite notions to the end that person has in view. This lion is supposed to be an enemy that will tear him to pieces. I have never seen this fabled lion presented to the world under any other circumstances; and, thus interpreted, there is not and cannot be any lion whatever in our path. There is no obstacle in the path before us except impediments which we have created ourselves. Nature has created no obstacle. That principle of Divine Goodness—call it what you may—which exists, and overrules the world, has created this fair land of Australia, situated as it is,—wisely created it for a grand experiment in human government, and there is no lion, and no natural difficulty before us. The path is plain and bright with the genial sunshine of our own blue heavens, with no impediment in it whatever. If we are only wise, and can only agree among ourselves,—if we acknowledge that bond which unites us as one people, whether we will or no,—if we acknowledge frankly that kinship from which we cannot escape, and from which no one desires to escape—if we acknowledge that, and if we subordinate all lower and sectional considerations to the one great aim of building up a power which, in the world outside, will have more influence, command more respect, will more securely enhance every comfort, and every profit of life amongst ourselves—if we only enter into the single contemplation of this one object, the thing will be accomplished, and accomplished more easily, and in shorter time, than any great achievement of the same nature was ever accomplished before. But let there be no mistake. We cannot become a nation and still cling to conditions and to desires which are antagonistic to nationality. We cannot become one united people and cherish some provincial object which is inconsistent with that national unity. We have grown, as this resolution says, in population and in wealth, and I have taken the liberty of proving both facts. We have made great advances in the discovery of resources, and we have done a wonderful work in developing them within the last seven years. Resources which were hidden seven years ago are now familiar and are familiarly acted upon. And in regard to self-governing power, the few allusions I have made to the product of our Parliamentary labours are sufficient to show how wonderfully we have exhibited our capacity for self-government. In answer to the question which is sometimes asked, "How much better shall we be for Federal Government?" I will endeavour to show, briefly from my limited point of view, how much better we shall be under those conditions. There are numberless sources of wealth which would be developed by one wise and powerful government which are not likely to be developed or matured by the provincial governments which now exist—notably, the splendid sea-fisheries which Australia possesses. There is no limit to, almost no knowledge of, the extent of the fisheries belonging to Australia. They certainly could, under one authority, one system of regulation and management, be developed to an extent which is never likely to be done otherwise. Then there is the safety of our coasts, their efficient lighting, and the completion of surveys. The security of our coasts could be infinitely better attended to by the central government than can ever be the case with the separate governments. Then, again, the means of communication, without trenching upon the rights of the several governments, could be greatly advanced by the sagacity, the wisdom, and the uniform power of a central government. Did time permit, I might enumerate the subjects with which it would be directly the province of a Federal Legislature to deal. We cannot hope to be secure from molestation from without. I for one, and no doubt I reflect the feeling of a great number of other men, earnestly pray that Australia may remain for ever at peace; but much as we may desire it, and no matter how much we may do to conserve that state of things, we know well enough that when nations are at war they know but one law, and that that law is the law of power and force. We have seen throughout all history that what has been done in the past will, as long as human nature is human nature, continue to be done in the future. We have seen that countries are attacked for the mere purpose of armed disturbance, and that, however much they may desire to be at peace, they are not allowed to be at peace. That was most strongly illustrated in the war between England and America, which commenced in 1812. The young United States—so conscious of weakness, so anxious to follow the maxims of peace, so entirely opposed to conflict of any kind—a country which had been living under the presidency of Mr. Jefferson and Mr. Madison, who of all men that ever held power were averse to war, and who made every possible effort to keep their people out of the terrible struggle between Napoleon and the rest of Europe—were obliged to go to war. That young Republic had her ships seized on the high seas, one after another, to the number of some 1,200, and I am sorry to say that the greater part were seized by Great Britain—lawlessly seized—while large numbers were seized by France. Although America desired to remain at peace, one great power at war in Europe was jealous of that young country stepping into her place in carrying the commerce of the world, and the usurper who governed France was determined to compel her to side with him. And from these unworthy motives the sea-borne commerce of the United States was almost entirely destroyed. We do not know when there may be war, and do you think that we shall be safer than were the United States in the years 1810, 1811, and 1812—until, indeed, the ravages made upon the marine of the United States by these two great contending Powers, France and England, at length compelled her to declare war when she was utterly unfit to fight so powerful an opponent as Great Britain. Do what we may we cannot be more secure than our countrymen were in the case to which I have called special attention. We cannot, indeed, be secure at all against the unlicensed force of a great armed power. In a state of war men do not consider what is right, but what is possible—they do not consider what is essentially just, but what directly or indirectly may forward their cause. If a great Power had any excuse for plundering these colonies the wealth of Australia would be of the most essential importance in promoting the elements of war. Nothing whatever can save us in any such event as that except a reasonably efficient, a reasonably strong, armed force, and the training of our young men to the defences of the country. I do not know, Mr. President, whether I need dwell much more upon the value of this union government, for it seems to be generally admitted. I find few men, hardly any, who will openly say it is a good thing for us not to be united. Nearly all that I have met with, or have heard of, will tell you that at some time or other these colonies ought to be united. The men who lived at the time when the Constitution of these colonies came into operation told us that the time had come then. Most of those men are now in their graves, but I venture to say that few of them ever supposed that a generation would pass away without anything having been done in a true direction of placing the Australian lands under one form of government. What we really want, from my point of view, is a complete form of government—a Legislature with full power to make laws for the whole country, and an Executive with full power to administer those laws and conduct the affairs of the country; and it seems to me that the founding of the United States affords us this one warning against anything short of a complete Constitution. We know that after the struggle for independence the United States tried to live under what are known as the Articles of Confederation. They tried to live as federated but independent States; but year by year they grew weaker, more dissatisfied, more incapable of attending to the real wants of even one of the States, and, as was pointed out all through by Washington, nothing could follow from the confederation but disaster, ruin, and acquisition by a foreign Power. It was only the failure of this system which compelled the States at last to accept the Constitution under which they have lived and thriven in such comparative happiness and prosperity, and in such comparative glory. That Constitution—and I know of nothing so instructive as the life of Washington in regard to it—was brought about by the disastrous effects of the experiment of trying to secure to the States their separate rights and separate sovereignty. By Washington alone it seemed to be seen clearly, from the first, that it must fail; and so complete was the union accomplished afterwards that in the result, as I have had many occasions to point out, the whole of that great territory now possessed by the United States of America is as free as the streets of Boston or the streets of New York. Since I came to Melbourne I have met with a curious case, illustrating the doctrine implanted in the Constitution in regard to the freedom of the separate States. If the Conference will bear with me for two or three moments, I will quote the case referred to. The General Assembly of Maryland passed a municipal law enabling the City Council of Baltimore to impose wharfage dues. It was a purely municipal law, limited to the municipal council of Baltimore. A little vessel, laden with potatoes, arrived in that port, and, in pursuance of this law, the municipal council levied wharfage dues to the extent of four dollars and some cents, which the resolute captain refused to pay. The ship itself had nothing but potatoes on Board, and not a great quantity of them, because the wharfage dues, according to the municipal law, only amounted to the sum I have mentioned. The captain, having refused to pay, was taken before the local Court, which ordered him to pay the money. The captain appealed to the Supreme Court of the State, which sustained the verdict of the Court below. But the sturdy captain, strong in his knowledge of the Constitution, appealed from the Supreme Court of that State to the Supreme Court of the United States, and the Supreme Court of the United States reversed judgment. After quoting a number of decisions, the judgment of the Court goes on to say:—

"In view of these and other decisions of this Court, it must be regarded as settled that no State can, consistently with the Federal Constitution, impose upon the products of other States, brought therein for sale or use, or upon citizens because engaged in the sale therein or the transportation thereto, or the products of other States, more onerous public burdens or taxes than it imposes upon the like products of its own territory."

The case seems to set at rest, in the most emphatic manner, what is sometimes disputed—the question of existence of entire freedom throughout the territory of the United States. As the members of the Conference know, she has created a tariff of a very severe, and in some cases almost prohibitive character against the outside world; but as between New York and Massachusetts, and as between Connecticut and Pennsylvania, there is no custom-house and no tax-collector. Between any two of the States—indeed from one end of the States to the other—the country is as free as the air in which the swallow flies. We cannot too fully bear in mind this doctrine of the great republic, a doctrine supported in the most convincing manner by the case to which I have alluded. Now, I am one of those who believe, as far as my opinion is of value, formed upon a rather long experience, that whatever may be the decision of the Conference, it will be playing at federation if we attempt to create a Federal Constitution with anything less than the full powers of a Federal Government. I am as anxious to preserve the proper rights and privileges of the Colony of New South Wales as any person can be of preserving the proper rights and privileges of the Colony of Victoria. Indeed, I should almost fear to go back to the colony which has treated me so well if I did not do my utmost to preserve her independence in all that is consistent with the province of one great Federal power. But the Federation Government must be a government of power. It must be a Government especially armed with plenary power for the defence of the country. It must be a Government armed with plenary power for the performance of all other functions pertaining to a

National Government, such as the building of ships, the enlistment of soldiers, and the carrying out of many works in the industrial world which may be necessary for the advancement of a nation. It may possibly be a very wise thing indeed that some of these powers should come into force with the concurrence of the State Legislatures or the Provincial Legislatures. It may, perhaps, be a wise thing that some condition of gradation should be stipulated for in completing the machinery of this Federal Government, or in consummating its full power; but that it should be in design, from the very first, a complete legislative and executive government, suited to perform the grandest and the highest functions of a nation, cannot, I think, be a matter of doubt. I do not know what may be the feelings of the members of this Conference. As most of my co-representatives must be aware, I have had little communication with them. In coming here, I have not sought communication with any person of influence. I have abstained from seeking consultation of that kind, because I desired to come to the Conference with my mind untrammelled, and because I desired to meet the representatives of other colonies on fair and open ground, with the one great object of resolving ourselves into a nation before us, and that alone moderated and controlled by a jealous regard for the separate rights of our individual colonies. I, for one, say that it is the duty of the whole of the delegates to have a jealous regard for the rights and just privileges of the colonies they represent. It would be impossible for any Federal Government to expect to give satisfaction unless its powers—which I still contend must be sufficient for its high purposes—were in harmony with what is justly due to the several colonies. I would ask the members of the Conference to keep steadily in mind the fact that they represent the whole population of Australasia, that in that population there is a wide, rapidly-increasing, wave of Australian-born men, many of them standing, as it were, in the early dawn of manhood ; and we cannot think so lightly of our country, and the men it has bred, as not to believe that in that new wave of life, with which we shall all be overwhelmed very shortly, there may be greater men than we. Indeed, the great old Universities of the world already bear testimony to the genius of young Australia. The young men of these fair regions have shown themselves in no degree behind their brethren of the old world. We have everything to look for in the generation that will follow us. We may have—and why should we not—as gifted men here as ever breathed the breath of life. They are upon us in thousands, and they will fill our places immediately. We ought not simply to look to the accidents of the time which may have put us in places of rule—we ought not to look for the auxiliary influences which may affect us as men—but we ought to look to those who are coming in such countless thousands after us, to the higher aims which they may have, and to the higher powers of achievement which they may manifest to the world. We ought not lightly to disregard all the powers which the imagination can call forth, in picturing the future of these great colonies. Their destiny is assured, and their Federation is assured. The union of the Australian people so commends itself to the most far-seeing of those who have come from other lands, so intertwines itself with the very life of the native-born, that no opposing effort can possibly stop its progress. I trust we have not entered upon the consideration of the question too soon, and I trust we shall make no mistake. I do not see how it is possible to shut our eyes to the fact that our duty, at all events, is to ask the Parliaments of the different colonies to consider whether or not the time is come. I submit this resolution at a time when, I am bound to confess, I have not strength to treat it in the way I would wish to treat it ; but I trust it has sufficient merit in itself to commend it to the serious consideration of the Conference. I submit it, Mr. President, with the full belief that it will be supported, and with the full belief that it will meet with the concurrence and emphatic approval of a large majority of the people of all the colonies.

Mr. DEAKIN.—Mr. President, I have great pleasure in seconding the resolution which has just been moved by Sir Henry Parkes.

Sir SAMUEL GRIFFITH.—Sir, I rise with some diffidence to follow my honorable friend Sir Henry Parkes, after the very able and eloquent speech with which he has favoured the members of this Conference, a speech full of historical information and deep research. I think I may take it for granted that all of us present here to-day show by our presence that we believe that the time has arrived for a more complete Federation of the Australian Colonies than has hitherto been attainable, and that, practically, the object for which we are met is to consider how far it is practicable, at the present time, to go on towards the end which I again assume we all have in view. I apprehend there can be no difference of opinion as to the end we all have in view—that end must be a complete Federal Government of Australia. Whether or not that Federation shall include New Zealand may be a matter for further consideration, and I speak of a complete Federal Government leaving that question open. I take it, therefore, that we are all agreed as to the end that is coming, and that what we are here for is to exchange ideas, and to consider, as practical men, how far we can go with any hope of success in asking the legislatures from which we come to entrust powers to a convention to frame a Federal Constitution. Sir Henry Parkes referred to a very able and eloquent report that was drawn up by a committee of the Legislative Assembly of Victoria in 1857, and alluded to the long interval which has elapsed since that time without much being done in the way of carrying out the aspirations expressed in it. Now, I am not quite so disposed to blame all the men who have been engaged in Australian statesmanship in the intervening time, and I think that the figures which were given by Sir Henry Parkes himself show how very different a place the Australia of to-day is from the Australia of 1857. What, in fact, was known of Australia then? Portions of this vast continent that are now known to be some of the richest and most fertile tracts on the face of the earth, were then regarded as stony deserts, or places certainly uninhabitable except by black-skinned people. We know a great deal more of the country now than we knew then. We know something of one another, but even at the present we don't know nearly as much about one another as we ought to do. Still, we have now means of communication which had then no existence; the colonies have very much larger populations, we are in short in closer touch with one another; so that the conditions are very different now from what they were then. Passing from that Report of the Select Committee in 1857, Sir Henry Parkes referred to the Convention that sat in Sydney, in 1883, and of which Mr. James Service was the prime mover. I think my honorable friend is quite right in saying, in fact there can be no doubt, that Mr. Service and his Victorian colleagues went to that Convention with the expectation that it would do a great deal more than it did, with the belief that the proposals they would make for the acceptance of the various colonial parliaments would go much further in the direction of Federation than the proposals which were actually made. And they were not the only ones who went with that expectation, and with that intention. Certainly I can say, speaking for myself, as one of the representatives of Queensland at that Convention, and the only member of this Conference who was a member of that Convention, that I hoped that we should go a great deal further than we actually did. However, it was our business to exchange ideas, and to consider what was both desirable and practicable, because the two things are often quite different. I take it, for instance, that we all agree that the Federation of Australia is desirable. Whether it is practicable is another matter, depending not upon our opinions, but upon the public opinion in the different colonies at the present time. The question is: Will these different colonies, through their legislatures, permit such a Federation as we may deem desirable? It is no use for us to pass abstract resolutions here, or any resolutions, unless effect will be given to them by our respective legislatures. I think myself it would be most unfortunate, in a double sense, if any conclusions we may come to, or any steps we may initiate at this Conference, should fall through owing to the refusal of the various legislatures of the colonies to give effect to them. I believe that that would have more than a merely negative influence, that it would not only delay the work of Federation until the parliament or parliaments that stood out of the union chose to come in, but it would have the effect of undoing all that was done before. Therefore it is very important that we should see exactly on what ground we are standing, so far as we can do so. We can only, after all, express our opinions on the matters of fact before us, but it is important we should know and consider the lion in the path, or any number of lions there may be in the path, and I confess, with my honorable friend Sir Henry Parkes, that I do not feel alarmed about any of these lions in the path. Well, at the Sydney Convention, in 1883, we came to the conclusion, after full discussion, that the colonies were not prepared to establish a Federal Government or a Federal Executive, especially a Federal Executive. That was one of the most important questions for discussion, because a very little consideration must show that there can be no real federation without a Federal Executive. The one question of defence is sufficient to show that. It is impossible to organize and manage a Federal Army without a Federal Executive, and that Executive Government, under any system with which we are familiar, or are likely to adopt on the Australian continent, must be practically appointed by or hold office with the approval of a Federal Parliament directly elected by the people. I do not think that the local parliaments would submit to any other mode of nomination than that with which we are familiar. More than that, the Federal Executive must, in order to give effect to its decrees, have a federal revenue, which could only be raised by the direct representatives of the people. We, therefore, felt that as soon as a Federal Executive was established for any purpose it was necessary that there should be a Federal Treasury, and a Federal Parliament, which to a certain extent must supersede the provincial parliaments, and compel them to surrender some of their functions. At that time we thought that it was not possible to do so much, as we believed that the provincial parliaments would not then consent to surrender any of their functions. We therefore adopted what we conceived to be a desirable course—not absolutely desirable, perhaps, but which was something better than we had, and was also practicable, and that was the establishment of a body in many respects like the conferences of representatives of the different colonies which had been held periodically, but with power to give effect to the conclusions it came to. Many such conferences had been held, many resolutions come to, many promises made, but somehow or other they had fallen through—the decisions were not acted upon, and nothing came of them. The constitution that was then devised for the Federal Council was like that of a conference; it might be called a treaty-making body, but with power to give effect to any conclusions to which it came. That was the scheme we adopted, and I believe that those who shared in that work have no reason to be ashamed of the result of their labours. What they did was never regarded as more than a step to something better. I have always said that I thought the time had come then—and the necessity is becoming more urgent every day—when something more should be done; and I do not think that it indicates any disrespect to the Federal Council, or to the gentlemen who were concerned in framing its constitution, to propose to give effect to what they themselves would have proposed if they had thought that there was any prospect of carrying it. We did then all that we could see to be practicable and desirable. Now, I have no doubt of it being desirable, and I believe it to be practicable, to do more. How much more is a question very difficult to answer, and upon that opinions may differ. But I for one take the same position now that I did six years ago. I have no doubt, or very little doubt, in my own mind, as to how much is desirable. If possible let us get a complete Federal Parliament and Federal Executive, one dominion with no rivalries—no customs rivalries at any rate, amongst ourselves. If we cannot get all that let us get as much of it as we can. That is the point of view from which I approach the subject. If we cannot get everything how much can we get? Every step in advance is something gained. If we can get a Federal Government even with limited powers, let us have it; but of course we should prefer to attain the end we have in view at the earliest possible moment, and with the least intervals, because I recognise this, that every imperfect step we make is a halting place, and it may be some time before we can move from it. Therefore, I would desire to go on as far as we can now. How far can we go? That is the question we have to consider. There are some questions about which there can be no doubt. I shall not occupy the time of the Conference in saying anything about the general advantages of Federation. I wish to deal with some of the practical difficulties which I believe we are here to face and to meet. There are some things which it is quite clear, the separate provincial governments cannot do properly or efficiently, although they may do them in some sort of way. We have been accustomed for so long to self-government that we have become practically almost sovereign States, a great deal more sovereign States, though not in name, than the separate States of America. We have been allowed absolute freedom to manage our own affairs; and I know that there are many people who, although they are favourable to the idea of Federation in the abstract, would yet hesitate to give up any of those rights which we have been in the habit of exercising. The advantages of Federation like everything else will have to be paid for; we cannot get them without giving something in return, and every power which may be exercised by the Federal Government with greater advantage than the separate governments, involves a corresponding diminution in the powers of the separate governments and legislatures. That is the first objection with which we shall be met; but there is an answer to it. There are some things which the separate parliaments and executives cannot do. First and foremost there strikes one the question which was the occasion of the suggestion made by Sir Henry Parkes which led to our being brought here. That is the question of defence. The several colonies may have separate armies of their own;

they may even have identical laws governing their armies; these laws may actually be in force beyond their own territories; nevertheless they will all be separate laws, so that a curious result may be brought about. Each of the colonies on the Australian mainland may pass a Defence Act identical in terms, authorising the removal of its troops beyond its own boundaries. Six armies might under these laws be concentrated in the one colony, Victoria for example, and yet they would actually all be governed by different laws. The Queenslanders would be governed by the laws of Queensland and amenable only to the tribunals of Queensland; and it would be the same with the New South Welshmen, the South Australians, and the Tasmanians. That is a state of things that is obviously incompatible with the existence of anything like a combined and well-disciplined army, and it could not be got over without a Federal Government. It could be got over so far as the legal difficulty is concerned, by a law of the Federal Council; but the difficulty with regard to the executive head could not be got over in that way. For the purposes of defence, at any rate, there must be a central government in Australia. I know quite well that there are a great many persons in Australia who do not believe in the danger of invasion at all. It is no use differing from them; they believe that it is only a device of a military caste, of persons with military fads, to spend money, and do foolish things. These views are very strong in some places, and the persons who hold them have to be reckoned with. It will be taken for granted that I am not saying this because I suppose there is anyone present who holds such views. As Sir Henry Parkes pointed out, we may at any moment be in imminent danger of invasion, and we cannot under existing circumstances protect ourselves satisfactorily. Another matter which must have occurred to everyone who has had experience in government, is that of external relations. The question has often arisen in the colonies. Communications frequently have to be carried on with the Colonial Office in London, and every country of the magnitude of Australia must have external relations with the rest of the world, and it is impossible for six or seven separate colonies to carry such affairs on satisfactorily. Matters relating to trade and commerce, copyright and patents, costly and unsatisfactory appeals to courts of justice in Great Britain—are things which the colonies cannot manage by themselves. I suppose every member of this Conference is familiar with the enumeration of subjects of general and local legislation in British North America. That list at once suggests that many things can be done with great advantage by a Federal Parliament and central executive. A central executive of course involves a central parliament. I wish to advert to another difficulty, and that is with respect to the Federal Executive. How far would the other colonies care to submit to any distinct acts of government by an executive with which they are not familiar? That difficulty arises from our common ignorance of each other. The difficulty arose when the three eastern colonies were governed from Sydney, and since that time a strong dislike has been shown to anything like centralised government. That is particularly the case in Queensland, where dissatisfaction has arisen just as it arose in an earlier period when Queensland and Victoria were governed from New South Wales. The establishment of a central executive would appear to many persons like going back to that old state of things, and it will be very necessary to explain, when bringing the subject before our several parliaments, that it is not intended to transfer to the executive government anything which could be as well done by the separate governments of the colonies. Then there is the question of fiscal union, which Mr. Service called "the lion in the path." It is only a question of time. There must be some day a fiscal union. Whether it can be brought about just now or not is a matter upon which opinions must differ very much. I think, for my part, although I admit freely that Federation without fiscal union would be unsatisfactory, that its absence would not be an insuperable obstacle. I maintain that Federation without fiscal union would be better than no Federation at all. I hope we shall get complete Federation, but it is of no use disguising that difficulty. However, as I have said, I do not regard that difficulty as being an insuperable one. Suppose we had a central government for defence, uniform laws, the regulation of trade and commerce externally, the post-office, sea fisheries, &c., and the colonies still had separate customs tariffs, we should be so much the better off by reason of the regulation of the things I have named by a central government, and as regards fiscal matters we should be no worse off than we are now. And there would be this advantage, that under the new arrangement the absurdity of fighting one another by customs tariffs would become so apparent that before very long they would be given up. It has been said that there can be no Federation without absolute freedom of interchange of products. But surely that is not so. What is the difference in principle between a duty collected on the border of a colony and an *octroi* duty collected on the outside of a municipality? The collection of such duties is a most disagreeable thing, but it is not inconsistent with Federation —not a perfect form of Federation, but an arrangement very much better than anything we have at the present time. That is the "lion in the path," and it seems to me to be a very harmless creature after all. It is of no use disguising the fact that the protective duties in many of the colonies are designed quite as much with a view to protect the colonies against their neighbours as to protect them against the outside world—indeed a great deal more so. This is not the place in which to discuss the wisdom of it. Moreover, in some of the colonies the revenue raised by tariff duties imposed upon their neighbours' products forms a very large proportion of the income of the Government; and when the great question of *cui bono* comes to be asked in the Parliaments these colonies will require a satisfactory answer as to what they are going to gain by surrendering their protective duties. My own opinion is that it is desirable to get rid of all these tariffs, and no doubt they will be got rid of some day, but their existence ought not to be regarded as an impediment to our doing the best we can. I should be sorry to be supposed to attach too much importance to these difficulties, or these practical aspects of the question before us. At the same time when we remember how many years have passed since the Act authorizing the making of treaties by the colonies for the imposition of differential duties was passed by the Imperial Parliament, and that no such treaty has yet been made, we must recognize that the question is one requiring very serious consideration. It may happen that there will be union between some of the colonies before there is a general union between the whole. That is a contingency to be contemplated. Whatever may be thought of a larger and more complete union, there is every reason to suppose that some of the colonies may agree to form a customs union. If that is done, the moral force of gravitation will compel the others to join. I hope, however, that these difficulties will not be allowed to stand in the way. Let anyone look at the list of subjects which may be dealt with by a general parliament and general government with so much greater advantage than by separate parliaments. I would like to trespass on the time of members of the Conference for a few moments for the purpose of mentioning some of the subjects which are enumerated in that great Act of British North America. I have before me a list of the subjects which are the exclusive business of the general legislature. These subjects include the following:—Public Debt and Property, Regulation of Trade and Commerce, Raising of Money by Taxation, Borrowing of Money on Public Credit, Postal Services, Census and Statistics, Militia, Military and Naval Forces, Defence, Beacons, Lighthouses, Navigation and Shipping, Quarantine, Ferries between Provinces, Currency and Coinage, Banking and Paper Money, Weights and Measures, Bills of Exchange and Promissory Notes, Interest, Bankruptcy and Insolvency, Patents, Copyrights, Naturalization and Alienage, Marriage and Divorce, and Criminal Law. To the latter, I think, may here be added the question of the regulation of the admission and exclusion of undesirable immigrants, and the establishment of a Court of Appeal. These are subjects in respect of which there is so little difference of opinion amongst intelligent men throughout Australia, that they could certainly be dealt with much better by one parliament, and the laws be better executed by one executive than by many. The work left for provincial parliaments would still be large and important, and it would be work which, in the main, could not be so well accomplished by a general government. This matter, however, is one which can be considered at a subsequent period. What I am anxious to insist upon is this: That we should not be deterred by any fear of not being able to do everything, but that we should do the most we can, remembering the old saying that half a loaf is a great deal better than no bread. Another difficulty which will meet us has reference to the want of knowledge which one colony possesses of another. If, for instance, the legislature of a country is asked to surrender its great powers of legislation to another body, people will naturally want to know of whom that body is to be constituted, and whether the members of it would consider their interests as well as they would consider them themselves. I would counsel all public men, during the two or three years which must elapse before any definite result can be achieved from our labours, to take every opportunity, both in public and private life, of making themselves acquainted with the different powers of Australasia, and of making the different powers of Australasia acquainted with them. Let us endeavour to distinguish, as far as possible, between means and ends. The end we have in view is the establishment of a great Australian nation. The means which may be adopted for attaining that end may be various. I remember, when I was a boy, a gentleman, for whom I had the greatest respect, saying that the practical definition of wisdom was the proper adaptation of means to ends. We shall require a great deal of this kind of wisdom in bringing about the end we have at heart. Matters such as those of fiscal policy are, after all, only means, not ends, in themselves. Whatever conclusion may be arrived at in regard to such matters, it is our business not to lose sight of the one great end in view—the establishment of a nation. The moral effect upon the people of Australia of the accomplishment of such an object would be very great indeed. Look how much wider will be the field for the legitimate and noble ambition of those who desire to take part in the affairs of a great nation—as it will be—a nation practically commanding the Southern Seas! The energies of men are cramped when they are confined to matters which, although of considerable magnitude in themselves, are, nevertheless, to a great extent, local in their character. I need not refer at any great length to the advantages which will accrue from the end we have in view being attained. Upon that point members of the Conference are likely to be all agreed. I hope that, in the discussion which will take place, members will direct themselves to the practical aspect of the question, with the view of enabling themselves and the public to arrive at a just conclusion as to what is the extent to which it will be desirable to ask the different parliaments to empower their representatives at a Convention to go in the framing of a Constitution. Some parliaments may be prepared to go further than others. Some of them indeed may refuse to give *carte blanche* to their representatives ; and they may even refuse to allow them to negotiate upon certain subjects. That, however, need not be looked upon as an obstacle. At the same time it would be very desirable that, in the Convention. the delegates should, if possible, possess co-extensive powers. Before closing. I wish to call attention to a provision in the Act to which I have already referred more than once—a provision for making the laws of property uniform in the three provinces of Ontario, New Brunswick, and Nova Scotia. The provision is to the effect that the parliament of Canada may deal with the question of assimilating the laws of property and procedure, but with this qualification: that their laws should be subject to adoption by the legislatures of the several provinces. Sir Henry Parkes, I think, referred to this matter in the course of his speech. The adoption of this idea may. I believe, be found to solve many of the difficulties which are apparently in the way. These, however, are matters which will have to be considered at a subsequent stage. I shall most cordially support the motion which has been proposed by Sir Henry Parkes—a motion which sums up, in the most happy manner, the present position of affairs. I shall be deeply disappointed if, as the result of this Conference, there are not laid the foundations of a real, strong, permanent, and complete Federal Government of Australasia.

Mr. T. PLAYFORD.—Mr. President, I understand that no other honorable member is just now ready to address the Conference on this subject, but I think it would be a pity to waste any time; and although I am not quite prepared myself, as some of my papers are locked up in a portmanteau, the key of which is in the possession of my servant, whom I cannot find, I think it would be better we should utilize the time at our disposal, and not adjourn at such an early hour in the afternoon. For the reason I have explained I shall have to trust to my memory for certain facts and figures, and also for the general tenor and effect of quotations which I had intended to read to the Conference in the course of my remarks. In the first place, Sir, allow me to say that I am somewhat disappointed with the motion that has been introduced by Sir Henry Parkes. I had anticipated something more than is contained in this motion. Very possibly it may be followed by a further resolution or resolutions, of which I have no knowledge at the present time, and, if so, I may have misunderstood the honorable gentleman; but if it is not to be followed by some further proposal on the subject, then I must say I am somewhat disappointed at the bald resolution which the honorable gentleman has introduced to our notice to-day. In reading the correspondence which took place between yourself, Mr. President, and Sir Henry Parkes—the correspondence which gave rise to this Conference being held—I notice that Sir Henry Parkes anticipates that the new parliament which is to be established for the whole of Australia will be built up on the lines of the Canadian parliament, and from that I took the cue that it was his intention, at all events at that time, to submit to this Conference a series of resolutions, which would not merely baldly affirm the desirability of a general parliament for the whole of Australia, but would at the same time indicate—I do not say in every detail, but at all events in the leading lines of detail—the powers and functions proposed to be vested in the general parliament. However, we have before us only a bald resolution, affirming, in its first clause, that in the opinion of this Conference the best interests, and the present and future prosperity, of the Australasian Colonies will be promoted by an early union under the Crown. I think we can all agree to that. There is no doubt about that. We have all agreed to it in the past—all of us, at all events, who have taken a prominent part in political life throughout the Australasian Colonies. With hardly an exception, we have agreed that sooner or later the time will come when Australia must be united under one government. The only points of difference have hitherto been as to whether the time was ripe for union, and as to what powers should be given to that parliament which is to be the general parliament for all the Australasian Colonies. The unfortunate part of the matter has been, that this question of the federation of the colonies has been taken up by the leading statesmen of the colonies. Now it has been asserted, by one who spoke with authority, that "all great reforms spring from the people;" and if the people of Australia had taken up this question in the first instance we should have had it brought to a conclusion long ago. But it has been taken up by the leading statesmen of the various colonies, and, as a consequence—well, I won't say as a consequence, but as a fact—the question has not been taken up by the people. It has not sprung from the people, and we are met here to-day, so far as South Australia is concerned, with the people not so educated on the question as to enable us to state that they, at all events, are distinctly and unmistakably prepared for Federation, and to what extent they are willing to go. The leading statesmen of the colonies have discussed this question for many years past. As far back as the first institution of responsible government in New South Wales, Mr. E. Deas-Thomson—I forget the particular position he occupied in the government of the day, but Sir Henry Parkes will, no doubt, remember it—pointed out, in the discussion of their Constitution, the necessity of having a general parliament to deal with certain subjects which he specified, and amounting, I believe, to a total of eight. Among those subjects were some of the very questions we are considering here to-day as questions which should be dealt with by a general parliament for the whole of Australia. You have only to go on to a little later period in Australian history, when you find that a gentleman of the name of Wakefield, in London, drew up a letter to Lord Derby, the Secretary of State for the Colonies at that time, in which he most clearly pointed out the desirability of establishing a general parliament of Australia to deal with such questions as the gold-fields questions—they have been settled; the land question—that has been settled; immigration —well, I think a general parliament of Australia would never have to deal with the question of immigration; and a variety of other subjects which have been practically settled among ourselves, and which would never form part of the deliberations of a Federal Parliament, but which at that time were looked upon as subjects which did unmistakably form part of the duties and functions of a Federal Parliament. But among the subjects to which Mr. Wakefield alluded, was that exceedingly important question of a uniform railway gauge for the whole of the Australian Colonies, and, if a uniform railway gauge had been adopted in the first instance, what a large amount of public money would have been saved which will be practically wasted when we come to break up all the railway gauges but one in these colonies. On other subjects, too, such as a Customs union, Mr. Wakefield hit the right nail on the head, and showed even in those early stages of Australian history how necessary it was in the best interests of the colonies as a whole that they should have a general parliament to deal with these most important questions. All these things were then pointed out by Mr. Wakefield and re-echoed by leading statesmen throughout the colonies, but even up to the present time the people of the various colonies have not taken up the question, and although it has for years past been discussed by the leading statesmen of Australia, who have expressed almost unanimous opinions on the subject, yet in consequence of the people not having taken up the subject heartily, we have not at the present time a general parliament for the whole of Australia. And I contend that our position with regard to the establishment of a general parliament for Australia is far more difficult than the position of any country that has federated in times past. In the United States of America federation was brought about because England insisted on taxing the colonies without giving them any voice in determining that taxation—taxation without representation. Those who agreed with taxation without representation stood on the side of the Crown, and those who did not agree with taxation without representation stood on the side against the Crown. The colonies were divided into two unmistakably hostile camps, and the sons of those old Puritans who landed in New England, true to their instincts of liberty, decided that they would never vote for allowing the Crown to tax them without their consent. They fought for their liberty, and gained it. In that case there was an unmistakable cause of appeal to the feelings of the people, and we can thoroughly understand how it was that they joined together to assert their rights and liberties, and how it was that they were so successful. And a lucky thing it was for England that they were so successful. As Lecky says in his *History of England in the Eighteenth Century*, on the result of that struggle for freedom depended the question whether the power of the Crown should continue to be paramount in England itself, or whether the English people should lose a portion of their liberties. Then, coming later down, leaving out the case of the people of Switzerland, who joined for the protection of their liberties, and the case of the United States of Holland, we come to Canada, the latest example of Federation, and what do we find there? Precisely the same reasons for Federation. Canada has a frontier of some 3,000 miles to the United States. At that time the great Southern rebellion was going on, and the North was making every effort to crush the South. A conference of delegates met at Prince Edward Island. At that original conference it was only intended that the maritime provinces of Canada should join together in federation. But Upper and Lower Canada were in a very peculiar position. When they decided among themselves to have one house of parliament and one legislature—one assembly and one council—it was agreed that Lower Canada should have precisely the same number of members in the assembly as Upper Canada; but Upper Canada grew quickly in population, and demanded that population should be the basis of representation so far as the Lower House was concerned. Lower Canada resisted, because she knew that if she allowed it to become the law of the land her power in the State would be seriously decreased, and from being the dominant power she would practically be in a minority. The resistance of Lower Canada brought about a deadlock. An appeal to the country took place. That resulted in another deadlock, and they saw no way out of the difficulty except Federation. At that time the people of Upper Canada sent a deputation to meet the representatives of the maritime provinces at their Conference. They met in Conference, and the question under discussion was the Federation of the whole of the States of Canada—Brunswick, Nova Scotia, Prince Edward Island, and Newfoundland. It was resolved that the colonies that had no power to be represented at that Conference should get those powers, and that the next Conference should meet at Quebec, and consider the whole subject. The position of affairs regarding Canada at that time was that there was a great war going on between North and South America. Just then the *Alabama* was let loose—possibly that is not a correct expression, although Lord John Russell is charged with having allowed the vessel to go from an English port. At all events the *Alabama* was destroying American commerce to a large extent, and the American people were very wroth against the English people and the English Government in consequence. Canada did not know at what moment war might break out between the United States and Great Britain, but the Canadians felt that if war did break out they would be the first, at all events, to suffer the injuries that such a war would inflict, and that most likely they would be attacked by the United States immediately on the declaration of war. Therefore, the question of defence, as far as Canada was concerned, was a question of paramount importance. There was also another reason which strengthened their desire for Federation. During the whole of the winter months Canada depended for its intercourse with the mother country and the continent of Europe entirely upon the communication through the United States of America—its own rivers, lakes, and canals being frozen —and the United States being at that time annoyed with England on account of the doings of the *Alabama*, began to put obstacles in the way of getting goods through bond from New York, and in other ways showed their teeth so unmistakably as to induce the colonies of Canada to join in Federation, so as not to be so dependent on the United States for their means of access to England and the rest of the world. For a long time the project of constructing a railway from Halifax to Quebec had been mooted—a line which would enable Canada to have intercourse with the mother country without going through any portion of the United States. Now between Canada and the maritime provinces there is a desert of a great many hundred miles in extent. This railway would have been a very expensive one, and it was thought that the colonies should join together in its construction, as the cost would be more than any one Colony, such as Nova Scotia or Lower Canada, could afford. That was another inducement to Federation. Then there was the fiscal difficulty, which was precisely the same as that with which we have to deal at the present time. The provinces had hostile tariffs - they had border customs duties which were collected by one province from the producers of the other provinces —and this matter also had to be adjusted. We can, therefore, understand why a Convention held in Quebec came to practically a unanimous resolution in favour of a draft bill, containing some seventy-two clauses, for submission to the Imperial Parliament, as forming a basis for the federation of the provinces. But even

then the dominion would never have been erected had it not been
for a circumstance which occurred while the various States were
engaged in the consideration of the resolutions of the Quebec
Convention. I refer to that wanton Fenian invasion of Canada,
which took place just when New Brunswick and Nova Scotia had
positively refused to adopt the bill agreed to by the Quebec
Convention. That wanton Fenian invasion on a peaceful community, across the borders of the United States, roused the
people of Canada. Those who had previously been opposed to
federation then saw the necessity of it. A dissolution of the
Parliament of New Brunswick, and I think also of the Parliament of Nova Scotia, took place; an appeal was again made to
the constituencies, and the constituencies reversed the decision
which they had given only a few months before. The Dominion
of Canada, as we see it to-day, was then formed. But even then
the provinces had difficulties and troubles in their path, and it
was not, after all, until they had got the Imperial Government
to guarantee them a loan of £3,000,000, that the lower maritime
provinces of Nova Scotia and New Brunswick agreed to form a
part of the confederation. What is our position compared with
the position of the Dominion of Canada? You have listened to
the speech of the Premier of New South Wales, and heard his
statement of the glorious progress made by the colonies under
our present form of government. Consider, then, what an argument he gave to those who are opposed to Federation: "If we
are the wealthiest people in the world without Federation, if we
are the best governed and the most prosperous communities that
exist in the world at the present time, without Federation, why on
earth," say the opponents of Federation, "should you go in for
Federation?" "If you have accomplished so much under the
present system of government why change it for Federation?"
We shall have to meet all these objections, and therefore I contend
that the difficulties in the way of Federation in the Australian
Colonies are greater than they were in any country in the world in
which Federation has taken place. We have difficulties to encounter
they never had. We have no enemy at our doors who is likely to

burn our cities, to levy contributions upon us, to kill a number of our people. We have nothing of that sort to fear, although all those countries which have federated in the past have had it to fear. Therefore we have to build up, and to build up slowly and carefully, a public opinion in the colonies, without being able to appeal to any catastrophe that might occur through war. We can only appeal to injuries that might be occasioned by our hostile tariffs, and to the advantages of union. We cannot do this at a bound, and therefore I contend that those gentlemen who were at the Sydney Conference of 1883, and agreed to the very small advance then made, to the very moderate powers given to the Federal Council, were wise in their generation. If they had attempted any more they would have failed. Sir Henry Parkes alluded to this Conference, but he neglected to allude to the Conference of 1881, of which he was a member. That Conference considered the subject of the formation of a Federal Council, and a draft bill was submitted by Sir Henry Parkes. It was thought then that the subject was hardly sufficiently ripe, but the bill was printed, and it is to be found in the proceedings of the Conference. The Conference did not come to any decision either for or against the formation of a Federal Council; the fact is, the matter dropped, but there is the bill. Sir Henry Parkes was not a member of the Conference of 1883; but that Conference practically adopted the honorable gentleman's bill, and the present Federal Council Act is based upon it. It may be said, I believe it has been said, that harmony is sometimes improved by inserting a little note of discord now and again into the music. Perhaps I shall insert one or two notes of discord regarding the Colony of New South Wales on the one hand, and the Colony of Victoria on the other hand. I do not wish to do that in any offensive manner, or with any other object than that of enabling me to answer questions which have been and will be again asked in South Australia. In the first place I would like to ask Sir Henry Parkes how was it that, after he had introduced the Federal Council Bill in 1881, the Colony of New South Wales refused to come into the Federal Council when it was formed, and how was it that he himself opposed its coming in? I do not know the reason, and I should like to know it.

Sir HENRY PARKES.—I will tell the honorable gentleman how, if he thinks well.

Mr. PLAYFORD.—I don't know which is the better course. I will appeal to the President.

The PRESIDENT.—It is a mere matter of convenience. If the honorable gentleman thinks that it would assist his argument he can hear the explanation now.

Mr. PLAYFORD.—No. It would perhaps be well to give Sir Henry Parkes time to consider the question.

Sir HENRY PARKES.—There is not much consideration required.

Mr. PLAYFORD.—Possibly not. I put the question in good faith, because it has been put in our colony and in our legislature, and it will be put again by the enemies of Federation. I should like to be able to give a straightforward honest answer to it.

Sir HENRY PARKES.—You had better have the explanation now, it will only take a few minutes.

Mr. PLAYFORD.—No, it will come better in the proper order. Sir Henry Parkes will have a right of reply, and he will have every opportunity of going into the question. Then I would like to ask Sir Henry Parkes a question concerning another matter which has been spoken of in our colony. Of course we all understand reasoning like this—that a gentleman who comes forward and says that he is in favour of Australian unity should be a gentleman who would desire to work harmoniously with all the colonies. We had a Conference not long ago on the Chinese question. We were then unanimous that a certain bill should be introduced in the local legislatures, and Sir Henry Parkes promised, on behalf of his government, that that course would be taken in New South Wales. The governments of the other colonies have introduced and passed the bill; but no such action has been taken in New South Wales. Does this conduct on the part of Sir Henry Parkes show that sincere desire for Australian unity which we would be led to suppose from the speech he delivered to-day, actuates him. There is another point I took a note of while Sir Henry Parkes was speaking. It appeared to me that he made an omission, but he will no doubt supply it when he replies. During the whole of his address he did not say a single word about our relations with the mother country. Whatever happens, I intend to remain loyal to the mother country, and so does the colony I represent. No matter how affairs are managed, we intend to continue to belong to that great Anglo-Saxon people whose home is Great Britain. If the mother country is unfairly attacked, we intend to defend her, as we feel that if we are unfairly attacked she will defend us. Although we may claim great powers of self-government, I maintain we should make it thoroughly and distinctly known that as far as we are concerned we are loyal to Great Britain; and I believe that is what Sir Henry Parkes means, though he did not refer to that particular point. There are two especially important points upon which we are asked to federate. The most important question calculated to drive us into Federation is undoubtedly the fiscal question. As far as we are concerned, it is more important than the defences, because, as long as we fairly do our duty in taking measures to defend ourselves, we may rest assured that we shall have the might of the British empire at our back to assist us. I do not fear this matter of the defences at all, but I look upon the question of rival customs houses established between the various colonies as a thing we ought to break down as soon as we can do it with reason and fairness to the colonies concerned. Now I ask the colony of Victoria and her representatives, who have been the greatest sinners in building up this wall between the various colonies? Which was the first colony to step forward and tax the natural products of her neighbours? Victoria, I reply. A necessity has arisen to federate and put a stop to the existing state of things simply because Victoria chose to erect these barriers. She was the first to start the system.

Mr. DEAKIN.—Hear, hear.

Mr. T. PLAYFORD.—The people of the colony I represent are asking what reason has Victoria for wishing to break down these barriers of her own erecting? Is she not actuated by self-interest in some form? The answer is, say the people of South Australia, that Victoria having been the first in the field with protection, having built up her manufactures, established her industries, and got her skilled workmen around her, she does not fear competition now with any of the colonies. She can now compete successfully against them, and by breaking down the barriers she will gain an advantage over the neighbouring colonies; by adopting that course she will reap the greatest benefit and pocket the most "tin." Speaking plainly and straightforwardly that is what the people in South Australia say, and I ask the representatives of Victoria to give us one or two answers to this. I think I have put the matter in a straight way, and I hope that when Mr. Deakin addresses the Conference there will be no beating about the bush.

Mr. DEAKIN.—There will be no disputed territory this time.

Mr. T. PLAYFORD.—Victoria has constructed this hedge and cemented this stone wall between us, and we have retaliated.

Mr. DEAKIN.—Imitation is the sincerest flattery.

Mr. T. PLAYFORD.—It is not flattery, it is pure retaliation.

Sir HENRY PARKES.—You should turn the other cheek now.

Mr. T. PLAYFORD.—When we found what had been done in the colony of Victoria we could hardly believe it. We had to adopt protective measures, and we should never have done that had not Victoria started it. We should on no account have taxed her natural products—her cattle, her sheep, her butter, her eggs, or anything else that was hers—but for the example set by Victoria. We were obliged to follow suit. Our people found that it was to their advantage to establish protective duties.

Sir HENRY PARKES.—That is unchristian.

Mr. T. PLAYFORD.—I do not know that we are arguing the matter from the Christian ethics standpoint. I am only putting the pertinent question which will be asked my colleague and myself when we return to our colony by people who will expect a satisfactory answer to it. Although I may agree with Sir Henry Parkes that there is no special lion in the path, there are difficulties in the way, and the people of South Australia will require a great deal of explanation in regard to the action of Victoria. I am waiting anxiously to hear a word or two of explanation from Mr. Deakin in regard to the action of the colony which, having erected a wall, is now the first to want to kick it down. I am quite certain that if we are to build up a Federation on the Canadian lines, the colony of South Australia will never agree to it. Sir Henry Parkes having, in his letter to Mr. Gillies, alluded to the Constitution of the Dominion of Canada as a basis of agreement, we naturally looked at that Constitution to see if it would suit our circumstances. Although unity is a grand thing, it is not everything. As far as the local legislatures are concerned, I contend that it will be the wiser course to adopt to leave to them all the powers we possibly can, apart from such powers as they cannot exercise individually.

Sir HENRY PARKES.—We all say that.

Mr. T. PLAYFORD.—Exactly the contrary course is pursued in the Constitution of the Dominion of Canada. There the local parliaments are only a little bit above municipalities. Railways and roads are under the general parliament. The local parliaments have a little to do with education, police, the destitute poor, and lunatics; and that is all. And above them is this great general power, which says—" We will veto any laws you pass which we disapprove of, and we have two years to do it in." It is said that a court will be established to save the expense of sending home appeals to the Privy Council; but though an appeal to a local court is provided, there is an appeal to the Privy Council after all, so that the rich man is simply given another string to his bow. He may appeal from the local magistrate, and from the local court of appeal to the Privy Council, and he is given another halting place and another means of putting money into the pockets of lawyers. If we have a court of appeal in these colonies that court of appeal must be final. After looking through the Constitution of the Dominion of Canada and the Acts passed under it, I say unhesitatingly that, as far as the colony I represent is concerned, we will have to go upon exactly the opposite basis, and instead of giving the whole of the powers not specified to the general parliament, we must give the whole of the powers not specified to the local parliaments. Of course the Constitution of the Dominion of Canada was framed under peculiar circumstances. While the Convention at Quebec was sitting North and South America were at war, and the Convention thought it desirable to put something in the Constitution to prevent the settling of matters with the sword. The Constitution was therefore made to provide that all the powers not specially given to the local parliaments should be given to the general parliament. When the Convention did that, it did not realize the immense power it was giving to the general parliament—an amount of power which these colonies will never consent to give. It will be for the best interest of the Australasian Colonies that the general parliament shall have its powers and duties clearly and specifically defined, everything else to be left to the local parliaments. The general parliament should only have entrusted to it such matters as relate to customs duties, the marriage laws, or a court of appeal. I do not believe in the powers of the local parliaments being curtailed, and in

South Australia the people will not give up any of them except such as can be better exercised by the general parliament. We want our local parliaments to become nurseries for the higher general parliament, and the more powers you give the local parliaments the greater responsibilities they will feel, and the better it will be for the community as a whole. I think it would be well if we were to pass some resolution which would clearly set the minds of the local legislatures at rest on this particular point. Sir Samuel Griffith pointed out that the jealousies of the local parliaments formed one of the difficulties we have got to face, and anything calculated to smooth the way—to show that we do not want to deprive them of powers which can be safely and properly left to them—would very considerably conduce to the carrying out of our wishes in the future. Although I am favourable to the adoption of the resolution, I consider it should be followed by further resolutions, showing the local parliaments the position we assume. We do not require a great dominion parliament, such as exists in Canada, relegating, as it does, all local legislatures into mere parish vestries. We require something in the shape of the government of the United States, where clearly defined powers are given to the senate and the house of representatives, and where all other powers not specified are left to be exercised by the local States and constituencies. I have endeavoured to point out to the Conference the difficult problem which besets it. We find that this desire for Federation has sprung from the top. It has commenced in the higher and not the lower branches of society. In South Australia, as in Victoria and New South Wales, there are people who will reap advantage from Federation, and the doing away of border duties. Some of these people will clamour for Federation. The great mass of the people, however, remain quiescent in regard to the question. They listen to what is going on, and they read their newspapers, but they do not appear to be greatly moved. There is no war impending; they are not much troubled by the officers of the custom-house; and the result is that they do not take much interest in the subject of Federation. Those who have occupied public positions for many years past, however, have felt the colonies ought to federate. This feeling has existed since the inauguration of responsible government itself, and nowhere more strongly than in the mother colony. The members of the Conference have met but there has been no great wave of public opinion to carry them on to success, and without this success will never be achieved. I have always been in favour of advancing, step by step, towards Federation. One step in advance has been taken in the formation of the Federal Council. Two or three further steps in advance ought to be taken by this Conference. But if we go too far, and endeavour to secure a dominion like that of Canada, the chances are that we shalll ose all, and Federation will be put back to a future time and generation. This, I take it, is only what may be termed a preliminary gathering. It is, I believe, understood that the members of Conference will recommend their parliaments to appoint delegates to a Convention, which shall have the power of drafting a bill to be submitted to the various governments. The resolution does not bind us to any great or small step in advance. Consequently it would be wise, in order that the existence of local jealousies may be avoided, to clearly define the principles upon which we think the Convention should be guided in framing the bill to be submitted.

Mr. DEAKIN.—Mr. President, I think the Conference will be much indebted to Mr. Playford for the frank, forcible, and extremely vigorous speech he has done us the honour of delivering—a speech in which he has certainly carried out his stated intention of facing, in the boldest manner, what he conceived to be difficulties of the situation. I was delighted to perceive that, notwithstanding a certain amount of antagonism which he endeavoured to infuse into his remarks and manner, he felt himself compelled, again and again, to confess what I take to be as complete an adhesion as is necessary to the principle embodied in the resolution before the Conference.

Mr. T. PLAYFORD.—Hear, hear.

Mr. DEAKIN.—I believe that, after fuller discussion shall have cleared the air, and more defined issues have been submitted, we shall find the honorable gentlemen side by side with us, co-operating to bring about the end we all desire. We shall then discover that he has served one of the best purposes of discussion, which is the study, not merely of the plain and easy paths of agreement, but of possible sources of disagreement, and of the question whether those sources of disagreement may not be removed. It was probably on account of the unfortunate absence of his papers that he failed to note that the particular omission to which he called the attention of Sir Henry Parkes was actually embodied in his resolution. The honorable gentleman will notice that the motion affirms, not simply that the interests of the Australian Colonies will be furthered by more complete Federation, but this is to be a union under the Crown. Again, in his concluding observations, Mr. Playford endeavoured to impress upon us the necessity of protecting the rights and privileges of the legislatures which we represent, and which represent the several colonies. I venture to think that all that could be demanded or expected by the most exacting of them is also contained in the resolution—in the last words, which come as a proviso to the whole—requiring that any Federation which may be adopted shall be one which shall be founded on principles just to the several colonies. Personally, I do not believe that any colony desires to have more than just treatment under Federation. Reserving this matter, however, I find that one of Mr. Playford's difficulties is, that we have no difficulties. He considers that one of the misfortunes of the present Conference is that it meets without a sufficiently great occasion; without that force of circumstances, such as existed in Canada and the United States, which might compel us to form a union *nolens volens*. As far as my memory serves me, his political sketch was perfectly correct. It is true that the two great Anglo-Saxon organizations to which we must necessarily direct our attention were consummated under the strongest pressure from without, so that the States or provinces, which up to that time had shown little disposition to agree, were compelled to form a union. Will the honorable gentlemen venture to advance the opinion that he can see nothing in the future possibilities of this continent which may compel Federation? Will he not admit, if he views the situation frankly, that, so far from being unlikely, it is practically a matter of certitude that, sooner or late, we too shall be faced with circumstances which, with or without our will, will force us into alliance? How much better then if, recognising this as one of the inevitable future events of our history, we face the question in a time of peace and quiet, and without any severe external compulsion. How much better to meet, as we do now, at our leisure, with a clear prescience of what must be the character of our future, to consider how deep we can lay the foundations of our national strength. Instead of being forced into partnership by a crisis, it will be far better for us to be united before the crisis arrives, so that we may face it with a bold and unbroken front. In the meantime we are now at our ease, and may consider not only the greater but the smaller conditions which should attach to a federation. This is a position rather of advantage than of disadvantage. It is a position which will enable us to devote even to the minor issues of the question an amount of attention which could scarcely be expected if we were met under the imminent hazard of a foreign war, or under circumstances of a like nature. I note that Mr. Playford spoke of the colonies and of their peoples —not intentionally, I am sure—with a certain implication throughout that there was something which distinguished the Victorian from the South Australian; the South Australian from the New South Welshman; the New South Welshman from the Queenslander; and the Queenslander from the Tasmanian.

Mr. T. PLAYFORD.—No, no.

Mr. DEAKIN.—The honorable gentleman must recollect that the attitude he has taken up might have been justified had it been assumed by himself as a citizen of a European State, and had his remarks been addressed to those of a different race, language, and creed, living under a different form of government. We cannot forget, however, that, in this country, we are separated only by imaginary lines, and that we are a people one in blood, race, religion, and aspirations. It is impossible for any man born in or belonging to one colony to pass to the other and to feel that he has gone to a foreign country. It is because of the intense closeness of the tie which unites us that we notice the line of Customs-houses along our borders, which remind us that we have created a difference where no difference need exist. The honorable gentleman seems to imply that there would always be the same separateness existing between the residents of the Australian Colonies as there may be between the residents of adjoining but differing nationalities. We have, however, to recollect that we have sprung from one stock and are one people, and whatever the barriers between us may be they are of our own creation. That which we have created we are surely strong enough to remove.

Mr. T. PLAYFORD.—I know that.

Mr. DEAKIN.—Well, then, let us brace ourselves to the task. Although we are here to consider the purely intellectual aspects of this question, we cannot avoid a reference to the sentimental aspect, which is so apparent in connection with this great issue. After all, it is upon the existence of the tie of affection between us that we rely when we ask assent to a resolution which expresses an aspiration native to every citizen of Australia, which cannot be rooted out of our hearts—which should inspire our lives—the aspiration of seeing these colonies united in one great nation. I do not wish to dwell on this aspect, but still it indicates a powerful factor which will infuse itself into this discussion at every turn, and it would not be well to pass on without noticing that we have always this to rely upon to help us over the difficulties that will face us. This sentiment of our nationality is one which, I believe, we shall see increasing in its intensity year by year, and it will count for much more than it now does when the people of these colonies have become a

people sprung from the soil, a people the vast majority of whom
will know no other home than the soil of Australia. I believe
that this passion of nationality will widen and deepen and
strengthen its tides until they will far more than suffice to float
all the burdens that may be placed upon their bosom. I quite
agree that the considerations we are bound to address ourselves
to are for the most part considerations of self-interest, and that
we should not seek to lay too great a strain on the feeling to
which I have alluded. But as a wise seaman steers his ship to
take advantage as far as possible of wind and tide, so should we
shape our course so as to secure for this great movement every
possible assistance, whether from the forces of sentiment or
motives of self-interest, and thus be enabled to reach the haven
of Federation. The honorable gentleman who preceded me said
that all great reforms spring from the people. That is perfectly
true. They spring from the people when they are ripening for
execution. It does not follow that the idea springs from the
many, but rather it must of necessity take its birth in the mind
of one, or, at all events, in the minds of a few. Unless the
honorable gentleman accepts some doctrine of an outpouring of
inspiration which falls on the million and neglects the unit, I do
not see how he can take any other view of this matter. So far
as our colony is concerned, I can assure him that throughout
the whole of Victoria there is in the hearts of the people a
strong desire for Federation. Now, I believe I can modify
Mr. Playford's statement with regard to the attitude of the
people of South Australia towards Federation in a way
that would make it more palatable even to himself.
Instead of saying that the people of South Australia have
not been moved by what he termed the federal wave, I fancy
he would more accurately define the situation by saying that the
people of his colony have the feeling for Federation, but they
require to see that this feeling, if given full play, will not run
counter to their interests and the development of their own
colony. I must say that, as far as I am acquainted with representative men in South Australia, I have always found them quite

as warm in the cause of Federation as any representatives from the other colonies in the group. A considerable section of the Victorian public will require to know how the new proposals may affect their own interests before they commit themselves to Federation. But it does not alter the general statement I have made with perfect accuracy, that the whole of the people of Victoria are moved by a desire for Federation, merely because numbers of them will need, before they give that feeling sway, to see that their interests are properly preserved and adequately protected. On the other hand, a large body of them are prepared to make sacrifices in the cause of Federation. However this may be, we certainly could not say that there is no popular zeal for Federation; on the contrary, it has been one of our current common-places for a long time past that the surest utterance to awaken a cheer at any Victorian gathering was one declaring for Federation. And if I were to point to the opinions of the press, I do not think I could lay my hands upon a single journal published in Victoria that takes up a position antagonistic to Federation. Some of them desire to see the conditions of union before they give in their adhesion to any particular plan of Federation, but I could quote scores of Victorian newspapers which are strongly and warmly in favour of the principle embodied in the motion now before us. "The crimson thread of kinship," as Sir Henry Parkes so happily and poetically termed it, running, as it does, through all the colonies, has not merely the strength of a thread, but is stronger than links of steel. When we are inclined to doubt the prospects of the future it is upon considerations such as these that we may for the time rely, confident that they will inevitably bring about that consummation which we all so earnestly desire. Mr. Playford offered some comments upon the past policy of the Premier of New South Wales, and the honorable gentleman was good enough to devote a small part of his attention to the colony which, in conjunction with our President, I have the honour to represent. He inquired, with a sufficient amount of warmth to indicate the genuineness of his sentiments, why it was that Victoria was now found among the federationists? Why Saul was found among the prophets would be the Biblical form of putting the question. The honorable member told us that this was a question he would be asked when he faced his constituents: Why Victoria, which was the first colony to adopt a Protective tariff, falling not only on the manufactures but also on the natural products of her neighbours, was now found among the first who were willing to join in an Australian Confederation? Well, if I were so disposed to divert the honorable gentleman's statement, I might point out, as a strong argument in favour of Federation, that if Federation had taken place years ago the barriers of which his people now complained would never have been reared at all, and he must, therefore, see that when he was complaining of the present condition of things he was supplying an argument in favour of union. The honorable gentleman asked if Victoria had not imposed these protective duties in her own interests, and whether the present movement, so far as it promised the removal of those duties, was not made by Victoria with a similar motive? That is a very natural question, to which there is a very ready reply. Certainly Victoria imposed protective duties with the idea of self-benefit, and without considering the interests of her neighbours in the slightest degree. Most assuredly self-interest was the impelling motive, because Victorian statesmen, like the statesmen of every other colony, are studious of the welfare of their own people. Under the present system their own people are to be found only within the borders of one colony or another, and these limited interests are the only interests which they are bound to consider. And why is it thus? Because you have created in these colonies a series of centres of independent life, and each of these centres of independent life will seek to maintain and multiply itself without regard for, and in more or less hostility to, the others. While these colonies are independent powers, and their legislatures enjoy full authority, those legislatures will be bound to exercise all the powers with which they are entrusted for the benefit of the people they represent, and the benefit only of the people they represent; and that has been the Victorian policy.

The one remedy, if you desire a remedy, for the present condition of things is to create another centre of national life, which shall so far absorb these minor centres as to give the people of the several colonies one common interest, instead of antagonistic interests. You cannot by any means short of Federation modify the present independent lives of the colonies so as to develop a national force, to which all individual forces shall minister. If Mr. Playford asks whether this proposal is not made at the present time by Victoria from self-interested objects, I say. "Yes, most assuredly." Do I believe that it is to the interest of Victoria that there should be a federation of the colonies? Certainly I believe it. If I did not believe it I should require stronger arguments than I do now to convince me that the Federation movement is one to be supported. If he asks the equivalent question, "Do I believe it to be to the interest of the other colonies of the Australian group that there should be Federation?" I answer with equal frankness that I believe it to be just as much to their interest as to the interest of Victoria. We have a mutual interest, and if I did not think that there was this mutual self-interest to assist the racial and national feeling we have already, I might anticipate much less from the result of this Federation movement. I answer Mr. Playford's inquiry with perfect frankness when I say that I believe we can all assure our own people that it is to our common interest to unite on all subjects on which union is possible, and that our highest interests are the joint interests which can only be effectually studied in unison. The comments which I desire to make upon the resolution itself will be of a rather fragmentary character, and supplementary only to those which have already been so ably placed before you by Sir Henry Parkes in his opening address—an address my own concurrence with which was so complete that I contented myself with merely formally seconding the motion, in order that some other speakers who felt more critical might exercise their skill upon it. That able address was then criticised in a perfectly fair spirit by Sir Samuel Griffith, who certainly called attention to all, or almost all, the

F

obstacles which would have to be surmounted before the situation could be considered to have been completely cleared. It is rather by way, therefore, of supplement to what has already been said that I venture to add a word or two upon some of the difficulties of union which must be taken into account. One of them was that noticed, in passing, by Sir Henry Parkes as the "something more than rivalry" which at present exists between the colonies. That is a consideration which should weigh with us most seriously. The spirit of partisanship is inherent in human nature, and it is perfectly certain that it is nowhere more vigorous than in Anglo-Saxon communities. The amount of feeling that can be aroused, even by the local contests which are waged by the young men of our country in friendly rivalry the one against the other, is often intense. It must be the experience of many gentlemen who have represented country constituencies that where there are two townships of about the same size within reasonable distance of each other the vigour of the antagonism that can be kindled dwarfs all general political antagonisms. Another illustration that suggests itself is that of the defender of the privileges of one house of parliament as against the other house, who, when he passes from one Chamber to the other, espouses the authority he previously attacked with as much energy as he has been accustomed to assail it. In all these directions, and in others, we find that the least possible reason for partiality is quite sufficient to set up a ground of difference, and sooner or later to create a distinct hostility. I believe there is a feeling existing between the different colonies of Australasia at the present time—that is, between some people in one colony and some in another—which is of an entirely regrettable character. One has only to observe the comments which appear, even in the best newspapers of one colony upon events taking place in another colony, to see that there is not a generous spirit of kinship exhibited by the critics. Representative journals even rejoice over the difficulties experienced by another colony, perhaps because it may suit the political policy of the paper to do so, but sometimes apparently without that cause, and for no other reason than that there is a kind of rivalry existing between the colonies. This is an unfortunate factor, and one the existence of which should not be disregarded. We cannot be sure that circumstances might not fan these latent oppositions into something far stronger and more difficult to cope with. They are too strong already, and it belongs to us to provide such measures as shall prevent their growing stronger. We must direct much of the loyalty which is now attached to individual colonies to a central ideal of the national life of Australia, so that our countrymen shall exhibit their loyalty to the nation, and the nation only, and shall feel that what transpires in any part of the colonies has as much interest for them as events occurring in the particular spot in which they dwell. Unless we have this centre of feeling, I am perfectly certain that the local sentiment which now exists may hereafter prove to be a serious stumbling block to any one who endeavours to solve the problem of union. One cannot but be struck with the fact that we have now reached a stage of our existence which points in many ways to theti meliness of Federation. Curiously enough, when the United States entered into their union, they had, roughly speaking, about the same population as we have at the present time; and the same remark applies to Canada. Curiously enough, also, the territory of the United States is almost exactly the same in area as that of Australia. The territory of Canada is somewhat larger, because the immense ice-bound districts to the north are included in it. The climatic differences which were considered to be so great a barrier to the union of the United States are greater than the climatic differences here. The geographical difficulties which had to be faced by the early delegates to Congress in the United States were infinitely greater than we would have to face in attending a central meeting of the representatives of Australia. And as Sir Henry Parkes pointed out, the prosperity of these colonies— their wealth, revenue, resources—are enormously larger than were those of the United States, and also larger than were those of the Canadas at the time of their union. All these circumstances seem to point to the fact that if we are to follow on the same lines we should be to-day close to the same point at which they found it to their interest to merge their separate selves into a common nationality. We should note, finally, that the United States and Canada had to deal with bodies as free and independent as our own. Each State of the United States, and each province of Canada, was as independent of every other State or province as each colony of Australia is of every other colony. Yet, in both of those instances, our own kinsmen, enjoying local self-government to the same extent that we enjoy it, found it to their mutual interest to create another and higher form of government. If we take the verdict of those countries to-day, if we ask any intelligent American or Canadian whether he would wish that the wheels of time should be rolled back, and the union his country enjoys dissolved, he would regard the question as so preposterous as scarcely to demand an answer. In each case they point with pride to their union; they celebrate it, and there is not a voice raised to regret it; on the contrary, they date from them all the progress which has been made. While Mr. Playford was perfectly right in saying that our horizon abroad is calm and clear, compared with the horizon that surrounded the men who federated the United States and Canada, yet, at the same time, it is not without its threatening clouds. We have, in the first place, in the neighbouring islands of the Pacific, a storehouse of confirmed criminals, whom we have not yet succeeded in either confining to the place to which they were sent, or, in more than a modified way, diminishing their influx. We may be faced at any time by serious difficulties in connection with the *recidivistes*, who will seek in our cities the means of pursuing the infamous practices, from which they are debarred in their place of detention, and it may be necessary to take strong action at any moment to protect our homes and our people from the consequences of this invasion. Then, again, in the islands of the New Hebrides and the Samoan group, it must be confessed that the political equilibrium is extremely unstable; the present condition of things may not continue for any length of time, and it may be highly desirable, when the hour arrives for finally settling their affairs, that the voice of Australia should be a strong and a united voice—a voice which will be listened to in London, echoed in the other capitals of Europe. We should claim to be recognised as the United States is making itself recognised in dealing with the destinies of these groups. United Australia will be called upon to face the largest problems. One has been in some measure already dealt with, but not yet finally solved—that of the influx of inferior races into the northern parts of the continent. There are questions arising with the Chinese Government which yet remain for final settlement; and in regard to which it is necessary that the peoples of these colonies should be able, through some recognised body, to speedily and effectually express their will. They must be prepared to support that will by united action when necessary. The immense importance of the issues involved is such as to furnish the strongest argument in favour of an early union—indeed they are so strong as to suffice in themselves to justify it. In connection with this and other questions, none of us doubts that the weight attached to our wishes would be enormously increased if we had a supreme representative of the Crown, in the person of a Governor-General, and one Agent-General in London, through whom United Australasia could express its views with the certainty that they would receive courteous and considerate attention. I say that in these respects we have everything to gain, and if our neighbours in those superb islands a little removed across the sea will realize how closely their interests are bound up with our interests in the Pacific and how necessary it is to gain the ear of Ministers in London, and impress the great powers of Europe, they will see that they too have much to gain by inclusion in such a dominion. There is yet another class of cases that are dealt with in the United States and Canada by means of the Federal authority, and which, in a lesser degree, will be required to be dealt with in these colonies by the same authority. I refer to the settlement and supervision of territories outside the States of the Union. It is proposed, I believe, by the Bill which will shortly grant Western Australia the local government which all Australasia has long wished her, to confine the new colony to the territory south of the 26th parallel, while the territory north of that is to be governed by Western Australia under the control of Ministers in England. We have already in New Guinea a Crown colony of a certain type which would also require to be administered, and it is possible, of course, that there may be yet other territories carved out of Australasia or the surrounding islands. Can it be doubted that it would be better that the executive of Federal Australasia and the general legislature of Australasia should be the bodies entrusted with their control, watching the gradual development of their resources, and providing for their gradual entry upon the rights of self-government, until they had become sufficiently advanced to justify their full admission to the Union. Such territories would be more sympathetically and more satisfactorily controlled by a parliament of Federated Australia than by the best Cabinet of Ministers that could be collected in London. The action of an executive in London must be tardy, costly, and hampered by want of local knowledge, while an Australasian parliament would have the advantages of proximity and better acquaintance with the circumstances of the new lands, thus fitting it to watch over them with the parental care which young communities require. I shall say nothing of the control of our defences, which was the occasion of the summoning of the present Conference, because what the mover of the motion and Sir Samuel Griffith have urged renders further comment unnecessary. The facts that we have already an army of 31,000 men maintained on this continent, that we shall shortly have our own fleet, and that the annual expenditure on our military and naval establishments amounts to £800,000, afford evidence that the military and naval establishments of Australasia are reaching a point in their development at which they call for central executive control. In addition to the new fleet, which will shortly form our first line of defence, there is a second line of defence (if I may use that term) which has developed in some measure in most of the colonies, especially in Queensland and Victoria, by the creation of a minor flotilla of torpedo and gunboats suitable for coast defence. These gunboats and torpedo boats would form an additional arm, which the Federal Executive would be able to largely increase, to the great advantage of the colonies. Whatever land defences we may possess, we may find use in times of peace, and fullest use in times of war, for an Australasian coastal squadron, which would protect our ports and harbours from any danger which may threaten them. With regard to work which might be better done by a Federal Government than by the separate Governments of the colonies, it is questioned whether, when the Convention comes to consider all the issues raised (which I do not enter into), it will not be decided that the larger part of the work should be left to the local Governments. It is argued that public works, for instance, would be more satisfactorily carried out by the local Governments than by a Government more removed. This is certainly open to discussion, though there seems no reason why the public works of these colonies should not, like those of America, be carried out by the individual States, and it may well be advisable for the railways, telegraphs, and post-offices to continue under the management of the several colonies within whose borders they may be. But what is clearer is, that the great cable and mail lines between this continent and the old world would inevitably pass under the control of the Federal Government. There is one land line already across the continent of Australia, which it might be necessary to hand over to the central government, and there is a cable projected towards North America, which will greatly affect the interests of the inhabitants of Australasia and the Pacific islands and our countrymen across the sea. The question of the Pacific cable is of the greatest consequence to all English-speaking peoples and to the Empire in particular. These lines would naturally fall under the direction of the Federal Government, and that government, owing to its magnificent credit, would stand in a better position in regard to any necessary expenditure than the separate governments of any of the colonies. The Federal Government would also be able to manage these means of communication with a success that even all the colonies in union could scarcely hope to attain to. Mr. Playford, I was glad to notice, agreed that the marriage, patent, and currency laws should be dealt with by the Federal Government, instead of by the separate authorities. These admissions of the honorable gentleman showed how truly his co-operation may be relied on in almost every direction. Then we are faced by the "lion in the path"—a Customs Union. This obstacle has been considered as presenting various aspects of menace and terror. Mr. Playford considers it formidable, but Sir Samuel Griffith does not, and both gentlemen have considered the means by which the lion may be made a serviceable animal. There are to be a few more years in which he is to satiate his appetite, and after that he is to become the obedient humble servant of the Federation. Until then he is to be allowed to prey upon neighbour and stranger alike. If this suggestion is to be adopted, the position which the Federal Government would find itself in would be the rather uncomfortable one of a government without any great source of revenue, unless it be specially endowed with some new powers of taxation, the operation of which would hardly introduce it in a favourable light to the inhabitants of this continent. Knowing that this subject will have to be thrashed out by the Convention, I pass it by with scant treatment. I desire to say, however, that if the suggestion be adopted there will be one essential condition, without which a Federal Government will be an impossibility, and this is, that if the local tariffs are to be maintained for a period of years it will be absolutely necessary that their collection should, from the first day of the formation of a Federal Government, be undertaken by the officers of that government, even if the revenue has to be afterwards paid over into local treasuries. There must from the first be a Federal control over all the ports of Australasia by Federal Customs officers. It will be necessary for the Federal Government to have the means of maintaining itself. It must receive the Customs revenues, and deduct what it is authorized to deduct, paying back to the several colonies the surplus there would be over the small expenditure upon such a form of government. I cordially agree with the statement that a common tariff is a *sine qua non* of national life. There can be no true union which does not include a Customs union. I will not yet admit that it is necessary that it should be even postponed. Another matter to which I would wish to call special attention is that in a Federal Judiciary we shall have one of the greatest gains and one of the strongest powers of the Federation—not simply by the creation of a court of appeal in Australasia, which should avoid the necessity of appealing to the Privy Council in London, but by the establishment of a judiciary in which, if we adopted the model of the United States, we should obtain one of the organizations by which the power of its union makes itself felt and obeyed in all portions of its vast dominions. In that monumental work by Mr. Bryce, *The American Commonwealth*, are summed up, in the most perspicuous and able manner, almost all the lessons which the political student could hope to cull from an exhaustive, impartial, and truly critical examination of the institutions of that country with which we are so closely allied. As a text-book for the philosophic study of constitutional questions it takes its place in the very first rank. In this volume Mr. Bryce points to the fact that the authority of the judiciary in the United States is not, as is often imagined by Englishmen, an authority only of a court of appeal sitting at Washington. On the contrary, while nine judges sit as a supreme court of appeal, there are sixty other judges scattered through the States, composing the Federal Justiciary. The powers with which the courts are entrusted, and the cases with which they have to deal, indicate the reality of the federation of the States comprising the Union. The cases dealt with by the Federal Courts include, " cases in law and equity arising under the Constitution ; the laws of the United States and treaties made under their authority." They also deal, according to Bryce, with " cases affecting ambassadors, other public ministers, and consuls ; " " cases of admiralty and maritime jurisdiction ; " " controversies to which the United States shall be a party;" and "controversies between two or more States, between a State and citizens of another State, between citizens of different States, between citizens of the same State claiming lands under grants of different States, and between a State, or the citizens thereof, and foreign States, citizens, or subjects." If a resident in Massachusetts has an action against a citizen of New York, and he does not feel justified in having his case tried in New York, it can be taken to the Federal Court. If one State has a cause of difference against another State, neither need consent to its cause being tried in the Courts of the other. Exactly similar circumstances must arise throughout Australia. What we shall require will be, not simply some Federal Court of Appeal to hear cases after they have been dealt with in the Courts of the colony, but a Federal Judiciary, with Federal Courts in all the colonies.

Mr. T. PLAYFORD.—We shall establish a lot of additional courts at a great deal of unnecessary expense.

Mr. DEAKIN.—If the honorable gentleman will look at the proceedings of his own parliament he will find that, two sessions ago, an important Act was passed to enable creditors on the South Australian side of the border to recover from debtors passing to our side. In the course of the debate on the subject numbers of instances were mentioned in which the people of South Australia had suffered great hardships for the want of such a law. If the honorable gentleman will question mercantile men and others, he will find that the present law by no means meets all their wishes. In fact he will find that the laws and the Courts at present provided are in many respects inadequate to meet requirements. The honorable gentleman need have no fear on the score of expense. The several existing Colonial Courts would probably be to some extent superseded, and their jurisdiction limited, or else they would be federalized. The expense of maintaining these Courts would be infinitesimal, not a decimal per cent. of the income of the smallest of the Australasian Colonies, while the benefits conferred by them upon large

classes would, I am sure, be found to be of the greatest value.
Leaving these details, which I have only ventured to touch upon
in a fragmentary way, and sympathizing with the strong stand
made by Mr. Playford on the supposition that the powers and
privileges of the different local governments were to be assailed,
and being as prepared as he is to do my utmost in their defence,
I believe that we would act idly unless we admitted from the
first that in the creation of a Federal Legislature and a Federal
Executive we meant them to be the organs of a Sovereign State—
a State which would not be a figment or shadow, nor exist only
on the sufferance of the local parliaments, but which would
draw its authority straight from the people of the different
colonies, obtaining from them the plenary powers to be exercised
by it within certain limits. The great lesson taught by Mr.
Bryce in his magnificent work is that the strength of the United
States Government lies in this, that although it is a Federal
Government, under which each State of the Union is theoretically and actually independent in respect to all concerns of local
life and legislation, it has nevertheless sovereign authority in
that it is gifted with powers which act directly and immediately
on every citizen of the entire country. It is not dependent on
any State for one cent of its revenue, nor upon State officers
for any act of administration, nor upon State courts for any
decision in its favour. Except that the State legislators elect
the members of the Senate, there is no connection between the
States and their central government. The Union is not concerned to have their support, nor does it seek their aid for the
forces it maintains. It is a sovereign State acting directly,
without any intermediary, upon the citizens from which it
springs. (Hear, hear.) I am glad that view is concurred with.
I am glad to think that we shall see a sovereign State in Australasia which will be able to act directly through its judiciary, and
in other ways, on every citizen within its borders, and be in every
respect and in all its powers the equal of any State in the world.
Were we to aim at crippling, maiming, or enfeebling the local
legislatures, we would aim at doing something not only wholly

unnecessary for our purpose, but something which would actually injure the Federal Government we are seeking to establish. There should be and must be nothing antagonistic between a Federal Government supreme in its sphere, and local governments supreme in their spheres. It is perfectly true that there must be a division of authority, that some of the powers of the local governments will have to be transferred to the Federal Government; but the judges of the powers to be given to either body must not be either the local governments with their jealousies, or the central government with its ambitions. The judgment must come from those whom both exist only to serve— from the people themselves. So far both the local and central authorities must be regarded as on the same platform, because as it is in the national interest that there should be a differentiation of the powers of government into central and local governments, so in settling that division only national interests ought to be considered. What we have to study is how to give the central authority all the powers which can be best exercised by such a body to the distinct advantage of the whole of the people. Those powers it ought to have; but it is not to be entitled to acquire them in such a way as would enfeeble the different local governments, on whose healthy life its successful existence must largely depend. As well might it be attempted to enfeeble municipal institutions in order to aggrandize parliament, the fact being that parliamentary government depends very much for its smooth and easy working upon the smooth and easy working of the minor local bodies. There are an infinite number of issues which no central parliament could deal with, but which necessarily belong to the local legislatures, and which they should be able to deal with in the present manner. For my part, I think we should seek to strengthen the local legislatures by every possible means. We should, as Mr. Playford says, leave them every power it is possible for them to exercise in the interests of the whole community. If more power can be given them for that purpose than is conceded elsewhere, let it be granted, but let us give the central government just as emphatically a full and unfettered power so far as the interests of the whole people demand it. I find Hamilton, one of the greatest of the founders of the American Constitution, saying—

"The establishment of a Constitution in time of profound peace by the voluntary consent of a whole people is a prodigy to the completion of which I look forward with trembling anxiety."

And I think that, although it would be arrogance indeed for the founders of an Australasian Constitution to measure themselves with men of the exalted moral character and splendid abilities of the founders of the great Republic, they may still approach their smaller task with much the same feeling. I do not quite concur in the statement that all great reforms spring from the people, but I fully admit that success in carrying out such reforms must come from the people. No success is possible without their sanction. All that is possible for this Conference or a Convention to do is to present to the Australasian people a means by which they can, if they so please, transform themselves and their separate segments into a great and united nation. I do not fear the result of an appeal to the people. Indeed, when the question is submitted to them, and a Constitution thoughtfully drafted by the representative men of all Australasia is presented to them, I shall be much astonished if the verdict from one end of the continent to the other is not an emphatic approval of what has been done. I would be alarmed if I could conceive of any other possibility. But that lies in the future. One thing we shall do in creating a central government will be to call into active political existence a class of men who have hitherto shown themselves unfitted or unable to deal with local politics, or who have, perhaps, not desired to deal with them. We shall, I believe, bring into the field of federal legislation a large body of trained political intelligence and also a number of minds not at present employed upon political issues, and we shall enable these to place at the service of the Union an ability and culture which shall be capable of conducting the business of the nation in a manner befitting its powers and its promises. The task which has fallen on the members of this Conference is in every sense preliminary, but it is a task which we can discharge, in all humility, yet with perfect confidence that the parliaments from which we have come will subsequently consider this question in a truly national spirit. A far greater task awaits the Convention, which will be called upon to frame a Federal Constitution. This will be a work of transcendent responsibility, yet the Constitution then shaped will, after all, however admirable, not be a final Constitution. There is not the least need to suppose that the Convention, when it addresses itself to its task, will do so under the impression that it is required to frame such a scheme as can never be improved upon for all time to come. Let that Constitution be what it may, if in any respect it fails to meet the wishes and needs of the people of Australia, they will still have the right, and certainly should be specially endowed with the power, of moulding it from time to time more and more into harmony with their needs and desires. We, in this Colony, obtained our Constitution in 1855, but it has been amended, and may be amended again. It was amended in 1858, again in 1862, again in 1864, and again in 1865, until at present out of the sixty-three sections of which it was originally composed, some twenty have been wholly or almost wholly repealed. The prospect of an eternal flux in a Constitution is not to be wished. But a Constitution lives for and from the people, and except so far as it coincides with their character is a dead burden. In national growth there must necessarily be constitutional changes suited to that growth, and such changes have been made, not only in this colony but in every other colony in the Australian group, so that we should not entertain too great a sense of the responsibility resting upon the Convention. It is a certainty that the Australasian Constitution adopted in our time will not be absolutely perfect, and that if ever it is found not completely adapted to the circumstances of the Australian people it ought to be altered, and will be altered by them to suit themselves. In conclusion, I think we need have no doubt that the people of these colonies, who have so wisely and well amended the Constitutions they obtained from the mother country, will be found perfectly able, not only to frame a constitution, but also, if necessary, to amend it so as to enable it to satisfy all reasonable needs. Indeed, it is upon this confidence in the capacity of our people for self-government that all our aspirations rest. It may be said of them, as Milton, in one of his pamphlets, said of the people of England—

"Lords and Commons of England, consider what nation it is whereof ye are, and whereof ye are governors; a nation not slow and dull, but of a quick, ingenious, and piercing spirit, acute to invent, subtile and sinewy to discourse, not beneath the reach of any point the highest that human capacity can soar to."

If Milton could say that of the superb generation of which he was one of the most glorious representatives, I believe that, with all deference, we may say as much of the picked race of men who founded these colonies not half a century since. The generation now passing away has, first with the consent of the Imperial Government, and afterwards with the consent of our own parliaments, moulded our local institutions so that whatever may be the few small flaws in them, we have Constitutions of which we are proud, and of which the wisest political thinkers have expressed their approval. Upon the generation now coming rests the greater task of framing a Federal Constitution which shall be for all the colonies what our present Constitutions have been to each of us; and when I recollect the fathers who have taught and trained them, and their achievements in this very sphere, I cannot despair of the result of the task committed to them, nor question the ultimate triumph of those who are now entering upon the hour of their labour and their trial.

The Conference adjourned at a quarter to six o'clock p m., until eleven o'clock a.m. the following day.

TUESDAY, FEBRUARY 11, 1890.

The Public were admitted to the Conference Chamber at five minutes to Noon, the PRESIDENT (Mr. D. GILLIES) being then in the Chair.

UNION OF THE COLONIES.

Discussion on Sir Henry Parkes' motion, in favour of an early union under the Crown of all the Australasian Colonies (proposed the previous day), was then resumed.

Mr. A. INGLIS CLARK said—Mr. President, the honorable mover of the proposition now under discussion by the Conference stated, at a very early stage of his speech, that the question of Australasian Federation had engaged the attention of leading statesmen in New South Wales and Victoria very soon after the adoption of responsible government in those colonies, and that since then the subject had been discussed by them from time to time until the meeting of the Convention of 1883, which resulted in the production of the Federal Council Act. Mr. Playford, one of the representatives of South Australia, followed that statement with another to the effect that the question of Federation had never got beyond the stage of being considered by the leading statesmen of the colonies—that it had never yet been taken up by the people of the colonies—and that until it was so taken up we could expect no good result either from this Conference or from any number of future Conferences like it.

Mr. PLAYFORD.—I alluded to complete Federation, and I spoke for South Australia only.

Mr. CLARK.—I assume that none of us can speak very decidedly for any colony except the one in which we live our daily life, and I feel that I can speak for the people of Tasmania, and say that they are quite ready, and even anxious for Federation; and perhaps I may be permitted to add, as a frequent visitor, during the last ten years, to Victoria and New South Wales, that I have formed the impression that the majority of the people of those colonies are animated by a very similar sentiment. Surely, if that is the case, I may fairly trust that this conference will be productive of solid results. Of course, as to public opinion in South Australia, I can offer no opinion whatever. I take it for granted, however, that the honorable gentlemen who represent that colony in this Conference are perfectly qualified to tell us the state of popular feeling there on the Federation question, and if it is as backward as Mr. Playford seems to indicate, I may nevertheless hope that this Conference, which speaks to all the colonies, will assist the education of the South Australian people on the subject. I will hope, also, that the representatives here of South Australia will be so impressed with the sincerity and earnestness of the representatives of the other colonies, that when they return to their homes they will do so convinced that they have a mission to strive all they can to persuade their fellow colonists to take an interest in, and to be eager for, the Federation that is bound to come. Perhaps I cannot do better, at this stage of my remarks, than express the feeling, which I believe exists throughout Tasmania, namely, that it would be a very good thing, supposing all the colonies to be not quite prepared to bind themselves at once into federative union, if as a beginning, four or five of them were to do so. For myself, I would be perfectly willing, and I am sure that so far I simply echo the voice of the colony I represent, to advocate a Federation including the colonies of Victoria, New South Wales, Queensland, and Tasmania—four contiguous colonies. Of course I greatly hope that this Conference will produce larger results than that, but I am reminded that such was the beginning of the federation of the Canadian Dominion. Originally only four colonies joined. Three others subsequently came in at different dates, and others are still standing out.

Mr. PLAYFORD.—Originally, only three colonies joined—Canada, New Brunswick, and Nova Scotia.

Mr. CLARK.—Upper and Lower Canada were two provinces.

Mr. PLAYFORD.—But under one Parliament.

Mr. CLARK.—At all events the representatives of four provinces met together for the purpose of federating.

Mr. PLAYFORD.—That is correct.

Mr. CLARK.—Again, lest four or five colonies should be thought too small a number to federate, I would beg to call attention to the fact that when the subject of Federation was first taken up in Australia, as mentioned by Sir Henry Parkes yesterday, there were in the whole of Australia only four self-governed colonies, namely, New South Wales, Victoria, South Australia, and Tasmania, and, in the Federation then proposed, only those four colonies could have been invited to join. With these facts before me I cannot help thinking that even supposing South Australia or any other colony could not see its way to federate at once, it would be quite open to the four contiguous colonies I have mentioned to join in a Federal Union forthwith, at the same time making provision for any other colony standing out to join them when it felt inclined to do so. Mr. Playford went on to say that, in his opinion, the difficulties in the way of Australasian Federation are greater than those which the people of Canada, or the people of the United States, had to grapple with when they federated. Well, I believe that with respect to Canada that statement was to a large extent correct. The honorable gentleman supported his assertions by an unquestionably very interesting and very correct account of the way Federation was brought about in Canada. He reminded us that the question was first taken up there during the Civil War in the United States of America, and that fear of invasion from the United States greatly accelerated the Federation movement in Canada. It is quite true that we have no similar difficulties or dangers to force us into Federation; but, let me observe, neither had the people of the United States when they adopted their present Constitution. They had achieved their independence, and they were at peace with the whole world. ("No.") Notwithstanding that contradiction, I think I can prove my statement by referring to an authority I scarcely think any honorable gentleman here will attempt to contradict. The great difficulties which the United States had to contend with at the time I speak of, and which induced them to adopt their present Constitution, were, in fact, exactly the same as those which we have to contend with.

Sir HENRY PARKES.—Hear, hear.

Mr. CLARK.—If there is an author who has more than another the right to be heard on this subject, it is the famous American statesman who is prominently known in the literature of that country as the great expounder and defender of the American Constitution, and as the most powerful intellect that ever appeared in the political arena of the United States. In fact it was on account of his enormous abilities, together with his intense love of the Union, and the vast service he rendered in educating his fellow-countrymen up to the standard of union, and in indoctrinating them with that affection for it which eventually carried them successfully through the Civil War, that a large proportion of his countrymen forgave him the action taken by him on the great moral question of slavery. I need scarcely say that I refer to Daniel Webster, who had during his life frequent occasion, both in the Supreme Court and in the Senate of his country, to refer not only to the origin of the Constitution, but also to the motives which induced the different States to enter into it. Here is a deliberate statement by him on the subject I have referred to. Before the Supreme Court, in the case of *Gibbons and Ogden*, he said—

"Few things are better known than the immediate causes which led to the adoption of the present Constitution, and there is nothing, I think, clearer than that the prevailing motive was to regulate commerce,"——

Not any necessity to arm in defence against a foreign foe, nor any dread of civil war between different States, nor any difficulty of the kind, but—

"to rescue it from the embarrassing and destructive consequences resulting from the legislation of so many different States, and to place it under the protection of a uniform law. The great objects were commerce and revenue, and they were objects indissolubly connected."

Are not these the great difficulties which we in Australasia have to contend with? Is it not motives of a precisely similar character that are urging us towards Federation? Again, in his great speech in the Senate, on the Sub-Treasury, he spoke as follows:—

"Sir, whatever we may think of it now, the Constitution had its immediate origin in a conviction of the necessity for this uniformity or identity in commercial regulations. The whole history of the country, of every year and every month from the close of the war of the Revolution of 1789, proves this. Over whatever other interests it was made to extend, and whatever other blessings it now confers, or hereafter may confer, on the millions of free citizens who do or shall live under its protection, even though in time to come it should raise a pyramid of power and grandeur whose apex should look down on the loftiest political structures of other nations and other ages, it will yet be true that it was itself the child of pressing commercial necessity. Unity and identity of commerce among all the States was its seminal principle. It had been found absolutely impossible to excite or foster enterprise in trade under the influence of discordant and jarring State regulations."

But I will offer no more quotations, for we are here, I presume, rather to give our own reasons for Australasian Federation than to refer to other authorities, however admirable or eloquent they may be. I will therefore content myself with what I have already cited in support of my contention that the difficulties we have to grapple with are in the main exactly those which the United States of America had in their way in 1787. On these grounds I regard some of the statements on this subject which Mr. Playford put forward as scarcely correct, although I believe he was substantially accurate in his assertions with respect to the formation of the Canadian Dominion. After the very able and interesting speech of Sir Henry Parkes came one of the most important and practical utterances we in this Conference have yet listened to, namely, that delivered by Sir Samuel Griffith, one of the representatives of Queensland. He very frankly and properly submitted that while we all admit the advantages of Federation, and are willing to anticipate its coming glories, we are nevertheless bound at the present time by every reasonable consideration to look fairly in the face the difficulties which stand in the way of its accomplishment, and to attempt to discover, through careful discussion and deliberation, some means of obviating them. The principal difficulty which he seemed to think lies in our path is that connected with the revenues of the respective colonies, and he pointed out that the majority of each of those revenues is largely derived from duties on goods imported from other colonies. What he laid stress upon was that in every colony the Customs Department produced the largest portion of the total revenue, and that that portion chiefly consisted of duties imposed on intercolonially imported articles. Now, I don't think that this state of affairs presents such a difficulty in the way of Federation as Sir Samuel Griffith appears to imagine. Certainly, if we were to do in Australasia what was done in Canada with regard to the public debt, the difficulty, if it is one, would immediately vanish. We know that the Dominion Government of Canada took over the whole of the public debts of the various colonies included in the Federation, and made an adjustment on the subject which put each colony in an equally fair and advantageous financial position. Well, if the government of the coming Federation of Australasia were to similarly take over the public debts of the several colonies of the group, surely each of them could very well afford to surrender the revenue derived by it from the particular source alluded to. I think this will appear clear from a few figures which I have put together since yesterday, and which show the proportion of revenue derived by each colony from Customs duties on goods imported from neighbouring colonies, and also the amount paid by each colony as interest on its national debt. Let us first take South Australia : We find its total annual revenue to be £2,354,743, about one-fourth of which, namely, £531,964, comes from duties of Customs. On the other hand, South Australia pays annually, as interest on its national debt, the sum of £794,922, or about £160,000 more than the whole of its Customs receipts. Now, it seems to me that if the central government undertook to pay that interest the colony could very well afford to part with its Customs revenue.

Sir SAMUEL GRIFFITH.—But from where is the Central Government to get the money wherewith to pay the interest?

Mr. CLARK.—I cannot quite understand the question. Will not the central government be able to collect what it wants?

Sir SAMUEL GRIFFITH.—Without Customs revenue from intercolonially imported goods the aggregate income of each colony would be diminished by at least half a million sterling.

Mr. CLARK.—But the loss could be made up by duties on goods imported from other parts of the world. For instance, I find that South Australia imports from the other colonies less than half the quantity of the goods she imports from elsewhere. Speaking roughly, the difference is that between 44 per cent. and 97 per cent. The revenue which she would hand over to the central government would be, in fact, about £260,000, so that her bargain in the matter would be a good one.

Mr. PLAYFORD.—South Australia would have to pay heavier Customs duties in order to make up the difference.

Mr. McMILLAN.—Don't go into figures.

Mr. CLARK.—I simply wished to show that South Australia, which I only referred to as an example, would be a gainer instead of a loser by the proposed transaction. There are also other aspects of the question to consider. I don't suppose that any one will imagine for a moment that when the central government is established it will for all time derive the whole of its revenue from Customs duties. It will have other sources of revenue. I never intended for one moment to convey that the central government would be able to obtain in the way I have alluded to all the revenue it would require in order to pay interest on the different national debts of the colonies, and at the same time to carry on its other work. Every government in the world goes in for both direct and indirect taxation, and possibly the central government will adopt some sort of direct or territorial taxation. Sir Samuel Griffith said himself that a uniform intercolonial tariff must come some day. Well, if a uniform tariff is to come, what good is to be gained by delaying its advent? For my part I don't think the position of affairs will be much improved by time. I have no wish to make this discussion turn in any degree upon the fiscal policy of the different Australian Colonies, but I cannot shut my eyes to the fact that some of the delegates who have spoken have done so on behalf and as the mouth-piece of colonies in which a protective policy is in force, and, I presume, as advocates of that policy.

Mr. DEAKIN.—Hear, hear.

Mr. CLARK.—That being so, I may be pardoned for looking at this question from the point of view of a free-trader. Well, taking the subject in that aspect, I don't think that delay will at all improve the position of affairs, by making the people of the various protectionist colonies more willing than they are now to give up their protective tariffs. We have often heard it said : "Give us a protective tariff for a time and by-and-by we will be able to stand up by ourselves;" but that time never seems to come. Instead, the cry is always for a little more protection, and with that sort of thing going on of course delay will only make matters worse. So far as South Australia is concerned it will, therefore, be far better for her to come in now, when her protectionist tariff is only two years old than at some future date—say, when it is twenty years old. Mr. Playford also said that he thought Sir Henry Parkes' speech was in reality as much against Federation as in its favour, because he painted such an admirable picture of Australasia as she is, that the question arises : " If we have done so well in our present state, would it not be better to leave well alone ?" No doubt we have done very well in the existing position of affairs, but who will say that we would not have done much better with Federation from the start? I do not think it has been hitherto generally known that when the draft Bill " for the better government of the Australian Colonies" was first submitted to the Imperial Parliament in 1849, there was a provision in it for the establishment of something like Federation, that is to say, for the adoption of a uniform tariff by a central body representing the several colonies. That Bill was supported by both sides of the House of Commons, and it passed there by a majority of 98, but for some inexplicable reason some member of the House of Lords moved the excision of the Federation clauses, and they were struck out. Who can say what the history of the Australian Colonies would have been had not a foolish lord—if I may use the expression—proposed the omission of the clauses I refer to, which, if they had been retained, might have given us, more than a generation ago, the very uniform tariff and Federal Executive we are now seeking to establish? Mr. Playford shakes his head.

Mr. PLAYFORD.—It was at the expression "foolish lord."

Mr. CLARK.—But whether things would have been better in the past or not, we know that nothing in the world remains always in the same condition. Change is the law of life, and if we are to live in the best sense of living, that is to say, attain to a wider, fuller, and higher life with regard to public matters, each of the communities we represent must emerge from provincialism and enter upon something better and larger than the separate existence of a separate colony. But if we remain apart for any considerable length of time it may be that unforeseen difficulties and dangers—such difficulties and dangers, for instance, as forced the Canadians into Federation—will arise on Australasian soil to overwhelm us. I don't pretend to indicate how such dangers and difficulties would develop themselves, or what, if they came, their nature would be, but I think it quite reasonable to suppose it to be possible that were we to continue as separate as we are for an indefinite period, contingencies of an unforeseen character would occur to cause some generations yet to be born to look back upon past events with the thought—"Oh! would that the delegates at the Melbourne Conference of 1890 had taken the step forward which was so necessary for the interests of the Australasian Colonies—that they had looked more to the possibilities of the future—and given us then that Federation which we are now with toil and suffering endeavouring to obtain." I hope, however, that this Conference will not, in future history, be characterized in any such fashion, but that, on the contrary— although we may have to be followed by a Convention, clothed with full authority to prepare an Australasian Constitution—we will be remembered as having done all in our power to promote, rather than retard, the great movement. Mr. Playford also dealt to some extent with the question of the Victorian tariff and retaliation. Well, I thank him for the frankness with which he approached the subject. I think it would be a pity were this Conference to dissolve without the representatives of each colony stating, with the utmost plainness, what they think of the past action of the different colonies towards one another. For myself, I propose to endorse nearly everything Mr. Playford said with regard to the Victorian tariff, because I think Tasmania has suffered from it even more than South Australia has. In fact, I might accuse Victoria of having actually broken faith with my colony in the matter of a certain reciprocity treaty. But I have not come here to indulge in retaliatory speeches. Indeed, I am willing to forget all the past, and to fight for the union of Victoria and Tasmania in the future, even if I do so on the low and selfish ground that with such a union we would no longer suffer from hostile tariffs, and no breach of faith, such as I have referred to as occurring in the past, could possibly be repeated. I hope the representatives of South Australia take a similar view. If South Australia has in the past suffered from Victoria ——

Mr. PLAYFORD.—Oh! we are quits now.

Mr. CLARK.—The question of the Canadian Constitution has been several times mentioned in the course of our proceedings, and its difference from that of the United States has been somewhat touched upon. On this point I would say that I think it would be well were each of us to state more or less precisely what kind of confederation we would individually advocate, and also what kind of confederation each colony represented by us would respectively be satisfied with. For my part I would prefer the lines of the American Union to those of the Dominion of Canada. In fact I regard the Dominion of Canada as an instance of amalgamation rather than of Federation, and I am convinced that the different Australian Colonies do not want absolute amalgamation. What they want is Federation in the true sense of the word. The British North American Act, under which the Dominion of Canada was established, not only goes on the principle of defining the powers of the local legislatures, as well as the powers of the central legislature, but also says that everything not included in the jurisdiction of the former is included in the jurisdiction of the latter, and it enables the central executive to veto the Acts of the local legislatures. Well, I believe that, in the course of time, those who live to see the outcome will find the local legislatures of the dominion reduced to the level of the position of large municipalities, and that Canada will have ceased to be, strictly speaking, a Federation at all. On the other hand, the American Constitution, as we all know, defines the powers of the central legislature, and reserves everything not included in them for the local legislatures. It has been supposed that this has been a source of a deal of controversy and trouble in the United States, and the real cause of the Civil War. I differ from that opinion. I believe that the cause of the political controversies of the United States, which resulted in that war, was the question of slavery. If we have a lion in the path in the way of the tariff, certainly the American Union had a serpent in its way in the form of that tremendous question. It roused all the passions and the faculties of human nature, good and evil, on one side or the other, and induced attempts to give the most tortuous interpretations to the Constitution, either to assist or resist its encroachments. Well, Mr. President, we shall be cursed with no such question in Australia. Therefore, I do not think we need fear to go upon the lines of the Constitution of the United States in defining and enumerating the powers of a central legislature, and leaving all other powers to local legislatures. Readers of

American history must have been frequently struck with the merits of the American system, in preserving that local public life of the various States which is so dear to the native American of every State. And when we notice to what a large extent the United States has grown, both in territory, population, wealth, and industry, we can scarcely imagine that that great community could flourish with such a variety of interests and industries and with such a variety of national life, under any other system than that under which it lives. So far from the local life of the States being the cause of political irritation, controversy, and dissension, I firmly believe that if the American Union were now constructed on the lines of those of Canada, there would be far more danger, dissension, irritation, and disunion in the future than exist at the present time. In fact the opinion of many of the most eminent publicists of Europe is that the salvation in the future of America as a united nation is the large amount of the local autonomy of the States. When we observe the large territory which we have in Australia—territory which we hope will some day be peopled to the same extent as is that of the United States—and when we notice the variety of climate and soil which will produce so great a variety of industrial and social life, we must come to the conclusion that we also ought to have a system which will preserve local, public, and national life in the same manner as it is preserved in America. It is quite possible that we may profit by the past experience of America, and give to the central legislature some few more powers than is possessed by that of the United States. It may be that we may even actually learn something from the Constitution of the present small Federal Council of Australasia, which has a provision not possessed by any other Federal Constitution in the World, and that is a provision that two or more colonies may refer any particular subject to the Federal Council to ask it to legislate upon it, and that it will then become law in those colonies, and, thereafter, in any other colony which may choose to adopt it. I firmly believe that many of the difficulties which have arisen in America, which the local States can not deal with, and which the central legislature, for some reason or other, has not seen fit to deal with, might have been met in that way. We can scarcely imagine that the Congress at Washington would refuse to legislate on any particular matter at the request of four or five States if it had the power to do so, and if the legislation so requested would affect only the States that asked for it. Congress would undoubtedly say, "it affects only the States which have asked us to legislate, and by all means let the power asked for be so exercised by those who desire it." The question of the management of post-offices and telegraphs has been touched upon by Mr. Deakin, who seemed to think that these institutions were amongst those which must be left to local legislatures. I am not, at present, prepared to follow the honorable gentleman in that opinion. I think the post-office ought to be, in a sense, a national institution; and I very much doubt that a uniform rate of postage can be secured unless it be under a central government. If the post-offices and telegraphs were under the control of the several colonies, and power were left to the local legislatures to create inequality of rates, irritation and discontent would certainly be produced. This would not be carrying out the principle of the local legislatures being sovereign within their own spheres, and in regard to the matters especially committed to their care. In order to secure uniformity of rates, as well as efficiency of management, I should be inclined to follow the example of America, and place the post-office under a central government. This, however, is a matter of detail, which may not properly be within the range of our discussions at the present time. As Mr. Deakin mentioned the matter, however, I thought I was perfectly justified in also referring to it. The honorable gentleman also referred to the advantages which would arise from a Federal Judiciary. I think he said all that could be said upon that question. I would add to his remarks upon that head, the opinion that the colonies would be able to obtain from such an institution what, to me, as a lawyer, and I presume to Mr. Deakin and Sir Samuel Griffith as lawyers, is of great consideration, and that is a higher education for our colonial judges. A judge, if he is to be worthy of his position, and desires to do good work for his country, must continue to learn after he goes on the Bench as well as before. It appears to me that where a system of gradation of courts exists, the judges will learn both from above and below. Every judge who knows how to take advantage of his position can, and does, learn from the able men who practise in the court before him. He will also learn from the judges of the court above him, to which an appeal lies from his decisions. At the present time, the only appeal we have is to the Privy Council. It is rarely invoked in Tasmania, and I find it is rarely invoked in some others of the smaller colonies. I do not know that it can be said to be frequently invoked even in the larger colonies. The consequence is, that the judges in several of the colonies sit without that sense and feeling of responsibility which we know would have a beneficial effect did they but realize that their work is open to the review of a higher court. If we had a Federal Court of Appeal, its aid would be invoked much more frequently than is the aid of the Privy Council now invoked, and the results, I believe, would be beneficial. Sir Samuel Griffith has very properly said that this question of federation after all, is one to be dealt with by the public opinion of the several colonies. The honorable gentleman expressed the opinion that the absence of any results of the Act of the Imperial Parliament enabling any two or more colonies to enter into a reciprocal treaty with regard to Customs duties proved, to some extent, the absence of public opinion on the subject, and the difficulties which lie in the way of anything like Federation. I feel tempted to reply to that observation by saying that it is only another illustration of the inefficacy of half-measures. It is said that a half-truth is the worst of lies, and that half-measures at all times are worse than none. Although great things were expected of it at the time, and although I believe it is capable of producing good results, nevertheless this Imperial Act is one of those half-measures which always disappoint. I would ask the Conference to let this be a warning to them in regard to the adoption of half-measures. Let us go the full length of a complete Federation, or else we shall discover that the results of an incomplete Federation which some advocate will be similar to the Act of the Imperial Government to which Sir Samuel Griffith referred. I regard Federation as such a great and grand thing in itself, that I do not for a moment believe that even a measure of it, if productive of positive results, can in any way be disadvantageous. I believe even in the measure of Federation which we possess in the Federal Council. That body has done some good work, and it would be capable of doing much more if all the colonies were represented in it. Speaking for the people of Tasmania, I believe I am justified in saying that if a complete Federation cannot be obtained, they would be content to accept an incomplete Federation. They would be content to take one step further, hoping for a still greater step to be taken in the future. But it appears to me that there are more difficulties in the way of incomplete Federation than of complete Federation. If we take another step, and attempt to add to the powers and increase the numbers of the members of the Federal Council, we shall immediately be faced with the problem of the taxing power. If you are going to increase that body and to give it greater power and dignity and larger functions, you must inevitably give it a revenue and an executive, and if you are going to give it a revenue you will immediately be met with the question as to the proportion of the representation of the various colonies. Are you prepared to give equal representation to all the colonies in a single legislature possessing taxing power? I am afraid that the larger colonies would object to this, and if there is unequal representation with taxing power, it is likely that the smaller colonies would think that they stood in danger of being swamped and out-voted. The only solution of the problem is the adoption of the bi-cameral system. But if it is once determined to go in for a bi-cameral legislature with taxing power and an Executive of its own, all other questions would be matters of such detail that they would not be worth while reserving. The partial measure of Federation which some people talk about has been already taken in the formation of the Federal Council. That is the full extent to which a partial Federation can practically and successfully go, and immediately you attempt to go further you must go the whole distance. That is the conclusion I have formed of this matter. In the course of this discussion, Mr. President, we have occasionally heard the sentimental side of the question mentioned, that is to say, one aspect of the question has been referred to as the sentimental aspect. 1 have tried, up to the present moment, to deal with what appeared to me to be the practical side of the question, but I do not hesitate to say that I value very highly the sentimental side. Perhaps I value the sentimental side of the question more than I do the practical side, and I will give my reasons for that statement. It is generally supposed that we take a sentimental view of things when we are young, and a practical view when we get old; and they say that part of the discipline of life is to knock the sentimental view out of us. I always sympathized with, and admired very much, that utterance of Charles Sumner when he said, "I hope we are not going to exchange the visions of youth for the calculations of age." I hope that the vision of a future Australian nation which is now before the eyes of young Australians, is not one to be laughed at or knocked out of them by rough contact with the world. I remember very distinctly once reading an article in the *Princeton Review*, by Professor E. A. Freeman, the historian of the Norman Conquest, entitled "The Sentimental and Practical in Politics"; and with that wealth of historical illustration which he has at his command, and which he uses so skilfully, he demonstrated—at least to my judgment—that what had been in the early stages of every political question derided and ridiculed as its sentimental aspect afterwards proved to be its real practical aspect. I believe it will be the same with regard to Australian Federation, and that the sentimental side will prove to be the practical, or the basis of the practical. After all, sentiment is the basis of more than one-half of human life. We are sometimes asked what we mean by a nation and by national life. I believe a nation, as was stated by Sir Henry Parkes, is, first of all, a sufficient aggregate of population. You cannot have a nation with half a dozen individuals, nor yet with a few hundred; you must have a more or less extensive aggregate of population. But that population to be a nation must be localized. It must be located within certain physical limits, and must be responsive to the influences of its physical environment. I believe that it is to such conditions we owe all the nationalities existing in the world. Where a number of living units are brought in contact with each other within a given physical environment, there will be produced a distinct type of life, and, in the case of nations, a distinct type of national life. I believe that the physical environments of the French, the Italians, the Spaniards, and the English, combined with the inter-action of the units composing those peoples upon one another, have produced the several distinct national types of manhood found in those countries. In Australia we have a population which is encircled by a definite physical environment, with a climate, soil, and other physical components peculiarly its own, and human nature in Australia is not going to be an exception to human nature all over the other parts of the globe. It will be influenced by its environment, and it will undoubtedly, in time, produce its definite national type of manhood in response to the action of that environment. We are proud to have sprung from the same race as the inhabitants of the British Isles. I believe, however, that it is our destiny to produce a different type of manhood from that which exists in those islands. I believe a different type of manhood has already developed itself in the United States of America, and the same process is going on in regard to the countries of South America. But I believe that the distinct type of national life, which is produced by the causes I have attempted to describe, will never come to perfect fruition, will never produce the best results, without political autonomy. It is political autonomy which we are now asking for Australia as a whole. We have political autonomy in the several colonies, but we have come to the conclusion, I believe, upon the sentimental side of the question, that the several colonies are not large enough in their territory and population to produce that national life which we believe can be produced upon the wider field of a United Australia. We are asking now for the political autonomy of a United Australia, in order that that national life, which we believe will exist under those conditions, may be produced and may bear the best fruits. I believe this national life can exist without political independence and without political autonomy as a germ, or even as more than a germ. But it will never be satisfied, it will never do that which it ought to do, until it obtains political autonomy. Sir Henry Parkes has spoken of the movement now on foot in Australasia as the birth of a nation. We have all lived in a time, I believe, in which what is called the birth of a nation has taken place in Europe. I refer to Italy. I do not believe that Italy was really born when she became united under one central government. It used to be said that Italy was only a geographical expression—that there were Tuscans, Romans, Venetians, Sardinians, but no Italians. But there was one Italian people, one Italian language, one Italian literature, one aspiration common to the Italians, to live a national life, and to obtain that political independence and unity to which they, at last, through much suffering, toil, and difficulty, eventually did attain. I believe that in Australia a similar national life to that which existed in Italy for generations before she had political unity and independence has commenced. It will go on and grow in the several colonies whether we now assist or not in giving it that political independence or autonomy which it craves for, and which it deserves. That wave of Australian feeling to which Sir Henry Parkes has referred will go on in the future, and, in spite of us, or in spite of any other Conference which may refuse to rise to the dignity of the occasion and do the work laid upon it, will produce that federation, unity, and political autonomy which our national life and aspirations require and demand, in order that they may have a free and adequate field for their expansion. There have been many Conferences amongst the colonies on various questions. This, however, is the first that has been expressly called for the purpose of exclusively discussing Federation. I will conclude by stating that I hope it will be the last. I hope it will be the last, not because we will have found our labours vain, not because we will have discovered that we have been chasing a dream, and that there is no room for a United Australia. No! but because I hope we may do our work so well that we may go back to our several colonies and obtain the assent of their several legislatures to the meeting of a Convention, which, within a very short period, will produce a Constitution under which a United Australia will progress and flourish, and take its place among the nations of the world.

Sir J. G. LEE STEERE.—Mr. President, I cannot hope that any effort of oratory or rhetoric on my part will be sufficiently great to arouse the imagination of members of this Conference as regards the question of Federation, because my mind is eminently a practical one, and I have little imagination in my constitution. I think, if I may say so without offence, that the debate that has hitherto taken place has had rather too much of an academic character, and has been a little too full of sentiment. We should now take the more practical view of the question. I have heard a great deal during the last few days about Federation being in the air. I think there is a deal of Federation in the air. We want to grasp it, and bring it down to the earth in order that we may grapple with it, and try to remove the difficulties which lie in the way. It is no use blinking the fact that there are difficulties in the way. It is a very happy omen indeed that in discussing this question we have with us representatives of New South Wales, because, whether it is true or not, there has been an impression throughout the Australian Colonies that the cause of Federation has been delayed in consequence of New South Wales refusing to take any part in the Federal Council. I am very glad indeed to see the representatives of New South Wales present now, because I hope that before this discussion ceases either one or the other of those representatives will give us their reasons for having hitherto refused to join that body, and thereby, as I contend, delayed the cause of Federation. From the correspondence which has been circulated in the different colonies, I am aware

that Sir Henry Parkes has stated that for the last twenty-five
years he has been in favour of Federation, but the course taken
by the honorable gentleman and by those who have followed him
in New South Wales must lead us to think that he really is not
so favourable to Federation as he has expressed himself to be,
and moreover that the general public of New South Wales are
not so favorable to Federation as they are supposed to be. I
think, too, that some confusion is caused in discussing this
question in talking about Federation. There is not one of us who
is not favorable to Federation. We are all most anxious to see
Federation brought about, but there are different kinds of
Federation. There is a complete Federation, based upon the
Constitution of Canada, and there may be an incomplete Federation, based upon a Constitution to be drawn up in future by us.
Now the resolution proposed by Sir Henry Parkes is one we cannot disagree with. We are all, I am sure, convinced that "the
early union under the Crown of all the Australasian Colonies"
is an end to be highly desired; but I have a very great objection
myself to discussing abstract resolutions of the kind now before
the Conference. I am rather surprised that an old parliamentary
hand, like Sir Henry Parkes, has not brought forward something
more definite, because, as a long student of constitutional history
and of parliamentary proceedings, I know that most leading
politicians deprecate bringing forward abstract resolutions, which
may to a certain extent excite public opinion, but, if they are
not followed up by something more practical, lead to nothing.
Therefore I was very sorry that Sir Henry Parkes did not follow
this motion up by some further resolutions which would lead to
some practical result. I believe myself that this motion was a
kind of blank shot fired across our bows by Sir Henry Parkes,
to make us show our colours. If that was his object he has to a
certain extent gained what he desired, because every member
who has yet spoken has declared what his views are. I gather
indirectly from Sir Henry Parkes that he is in favour of a complete Federation, that is, of at once founding an Australasian
Dominion based on the Constitution of Canada. I cannot say

that I am quite certain from what Mr. Deakin said whether he is in favour of a complete Federation based upon the Constitution of Canada, or whether he is prepared to accept something not quite so complete. There is no doubt about the views held by Mr. Playford. He decidedly thinks that we are not at present in a position to go in for complete Federation, while Sir Samuel Griffith is willing to take what he can get. Mr. Clark has stated that he would prefer a Constitution based upon that of the United States, but he is prepared to go in at once for a Dominion Federation. I myself am of opinion that it is impossible at the present time to form a Federal Dominion of the type of Canada. The difficulties that stand in the way are difficulties arising from the questions of finance and the fiscal policy, that every practical politician in the colony finds constantly confronting him. Of course, if we were to adopt a Federal Constitution based upon that of Canada or the United States we would have to give up all our Customs duties to the Federal Government. In doing that we would be following the lead of Canada, and my arguments at present are directed to the Constitution of Canada, and to the impossibility of our adopting it. Although I place these difficulties before members of the Conference, I hope that they will not think that I am at all opposed to a Federal Union. No one would rejoice more than I would if I could see a Federal Union of these colonies. We are in a very different position in these Colonies to what Canada was when it adopted Federation. Our position is very different financially—so different, that I see almost insurmountable difficulties to our following the lead of Canada in this respect. When Canada adopted Federation its public debt amounted to £21,000,000, and the interest upon it was £1,000,000 per annum. At the present time the total public debt of Canada is £40,000,000, whilst the interest is only £1,600,000. The loans have been consolidated, and less interest is paid now than before. The total amount raised by Customs duties in the dominion is £4,000,000 per annum, which is £2,400,000 more than is required to pay the interest on the public debt, and in addition to that the Federal Government have other revenues amounting to £3,000,000. They have, therefore, a revenue independently of the provinces, and after paying the interest on the public debt, of £5,400,000 with which to carry on the general government. Now, what is the case with Australasia? At the present time Australasia, instead of having a public debt of £21,000,000 like Canada, has a public debt of £168,000,000, on which she has to pay interest amounting to £6,365,000 per annum. These statistics are up to the end of 1888.

Mr. McMILLAN.—Does that include New Zealand?

Sir J. G. LEE STEERE.—Yes. How is this interest to be met? If we followed the lead of Canada the Federal Government would take all the Customs duties. Would the Customs duties produce an amount sufficient to pay the interest on the public debt alone. In Queensland the proportion of the total revenue raised from Customs duties is about one-third. In New South Wales—and this will astonish some people, because I have heard it said that New South Wales does not levy any Customs duties—the amount raised by Customs duties is nearly £2,000,000 per annum out of a total revenue of £8,800,000, or about one-fourth. In Victoria one-third of the total revenue is raised by Customs duties, in South Australia the proportion is one-fourth, in Western Australia one-half, in Tasmania one-half, and in New Zealand one-third. The total amount received for Customs duties in all the Colonies is nearly £8,000,000, and deducting about one-fourth for duties levied on intercolonial trade, which would cease altogether if we were federated on the basis of Canada, I estimate that there would be a balance left at the disposal of the Dominion Government of a little less than £6,000,000, which would all be absorbed in paying the interest upon the public debt, leaving nothing whatever for the general purposes of government.

Mr. PLAYFORD.—What about the cost of collection?

Sir J. G. LEE STEERE.—I would not be certain whether that includes the cost of collection or not. I do not think it does.

Mr. PLAYFORD.—It does not for South Australia.

Sir J. G. LEE STEERE.—Then there would not be sufficient to pay the interest on the public debt. How then is such a Government to be carried on? What other means are there of raising revenue?

Mr. PLAYFORD.—Excise.

Mr. J. G. LEE STEERE.—If we are to follow the example of Canada, the revenue from licenses and lands will be handed over to the provincial governments. I will tell you what Canada had, which we have not. It had a very large territory, independently of the provinces which came under the Federal Government. I allude to the whole of that splendid north-west territory, including the valuable lands of Manitoba.

Mr. BIRD.—We have Western Australia.

Sir J. G. LEE STEERE.—I am not surprised to hear that remark. Mr. Deakin suggested yesterday that the portion of Western Australia not to be handed over to the government of that colony should be placed in the hands of the Federal Parliament.

Mr. DEAKIN.—Instead of the government at home.

Sir J. G. LEE STEERE.—That was never intended. The honorable gentleman is under some misapprehension and perhaps he will allow me to correct him. It was proposed that a line should be drawn at the 26° latitude, as was done in South Australia. The legislature of Western Australia was to have precisely the same control over the lands south of that line as the other colonies of Australia have over their territory. North of that line the lands were to remain under regulations approved by the Secretary of State for the Colonies, and to be administered by the Colonial Government, the Imperial Government having nothing whatever to do with them. The rents derived from these lands were to be paid into the colonial exchequer, as part of the general revenue of the colony, but the proceeds of all sales of lands—and there are not likely to be many sales up there on account of the nature of the climate—were to be paid into a fund to be reserved for any colony that might hereafter be formed in that portion of the territory of Western Australia. Therefore there is no likehood of that land being made over to a Federal Government. We would far rather that it should be made over to a Federal Government than that it should be administered by a Government in England unacquainted with the circumstances of the colony, but I do not think that Western Australia would be prepared to make over the revenue of the northern portion of the colony for the purposes of a Federal Government. I have now shown pretty clearly that it is impossible, under the present circumstances of Australia, that we could enter into a complete Federal dominion on the basis of that of Canada, because of the financial and the fiscal difficuities in the way. I have been rather surprised to hear honorable gentlemen speak very lightly of those difficulties, as if they were cobwebs to be swept out of our way. That is not the best way to remove those difficulties; we must recognize them. The question next arises, whether, if we find it impossible to enter into a Federal dominion based upon the Constitution of Canada, we cannot agree to enter into a Federation not quite so complete as that. There was a phrase made use of in the letter of Mr. Morehead, the Premier of Queensland, on this subject, which struck me as being a very appropriate one, and which has my hearty concurrence. It is a phrase that will be long remembered by those who have to discuss this question. Mr. Morehead said that if the Federal Council was to be superseded it should be by a process of development, and not by a process of displacement. We should not entirely displace the Federal Council, but we should develop it until we made it available for the purposes for which we require it at present. I was not at the Conference held in Sydney, at which the Constitution of the Federal Council was drawn up, but I have been a member of the Federal Council since its formation, and I do not say that it is perfect, or anything like perfect. The members of the Conference who drew up the Constitution of the Federal Council recognized that it was not perfect, but they felt that they could not go further at that time. It is certainly capable of very great improvements. In the first place the members ought to be elected, and not appointed by any one; and then they would carry more weight than they do at the present time. In the next place the number of members ought to be increased very considerably. I do not think that two members for each colony is anything like enough to discuss questions in a proper manner. Then it is absolutely necessary for the purposes of defence, at any rate, that there should be an executive to carry out the decisions of the Federal Council. What is the use of our agreeing to have a federal defence force if there is to be no head? Suppose a war broke out and we wanted to concentrate all the colonial troops in one place, who is to give the orders? The Prime Minister of one colony would not allow the Prime Minister of another colony to give such orders. We must have a General appointed by the Imperial Government to take command of the troops, and we must have an Executive Government on whose orders that General would act, otherwise we cannot have federal defence. The initiatory step in connection with this Conference was taken by Sir Henry Parkes, who asked the Premier of Victoria what he intended to do in view of the report of Major-General Edwards. Sir Henry Parkes suggested a consultation. Mr. Gillies' answer was that more than a consultation was required; that action was necessary. A correspondence took place, and eventually Sir Henry Parkes recommended that the various colonies should appoint delegates to attend a Conference to consider certain resolutions with a view to the formation of a Federal Parliament on the model of that of Canada. I think that this Conference has a great deal more power than the majority of the members are disposed to attribute to it. We have just as much power as the Conference which met in Sydney, and which drew up the Constitution of the Federal Council. The members of this Conference have all been appointed by their Governments.

Mr. PLAYFORD.—No, we were appointed by Parliament.

Sir J. G. LEE STEERE.—So much the better. The representatives of New South Wales were appointed by their government, or rather they appointed themselves, because they are the government. Their parliament were perfectly aware that they were coming over here. How then can it be said that we are a self-constituted body, unable to deal with this question? I cannot agree with that view. We are bound to do more than pass an abstract resolution affirming that Federation is desirable. How can we ask our parliaments to send delegates to another Convention to discuss Federation? They will naturally ask, "What kind of Federation?" It is absolutely necessary that we should lay down some of the conditions of this Federation, so that our parliaments may express an opinion upon them. I do not think that the parliaments will be disposed to appoint delegates for such a purpose unless they know what those delegates are going to consider, and for that reason I think we should agree to something definite and practical. Then it will be impossible for us to persuade our parliaments to send delegates to a Convention unless we are prepared to show them that they are going to get some benefit from it. There is a good deal of self-interest being displayed by some of the colonies in this question of Federation. There is no doubt whatever that Federation will be of very great advantage to the larger colonies, but I am not sure that we will be able to show that the smaller colonies will get equal advantage from it. I am quite certain that Western Australia will not if the Federal Constitution is based upon that of Canada. We derive quite one-half of our revenue from Customs duties, and a great proportion of the amount is obtained from the duties levied on goods from the other colonies. If we gave up so large a portion of our revenue we would have to have recourse to direct taxation. What prospect would there be of Western Australia agreeing to enter into a Federal Union if the first thing we had to tell the people of that colony was that they would have to put their hands in their pockets and pay a direct tax.

Mr. CLARK.—You would be relieved of some of your burdens.

Sir J. G. LEE STEERE.—Yes, but to nothing like the extent to which we would have to contribute to the general government. There is another thing we should know before we recommend our parliaments to send delegates to the Convention. I hope we shall be told on behalf of New South Wales whether that colony is willing to come into anything less than a complete Federated Union. If that colony is not willing it will be waste of time to have a Convention, and I hope that Sir Henry Parkes will use his great influence to induce the colony he represents to enter into what he may call an incomplete union if he cannot obtain the complete union he desires. I shall welcome most gladly any scheme that may be devised to enable us to federate, if only for certain purposes. If we only federate for the purpose of defence it will be well to have had a Conference for that. Mr. Deakin remarked that it was all very well to ridicule the idea of the colonies being attacked by a foreign foe, but I do not see anything ridiculous in the idea. A day may come when England is at war, and our coasts may be ravaged by hostile cruisers, or attempts be made to land a foreign force on our shores. It is absolutely necessary that we should be prepared with a Federal defence force. For that reason alone, if for no other, I shall be glad to see Federation accomplished in some form. I looked over the Federal Council Act this morning to see what subjects can be referred to that body, and I find that almost every subject which concerns the colonies as a whole is included in the list, while subjects which are not included can be referred to the Council by the legislatures of the several colonies. Thus, under the Act, everything could be referred to the Federal Council, and we could obtain everything that is desired with the three alterations I have mentioned as desirable in the constitution of the Council—a larger number of representatives, these representatives to be elective, and a Federal Executive. I hope that the views I have put forth will do something to elucidate the question and remove the difficulties in the way—difficulties which cannot be ignored. We must do the best we can to conquer those difficulties. I hope that the efforts of this Conference will at any rate result in our agreeing to recommend that delegates be sent from our several parliaments to consider what is the best form for a Federal Constitution to be brought into operation at the present time.

Captain RUSSELL.—Mr. President, it was Sir Samuel Griffith, I think, who told us that it appeared that the sentiment of Federation was in the boughs of a tree—that it was descending from the boughs rather than springing from the roots of the tree. I think that is true to a great extent, and that the plant has not yet taken root, but that does not materially affect the point. We, who have come over here as representatives to this Conference are as the seed; when we go back to our several colonies we may plant it in fertile soil, and from that may grow the roots and branches of Federated Australasia. It will be my pleasure to go back under these circumstances and instruct my countrymen as I have been myself instructed in regard to the many advantages which may flow from Federation. Federation not only floats in the air—no person can doubt that; for the Australian Colonies it will very shortly be an accomplished fact. I hope that many years will not elapse before there will be a United Australia, which will be a great power in the southern seas. Coming as from a rather remote part of Australasia, I view possibly more dispassionately than any other member of the Conference (except my colleague) the various difficulties which stand in the way of a United Australasia. We have heard them compared to a lion standing in the way, to an opossum, and—after ideas had grown big at grand banquets—to an elephant. I believe the illustration of the mountain would be more correct, feeling sure that on examination it will bring forth only a ridiculous mouse. It has been said that we cannot federate without fiscal union. As a free-trader, such is my opinion. The true basis of Federation is that interchange of products which leads to the expansion of trade, and a consequent *rapprochement* between the peoples of different communities. It is said that if the extremely absurd duties on local products are not abolished, a Federal Union can come to nothing, and that must be so.

What reason is there why, in a country like this, where the climate and the habits and customs of the people are one, you should first create arbitrary distinctions and then say it is impossible to destroy them? Are you not all one people with identical interests, no matter what divisions into colonies there may be, and why should you not all work cordially together? Sir Henry Parkes said there were no natural difficulties—no boundaries to separate you. As far as my knowledge of the geography of Australia goes, I believe that parallels of latitude or longitude are in many instances the imaginary boundaries which separate the great colonies of the Australian continent. The only other so-called boundary is the River Murray, which, far from being a boundary, should be a great highway (for it is a road which ever maintains itself without expense) to carry the products of the neighbouring colonies to one another. There is no reason why the colonies should be separated. With climate similar, and soil so similar that, though the latter happily varies so as to enable one colony to produce that which is needed in another, there is nothing to compel the colonies to have artificial restrictions. I would avoid altogether going into the question as to whether we should federate on the principle of Canada or the United States. Australia will enjoy the advantage of being able to compare those two Constitutions, and she may take from them that which is material and necessary to her own Constitution. There is no reason why Australia should not adopt that which is best from every kind of Constitution in forming the Union. Then the question comes, can Australasia at the present moment join in this Federation? Though I believe that the feeling in all the colonies of Australasia is most kindly one towards the others, and though there is a desire that their interests should be identical, it would be absurd to deny the fact that when circumstances are so different as between the sister colonies of New Zealand, Fiji, and Australia, it is impossible to say at this moment that the people of the two former colonies would at once join in any scheme of Federation. There are very many points in which the colony which I represent would be glad to join in happy concord with the continental colonies, but to say absolutely that that colony would be prepared, at any rate for the next few years, to merge its young manhood in the more mature life of the Australian Colonies would be to lead the Conference to believe what I cannot hope. We have many interests in common, but it is probable we should not at once submit ourselves to a Government in which we should have so unimportant a part. Mr. Clark, the Attorney-General for Tasmania, remarked, when addressing the Conference to-day, that with every distinct physical environment there comes a distinct national type. With a population of 700,000 people in New Zealand, dwelling in an island where the climate is dissimilar to a very great extent from that of Australia, which has been colonized in an entirely different manner, and, speaking colloquially, having had a very much rougher time than the colonies of Australia, we are likely to develop a very complete individuality—a distinct national type. We have had to struggle against not only a more boisterous climate than Australia but against a dense vegetation; and we have had to carve our homes out of the wilderness which, though marvellously prolific and fertile nevertheless marks a country in which self-denial has had to be practised by its settlers to an extent of which the people of the Australian continent have no conception. Not only have the settlers had to struggle against the forces of nature but against a proud, indomitable, and courageous race of aborigines. That native race has been treated in a manner so considerate that the condition of no other native and savage race on the face of the globe can be compared to it. Their right to their lands was recognised from the first. I do not boast that our public men were more pure in spirit than those of other countries, but as the colonization of New Zealand was effected originally through missionary zeal, through that, to a large extent, our hearts and policy were softened. But in addition to this feeling, the natives could defend their own interests and look down the sights of a rifle better than any other savage people. They were many, and the white settlers were few, and when our hearts were not softened by the missionary, we were controlled by the thought of the Maoris' numbers, and of their rifles. Therefore we recognised their right to their own land, and instead of confiscating it we admitted their claim to its full possession, administration, and disposal. Members of the Conference may perhaps ask, why am I giving this short historical sketch? It bears materially upon the question of Federation. The whole of New Zealand politics for years hinged almost entirely upon the native question. That question destroyed more governments than anything else in New Zealand. All turned upon the necessity for keeping the natives at peace, and yet obtaining enough of their lands to further colonization. I am happy to say, and I thank God for it, that the day is past in which there is any probability —nay, any possibility—of another native war occurring. But one of the important questions in New Zealand politics for many years to come must be that of native administration, and were we to hand over that question to a Federal Parliament—to an elective body, mostly Australians, that cares nothing and knows nothing about native administration, and the members of which have dealt with native races in a much more summary manner than we have ventured to deal with ours in New Zealand—the difficulty which precluded settlement for years in the North Island might again appear. It is extremely improbable that hostilities would again break out between the natives and the white settlers, but the advance of civilization would be enormously delayed if the regulation of this question affecting New Zealand was handed over to a body of gentlemen who know nothing whatever of the traditions of the past. Another question which it has been said will come well within the scope of a Federal Government is that of a scheme of federal defence. Up to a certain point I hold that to be perfectly true. New Zealand has a large sea-coast; she may be open to attack on the part of hostile cruisers should they ever come into these waters, and we should be only too happy—I can speak with absolute certainty as to that—to join with Australia in any system of naval defence.

Mr. DEAKIN.—Hear, hear.

Captain RUSSELL.—I venture to say that, with our large sea-board and seafaring population, before many years are over we shall be able to furnish a considerable contingent who will be pleased to serve Her Majesty and her colonies on board ship. The most popular corps in New Zealand are those of the naval volunteers, and I have no hesitation in saying that if the time comes in which we are unfortunately involved in war with a European power, we could place upon the ships of war, Her Majesty might send out, a contingent which would vastly enhance Great Britain's maritime power in these seas. But I do not see how we are to benefit by a Federal Army. As an old soldier I recognise the importance of having a considerable force in which there should be promotion among the young officers, so that they may not stagnate in the junior ranks until they are old men, and finally leave the service as useless as they were when they entered it. It is necessary that there should be a Federal Army—and this would specially apply to Australia—that there may be promotion, and that you may be able to obtain that constant succession of young officers by which alone you can ensure those scientific soldiers who are absolutely necessary in these days. But would it be possible, in case of an attack upon New Zealand, to send over an army from Australia to help us? Of the willingness of Australia to do this I have no doubt, but in her power to do it I cannot believe. We should be assaulted, if at all, by a filibustering expedition, which would come, see, but I hope not conquer, long before you in Australia could hear of its appearance on our shores. A Federal Army would be of no use to us, and it might involve us in expenses we are not prepared to meet. But there are innumerable points to which we could agree in the union. For instance, all matrimonial laws should be of one currency throughout Australasia. So also should postal and cable communication. That, however, could probably be brought about without resort to a Federal Parliament, and also reciprocity with all the colonies. New Zealand would be happy to meet any other colony in some treaty; but if

I, who am a free-trader to the backbone, am to be told that New Zealand should join irrevocably in a Customs Union which might bring about more protection than exists at the present time, it is to tell me that which does not commend itself to my judgment. I do not believe that New Zealand would join in that. We are essentially an exporting country, depending materially on outside trade, and that being the case, our prosperity must depend upon a large, free inter-communication between the different nations of the earth. Speaking for myself, I would never consent to any scheme which would bring more protection upon the colony of New Zealand. There are one or two reasons in addition, which I jotted down while Sir Henry Parkes was speaking, which would make it a very dangerous thing for the smaller colonies to enter into this scheme of federal union, without grave consideration. Out of a population of 3,810,000, New South Wales, Victoria, and Queensland own the allegiance of 2,656,000 people; in other words, said Sir Henry Parkes, two-thirds of the whole population of Australasia belonged to those three colonies. It must, of course, be a matter for very grave doubt as to whether the influence which naturally must proceed from this large population might not work adversely to the interests of the more thinly-populated colonies. It is of no use attempting to blink these things. It must also be remembered that the three colonies I have named are united by natural circumstances, that they are side by side, and were originally part of the same colony. Local politics brought about the severance of those colonies, and there is no reason why they should ever have separated if they had been allowed a little more local government. There is no reason why they should not be reunited, and if they are reunited it will be a marriage of affection. It will be a case of neighbours whose sons and daughters have married together in order to bring divided lands into one solid property. It will be a marriage of affection if these colonies come together. But with New Zealand it would be simply a *mariage de convenance*, and her representatives must see that the marriage settlements are not drawn out in a hurry, that before the masculine power and strength of

Australia was united to the beauty of New Zealand the settlements are so arranged that the Married Women's Property Act shall have full force in case of any little dispute occurring hereafter. I had thought of moving an amendment upon the motion of Sir Henry Parkes, but as it is not my object to throw the apple of discord into this fair community, as I desire by every means in my power to assist the federation of the colonies, and as I wish that not only New Zealand but the remoter colonies of Australasia shall have an opportunity of coming into this Federation as soon as they can see any advantage to be gained by it, I hope Sir Henry Parkes will consent to change the word "Australasian" in his motion to "Australian." If he will consent to do that I will propose a motion additional, as follows:—

"That to the union of the Australian Colonies contemplated by the foregoing resolution, the remoter Australasian Colonies shall be entitled to admission at such times and on such conditions as may hereafter be agreed upon."

I think it would be a very great misfortune, not only to Australasia but also to Australia, if in the Convention which we may take it for granted will some day meet, and to which the New Zealand representatives at this Conference will ask their parliament to send delegates, New Zealand and Fiji are not represented. It would be a pity for Australasia, and for Australia too, seeing that if the latter is true to herself and has a motherly feeling for the younger colonies, which I believe she has, she should join in saying to them: "Although you do not at present feel that you can enter the Federation and throw yourself into our arms, here is a hand to help you whenever the day may come in which you see your way to join this magnificent union."

Dr. COCKBURN.—Sir, I feel that to-day a very great point has been gained. A large number of speeches have been addressed to the Conference from an absolutely practical point of view. I would like to say a word or two in reference to the most excellent address which Mr. Clark delivered. I think that among all the advocates for Federation who are here to-day there are none stronger or more enthusiastic than the representatives of Tasmania. But I should be sorry if this eagerness should lead to any undue haste, and I do not think that the particular form of union which Mr. Clark mentioned as something which might be obtained at once would be at all a desirable thing. Mr. Clark intimated that, pending the adjustment of differences, it would be a step in advance if the eastern colonies joined at once in a complete union. I do not think that this would assist the cause of Federation, or that it would be a good way to begin uniting Australia by dividing it into two. I am afraid that any such step would be more likely to have the effect of postponing the settlement of the questions at issue, or the formation of an Australian nation covering the whole continent, and taking in the colonies which form Australasia. Canada, certainly, had this form of union in the first instance, but the case is not a parallel one. Previous to Nova Scotia and New Brunswick joining with Upper and Lower Canada there was no Federal Government existing between the Canadas, except the union between Quebec and Ontario, which was in no sense a confederation, but was in every respect a complete union. In our case things are different. We have already made some steps towards union. We are not altogether disunited. We have taken the first steps, and embarked upon some form of Federation, and to drop this substance for a shadow, infinitely greater but more remote, would be an act which could only bring about disastrous consequences. I am afraid that Mr. Clark's suggestion would divide the map of Australia just about as near the centre as it could be divided, north and south, and I am afraid that a long time would elapse before those two parts became cemented again. And I am quite sure that it would be much better to first adjust our minor differences, even though that should take a few years—two or three years—to accomplish, than to embark on a one-sided union immediately. Now, Mr. Clark says, also, that in the United States there was a complete parallel for our present condition, and that the reason for the formation of the legislative union which now obtains between the

United States was the existence of a commercial difficulty. Well, that is no doubt one aspect of the case, which can very well be considered, but I must say that my reading of the history of America leads me to the conclusion that the causes which drove the different States of America together were of an altogether more pressing character than any commercial needs. Throughout the papers which were written at that time by those who were rightly called the fathers of the Constitution—Hamilton, Madison, and others—and published in the form of the *Federalist*, the greatest possible stress is laid upon the fact that a further union of the United States was necessary, because the loose federation which had previously existed was not equal to the demands made upon it by a prolonged war. Congress might levy for soldiers from the different States, but it had no means of securing their attendance on the field of battle; Congress might levy contributions from the different States, but it had no means of ensuring the payments of those contributions by the States— and it was in order to remove this state of things, and to put the country, in a time of peace, in such a position that it should never more be endangered in time of war—it was to carry out the essential principle of defence, and not so much the mere necessities of commercial affairs, which led to that strong union being formed. The United States were not absolutely at war, but they were surrounded by enemies, north and south, and the navigation of their rivers was impeded by foreign interference. Their case was, therefore, altogether different from that which now presents itself to us. Mr. Clark alluded to the question of a Customs union as affecting South Australia, and he seemed to indicate that if the financial difficulty was got over all that was necessary would have been accomplished. Now, admitting that the financial difficulty does stand very much in the way of an immediate Customs union, I may say at once that that is not the only aspect of the case in which South Australia considers the question of Federation. Our Customs tariff was not in any way initiated for the purposes of revenue. Those who formulated our tariff formulated it as a purely protective tariff, and it was not at all a spirit of raising revenue that dictated the imposition of that tariff. The mere fact of revenue being thereby raised was altogether a secondary consideration, and the attitude of South Australia, in considering whether the time is ripe for a Customs union or not, has no reference whatever to the financial question. Our manufacturing industries are, of course, in their infancy, and if a Customs union obtained between the colonies, they would have at once to be brought into direct competition with the long-established industries of their powerful neighbours. In saying this I do not wish to convey in any way the impression that South Australia means to maintain her hostile tariff against the rest of Australia; she does not look forward to hostile custom-houses continually harassing those who wish to cross her borders, but from the protectionist point of view she asks that some little time should be allowed to her industries before they have to face a competition which has been too severe for them in the past; some little time for those manufacturers who have lately embarked in their industrial enterprises under the fostering aid of a protective tariff to become firmly established. However, as I have said on other occasions, I don't think this difficulty would be lasting, and I don't think it would be long before it was overcome. I think that South Australia will say, on looking at the question all round, that she has quite as much to gain in some directions by intercolonial free trade as she has to lose in other directions. Standing as she does in the centre of all the colonies, holding out a hand to each of them, I think that her position would dictate that, after the mere temporary difficulties have been overcome, she of all the colonies would have least to lose by reciprocity and free trade among them all. But as the question of a Customs union has been so often raised, and as our arguments here are partaking very strongly of a free-trade character, I should just like to know this: Is it the impression of any member here that when the federation of Australia is consummated it is to be a vindication of the principle of free trade? I take it that any such hope is for ever past when the federation of Australia is consummated. When, as a portion of that Federation, the hostile custom-houses on the borders of the different colonies are removed, it will not be a vindication of the principle of free trade, but rather the institution of a more complete system of protection—the apotheosis of a strong protective policy. I think it is just as well that this should be understood. The voice of South Australia has pronounced emphatically, and by a large majority, in favour of that protection without which the history of the world presents no example, as far as my reading has been able to show, of a nation which has risen into prosperity. Mr. Clark, I know, will excuse me if I take up another point. He delivered a speech so full of points that it is quite impossible to speak on the subject without devoting attention to them. Mr. Clark expressed some regret that steps had not been taken by the Imperial authorities, when the Constitutions of the colonies were first given to them, to guard against such difficulties as those which now exist. Now, I think it would have been a great mistake had that step been taken by the Imperial Legislature. I think that the wisdom of the Mother-country, in dealing with her colonies, has always been shown in her leaving them as free as possible to follow their own inclinations, and to work out their own destinies. Any dictation, even although it had been at the very commencement of our Constitutions, would not, I am afraid, have led to the end desired; and I think it would have been a mistake, from every point of view, had anything been done in the earlier stage of the history of these colonies to lessen the development of that individuality which, after all, goes to make the strength of a colony. I take it, Sir, that, consistent with union for those purposes on which union is necessary for the good of all, the least possible sacrifice there is of individuality the better it will be for each of the colonies standing by itself, and the better for that union of the colonies which will represent them all. Because I don't think that we wish to see a homogeneous National union. We want to see a union of strong colonies, each with its own local traditions, each with its own local affections, each with its own peculiarities. I think that such a union, such a brotherhood of infinite diversity would be much better than a homogeneous union of colonies without a proper amount of differentiation. I quite agree with Mr. Clark in saying that we could not follow Canada in this respect. I think the members of the Conference generally agree in that opinion that in no regard can we look upon the example of Canada as one to be imitated. On the other hand, we should have considerable difficulty in following the example of America, because the whole constitution of the United States of America is so far removed from anything which has ever obtained under British rule. In America there is no such thing as responsibility of Ministers to Parliament, and in this respect, I am sure, no member of this Conference would suggest that we should follow the example of the United States.

Mr. CLARK.—I don't know about that.

Dr. COCKBURN.—Well, it would be so utterly different from any of those traditions which have enwrapped themselves around the growth of the British Constitution, that I don't think any dependency of the Crown ——

Sir HENRY PARKES.—It would be another growth of that prized variety.

Dr. COCKBURN.—But I don't think that any colony or group of colonies under the British Crown could effect such a radical change, even supposing the change were desirable, which, I think, most of us would agree it is not.

Mr. CLARK.—Party government is played out.

Dr. COCKBURN.—But party government obtains to the fullest extent in America.

Mr. DEAKIN.—Nowhere more so.

Dr. COCKBURN.—What do we see in America? What is the counterpart of our popular assemblies in America. The Congress, which presents in no respect, as far as I can see, save in the respect that representation therein is based on population, any analogy to our representative assemblies. The Congress is a large body of men with no governing power whatever. There are no Ministers responsible for the conduct of business. The Congress is split up into something like fifty committees, acting independently of one another, and the number of bills submitted in the course of a session amount to about 7,000.

Mr. CLARK.—How many are passed ?

Dr. COCKBURN.—A very small number of them.

Mr. CLARK.—So much the better.

Dr. COCKBURN.—The whole principle of our British Constitution is that of the responsibility of Ministers to parliament, and I think that the British Constitution being a gradual growth, and not a manufacture, is vastly superior to any Constitution even however carefully drawn up, as the American Constitution was. The very principle of the British Constitution is elasticity and development; whereas the principle of the American Constitution is rigidity and finality. I think that in a young country like Australia any form of government should be as expansive as possible, so as to adapt itself to the constantly varying requirements of the future life of the colonies. I don't think I need follow this matter any further, more than to say this: that a study of the American Constitution, as a manufactured article, as compared with the British Constitution as a gradual growth, leads one to the conclusion, I think irresistibly, that in all matters of constitutional government the form of government should be a growth, and not in any sense a manufacture. The very points on which the framers of the American Constitution prided themselves, those forms which they themselves invented, are the very parts of their system of government which have proved to be failures, while, on the contrary, those they adopted from England, which were the growth of centuries, have been found to be successful. What the members of the Convention that drew up the Constitution of America prided themselves most upon was the manner of the election of the President, and yet if anything has proved a failure and fallen short of the hopes of those who drew up that Constitution it has been the manner in which the election of President, for which they laid out such careful rules, has become modified by usage. And so I think that in every respect Federation should be a growth, and, as with all growths, anything like forcing is to be deprecated. As a rule, the slower the growth, the more gradual the development, the stronger is the product. Now, a good many members of the Conference, and still more, a large section of the public, have complained of the very slow advance, the small progress which has been made towards the consummation of Australian unity. For my part I have not been able to join in this view. I think that, considering all things, the colonies have been growing together very well indeed. I think that for every one who hoped to have seen a more speedy adhesion to Federation there are many who, looking closely into the matter, would come to the conclusion that the colonies might have done very much worse. It seems to me that the way the colonies have been federated in detail augurs very highly indeed for the success of their Federation in general. The colonies for many years have been growing together on such questions as the postal union. Some years ago I had the honour of being the Minister controlling the Postal Department of South Australia, when an arrangement was entered into with the sister colonies for a postal union with regard to the transmission of mails by the great sea route to and from Europe. In this respect we federated first in detail. And so it was with regard to legislation in reference to debtors absconding over the Border, with respect to which the colonies approached one another in the true federal spirit. Then again, in reference to the exclusion of alien races whose presence would we think be detrimental to our development, a Conference was held in the true federal spirit, and I hope that effect will be given to the conclusions of that Conference by all the colonies that were concerned in it. There is another matter in which, I think, without much difficulty we can exhibit the federal spirit in detail—a question which greatly concerns the Colony of South Australia—I mean the question of navigation and riparian rights of the Murray waters. That is a matter on which I think there is an opportunity for the colonies adjoining the Murray to exhibit the true federal spirit, and I trust that the Colony of New South Wales will very soon see its way to meet the wishes of South Australia in this matter. We have been pressing for a long time now for a Conference between the three colonies concerned to consider the matter, because hitherto no basis of agreement has been arrived at, and I do trust that the federal spirit which has prevailed amongst the colonies in regard to other matters will, in this instance also, have its due effect. For the reasons I have named we have nothing to complain of so far as the existence of a federal spirit between the colonies is concerned, but what we want to do is to give to this federal spirit "a local habitation and a name." And in doing that we are brought face to face with the question as to what form of union is best adapted to our requirements. Of course it is well known that States become united either by means of a federation or by means of what is known as a national union. In a pure federation the central government is not brought into immediate relation with the individual citizen, but deals only with him through the local legislatures. The mandates of the central government are enforced through the local legislatures, and any funds requisite for the transaction of the business of the central government are levied by the local legislatures. On the other hand, in a national union, the central government is brought into immediate relation with every citizen of the nation. And it was this difference between the manner in which the Congress was brought into relation either with the local States or with the individual citizen which led America to abandon the pure confederation which the States had at first—the first Congress America had being an example of pure federation. It was this fact, that the federation had no immediate influence on the individual citizen, but acted on the citizen only through the medium of the local government—the government of the local State—that led to the denunciation of the federation system by Hamilton, Madison, and other writers in the *Federalist*, and to their claims for something more nearly approaching a national union, which, in fact, led to the establishment of the present Constitution of the United States. That is neither a pure federation nor is it a pure national union. It is a compromise between the two. As far as Congress is concerned, the individual citizen is represented; as far as the Senate is concerned, representation only obtains through the medium of the State. Each State is there represented as a unit, irrespective of its population. But there is this advantage over a pure federation, that the central government is brought into immediate relation with every individual citizen of the United States, taxes are levied direct without the intervention of the local legislatures. One of the great arguments in favour of the existence of that state of things was the impossibility of enforcing contributions towards the support of the Federal Army, when the States were united merely by means of a federation. It was pointed out then that all the difference in the world lay between active resistance and non-compliance. When the States were joined merely by a federation, all that a State had to do, if it did not wish to contribute, was not to actively resist but merely neglect to comply with the demands of the central authority; but in the case of a national union mere non-compliance is not sufficient. In that case active resistance is required, and it is so much easier for the central government to deal with a case of active resistance than to deal with a case of mere non-compliance. Now, the federation in the United States of America was found not to be that success which its advocates anticipated, and the secret of that failure is the same as the secret of the failures of all federations which have ever existed, as far as my reading goes on the history of federation. That is to say, a loose union of States, although it is ample in time of peace, has proved to be utterly inadequate to the prosecution of a prolonged war. It was this cause that led to the breaking-up of the great Grecian Confederations; it was this which led to the breaking-up of the American Confederation; but because this cause has been effective in preventing the success of federations in the past, there is no reason whatever why, under different conditions, federations should not be more successful in the future. I don't think there is any probability of a United Australia ever being engaged in a prolonged war; at all events, it is not a likely occurrence; and, therefore, because federations have been unsuccessful in the past we must not conclude that the system of federation will not be applicable to our requirements. I quite agree with what Sir James Lee Steere said, that if the Federal Council—which is at present such a federation as obtained in America before the complete union, such a federation as obtained between the Grecian States—is to be superseded, it should be in the manner he advocates, namely by development. I do not think we are likely to advance the cause of federation by breaking with the past. But, for the Federal Council, I am sure this Conference could not have assembled with the prospects of success which I believe now await it. The Federal Council has done a great deal towards fostering the federal spirit, towards drawing the colonies together, and I do trust, whatever the outcome of this Conference and of succeeding Conventions may be, that in every respect the work of the Federal Council will be recognised, and that any union which may take its place will be as a development and an improvement upon the Federal Council, and will not be in any way founded upon its ruins. So much has been said on the subject of the Canadian federation, that I feel it is hardly excusable for me to deal further with it, but there is one aspect which I should like to present to the Conference as regards the formation of what is known as the Canadian Confederation, in 1867, and I quite agree with other speakers on this subject that in no sense is the Government of the Canadian States a true federation. It is in reality a national union, and the explanation of its existence is found in the circumstances which obtained in Canada in 1867. What took place in Canada in 1867 has always been looked upon as a movement towards closer union, but I confess that, as far as I have read on the subject, it can in no way bear such an interpretation. The action of Canada in 1867 was, in reality, an act of disunion. The causes which led up to it were the dissatisfaction between Ontario and Quebec—Upper and Lower Canada—with regard to the union which between the years 1841 and 1867 existed between them. In 1841, Upper and Lower Canada, which before that had been under different Parliaments, were united by an Imperial Act under one strong and coercive union. And the action of 1867, instead of being a drawing into closer union of those two provinces, was, in reality, an action of disruption. It was the union which chafed them; it was not their separation. They were already united in the closest possible bonds, but it was this close union which they objected to, and from which they strove to free themselves. In 1867 two alternative schemes were proposed. One was for a general confederation of the States of Canada, in which Upper and Lower Canada were to be represented, and also Nova Scotia and New Brunswick, and such other States as chose to come into it. But there was an alternative scheme, and that was, that, failing the joining of the other colonies in the federation, the disunion of the previously united Canada should be effected at all hazards. During the very last year in which the united parliament of Ontario and Quebec sat, an address was presented to Her Majesty the Queen, praying for what? A closer union? No! For centralisation? No! Praying for provincialism, praying for separate governments, praying for a release from that bond of union which they felt to have chafed and hindered their development. The whole history of Canada was an attempt to unite the different States, not with the view of ministering to the requirements of all the population of Canada, but with the view of stamping out one of the elements existing in Canada, or at least so overruling it that it should have no voice in the government of the country. Lord Durham, who in 1841 presented a report to the Imperial Parliament on the subject, made no attempt to conceal what the real object of the union then advocated was. The object was to denationalize the French inhabitants of Quebec, to give to the English-speaking portions of the community a preponderating influence in the deliberations of the legislature. I think nothing can be more foreign to our purpose than the spirit which animated the Canadians between the years 1841 and 1867. They had found their union oppressive. The whole government had become reduced to a deadlock. Between 1862 and 1864 there were no less than five changes of Ministries. The government could not be continued. They wanted no closer union or central government, but provincial legislatures to guard those local interests which they felt could not be properly dealt with by a central authority. The case of Australasia, of course, presents a complete opposite to what obtained in Canada. Here we have no diverse populations, speaking different languages. Here we have no desire to stamp out the individuality of any class of men who are loyal to the British Crown. In Canada the union was an absolute necessity, to counterbalance the continually increasing and preponderating influence of the United States. A coercive union was an absolute necessity, in order, as Lord Durham stated, to denationalize the French; and because not only was union, but coercive union, necessary, they established a form of government which practically vested all the powers in the central government. Here we have no desire to act in such a manner. Here we desire to preserve the individuality of every province and every colony which at present forms the Australian group. The coercion which was necessary in Canada is here unnecessary. We have no fear of one another. In Canada all kinds of local jealousies existed. Here we have no real jealousies, no racial distinctions. Therefore it is not necessary here, where the community is homogeneous and adhesive, to resort to those bonds which, in Canada, were found necessary to counteract the thrust of divergent elements. Fortunately for Canada the minor scheme, which only dealt with the establishment of local governments in Upper and Lower Canada, was not resorted to. By all manner of means the other provinces—Nova Scotia and New Brunswick, and eventually Prince Edward Island and other provinces— were brought into the union. But it must be remembered that each of these provinces joined the union for some immediate and substantial benefit. Nova Scotia and New Brunswick were allowed the special advantage of levying duties on the export of wool and coal. They also had reason to believe they would be largely represented in the Senate of Canada. Twenty-four members were to be allowed to Quebec, twenty-four to Ontario, and twenty-four to the maritime provinces; but as a matter of fact Nova Scotia and New Brunswick now only possess a small amount of that representation. The other provinces joined the confederation under strong dictates of self-interest. They had not all to surrender those individual and sovereign rights which the colonies of Australia possess. As far as Prince Edward Island is concerned she had no powers of autonomy at all. Her executive consisted of a Governor, who appointed his own Ministry. Prince Edward Island had everything to gain and nothing to lose by coming into confederation. Instead of losing liberties, she absolutely gained everything. She gained some share, at least, of autonomy. In addition to that, a powerful reason existed for the entrance of the island into the confederation. A great difficulty had existed owing to the greater portion of the lands being in the hands of landlords, and to the existence of the fact that settlers on the island found it difficult to make satisfactory terms with the holders. They were brought into confederation under the agreement that this difficulty was to be solved. Money was to be provided for the purchase of the land for the settlers, and by this means the settlers were to be relieved from the difficulties under which they were labouring. Again, Canada had another strong reason for federation. She had long cast covetous eyes on the north-west province, and it was understood, if federation were effected, that that province would be handed over to her. There are many features in connection with Canada which it would be a misfortune for the Australasian Colonies to follow. Not only is there no equal representation of the States, as such, in either branch of the legislature, but the Supreme Court in Canada is merely a superior court, and is subject itself to the higher powers of the Privy Council. So that, as has already been mentioned, the Supreme Court, instead of making justice final, as a matter of fact interposes another platform upon which the rich man can fight the poor. Another objection to the system of Canada is that, although many of the local legislatures have their franchise based on manhood—every man having the right to vote—no such rule obtains in the Dominion of Canada. In the Dominion of Canada manhood suffrage does not obtain, but property qualification, although not extensive, is imposed on every elector. Again, the power of veto, exercised by the central government of Canada over acts of the provincial legislatures, has always been found to be exceedingly irritating, and tends to make their affection towards the central government less than it otherwise would be. Any act passed by a provincial legislature might be vetoed by the central government within the space of one year, and any act passed by the Dominion of Canada as a whole might be vetoed by the Crown within the lapse of two years. I do not think that when we have formed our complete Federation we ought to have so extensive a power of vetoing as that which obtains in the case of Canada. The power of vetoing, if given at all, should be laid down within strict lines. In Canada, however, that power covers most debatable ground, and it is this latitude which renders the exercise of the vetoing power so disastrous in its consequences. Where the lines are strict and well defined no one feels the imposition, but where there is a doubt, at once there exists difficulty and disaffection. Then, in Canada, almost the whole of the revenues go to the central government, and have to be repaid in the form of subsidies to the local legislatures. By far the largest amount of the revenues of provincial legislatures is derived from subsidies from the central government. This, I think all will agree, is a most roundabout way of levying and disbursing the results of taxation. The consideration of the confederations which had existed previously—of the partial confederation, or compromise between the principles of federation and national union in the United States, and the complete union which obtains in Canada under the name of federation—leads us to the conclusion that, in the matter of framing our Constitution, we can have no precedent to guide us. From the very first we have presented to the world an unprecedented occurrence, and I think that, as our past history has been unprecedented, so our future history must be of a similar character. We must look to ourselves to draw out the lines upon which our great destiny is to be accomplished. We must take counsel of our own necessities, and not be blindly guided by any precedent whatever; I am sure that in this way only shall we arrive at the consummation of our desires. To blindly follow any example would be likely to lead to most disastrous consequences; whereas to follow our own destiny, to trust that power which has hitherto led us to shape a successful course for us in the future, is no more than our past records justify us in doing. Above all things—whatever is the result of this Conference and of succeeding Conferences—I trust that nothing will be done to unduly sacrifice the individuality of the various colonies. Our individualities, our very limitations, are our strength. To attempt to secure anything like uniformity would be most disastrous. Such union as we have must be the union of various elements. Our Australian concert is not to be one of unison, but of harmony, in which the difference of each part blend together in forming the concord of the whole. Considering the true federal spirit which has been animating the various colonies in the past, considering the strong public sentiment which is now growing up in favour of Federation, the wonderful growth which has attended this question even within the last few weeks—viewing the progress we have made towards union, viewing the fact that all great forces tend towards union, I do not think we need have any fear whatever of what the ultimate result will be. We can securely look forward to the consummation of Australian unity as a confederation, not as a crushing national union—we can look forward to the consideration of such Australian unity as will preserve our individuality, as an occurrence which is likely to take place before the lapse of many years, and very much earlier than even the most sanguine of us at present are capable of hoping. We have everything in our favour—the differences between us are small and temporary; the bonds of union are large and lasting—and, in common with other members of the Conference I trust that this meeting will yield no barren fruit, but will in future stand out as the preliminary step taken by the Australian Colonies towards bringing about the hope of their larger patriotism, a United Australia.

The Conference adjourned at twenty minutes past four o'clock until eleven o'clock the following day.

WEDNESDAY, FEBRUARY 12, 1890.

The public were admitted to the Conference Chamber at twenty-five minutes past eleven o'clock, a.m., the PRESIDENT (Mr. D. GILLIES) being in the Chair.

UNION OF THE COLONIES.

Discussion on Sir Henry Parkes' motion, in favour of an early union under the Crown of all the Australasian Colonies (adjourned from the previous day) was then resumed.

Mr. W. McMILLAN said—Mr. President, it seems to me that in debating the present proposition, which stands first on the notice-paper and is certainly of a more or less abstract character, we should keep clearly in view the second and third propositions which are also on the notice-paper, and which are really of a thoroughly practical nature, inasmuch as they indicate the goal towards which we, in this Conference, are moving. The second proposition sets forth that the delegates at the Conference should ask their respective Parliaments to send delegates to a Convention, to be held at a future period, to discuss the whole question of Australasian Federation; while the third simply refers to the number of delegates to be appointed by each Colony, which the proposal of Mr. Deakin fixes at seven. This leads me to point out the exact position we, the New South Wales delegates, now occupy. It may be well at the present stage to take, what has not been taken yet, a slight retrospective glance at the proceedings which preceded the Conference. It will be in the recollection of my fellow delegates that the Convention originally proposed by Sir Henry Parkes was very much on the lines of the plan since laid before us by Mr. Deakin, but the Premiers of the other Australasian Colonies concerned thought fit to suggest a different mode of bringing the public men of the several colonies together. It was considered probable that it would be well to take more initial steps in order to formulate the resolutions to be placed before their respective Parliaments. I may here point out that, although many of its members are also members of the Federal Council, this Conference has no direct sanction from the different parliaments of the several colonies represented. We are here wholly as a consultative body, and, of course, there can be no practical outcome from such an assemblage, except in the way of suggestion. It appears to me, therefore, that the references made by different speakers to certain details were quite unnecessary, and also that they are in many ways liable to embarrass us in our future action with regard to our respective parliaments. I quite admit that over and above the mere abstract proposition that the time is ripe for Federation, it is quite proper that some details should be entered upon, but I must protest against some of the more elaborate references which have been made, especially by Dr. Cockburn, one of the representatives of South Australia, and others, and which seem to require us. while trying to formulate a particular kind of government, to go into all sorts of complexities as to whether we should have a partial or complete federation of the colonies, and so on. However, as this course has been taken, it appears to me that it is my duty to a certain extent to reply to some of the remarks, at any rate to those bearing upon the more salient points connected with the Federation of the future. As a matter of fact, Sir Henry Parkes has been blamed for not going more into detail, and a very severe attack has been made upon him by my robust friend, Mr. Playford, on that account. But I think careful consideration of the observations which have fallen from my honorable colleague will show that attack to be wholly unjustifiable. Let me point out, for instance, that although in one of the letters written by him which brought about this Conference he unquestionably referred to the Dominion of Canada, he did so only in these words:—

"The scheme of Federal Government, it is assumed, would necessarily follow close upon the type of the Dominion Government of Canada. It would provide for the appointment of a Governor-General, for the creation of an Australian Privy Council, and a Parliament consisting of a Senate and a House of Commons."

Every one knows that it is often very difficult, especially in political matters, to separate principles from details, but surely the division is here most complete. In fact I defy any member of the Convention to indicate any reference made by my honorable colleague in which he does more than refer to the larger outlines of the Federation scheme. Again, Mr. Playford referred to my honorable colleague's remarks with respect to a court of appeal. He assumed that, besides a court of appeal in connection with a Federation Legislature, there would still be an ultimate appeal to the Imperial Privy Council. But no such thing has ever been intended, and I trust no such arrangement will exist. It is in order to get justice promptly, and afford the same finality that attaches to the supreme court of appeal now in existence, that we propose that there should be an Australasian court of appeal, composed of men familiar with the circumstances and also the laws and courts of the colonies, which we believe will be satisfactory, and productive of benefit to the whole Australasian people. I could not help feeling, to a certain extent, amused by the references made by different members of the Federal Council. For instance, it has seemed all along, in the case of my honorable friend, Sir Samuel Griffith, that he is really quite as enthusiastic for Federation as any of us—that, in fact, he holds a brief for Federation—but that, nevertheless, he wants, with the peculiarity belonging to the legal mind, to show us all the difficulties and disturbing elements in the way. Then we have had Sir J. Lee Steere, who intimated, in a very sweeping manner, that all the remarks preceding his had been actuated by pure sentiment, and that what he had in view was to bring us down to the *terra firma* of practical ideas. No doubt he did this to some extent, but what was the outcome of his remarks? To, so far, show us that every possible scheme of Federation—good, bad, or indifferent—was simply impracticable. In much the same way Dr. Cockburn began his remarks, with, apparently, a most dreary and hopeless feeling of the difficulties surrounding the case; but I was glad to notice that eventually he was found entering thoroughly, like all the other delegates, into the spirit of the movement, and declaring that he, for one, thoroughly believed in Australasian union. According to my view, the question really before us in this Conference is : Has not such a wave of feeling flowed over the minds of the Australasian people that the public men assembled here may well feel justified in asking their several parliaments to bring about a Convention to discuss the whole question of Federation, in an absolutely untrammelled way, from beginning to end? Let us see if that position can be maintained. I believe that there is no question as to the spread of the Federation spirit in New South Wales. For instance, the Federation idea there could have no higher sanction than that of the parliament of the colony. Well, at the commencement of last session the matter of Federation was adverted to in the Governor's speech, and the reply to that speech was adopted without a dissentient voice. Then there has not been for some time, throughout the length and breadth of the colony, a single public meeting where every speech, toast, or sentiment at all touching Federation was not received with the almost unanimous applause of those present. In short, there can be no question that the people of New South Wales, together with their neighbours, are determined to have Federation, and anxious for the public men of the different colonies to meet together in order to weave some scheme practical in its character for the adoption of the different local parliaments. Another question, perhaps even more important and more practical than any affecting the mere sentiment of the people of the different colonies, is: "How far are they united at the present time"? One delegate has told us that we, in the various colonies, have no knowledge of one another. But I think it will be conceded that, during at all events the last ten years, there has been a very considerable advance in the means of intercommunication in connection with the larger colonies of the group. During that period we have joined our railway systems, and in consequence an impetus has been given to commercial and other intercourse, which no one would have previously imagined. For instance, have not our principal commercial firms business ramifications extend ing throughout the whole of the colonies—Victoria, New South Wales, and Queensland? Are not the various colonial churches firmly welded together in ecclesiastical communion? Are not the families of the different colonies continually spreading out their tendrils right and left towards each other, the children uniting to create and increase intercolonial interests? Does any man travelling among the colonies, directly he has passed the wretched custom-houses on the Border, ever feel that he is in a foreign country? For myself, I feel that we have to-day, among the several colonies, greater elements of union than have ever before, in the history of the world, existed in connection with any community about to join, or which has joined, in federative connection. Between the various States of America there was never such an union, either in race, religion, or opinion, as there is here. Search as you will, you will find no foreign element whatever. In fact, in our intercourse with one another, there is but one disturbing constituent, namely, that contained in the question of Border duties. This may, perhaps, be regarded by some as a matter of detail, but I say most emphatically that there can be no union between the colonies worth calling union unless we abolish every custom-house along every Intercolonial border. Sir, what is Federation? The only Federation I want to see is not the Federation of my honorable friend, Dr. Cockburn—the mere federation of nations showing great versatility and variety in their different characteristics. I want to see a union of the several Australasian peoples so homogeneous, complete, and perfect that we would be but one Australasian nation, without any sense of discord; and no other attempt at nationality, such as the creation of a Zollverein for any mere commercial or other purpose of a partial character, will ever meet the wishes and views of, at any rate, the rising youth of Australasia, who, I believe, will be the great factor in bringing about the ultimate union of every portion of its different populations. We have been told by several authorities that what we want is, primarily, something in the shape of partial union. But what would partial union mean? I don't want to reflect for a moment on the Federal Council. It would not be wise, in a discussion like the present, to introduce any irritating element to affect the issues with which we have to deal. But it cannot be said that the Federal Council, with its partial and limited scope, has been a success in the past. Supposing, for one moment, that you attempted to establish a poor, meagre, half-and-half kind of government throughout these colonies, what would be the history of the future? Take the case of a colony like New South Wales, standing in her position of natural superiority to probably any of the other colonies, and with her rapidly increasing population. What will it be in a few years to come? I am not now boasting of the inhabitants of New South Wales, but simply alluding to her command of the Pacific Ocean, and to her marvellous resources—her coal, iron, and almost everything else that the civilized world requires. Do you think that a mere partial confederation, a mere make-shift Federal Parliament, would suit her—that the legislature of a great colony of that sort would bow to anything but sovereign authority? I don't mean for one moment to say that the other colonies should be in any way dwarfed, but I do mean that whatever federal authority you create in the future must be strong, potent, and acknowledged. It must be independent in its Executive and in its Treasury, or else you will be eternally subject to most serious consequences from sudden up-risings of the local powers against the central power. We have had a great many analogies drawn between the United States and the Dominion of Canada. No doubt there is a partial analogy in many respects between ourselves and those countries, but, on the other hand, there are essential differences. For example, we are an island continent. No matter how you subdivide the different parts of Australia into different sections, you must give to each of them a large sea-coast, with its harbours and valuable commerce, together with all the other possibilities of national life. But the position of the United States or of Canada is that of a congeries of littoral States depending for their commerce upon the interior States, which in their turn naturally depend upon the others for the means of getting their products to the markets of the world. Surely in the case of these Australasian Colonies, each possessing within itself, as it does, not only a sea-coast, but one touching the broad ocean, of the world, and so far having the great advantage for which countries like Germany and Russia are at the present time fighting so hard, namely, a means of getting out to the high seas, it is absolutely necessary that if we have a Federal Parliament it should not be a mongrel Parliament, but a sovereign body which would be respectfully recognised by every independent State, and which would have within itself such freedom of action and such power that no other country on the face of the globe would be able to override it. In this connection I may say that, while there is much to gain, there are sacrifices to be made. No really great effort of patriotism was ever yet unattended with enormous sacrifices. But I may say also, without egotism, that the sacrifices made by New South Wales in this union of the colonies will be greater than the sacrifices of any other colony in the group.

Sir HENRY PARKES.—Hear, hear.

Mr. McMILLAN.—What is our position? I do not imply that we have a nobler or better race of people than the other colonies have. I believe there was a time in the history of these colonies when the possessors of the best ability, the best brains, and the best energies in Australia had found their way to Victoria. I acknowledge freely and fully that the reflected energy of Victoria has done New South Wales an enormous amount of good. But the fact remains that we are now a colony which could be, if we wished, independent of all the other colonies. If we desired to impose heavy protective duties along our borders and against the outside world, we would be better able to carry out such a plan than any other colony of the group. No other colony could stand as we could stand. We possess, as I have already mentioned, all the elements that go to make up the wealth of Britain, and we have besides the finest harbour (which is almost a joke) on the Pacific Ocean. In fact we hold the key of the

Pacific. And I think that when free-trade New South Wales, with all her advantages, is willing to put out the right hand of fellowship to all the other colonies, small or great, she offers to give as powerful an impetus to the Federation movement as the sacrifices she is ready to make are large. No other colony could give an impetus so strong, or is in a position to make equal sacrifices. I don't say that what I refer to would be all self-sacrifice, for over and above what may come from other sources we have behind us the sentiment of a new nationality. I believe that the native youth of this continent, who have never known any other home, and with whom the sentiment of "home" as referring to the mother country is to a certain extent fast dying out, are determined that they will have a national union of all Australia—that they will appear to the world not as New South Welshmen, not as Victorians, nor as the citizens of any separate colony, but as Australians. We have had a good deal of cavil with respect to this matter of tariff, and it has seemed to me that in this Conference—it is only in accordance with human nature that such should be the case—some of our friends who have felt the heavy tread of Victoria have been anxious to give her a small unchristian slap on the cheek in order to show that the course pursued by her was resented. Well, it is a cause for great thankfulness that we now know that Victoria has seen the error of her ways. It is, of course, possible that she recognises that the time has come when Federal Union will be all to her benefit. No doubt she feels the geographical troubles that await her on the Murray, owing to the smallness of her territory. There is also no doubt that a large amount of the enterprise carried on in New South Wales, towards her southern border, is carried on by people who call themselves Victorians. At the same time it seems to me that even supposing Victoria does get some extra benefit out of union, the fact remains that from all matters of mutual interest the cleverest fellow concerned always derives the most advantage. Therefore, I am quite willing, in view of the smallness of the territory of Victoria, and her want of those natural riches which are said to be made up to her by the superhuman energies of her people, that she should have the difficulties in her path wiped out for her by the abolition of Border duties. But, after all, is it fair for us to go into the past? Are we likely to bring about the consummation of our great idea by harping on all the troubles and grievances of a bygone period? I think not. Let us bear in mind that up to a very short time ago these colonies were each almost absolutely isolated. Victoria was then, in many respects, almost as much apart from New South Wales as she is now from Western Australia. In short, we know very little of one another. There were no proper means of intercommunication. Let us trust, however, that had such proper means of intercommunication then existed, and we had been enabled to frequently meet each other, and, perhaps, marry our sons and daughters to each other, these hostile intercolonial tariffs would never have been imposed; and also that, with the earlier development of the fraternal spirit which has led to this Conference, we would by this time have been by so much the nearer to the result which we now have in view. Therefore what we should now consider is not whether certain colonies have or have not done wrong in the past, not whether a system of retaliation has or has not been built up, say by South Australia—for retaliation is the one thing at the bottom of this protection business—but whether we have or have not determined to let bygones be bygones. As for myself, I wish to emphatically assert that no union of the colonies can be worth anything without intercolonial freetrade, inasmuch, as I have said before, what is called protection is the natural germ of retaliation among the States affected. How, in the name of common sense, can we have any union amongst the different parts of Australia, with restrictions in connection with one of the most important matters of our daily life, namely, mutual commercial intercourse— one colony adding duties on duties, which another colony tries to cap—a system of retaliation underlying everything? Union under such circumstances would be an absolute farce. One or two of the delegates have referred to matters of finance. Sir J. Lee Steere made out a very dismal picture. But it seems to me that, speaking broadly, if any of the colonies are to be specially benefited by a Federal Union, it will be the smaller colonies. Yet there is the fact that it is the larger colonies that are most anxious to federate. Sir J. Lee Steere spoke with mournfulness, but when the Imperial Parliament has passed a measure giving Western Australia a Constitution, and that colony, with its 40,000, or thereabouts, of population, rises to the dignity of a young nation, and finds itself welded to the other colonies, surely it will consider it a great advantage to be able to borrow money at two or three per cent. below its present credit. Then, as to the larger colonies, shall we not present a firmer front to the commercial world of England when we are a united Australasia? Most of the colonies are, at the present time, working off six, five, and four per cent. debentures, but I look forward to the time when, as one of the necessary triumphs of Federation, we shall be able to borrow at three per cent., our credit being almost equal to the credit of England itself. The delegates who talked about finance seemed to forget that, whether we like it or not, and even whether we federate or not, we are fast becoming nations. If we federate, we shall be one nation; if we do not, we shall be separate nations. We are beginning to defend our ports, to raise volunteers, and to maintain standing armies. These are sources of expense which must grow. Surely, then, if there is any economy at all in concentration of administration, the matters which devolve upon us in the higher life of the future would be far more economically carried on by one central government than by a series of local governments, each acting according to its own sweet pleasure. As to the national debts of the colonies, that is a subject scarcely worth consideration at the present time, for each of those debts is represented to a great extent by substantial assets of a local character. The question of a central authority taking over the railways is, to my mind, one of a very remote character. There is nothing in it essentially connected with the idea of central government, except perhaps so far as concerns the adoption of an intercolonial gauge, and the control of the entire

Australian railway system being rested, under certain circumstances, such as a state of war, in central hands. Otherwise the affair is one of purely local interest. Let it be remembered that in dealing with the future debts of these colonies we do not deal with debts which are the result of extravagance or warfare, but only with debts incurred for representative public works, a large number of which are of an interest-bearing character. Coming back to the matter of defence, surely if any central power takes upon itself to be the sole administrator of the defences of the Continent, it must be a power of a truly royal character—one which would overshadow every other Australian power, and necessarily have large authority as to taxation, so that, in case of urgent times, each of the peoples concerned might be called upon to pay its quota of the expense of defending them. As far as I can see, the question before us ultimately resolves itself into this: Are we convinced that there is a sufficiently strong feeling among the different colonies to warrant us in having the second and third propositions on the notice-paper as well as the first, and so bring about a convention of the different colonies? I am glad to find, from what the different delegates have expressed, that they intend to ask their parliaments to send representatives to such a Convention. Even in the case of New Zealand its delegates will, if I mistake not, follow that course.

Captain RUSSELL.—Hear, hear.

Mr. McMILLIAN.—The passing of this motion simply pledges us to the opinion that the time has come for real and practical discussion. I believe that in this opinion we are upheld by some of the greatest thinkers in England; I believe we are also upheld by the different populations of the Australian Colonies, and I believe that when public opinion has sufficiently penetrated New Zealand, even New Zealand, separated from this continent by 1,200 miles of water, will come into the Federation of the Australasian Colonies. But it would be a lamentable and a deplorable thing if the smaller colonies outside New Zealand attempted to hold themselves aloof from this great

Federation of Australia. It is all well enough to pass resolutions for them to be admitted on certain terms at any time in the future, but nobody can foretell what the future may bring. I would like to point out to my honorable friend, Sir James Lee Steere, that one of the most vital parts along the coast line of our colonies is King George's Sound. Private enterprise has constructed a railway there which joins their main line at a place called Beverley, and if that point were not defended nothing could hinder an enemy from reaching the very heart of that little colony, and destroying even the house of Sir James Lee Steere.

Sir J. LEE STEERE.—They would find it a very difficult thing to do.

Mr. McMILLAN.—Now I just wish to sound this one warning note—that if the three great colonies on the eastern side of the continent—Queensland, New South Wales, Victoria, and also Tasmania, agree to form a Federal Union among themselves, it will be a thorough and complete Federal Union; and if the four colonies I have named agree to such a union, how in the name of common sense can they allow the other colonies hereafter to enter the union upon any partial conditions? It seems to me that they must be shut out altogether for a long time to come; but if the other colonies fairly and generously come to that union, declaring that they are willing to throw in their lot with the other colonies, then their position will be considered in the detailed arrangements that will be made. And it seems to me that that is a fair and a generous way of dealing with the peoples of the other colonies. Let me ask the representatives of those colonies once more to reconsider the positions they have taken up. My honorable friend, Mr. Playford, who is, I know, a fighting man, and one whom I should like to get behind in the event of an invasion, had a certain amount of antagonism to unbosom himself from, and now that he has done so, I have no doubt that, like every decent Englishman, when the fight is over, he is inclined to be generous. As regards my friend Dr. Cockburn, I believe that his opinions on this question are, to a certain extent—to use a medical phrase—in solution. I believe he is quite open to be converted, as I dare say he will be converted by my honorable friend, Mr. Macrossan, when he addresses the Conference. I have not much more to say. I don't intend to go back on my own principles. I consider that we are not here to discuss details. Changes rapidly occur in these colonies as well as elsewhere, and by basing our opinions too much upon details we might feel ourselves hampered in the future. We all belong to parliaments in which there is party government; we know that, no matter what may be the sentiments in connection with Federation, party purposes will come in and party antagonisms will be aroused, and as I have no mandate from the Parliament of New South Wales, but am simply here in my position as a delegate to discuss the proposal in regard to a future Convention, all I can now say is, that I believe such a Convention is necessary, that we are ripe for it, and that when forty or fifty men thoroughly representative of the different political creeds and different sentiments of the various colonies get together, with the same spirit which was given to our ancestors, to make a Constitution when it was necessary, rising to the exigencies of the present constitutional position, those men will do their duty, and the result will be something great for the future of Australasia.

Mr. B. S. BIRD.—Mr. President, representing as I do the smallest colony in the Australasian group, and happening to be the junior member for Tasmania in the Federal Council, I have waited, with the modesty, I hope, befitting that position, to hear what my honorable colleague in the representation of Tasmania would say for the colony we jointly represent, and also what the members for the greater colonies had to say upon this great question of Federation, before I addressed myself to it. In taking the opportunity which is now given to me to express my views on the subject, I may say at once that I do not intend to indulge in general criticism of those who have gone before me, as has been done by my honorable friend who has just addressed the Conference; but I will begin, in the first place, by bearing testimony, as my honorable colleague has already done, to the strong feeling and deep interest which exist in Tasmania in favour of Federation. Although we are so small a colony, the interests involved in this important question are in our measure, and in proportion to our population, as great as those of any other colony in the group. There are individual interests and there are sectional interests in connection with the producing and commercial communities, which for us as a people are as serious and as important as they are for the individual and sectional interests in any other part of Australasia. And therefore it is, I think, fitting that Tasmania, the smallest of the colonies in the group, should have taken her place in the discussions of this Conference, and that her voice—no uncertain voice— should be heard upon the very important questions we are brought here to discuss. And yet, Sir, I wish to feel, and I do feel, that I am not here so much as a Tasmanian, as representing a small colony, or as representing sectional interests, nor to point out sectional advantages, or to claim them for any one colony as against another, but rather I desire to feel that I am here as one of the people who are about, I believe, to be united in a great Empire which will sway the destinies of countless millions for generations yet to come. I wish almost to forget, while I am here, that I am a Tasmanian, and to feel that I am an Australasian, a term which I dare say may yet come to be used to designate every citizen of the great group of islands which are to be federated in these Southern seas. To every citizen in that important group of States—the United States of America—is given the designation of American, whether his local habitation be New York or San Francisco, or any of the vast territory lying between. Likewise to each citizen of the great Canadian Empire is given the designation of Canadian, whether his home be in Nova Scotia, or in any of the Central Provinces, or upon the shores of the Pacific, or in British Columbia. And so, Sir, I hope the day is not far distant when every citizen of these colonies, which I trust will soon be joined together in the bonds of a union never to be dissolved, shall be known the wide world over as an

Australasian, because, like a citizen of Canada or a citizen of the United States, he is an individual unit in one great Federation. I cannot help feeling that this great sentiment of unity, of oneness as a people, has found very forcible and gratifying expression, in spite of all the differences that have appeared in regard to the modes of union, in the speeches that have been delivered to us by members of the Conference during the last day or two. I feel sure that with such a spirit as this animating us we may look forward with confidence to the future, believing that whatever difficulties may lie in the way of the union of these great colonies, whether those difficulties may be characterized as lions, or as less or more formidable creatures, they will all be easily and wisely overcome, and that we shall speedily be brought together as a united people possessed of all the elements of expanding greatness. I would express my pleasure, Sir, that in the resolution which Sir Henry Parkes has introduced it is set out so plainly and positively that the union is to be under the Crown of England. In this I am glad to state that Tasmania will most heartily concur, for I am sure I may say, without boasting, that there is no people amongst the peoples of the British Possessions more loyal to the Crown of England than are the people of Tasmania. I have no doubt that in Tasmania, as in some of the other colonies, a few radical spirits may be found who would hoist the flag of separation to-morrow if they thought they could succeed, but at heart I am bound to say that the great mass of the people of Tasmania are loyal to the Throne of England, and desire nothing better than to continue their connection with the illustrious British Empire. And I very much mistake the spirit that animates the masses of the people in the whole of the Australasian group if it does not correspond with that sentiment, which as I have said, exists so strongly in Tasmania. I consider that it would be an act of very ill grace on our part, and on the part of any of these colonies, which are still certainly in what we may term the infantile stage of their existence—to dream of separation from that mother State which has with lavish hand, and some would say, indeed, with unwise liberality, bestowed upon us such a splendid inheritance of territory unsurpassed in fertility, and containing vast mineral and other resources. Having received such a grand inheritance as this, freely given by the mother country, and having received also at the same time the highly-prized privilege of self-government, it would ill become us, I say, to turn away from the parental hand that has so richly and so generously bestowed these things upon us. And the same spirit, which I believe will bind us to the mother country for many a generation to come, ought to bind all Australasians still closer together as citizens of the British Empire. I think, Sir, that the sooner we break down those barriers which hostile tariffs and varied laws have raised against the free intercourse of the peoples of these lands the better it will be for us all. I regard it as a most unfortunate circumstance that such barriers were ever interposed between peoples of the same blood, peoples with the same destinies, peoples with the same aspirations, because the existence of these barriers has caused, as we know, in the past, and is still causing, as was shown by the speech of Mr. Playford at this Conference, a large amount of irritation, and it has also called forth a spirit of retaliation. But here, Sir, we come upon one of the difficulties, the main difficulty—the "lion in the path" of Federation. Some of the colonies, as appears from the speeches of their representatives at this Conference, will be unwilling to, at once at any rate, enter into a Customs union, and give up the control of their Customs tariff. Now, Sir, I regret this very much, for while I will not go so far as to say, with Mr. McMillan, that Federation will not be worth having unless it bring with it a Customs union or intercolonial free trade, yet I do feel that such a Federation would be so imperfect and so comparatively disadvantageous, that I should very much regret to see it established. And I believe I speak the sentiments of the bulk of Tasmanians when I say that they also feel that a union which will not open the ports of the neighbouring colonies to all their products and leave their own ports free for the importation of the products of the neighbouring lands will not be such a union as would perfectly satisfy

L

their desire for colonial Federation. There are those who feel, as Mr. McMillan has told us he feels, very strongly that such a union would not be worth having; and I may say here that there are members of the Tasmanian parliament, among them colleagues of my own in the government of Tasmania, who entertain the very same feeling, and who would regard such a Federation as being practically worthless, and would almost be content rather to pursue the course we have entered upon in connection with the Federal Council until all the colonies could come to be of one mind in the matter, and could all unite together upon, among other things, the basis of a common tariff. I am quite prepared to admit, as Sir Samuel Griffith has clearly and forcibly pointed out, that a union of the colonies, although it did not embrace a Customs union, would be, or might be at any rate, in very many respects a very great advantage to the whole of the colonies; but at the same time, as the honorable gentleman also clearly showed, it would be so anomalous in its character, and would contain such elements of irritation as would result in creating greater bitterness and greater strife between the various colonies than has hitherto existed under the present fiscal arrangements. For, assuming that in any union each colony must contribute in one form or another to the Federal Treasury on an equal basis, the fact that Customs duties of a higher and more burdensome character were being levied against the productions of one colony than against the productions of another would produce such irritation amongst those who would be called upon to contribute, either upon the basis of population or upon some other uniform scale, that it is perfectly clear that the feeling of unfairness would become marked in the minds of those who suffered by having to pay first their regular contributions to the general revenue of the Federal Government, and then to be burdened with those additional Customs duties, which would be a further tax upon them. It is easy to see how they would kick against it, and that bitterness and strife, of a kind surpassing anything we have yet known in the colonies on account of Customs duties, would assuredly arise. Possibly, however, that would work its own cure, because the injustice, the unfairness, and the absurdity of such a system among a people who were supposed to be united, would become so obvious that those who suffered from it, and those who were inflicting their sufferings by the continuance of such a system, would ere long be compelled to come together and agree upon the adoption of that more complete union which is so desirable—a union based upon a uniform Customs tariff. Now, Sir, if a union is to be established, and I fondly hope it will, Tasmania, I know, would like to stipulate that one condition of the union should be the establishment of free ports as regards the trade between the colonies. I believe that she would be quite content to leave the question of a protective or a free-trade policy as against the outside world to be settled by the Federal Legislature. I am glad to find that this appears to be the position which the honorable members for New South Wales take up, whether they will have in that respect large sacrifices to make or less. I for my part do not see that their sacrifices will be so large as those of some of the other colonies, for I believe that those colonies which have the heaviest protective duties imposed will necessarily suffer most in loss of revenue by the establishment of intercolonial free trade. But I am glad to see that the disposition I have described is shown by the representatives of New South Wales, and I trust that it will be taken up and followed as an example by the other colonies of the group, so that there will be little or no difficulty in securing the formation of a union based upon a uniform tariff amongst the colonies. I confess I could not quite follow my honorable friend Mr. Deakin in the way of concurrence when he expressed the opinion that whether we have or have not a uniform tariff in the about-to-be-established Confederation, it would be absolutely essential that from the hour of the union the whole of the Customs duties should be collected by the Federal Government. I cannot agree in this, nor do I quite know the reason why Mr. Deakin insisted upon it, as he did so very strongly, unless he conceives that in this way alone the Federal Government would have that perfect control of the purse which is essential to a powerful Federal Government.

But I think it would be a clumsy way of securing that power, and that all the money which would be required to meet the necessities of the Federal Treasury could be secured by levying a contribution based upon the populations of the various States, provided there was some power behind it to enforce payment of the levy, if any of the colonies, from any cause whatever, appeared inclined to repudiate its obligation. The general advantages of union have been so fully and so ably pointed out by my friend Sir Samuel Griffith, as well as by other members of the Conference, that there is no need for me to enlarge very much upon that particular point. However, I would like to say a few words later on with regard to that ; but at this stage of my remarks I desire to say that the advantages of union to each colony of the whole group—although they would doubtless be less in the case of some than in the case of others—are, in my estimation, certain to be so great that it would be well worth the while of any of the colonies to make even some considerable sacrifice in order to take its place in the Confederation. I should like to see such a constitution framed for the Australasian Federation that all the colonies of the group without exception would, perforce, see and feel, and own that, balancing the advantages with the disadvantages likely to arise from such a union, the scale would turn decisively in favour of union, and that speedily. In fact, Sir, so anxious am I to see the foundations of a great empire in these Southern seas laid broad and deep that I desire the constitution of this proposed Confederation to be such that all the British possessions which cluster around Australia, and all those which are in proximity to her in the Pacific, should eventually be drawn in as members of the Dominion of Australasia. And further, Sir—and this is a point which, I think, has not yet been touched upon by any speaker who has preceded me—in view of what all Australasia takes to be the most unsatisfactory existence of the prison settlement of a foreign power in close vicinity to Australian shores, I should hope that the coming Confederation of Australasia would very soon be in a position to exercise such influence upon the Imperial Govern-

ment as to secure the early and amicable removal both of the
French prisoners and the French people from a country that lies
so near to our shores; and that, obtained by England in exchange,
perhaps, for some slice of territory elsewhere, or for some other
fair equivalent, that land might come into our possession, so that
it, together with the New Hebrides, Fiji, and the rest of the
islands which are the natural adjuncts of an Australasian Empire,
might be joined to the group, and have flying over it the flag of a
United Australasia. I would express my hope that this union,
on which it seems we are all in one form or another bent, will
when consummated be a great deal more complete than there
appears to be at present, judging from the speeches delivered,
any probability of its becoming. I think I have already said that
I regret the apparent indisposition on the part of one or two of
the colonies to enter upon a federation which will embrace a
Customs union; and I now express my regret that New Zealand,
which seemed to be somewhat favourably disposed to a Customs
union, yet appears, from Captain Russell's remarks, to hesitate
about casting in her lot with a legislature in which, having herself only a population of some 700,000, she would feel, to use his
own words, her comparative insignificance amongst a body of
representatives of a population of nearly 4,000,000. I do not
think the inhabitants of New Zealand need have any fear that
they will be overpowered by the weight of representation in a
body whose constituents number even so many as 4,000,000. We
in Tasmania, who number only 150,000 people, have no fear that
our interests will not be duly and justly conserved; and Western
Australia, numbering a little over 40,000 inhabitants, also enter-
tains no fears as to the results of joining a union in which there
will be such overwhelming numbers represented. I also judge,
from what has been said, that neither South Australia or Queensland, whose populations are less than those of New Zealand, have
any fear on this particular score. Of course everything will
depend on the basis of representation. But I apprehend that
whatever form this union about to be effected will take, it will
be, as Sir Henry Parkes very tersely puts it in the closing words

of his resolution, on principles just to the several colonies. If New Zealand joins, as I am happy to think she will, in a Convention at some future time to discuss and draft a scheme of Federation, she will have an opportunity of taking every care that her representation shall be such that she need have no fear of suffering from a sense of insignificance, even in a parliament which represents 4,000,000 of people. It was with some further regret that I found Captain Russell expressing hesitation in regard to joining in any scheme for a united military organization for the several colonies. His indisposition, and that of his colony, to join in such an organization appeared to be based upon the fact that New Zealand is some four or five days' sail from the Australian continent, and that there is every probability that before armed assistance could be sent to her from Australia in case of emergency the mischief intended by the enemy's cruisers would have been accomplished, and the foreign ships would have disappeared, so that a union from that point of view could not be of much service. But I cannot help calling attention to the circumstance that New Zealand in the past, as Sir John Hall reminded us elsewhere a few evenings since, has made application to the Australian Colonies (which were then in a sense further away, because of the less rapid means of communication) to assist her in a time of emergency, and that New Zealand was gratified to find the readiness with which a contingent from Victoria (and, if I mistake not, from Tasmania also) was sent across to help that colony in quelling the trouble that had overtaken it.

Captain RUSSELL.—Hear, hear.

Mr. BIRD.—As a civilian, I feel that I should speak with bated breath in the presence of a distinguished military officer like Captain Russell, and, perhaps, I ought not to offer suggestions to one whose military experience is so superior to mine; yet I cannot help saying than an emergency may arise in which New Zealand will be exceedingly glad to have assistance rendered to her by troops, though they have to go four or five days' journey to reach the land where the disturbance is. If I were a New Zealander I should consider it a grand thing to have even the right, which as a member of the great Federation of Australasia that colony would have, to call upon the neighbouring colonies for men or money in such a case. I hope (and I am sure that Captain Russell will pardon me for making the suggestion) that New Zealand will more fully consider this matter, and seeing that, as a member of the Confederation of Australasia, she would only have to bear her share in the general cost of military or naval defences, and that if an extra burden of expenditure should fall upon her, from any cause whatever, that burden would be shared by the rest of the colonies, she may fairly consider that it may, after all, be to her advantage to join the Federation of Australasia, and agree to it upon such a basis as would include in it federal defence, as well as a Customs union. I shall be very glad if any scheme of general defence can be devised, and any organization effected, under the powers which the Federal Council is already capable of exercising, so that we may have more speedily than we possibly can have under the proposed Federation some organization to meet the emergency of our being suddenly overtaken by war. Three or four years, at least, must elapse before we can secure Australasian Federation on such lines as are being discussed at this Conference, and it will be a sad thing if we have to wait all that time for the establishment of a more effective military organization than we have at present. I do not desire to anticipate anything Mr. Deakin may have to say upon the resolution bearing on this question of which he has given notice ; but if, under the Federal Council, as he evidently contemplates, we have sufficient power to organize and control general military defences, involving a Federal Executive and a Federal Treasury, it seems to give a hint that possibly after all in this Federal Council, which has been somewhat despised in some quarters, there is considerably more power than some people have thought, and that in it there are possibilities of united action and Federation which have been slightly looked upon by some of the members of the group. In the remarks of Sir J. Lee Steere and Dr. Cockburn in regard to this question there were hints and suggestions we would do well to think out and make effective at some future day, when the Convention meets. Before passing on to speak of the most suitable form of union, I wish to say something about the advantages and disadvantages, the gains and the losses, that are likely to attend on Federation, whatever form it may take. For we must not run away with the idea that Federation will be all gain to each or all of the colonies. If Federation includes intercolonial freetrade, and I hope most sincerely that it will, it will unquestionably mean a loss of revenue to such colonies as have levied border duties upon their neighbours' goods; and the higher those protective duties have been, the more serious the loss of revenue will be. And that revenue, as a matter of course, can only be made up by increased protective duties against the outside world, or duties in some other form—perhaps direct taxation. This, doubtless, will create in some colonies difficulties which will not be easily got over. It will involve sacrifices which some of the people in these lands, we have been told, will hesitate to make. It is not in human nature, and certainly not in that of Colonial Treasurers, to be ready to make sacrifices of colonial revenue, particularly when in the case of many of the colonies the Governments are troubled to make their financial ends meet. It is not every colony that is in the proud position of Victoria (or the position she was in a little while ago) of being blessed with a large surplus; and it is not too much to say that this difficulty will be a lion in the path of Federation as regards some of the colonies, whose inhabitants will be unwilling to make sacrifices unless it is shown to them most clearly that they will gain compensating advantages. Again, if the Federation includes federal defence, and it most likely will, the expenditure incurred in some of the colonies will far exceed the present amount. Here will occur again the same difficulty which will face some of the colonies in abandoning a portion of their revenue from border duties, and some of the Colonial Treasurers will feel it an unthankful task to have to say to their parliaments, " We have federated, and it means that instead of spending £100,000 on defences you will have to spend £200,000 ;" or that, " instead of spending £10,000 you will have to spend £20,000 or £40,000." Those who have to go to their parliaments and advocate Federation must be prepared to show some of the advantages which will compensate for such additional expenditure. I am sure that unless the peoples of the different colonies are fully convinced that they are gaining additional security against foreign aggression, they will think a great many times before they will enter upon a scheme of Federation which embraces federal defences. And it will be the same in regard to other matters which the Federal Government may be asked to take in hand. It is therefore very important that we should face all the difficulties at this early stage, and be prepared to fully meet them, so that those who hesitate about Federation, and some, I am sorry to say, do, will see clearly that on the whole the advantage lies in federating. Besides these purely financial sacrifices, which some of the colonies will inevitably have to make—some more than others—there are other sacrifices which will have to be made, such as the yielding up of local control over some of those matters which is generally admitted will be very much better managed and administered by a Federal Government. In regard to all matters like this, the self-governing colonies will certainly be most jealous of the loss of any of their existing rights, powers, and privileges, and we must be prepared to show them that while they are going to lose so much they are going to gain more. Nothing whatever should be taken away from the control of the local governments but such things as can be best administered in the interests of the individual colonies and of the whole group by the Federal Government. I think that whatever jealousy there may be as to loss of power, prestige, and privilege on the part of the local legislatures, they would be willing to consent to Federation if they could see that their powers were not going to be curtailed needlessly in this respect, but that only those matters will be taken out of their hands which can be best managed by a Federal Government. In this connection I also wish to remark that there is a set-off to the loss of revenue which would be sustained by the establishment of intercolonial free-trade in the shape of the certain large increase in the commercial transactions which would follow. The indirect advantages arising from this, I hold, would very largely compensate for the loss of revenue sustained by the establishment of free-trade, and would bring about a condition of things in the colonies affected that would fit them for bearing the burthen of taxation which would have to be imposed in some other form to make up for the loss of revenue sustained by opening the ports on the borders. As a small matter, showing that the Federal Government will effect savings in many directions, there will be the fact that, owing to the closing of our Customs-houses on all our inland borders, there will be the possibility of dispensing with a large army of Customs officers, while a much smaller staff will be required all along the seaports, because we shall not have to search and pass entries for goods coming from neighbouring colonies, but only for those coming by vessels from foreign ports. There is one item of peculiar advantage which has not yet been definitely remarked upon, though I think Mr. McMillan, in passing, alluded to it. I refer to the probable saving to be effected in the annual payments of interest upon the public debts of all the colonies, if, with Federation, the Federal Government takes over the loans of all the colonies. There is no doubt that with such a splendid credit as the Federal Government could command in the money market, we could secure loans consolidating all existing loans at something like three per cent. Canada has already borrowed at three per cent., though we know she did not obtain anything like par ; but I believe that a Federated Australasia will be able to go into the money market and borrow on terms almost as favourable as the British Government. That would represent a saving, on a very moderate calculation, of £1,000,000 per annum in the matter of interest alone in our present state of indebtedness. That would tend to remove some of the difficulties which some members of the Conference, such as Sir J. Lee Steere, feel in regard to giving up so much of the revenue of their colonies as must be involved in the establishment of the Customs union. Mr. Deakin referred, in passing, to one or two matters of a practical character following upon Federation, such as the more advantageous working of our postal and telegraph services, &c., under federal control than under the separate governments. No doubt with our postal services under the control of the Federal Government, contracts for the carrying of mails and arrangements for intercolonial and foreign mail communication could be more economically managed than under the present system of each colony making its own arrangements. Of course I do not forget that we have already done a little bit of Federation in regard to our postal services. At the Postal Conference held in Sydney, at the beginning of 1888, two or three of the colonies agreed to unite their interests in the Peninsular and Oriental Company's and the Orient Company's services, and since then Queensland has joined those colonies on the same terms. I say that the experience we have had in connection with the united postal service goes far to show that if it were extended throughout the whole of Australasia in the coming dominion, it would be more economical and better in every sense than the present arrangement. And the same remark applies to the telegraphic service. I regret that the Conference held in Sydney two years ago, which came to a practical agreement in regard to postal matters, did not do the same in regard to telegraphs. I believe that matters like this can be managed much better by the Federal Government than by the local legislatures respectively or unitedly. Under the federal system less time would be wasted in holding Conferences, and fewer difficulties would arise in getting the individual colonies to accept the recommendations of Conferences. Under the present system years elapse sometimes in carrying on correspondence before the results desired can be achieved, and it is in every way desirable that the Federal Government should take the control of these matters. I believe that if a Federal Government were established we should in six months have a cable tariff between these colonies and the mother country not exceeding 3s. or 4s. a word, as against the present rate of 9s. or 10s. a word. Proposals were made to the Postal Conference, two years ago, which, if carried, would have reduced the tariff to 4s. a word, but it has not yet been found possible to get the several governments to agree to those proposals. I believe that if that reduction were made such an impetus would be given to trade and commerce and social communication between different parts of the world that we should very soon find we had the advantage of the lower rate without any increased cost by way of subsidies paid by the several colonies. These are some of the advantages of a monetary character which Federation has to give. They are worthy of consideration, and I think that, added to all the advantages which other members of this Conference have already clearly pointed out, they will have weight in influencing the people of these lands in favour of Australasian Federation. But the question remains: What kind of union are we going to have? What sort of union will best meet the needs of this present time and the aspirations of the people of these lands? I confess, as I have already said, to a feeling that we have not yet exhausted the possibilities that exist in the matter of a Federal Government under the Federal Council Act. That measure might easily be amended so as to render it more suitable to the existing needs. I am aware that our venerable friend, Sir Henry Parkes, has told the world in a memorandum of his that there is no man or political party in New South Wales influential enough to induce that colony to join the Federal Council—as it exists, I presume. But possibly some slight alterations might make it acceptable even to our New South Wales friends; and if that measure, with a little improvement, would meet the needs of our time, it would be better, perhaps, to seek to bring into existence a union on such a basis as that affords, rather than some new-blown Constitution, which will not be, as Dr. Cockburn says, the gradual outgrowth from our people and their existing conditions, but an exotic transplanted from Canadian or American soil, and which possibly might not flourish so well here as would an indigenous product. I do not say that this is the best method of growing up into union—I do not even say it is practicable—but I do say that in discussing this great question of Federation it is very important for us to consider whether a union may not be procured which will meet all our needs by working under the Federal Council, or whether some important amendments might not be made in the Act which would give us for the time being all that we require. Mr. Deakin has already indicated his opinion that the Federal Council might take the control of a united military organization and general defence; and others, whose views are of great weight in a matter like this, consider that that is practicable; and if the Federal Council is competent to do this, involving as it would a Federal Executive and a Federal Treasury, as necessary to carry it out, would it not also be competent to take control of Federal Customs and of the postal and telegraphic services, as well as to legislate on any questions remitted to it by any of the local legislatures? There is no reason that I know of why we should not work on to a larger union from the Federal Council. The crux in the matter will be the question of representation. The Federal Council being a legislature of one house only, it would, I think, be essential that the colonies should be equally represented upon it. Democracies, however, stand in fear of such bodies, because they have too much power over the purse; but even if we adopted the bi-cameral system, which appears to be most in favour in self-governing communities, and is apparently in favour here, I take it that the representation in the Senate must be by colonies, and must be equal. But in that case money votes initiated in the Lower House could be rejected by the individual power of the other Chamber. I cannot see therefore why, if such a body can do this, a Federal Council might not be entrusted with the power both to initiate and carry a money vote. I make these remarks not with the view of showing that the form of government set out in the Federal Council Act should be adopted by us, but rather by way of suggestion, so that the question may be fully considered, in preparation for the larger Convention which we hope will be held before many months are past. I hope that the form of union which is eventually adopted will be of such a character, and on such lines, that all the colonies will from the outset be prepared, and even glad, to join it, so that we may all start together as one great confederation. I shall certainly support the motion, even if it is altered as proposed, because I shall regard it as a general expression of the opinion of this Conference that a federal union of some kind should be established. I sympathize somewhat with the remarks of Mr. Playford and Sir James Lee Steere as to the vagueness of the motion, and in their desire that something more practical should be submitted. But perhaps we have after all secured by the discussion that has taken place, which has embraced many of the details of the subject, all we could hope to secure at a Conference of this kind by a general resolution. It will be of great service in promoting the cause of Federation, and will materially assist the delegates to the proposed Convention. Debates will follow in the several Colonial Parliaments when the recommendations of this Conference are submitted to them, and these also will help to pave the way for the final settlement of the question. I think, therefore, we may congratulate ourselves on the fact that the proposal originally made by Sir Henry Parkes that a convention of delegates to be appointed by the several parliaments should at once be held was not agreed to by the colonies, and that we have taken the somewhat round-about, slower, but safer course of discussing the matter first in a preliminary Conference, and preparing the minds of the people for the great work which lies before us. Whoever are the members of the proposed Convention, they will have a most onerous and honorable position to fill, and work to do; but they will come to their work so prepared for it that they will be able to formulate a scheme which may for many generations exist as evidence of the wisdom of those men who will be known in future history as the founders of an Australasian Empire.

Sir JOHN HALL.—Sir, some remarks which fell from the last speaker on the subject of the position taken up by the delegates from New Zealand in regard to the resolution of Sir Henry Parkes induce me to say that although I rise to support the suggestion of my honorable colleague the Colonial Secretary for New Zealand, that for the present the proposed Federation should be confined to the Australian Colonies, yet I earnestly assure members of the Conference that that suggestion comes from no want of appreciation on our part, or on the part of those who have sent us here, of the value of a united Australasian Dominion, and from no indisposition to do all that circumstances will allow to further so great a cause. Were it not that this discussion has almost exhausted the subject, I should venture to trouble the Conference with some remarks upon the necessity for this great work, and the good it will do for us and our children. But the subject has been so ably treated by previous speakers that I should be wasting your time by recurring to it. I think it rather my duty to say a few words in addition to those uttered by my colleague, to show why it is that New Zealand does not see its way for the present to join in this movement. The speeches of Sir Henry Parkes and other gentlemen must have carried conviction to the mind of every listener that the time has arrived when a movement should be made in this direction, and I cannot help congratulating my venerable friend, whom I had the pleasure of working with at a Conference held in Melbourne, nearly a quarter of a century ago, that it has fallen to his lot to initiate the greatest movement towards the erection of a complete edifice of self-government which has ever been attempted in Australia. I thank Sir Henry Parkes for the admirable way in which he has brought this subject before us, but he must allow me to say that in one respect he was inaccurate, in so far as his speech applied to Australasia. He stated that Nature had made no impediment to the Federation of the Australasian Colonies. Nature has made 1,200 impediments to the inclusion of New Zealand in any such Federation in the 1,200 miles of stormy ocean which lie between us and our brethren in Australia. That does not prevent the existence of a community of interests between us. There is a community of interests, and if circumstances allow us at a future date to join in the Federation we shall be only too glad to do so. But what is the meaning of having 1,200 miles of ocean between us? Democratic government must be a government not only for the people, and by the people, but if it is to be efficient and give content, it must be in sight and within hearing of the people. If members of the Conference had lived in New Zealand, and knew how little we learn through the public press of what is going on in the adjoining colonies—no more, in fact, than of what is going on in Europe, Asia, and America—they would realize that no Dominion Government, the laws and executive acts of which are to be binding on New Zealand, could, under existing circumstances, give satisfaction to the people of that colony. There would be practically such an absence of influence or of control on our part as to prevent such a government ever being popular. My attention has been called to another impediment arising out of this distance by a remark which fell from Mr. Deakin. That gentleman stated with great force—and the statement must appeal to all thoughtful men—that a Dominion Parliament, exercising control over a large continent and dealing with large interests, would surely attract to political life many able, educated, intelligent citizens, who up to the present time have refrained from taking upon themselves a share of the burdens of government. That may be a great advantage resulting from a Dominion Government; but we in New Zealand, and you in Australia perhaps to a less extent, have very few men of realized wealth and leisure. Our most intelligent, energetic citizens are those who are still fighting the battle of life, who could not afford to absent themselves for three, four, or five months at a time from their business, and to agree that we are to be governed by a Dominion Parliament would mean, not that we are to include, but that we are to exclude from it, a great many of our best men. Mr. Bird threw out some hints from which one must infer that he expected some concession to be made in the matter of representation to the smaller and the remoter colonies.

No doubt remoteness from the seat of government reduces very largely the possibility of any influence being exercised by the distant constituencies. The same proportionate representation granted to a constituency remote from the seat of government would practically give the former much greater influence than the latter. So much is this said to be the case that, on the occasion of the last redistribution of representation in the United Kingdom, Mr. Gladstone stated as a reason why a relatively larger number of members should be given to Ireland the fact that a great part of Ireland was remote from the seat of government. If the fact of a part of Ireland being 36 hours' journey from the seat of government justified a larger amount of representation being given to that country, what number of representatives would the people of New Zealand not require in order that justice might be done to them? They would require a number which we cannot believe a Dominion Parliament would accord to them. I am anxious that honorable gentlemen who regret and rather deprecate our refusal to federate with Australia should be good enough to carefully consider these reasons. I can speak for my fellow-colonists in New Zealand as well as myself when I say that we should be glad to join if we could do so with fair regard to our own interests. And, if at the present time we cannot become a member of the Australian Dominion, we are anxious to go as far as we can in any action which will promote the interests of all the Australasian Colonies. But there are other reasons why we do not see our way to join. The first and most pressing reason given for the creation of a dominion is the necessity of organizing the military defences of Australia. The arguments set forth by Sir Henry Parkes on this subject, in the paper which has been circulated by him, appear to me quite irresistible. To think that Australian military forces, organized by five or six different governments, paid by five or six different governments, acting under the authority of five or six different governments, can equal in efficiency to any degree the same number of men belonging to one government and

M

acting under one head, is, I think, the merest dream. Students of history will agree that no lesson is more clear than that when allied forces have been opposed by an army belonging to one government, and acting under one head, they have always been at a disadvantage. The history of the great war at the commencement of the present century certainly tells us that if the allied forces opposed to Napoleon Bonaparte had not been composed of the forces of separate Governments, whose commanders were jealous of each other, and were constantly disagreeing among themselves—if there had been unity of purpose and obedience to one will amongst them, as there was in the French army—the fate of that war might have been very different. It would be a tremendous mistake if we Australians were to hug ourselves with the belief that anything like a temporary arrangement for uniting the forces of the separate colonies could provide effectually for the military defence of Australia. This is a pressing and urgent reason why a Dominion Executive and Parliament should be created. But I ask honorable gentlemen to consider whether it is possible that a military force in Australia, divided from New Zealand by seas patrolled by an enemy's cruisers, could be of any advantage to New Zealand, or a New Zealand force, under the same circumstances, to Australia? Mr. Bird has reminded us that in a well-known emergency the settlers of Australia came to the help of their brothers in New Zealand, with a promptitude and generosity which has made a lasting impression in the memory of the people of that Colony. That, however, was at a time when Australia was in no danger; but in the event of our being involved in a great war, the same danger which menaced New Zealand would menace Australia, and she could not then spare any of her military forces, as she did on the occasion alluded to. We must come to the conclusion that, under such circumstances, an Australian army would be of no use to New Zealand. Naval defence is an entirely different question. The naval defence of these seas must be undertaken by one fleet, because the same enemy which threatened one part of Australasia would threaten the other. In this defence the

New Zealanders have been perfectly ready to co-operate. If further measures are required, I feel sure that they will be ready to do their part without grudging or hesitation. While on this point I may say that I sincerely hope that the outcome of this movement towards an Australian Dominion will never be that we shall have to rely solely upon a naval force created by a Dominion of Australia. It would be a sad day for these colonies when they had not the immense naval force of the mother country to protect them. We would be living in a fool's paradise if we believed that any navy these colonies could support could cope with the naval forces that would be brought against us by Great Powers of the old world. Honorable gentlemen may, perhaps, say to the delegates of New Zealand: "If you are unable for these reasons to work with us, why did you come here?" We came here because we were invited to do so. It would have been discourteous and ungracious for us not to have come to a Conference convened for the consideration of so important a question, and to ascertain whether there was any way in which we could co-operate for the common good of Australasia. I still hope there may be some way. There is every disposition on our part to unite as far as possible with you. I hope that we may be able to take some steps towards the removal or diminution of those barriers which so impede commercial intercourse between different parts of Australasia. I agree with my honorable colleague, Captain Russell, upon almost every public question excepting that of free trade and protection. I have for twenty-five years been in favour of a protectionist policy, and I was in favour of it when it was not as popular as it is now. I believe that the manufactures and industries of a new country will never grow into vigorous life unless in the first instance they have some protection against the cheaper productions of older countries. It is impossible for them to thrive unless, for a time at any rate, they have given to them some compensating advantage against the cheaper labour, cheaper capital, and greater experience of older countries. But that does not apply as between the several Colonies. The cost of production in the several Colonies is pretty well on a level, and Victoria has no more reason to fear New Zealand than New Zealand has to fear New South Wales or Queensland. I much regret the large and increasing barriers that are being erected to commercial intercourse between the Colonies. I must say for New Zealand that, although we have to a certain extent adopted a protective policy, in no one case has that policy been directed against our neighbours. On the contrary, we allow preferential duties in favour of some of the products of Australia as against the products of other parts of the world. I wish I could say as much for our neighbours in Victoria. I do not abandon the hope that it may be agreed to be mutually advantageous to facilitate the exchange of the products of the colonies, some of which are fitted by soil, circumstances, and climate to the production of one class of goods and some of another, and to diminish some of the barriers which at present impede that exchange. Increased commercial intercourse will lead to increased social intercourse, and the more we know of each other the better friends we shall be, and the more likely it will be that we will be prepared to agree to a more intimate union than is at present practicable. There are other subjects on which we shall be very glad to work with our Australian brothers. I believe that an intercolonial court of appeal might be advantageously established, but I cannot agree with those who think that it must be a final court of appeal. They will never get that so long as the Queen, the fountain of justice, is at the head of the Empire to which we belong. But if we do not get that, I submit to Mr. Playford, who seemed to think that this would be a measure disadvantageous to the poor man, that an intercolonial court of appeal would, on the contrary, render practical to the poor man, who cannot afford to have recourse to the Privy Council, the means of appeal in the colonies.

Mr. PLAYFORD.—The rich man will go further.

Sir JOHN HALL.—I believe that in nine cases out of ten the decision of an intercolonial court of appeal would be satisfactory and final.

Mr. PLAYFORD.—I do not think so.

Sir JOHN HALL.—A principle of the British Constitution is that the Sovereign is the fountain of justice, and if Mr. Playford's experiments were tried it would cause greater dissatisfaction than results from the present system. The inability of New Zealand at present to join with Australia in this great work of Federation should be no difficulty to Australia. On the contrary, I submit that it will greatly facilitate and simplify your proceedings, because if New Zealand were brought into the Federation, her peculiar position would necessarily introduce a great many difficulties in the framing of the Constitution from which, if you were dealing with the Australian continent, you would certainly be free. I think, therefore, that honorable gentlemen should congratulate themselves on being freed from the complications to which they might have been introduced if they had had New Zealand to consider. Their task will be simplified. It may also be simplified in regard to the nature of the subjects which will be entrusted to the Dominion Government. We have been told by Sir Samuel Griffith, in sagacious and practical language, that, if they are wise and prudent, the framers of the proposed Constitution will be content " to take as much as they can get." I was sorry to hear Mr. McMillan state, as I understood him, that New South Wales would never be satisfied to take part in anything less than an absolutely complete Federation, including a Customs Union. The honorable gentleman's expressions remind me of the advice given by an English statesman to a young Parliamentary hand, who had declared that he would never agree to a certain proceeding. The statesman said, " I advise my young friend never to use the word ' never.' " I hope that Mr. McMillan, when he has gained more Parliamentary experience, will see the inexpediency of committing himself so positively to a refusal to accept less than he at the present time thinks desirable. Although some honorable gentlemen will not be bound to follow the Canadian and the United States' example, I think we should not refuse to be helped by them. If the framers of that Constitution had said they would not form any confederation unless they could get the whole of the North American Colonies to join, the Canadian Dominion would never have been formed. They were content to accept at first the greater of the Canadian Colonies, strong in the belief that the experience of working that limited confederation would induce other colonies to come in. I suggest to my Australian brethren that they should do the same. As Sir Samuel Griffith has said : "Take what you can get." Take what subjects you can get ; take what colonies you can get ; in the conviction that the union of Australia and Australasia is so beneficent a work, is so certain to conduce to the prosperity and happiness, aye, and the liberty of the people, that, if a partial dominion is formed, it will be the will of the people before long to make the dominion a complete one. One proposed feature of this dominion will, I trust, be loyally adhered to, and that is that it shall be a dominion under the Crown of Great Britain. I am induced to say this because one hears, not in this Chamber, but outside, allusions to Australian youth which knows no loyalty to the old country. Speaking for my fellow settlers in New Zealand, I can say that they are thoroughly loyal to the old land. We try to educate our children in a knowledge of the history of our great mother country. We try to teach them that that great history —with its glorious associations—are part of a precious heritage ; that they do not belong to a people insignificant and little known in the records of Empire, but to a nation which has accomplished great things in arms and still more in the more nobler arts of peace, in self-government, and the enjoyment of individual liberty. We teach them that they belong to a nation which is first in these respects in the history of the world. We are attached by the fondest ties of affection to the old country, but we are also attached by something more permanent and durable, that is by a conviction that our connection with the old country will best serve our material interests and be the best safeguard of our liberties. These are the days of great armaments, both military and naval. These are the days of rapid communication, and although during the last great war in which England was engaged—the Crimean war—such a thing as the advent of a large foreign naval force in these seas had never to be dreamt of, can we doubt that, in the event of our being now engaged in a great naval war, many months, weeks, or days would elapse before formidable enemies would make their appearance at our doors? We cannot hope, nor, I submit, can an Australian dominion hope, to be able to maintain a naval force so large, so modern in its construction, so perfect in all the latest appliances of naval science, as to be able to cope with the forces of the old world Powers. We know that if there is one thing more than another which these great nations hunger and thirst for, it is land with a temperate climate, which is open to settlement, and upon which they can pour their surplus population without losing their allegiance. And can we doubt that the one thing they would have in view would be to possess themselves of, or to prey upon, these colonies. We feel, therefore, that the protection of Great Britain which we are sure will be afforded to us in no grudging manner, will enormously serve our best interests. For these reasons New Zealand will not have part or lot in any movement which involves separation from the Empire. We do not question the right of others to work out their political salvation in whatever way they may think proper, but we would earnestly advise them to think twice, thrice, indeed many times, before they allow any proposal of that kind to be seriously considered. This union of the colonies of Australia is, in my opinion, sure to come. I have no more doubt that it will come, whether temporary difficulties bar the way or not, than that I have that the sun will rise to-morrow. Without any want of respect to the originators of the Federal Council, which has its friends here, I may congratulate my honorable friend, Sir Henry Parkes, the patriarch of Australian statesmen, upon the proud position of being the man to propose the laying of the foundation stone of so great an edifice. But, sir, we are not really laying the foundation stone. I was going to say that we were preparing the foundation, but the foundation already exists. The foundation exists in that feeling of kinship among Australasians to which so much eloquent allusion has been made. That is the foundation upon which we are preparing to build—upon interests which are common, upon community of race, language, and history. In conclusion, I must say that I almost envy my Australian brethren the opportunity of joining in the great work before them. I cannot help regretting that, for the present, circumstances render it impossible for New Zealand to do so. It is said that history repeats itself, and we shall, I feel confident, have another instance of it. In the northern hemisphere the old Empire has shown to the world how it is possible to combine the greatest amount of individual freedom and liberty with most absolute security for life, property, and order; and I believe it will be our great glory that in the southern hemisphere, and in these southern seas, we shall repeat the lesson which the dear old mother country has taught the north, and that this great Australian dominion will prove a centre of liberty, civilization, and light throughout the length and breadth of the Pacific.

Mr. MACROSSAN.—Before I enter upon the subject on which I wish to speak, let me say that I appreciate the motives of the delegates from New Zealand. I cannot help saying that I approve of their conduct. Whether they join the Australian Union or not, they can always be satisfied that they will have the best wishes of their Australian brethren for the material progress and prosperity of the colony they represent. I thoroughly approve of the resolution proposed by Sir Henry Parkes. I approve of the resolution word for word, with the exception, perhaps, of the word "Australasian," to which the New Zealand delegates have alluded. Although certain members of the Conference have thought such a motion is too vague and indefinite, I consider Sir Henry Parkes has shown his wise discretion in proposing it. Judging from the speeches which have been made, Sir Henry Parkes must have had the prescience that if he had proposed a motion more precise and definite, we probably should never have arrived at a unanimous decision upon it. Therefore

I approve of the motion most heartily. At the same time I expect we shall have to go further in other motions which are to follow. Although the motion proposed by the Premier of New South Wales may be considered to be an abstract one and vague, the speeches made by the honorable members of the Conference have been very far from vague. They have been very definite indeed. Many of the speakers entered very closely into the details of what they considered should form the union which Australia should adopt in the future. After the speeches which have been delivered, I stand in the position of having nothing to say. All the members of the Conference, with the exception of myself, have spoken, and they have exhausted the subject of Australasian Federation. Therefore, I am in the position of the needy knife-grinder who had no story to tell. Nevertheless, honorable gentlemen have left me some grounds, I will not say of criticism, because I do not wish to criticise the speeches of my *confrères*, but some arguments to advance which may be considered to have an important bearing on the subject under consideration. Objections have been taken to different points in what may be considered our future union. I shall not, however, deal with them at present. I shall, however, deal very briefly with some of the advantages of Australasian Federation, which some members of the Conference have perhaps overlooked. Those who have spoken have dealt more or less with what is called a Customs union. But there are other matters which, although not as important as that of a Customs union, and which do not present such great difficulties, have still an important bearing on the subject of Federation. I must say, at the outset, that I believe in Federation complete and simple. I believe we shall do no good in Australia until we have a complete Federation. I should like the advocates of an incomplete Federation to point out how we are to get along better, under such a system, than we have got along up to the present time, under the Federal Council. To premise what I have to say I will state, in a few words, what I consider to be complete Federation, by enumerating some of the subjects which the Dominion Government of Canada have power of dealing with exclusively. First, there is the public debt and the public property; second, the regulations of trade and commerce; third, the raising of money by any mode or system of taxation; and fourth, the borrowing of money on the public credit. The seventh item amongst the exclusive subjects dealt with by the Canadian Legislature has reference to military and naval defence and service. The control of these matters is, I think indispensable to a complete Australian Federation. There are many other subjects of legislation which might be spoken of, which I consider to be indispensable; but those I have enumerated are certainly indispensable. I consider that the dealing with the public debt and the public property ought to belong, exclusively, to our Federal Parliament, when we have the happiness to establish it. The subject was slightly touched upon by Mr. McMillan this morning. That honorable gentleman alluded to the public debt, and he spoke of the probability of a Federal Government being able to borrow money at a lower rate of interest than the several governments of Australasia are at present able to borrow. But we can go further than that. I think that a Federal Executive would not only be able to borrow at a much lower rate of interest than are the several governments at present, but that they would be able to convert existing debts to a much lower rate of interest than the several governments are at present paying. By this means we would probably save a million or two millions of money. I look upon the unification of the debt as a *sine qua non* to the establishment of a Federal Government and Federal Executive. This brings me to a few remarks I have to make on the observations of Mr. Bird, one of the representatives of Tasmania. That honorable gentleman seemed to be under the impression that if a Federal Customs Union were established, and if the Customs barriers were abolished between the different colonies, the colonies would suffer through being obliged to raise money to make up for the loss. I, myself, do not like the expression "Federal Customs Union," and I would rather speak of it as the giving of power to the Federal

Government for raising money by any mode or system of taxation. Well, the honorable gentleman overlooked the fact that if a Federal Government has the power given to it of raising money by any mode or system of taxation, it must, of necessity, take over the public debt. Therefore, the different colonies will be relieved from the interest they now pay upon their public debts, and, as I shall show presently, that will be full compensation for the abolition of the Customs barriers between the different colonies. The same consideration occurs in connection with the matter of defence. Mr. Bird seemed to think that if a Federal Government took up the duty of defence, the different States would be obliged to pay certain sums towards that defence. If defence is given—as I think it must be given—to a Federal Executive, that executive must undertake the whole control and expense of it, and not the States. This must be done if defence is to be effective. The several States will not be asked—at least I should hope they will not be asked—for anything in the shape of requisitions. Our experience, up to the present, in the way of requisitions, has not been very fortunate. A Federal Government must take the expense of a Federal Defence upon itself, and relieve the several States of that defence.

Mr. BIRD.—Where will you get the money from?

Mr. MACROSSAN.—The Federal Government will get the money from the proceeds of taxation which the separate colonies at present impose upon people belonging to those colonies. I do not know whether the honorable gentleman is aware of the total amount of taxation which is at present levied upon the different Colonies of Australasia, exclusive of New Zealand. In anything I have to say at present I wish it to be understood that I exclude New Zealand, as the delegates from that Colony have no intention of entering into a union at the present time. I was rather startled last night by the statement of Sir James Lee Steere, the delegate from Western Australia, when he said that the abolition of the Customs duties would lead to a deficiency of two millions a year. I thought that this could not be possible, and I took the trouble of examining the statistics of Australasia for the purpose of ascertaining whether the statement was correct or not. The result was that I found the honorable gentleman had made a mistake. The total amount received from all sources by the different colonies, excluding New Zealand, amounted, in the year 1888, to £8,655,661.

Mr. PLAYFORD.—But you are not going to give the whole of that up to general revenue?

Mr. MACROSSAN.—I hope so. My idea of Federation is that the general government will have the sole power of raising money by any mode or system of taxation.

Mr. PLAYFORD.—Then you snuff out all the local governments.

Mr. MACROSSAN.—No; the honorable gentleman is mistaken in thinking the local governments will be snuffed out. The total interest paid on the public debt of the whole of the different colonies amounts to £4,865,991. My figures are taken from the Government Statist of Victoria, so that I presume they are correct. The difference between the total amount of taxation raised in the different colonies and the total amount of interest paid on the public debt is £3,589,650. I think that this completely answers the statement made by Sir James Lee Steere yesterday evening, which startled me so much, and other members of the Conference as well.

Sir JAMES LEE STEERE.—My statement is correct, and the honorable gentleman's statement is incorrect. I have taken my figures from the official records.

Mr. MACROSSAN.—My statement is based on the figures to be found on page 456 of the *Victorian Year Book*, 1888-9. If my statement is incorrect Mr. Hayter is also incorrect. I prefer to believe that Mr. Hayter is not incorrect.

Mr. CLARK.—The figures are correct, but it is the use you make of them.

Mr. MACROSSAN.—It is Mr. Hayter's business to be correct in his statements. I have taken the figures as they stand, and I have used no others but those contained in the book. The source I have mentioned is the source from which the money will come, and there will be other sources as well. The representative of Western Australia also stated last night that, including New Zealand, we owed £168,000,000. I will now leave New Zealand out of the question. Leaving that Colony out of the question, we owe £130,000,000. Out of that £130,000,000 70 per cent. has been contracted for the purpose of making railways and telegraph lines. Taking every Colony in Australia, including Tasmania, the railways are actually paying, according to Mr. Hayter, 3·55 per cent., so that in reality, at least two-thirds of the public debt of Australia produces almost sufficient to pay the interest upon the capital expended upon them. I believe, when we have a Federal Government, as I believe we will have in a few years, that the interest will be so reduced by the unification of the conversion of the debt, that the railways and telegraph lines of Australia will pay more than they have actually cost. Thus the balance of 30 per cent. of the debt will be very easily met by the surplus amount I have mentioned as existing between the debt and the total amount of taxation. I believe that the abolition of the Customs duties between the different colonies will lead to a loss, but I do not believe it will lead to the loss of £2,000,000, as suggested by Sir James Lee Steere. It is absurd to think that it will lead to a loss of this character. My honourable colleague, Sir Samuel Griffith, thinks it will probably lead to the loss of half a million. Personally, I think it will lead to the loss of about a million. We have, however, no means of ascertaining what the actual loss will be. I think it is far more likely that it will not exceed a million, than that it will reach two millions. A point which has been overlooked by members of the Conference has reference to our railways. If the Federal Government takes over, as it must, the whole of our debt, it will, of course, take over the property upon which that debt has been contracted. This naturally follows in any matter of State business. Some objection may, perhaps, be raised in reference to the management of the railways by the Federal authorities, who may not be so conversant with local wants and requirements as the present governments. In order to meet that objection I would point out that in three of the colonies I know of, and perhaps in the fourth, Railway Commissioners have been appointed for the control and management of the various railways. All that the Federal Government have to do in a case of this kind is to make the Railway Commissioners federal officers, and the management will remain the same as at present. A system of this kind will have the advantage of still further removing the management of the railways from that political influence, the existence of which was the chief reason why Commissioners were first appointed. The result will be very advantageous. I believe that the people generally will approve of a Federal Government taking over the management of the railways. If the management of the railways is left entirely and solely under the control of the different local governments, the same wars of tariffs will go on in the future as they have done in the past. Human nature will always remain the same. Whether we have a Federal Government or not we cannot alter the human nature of the people of Australia; but if we place the management of the railways under the control of a Federal Executive we shall be relieved from any apprehension of a federal war, whilst the railways will still be managed as well as they are now, and by people who will be as conversant with local requirements as they are at present. These are two advantages which we shall gain from Federation. Then there is the question of the public lands. I confess I have not quite made up my mind on that question, although I may say that I think the public lands should be under the control of the Federal Executive. We have two examples before us of the federation of peoples of our own race, in the cases of Canada and America. In the United States of America the Federal Government has the full and sole control of all the public lands, and no one can say that the public lands of the United States have not been well administered and well managed. In Canada the Dominion Parliament left the control of the public lands to the local governments. Whether the public lands of Canada have been as well administered as the public lands of the United States I cannot say; probably other members of the Conference are better informed on that point than I am. But we have these two opposite systems to consider between this and the meeting of the Federal Convention, which I hope to see assemble in a few months. In the meantime I think myself that the balance of opinion is in favour of the Federal Government having control of the public lands. Now these are some of the advantages of Federation which members of the Conference who have already spoken have not examined perhaps so closely as I have; at any rate they have not broached them. I shall now come to some of the objections which have been made to Federation, notably by the representatives of the two colonies of Western Australia and South Australia. The colony of Western Australia, through its representative, Sir James Lee Steere, has expressed a fear, that, if the Customs revenue is taken away from the local authority, they will have no means of carrying on their present local government. Now, I have pointed out what I believe to be a mistake which that honorable gentleman has made in his calculation, but the honorable gentleman should also recollect this, that it will be within the power, and no doubt will be the duty of the Federal Government to subsidize the different local governments to whatever extent may be deemed fit. That is the case in the United States of America, and that is the case in the Dominion of Canada. In Canada a certain amount of subsidy is provided by the North American Act; and in America a certain amount of subsidy is apportioned amongst the different States in the Union for certain special objects, according to the amount of revenue which the National Government has the means of distributing. I do not think that any colony, and least of all a colony like Western Australia, which has so small a population at the present time, and no doubt has difficulties to encounter which the greater colonies have not, need be afraid that the Federal Government would not do justice to it and see that justice was done to it in every respect as far as revenue was concerned. I believe that the Federal Government would not take advantage of the position of a colony like Western Australia to injure it, or in any way to impair its local administration. The two gentlemen from South Australia, although they are in favour of Federation in the abstract, seem to be in the concrete rather afraid of throwing down the Customs barriers. Well, I really don't know why they should be afraid of doing that. South Australia is inclined to be protective, as all the colonies of Australia are, more or less, with the exception of New South Wales, but South Australia will be placed in exactly the same position as the other colonies will be placed, if a uniform tariff be adopted. The representatives of South Australia are afraid, no doubt, that Victoria has got the advantage of starting in the race, but I think that they need not be afraid of that. South Australia is able to produce many articles much cheaper and better than Victoria, articles of very common use, such as flour, for example. Now, I think that if the gentlemen representing South Australia will compare the position of their colony with the position of Queensland, they need not be in the least afraid of throwing down the Customs barriers. There is no doubt that Victoria has been very selfish in the past, and probably she is selfish in the present, but can those honorable gentlemen point to any State in the world, great or little, that has not been selfish whenever it has had the chance to be so? It is in the nature of States to be selfish, and I don't think that we should allow that notion, or that fact, rather, of the selfishness of Victoria, to stand in the way of a complete Federal union of the Australasian Colonies. I believe that the people of Queensland are not afraid to throw down the Customs barriers, neither are they afraid of any start that Victoria has got in the race, although this colony has got as large a start, in the way of protection, against Queensland as it has against South Australia. I know that in several items of manufactured goods which the Victorians pride themselves on manufacturing, we, in Queensland, are able to hold our own even under the most open free-trade, and if we cannot continue to hold our own in the future as we have done in the past, then I think we ought to go to the wall. But although Victoria will, no doubt, have a slight advantage after the throwing down of the Customs barriers, still I believe she will not have that advantage very long; and as far as Queensland is concerned, and I think the same may be said of sections, at all events, of South Australia, the distance and the extra cost of freight ought to be a sufficient protection on almost every item which is manufactured in Victoria. Then, I know that the colony of South Australia has been extremely anxious in the past to enter into a reciprocity treaty with Queensland, and, that being so, what objection can it have to such a complete system of reciprocity as the throwing down of all the Customs barriers in the colonies would be? No reciprocity treaty would give equal advantages to that. Different governments of South Australia have, to my knowledge, made it their business for several years past to try and induce different governments of Queensland to enter into negotiations with them for the purpose of adopting a treaty under which certain products of South Australia would be admitted free into Queensland, or admitted at reduced rates of duty, and certain products of Queensland would be admitted to South Australia duty free or at reduced rates of duty; and if different governments of South Australia have been so anxious for that limited measure of reciprocity, why then cannot they adopt the higher and greater form of reciprocity—free trade with all our colonies? I really think that the South Australians are standing in their own light, although I do not believe for a single moment that the people of South Australia, when the question put by both of their representatives at this Conference comes to be settled, will declare against free trade between the colonies. I am a protectionist in principle in my own colony, and I believe that one outcome of the establishment of a Federal Parliament and a Federal Government will be intercolonial free trade and protection against the outside world. Now, anyone who is at all acquainted with the

N

history of America must know that the greatness of America has partly risen from the fact of there being free trade between all the States, from north to south and from east to west, with protection against the whole world outside. Nothing has contributed more to the advantage of America than that simple fact. Of course I know that I am speaking in the presence of a great freetrader—Sir Henry Parkes—who does not believe in protection at all. At the same time he must admit that it is much better to have free trade between all the colonies than to have only one colony a free-trade colony, even although the union may ultimately lead, as I think it will, to protection in all the colonies as against the outside world. Now, Sir, I come to some of the difficulties which have been stated by gentlemen who have spoken before me, some of them by my own colleague in the representation of Queensland, Sir Samuel Griffith. One of these objections is that the people of the different colonies are not prepared to go the length that we, the delegates in this Conference, are prepared to go. Another objection is that the people of the different colonies do not know each other sufficiently, and that they are opposed to the centralized system of Government, and my honorable colleague specially instanced Queensland as being opposed to a centralized system of government. Now, Sir, I believe that the people of these colonies are far more ripe in the cause of Federation than some honorable gentlemen in this Conference give them the credit of being. I thoroughly believe that if the question was put to the colonies to-morrow, as certain questions are sometimes put in Switzerland and in other countries under what is called the Referendum, the majority of the people of Australia would vote for Federation as against no Federation. And I believe, also, that they would give their votes intelligently, knowing what Federation meant, what sacrifices would have to be made by the different local legislatures; knowing, also, that it would mean the establishment of a Federal Executive and a Federal Parliament, with which they would have very little or no intimate connection. Now, if my honorable colleague believes that, as I think he does, why should he, or any other member of this Conference, be afraid to give expression to the opinion? Why should we, who believe so thoroughly in Federation, be afraid to raise the standard of Federation, which we feel ought to be raised, but which seemingly we are too timid to raise for fear of offending the susceptibilities of timid conservative people? Then, again, my honorable colleague thinks that the people of Queensland might be opposed to Federation because they are opposed to centralization, being separationists in some parts of the colony; but the honorable gentleman ought to know, and I think he does know, that those people who are actually the strongest separationists are the most ardent of federationists.

Sir SAMUEL GRIFFITH.—Hear, hear.

Mr. MACROSSAN.—The whole of the people of Northern Queensland, who are separationists, are as strong in the principle of Federation as I am, therefore the argument that the people are opposed to Federation because they are afraid of centralization has no force or effect whatever, as far as Queensland is concerned. Centralization has no terror for anyone who thinks upon the subject, if sufficient local autonomy is left to the local legislatures. If we were to have a Legislative Union it would be a different matter; if we were proposing to destroy the local legislatures it would be a different thing entirely; but if we leave sufficient authority, as we ought to do to the local legislatures, Federal Government or centralization can only have the effect of making men believe that which we wish them to believe—that they are first Australians, and then Queenslanders, South Australians, or Victorians. Then, again, on the other hand, we must, I think, give to the Federal Parliament the full control of the waste lands of the Crown. I have said already that I am in doubt whether I would give the Federal Parliament the control of all the Crown lands, but there is a large amount of waste lands of the Crown almost outside of civilization which I think the Federal Parliament should have the full control of, and the Federal Parliament should also have the same control over the territorial jurisdiction of such outside parts as portions of Western Australia and the Northern Territory for the formation of new States. Every power and authority now exercised by the Imperial Parliament over those parts of Australia should be exercised by the Federal Parliament, and I believe that those powers would be exercised by the Federal Parliament in a more beneficent and intelligent manner than obtains at present, because the power would be exercised by those who know the character of the country and the requirements of the people they are dealing with. I believe also that power should be given to the Federal Parliament—as it is given to the Imperial Parliament—to cut up, if thought necessary, the different existing colonies of Australia, and form them into smaller States. I consider that the colonies of Australia are too large for good government. Some of the existing colonies, such as Queensland, South Australia, and Western Australia are far too large for good government.

Mr. PLAYFORD.—No.

Mr. MACROSSAN.—I do not say South Australia only—New South Wales is also too large. If we look at the geographical position and area of the United States of America, we shall find that not one of those States is as large as the Colony of New South Wales. Texas, the largest State in the Union, is only about one-third, or, at most, perhaps half the size of Queensland. There has been an agitation going on in Texas for years for the cutting up of that State into several smaller States. I believe that the small extent of territory in each State in America has had much to do with the good government which obtains in that country, and that Victoria has been the best governed colony in Australia because of the smallness of its territory.

Mr. PLAYFORD.—Query.

Mr. MACROSSAN.—There is no query about the matter. To a large extent, the good government which has prevailed in Victoria has arisen from the smallness of her territory. Large

States are never so well governed as small ones, and, therefore, the Federal Parliament ought to be empowered to cut up the larger colonies into smaller colonies, as the Federal Government of America has cut up the larger States into smaller States when it has been deemed expedient and just to do so. This may be an extreme opinion, but it is one I have held for a long time, and it is one which I am certain will not be opposed by my constituents in Queensland. I have heard a good deal from the speakers who have preceded me in regard to the Constitutions of Canada and the United States. Some reference has also been made to the establishment of a Federal Court of Appeal. The only representative, however, who really approached the subject, seemingly, with a full knowledge of it, was Sir John Hall. It must be known to every member of this Conference that the Sovereign is the fountain of justice, and that a subject cannot be prevented from appealing to Her Majesty for justice if he has not obtained it elsewhere. Therefore the establishment of a Federal Court of Appeal would not prevent an appeal from that judiciary to the Privy Council in London.

Mr. PLAYFORD.—We want the court of appeal in the colonies to be a final court of appeal; and a court of appeal in the colonies will be a Queen's Court as much as the Privy Council is.

Sir HENRY PARKES.—It would not be of much use if it were not so.

Mr. MACROSSAN.—The Federal Court of Appeal will be a court under the Crown, no doubt, but no one can prevent an appeal being made to Her Majesty, who sits figuratively in the Privy Council.

Mr. PLAYFORD.—Her Majesty will also sit figuratively in the court of appeal in the colonies.

Mr. MACROSSAN.—I would be quite as anxious as Mr. Playford to prevent any appeal going beyond the bounds of

Australasia if it could be done, but the limitation does not exist in Canada. An appeal lies in Canada to the Privy Council in London, though only in certain cases.

Sir SAMUEL GRIFFITH.—Only by special leave of the Privy Council.

Mr. MACROSSAN.—There are some other points in the Canadian Constitution which I certainly would not like to see brought into the Australasian Constitution. First, there is the question of the Senate. The Canadian Senate is a body appointed by the Governor in Council for life, and I would be utterly opposed to the adoption of that plan here. I think the Senate ought to be a representative body, and that to allay the fears of the smaller States, such as Western Australia and Tasmania, the second chamber should in some way represent the colonies themselves as separate sovereignties. I regard the Senate of the United States as being one of the grandest representative bodies in existence. It is quite equal to, if it does not surpass, the British House of Lords. It is the best elective House of Legislature in the world, the reason of that being that it represents the different States, and is composed of men who have had vast experience of political life in some capacity or other before entering the Senate. Then, in Canada, the Governor in Council has the power of vetoing the legislation passed by the different local legislatures. That is a power I would not like to give to any Federal Government established in Australia. When we have established a Federal Constitution in Australia I think the Governors of the different colonies should be elected by the people of each colony, and that the Governor should only have a veto upon the legislation of the legislatures of the colony over which he presides. Those are two very material points in regard to which I differ with the system that prevails in Canada. I think that too much authority is given to the Federal Government in that country, and too little to the local legislatures. I think that a happy medium might be established between the Canadian system and that which obtains in the United States.

Coming to another point, Mr. Playford complained in a kind of way that this movement for Federation did not originate with the people of the colonies. I would like to ask him what great movement has ever originated with the people? Have not the people always been urged on by their leaders in every matter of improvement and reform?

Mr. PLAYFORD.—The people have always forced their leaders.

Mr. MACROSSAN.—It is the leaders who begin reforms, and the people take it up from them. We can move the people if we try to do so, and if we believe in Federation it is our duty to endeavour to influence the people to bring it about. Mr. Playford is under the impression, I suppose, that the United States of America in forming their present Constitution had fewer difficulties to contend against than we have in these colonies, and that in America the movement originated with the people. The fact is it was quite the opposite.

Mr. PLAYFORD.—Did not the action of Great Britain move the people?

Mr. MACROSSAN.—The difficulties the Americans had to contend against were enormous. The only real difficulty we have is the fiscal one. The Americans had that and half-a-dozen others besides. They had the fiscal difficulty to a larger extent than we have. They had also the difficulty of slavery, the difficulty of dislike and hatred existing between the different inhabitants of different States, and the difficulty of living under a government which had come to be despised. Our governments are not despised. The Americans had also the difficulty of being so impressed with democratic ideas that the people would not trust a man to represent them for more than twelve months without retaining the power of withdrawing their confidence from him and withdrawing him from the assembly into which they had sent him. The sturdy independence of the old Puritan spirit was such that they would trust no member of parliament. We have no fear of tyranny in these colonies, or that a Federal

Government will not act honestly within the limited sphere of its jurisdiction. But the American Government was scarcely a government at all, and at the same time the people were averse to having a government which exercised more power than the Articles of Federation gave to the Congress at that time. The Convention which established the present Constitution of America sat four years after the war with Great Britain was finished. There was no fear of any war at that time, but the country was tumbling into a state of anarchy. Rebellion had existed for months in Massachusetts, and there had been riots in other States. In America the impelling power to federate was greater than in Australia, but the difficulties were also greater. With us the impelling power is the desire for nationality, and the desire to abolish the Customs tariffs. When the American Convention was held it was not held at the instance of the people—it was held in a sneaking kind of way. James Madison, who was an advocate for a strong central government, was actually afraid to bring forward a motion in his own State of Virginia for the holding of a Convention. He got a man who was opposed to the idea to do it, so fearful was he of the effect on public opinion of a proposal to have a strong government. The father of one of the American Presidents, Mr. Tyler, was the man who submitted the motion. Then, when the Convention was held, all the States were not represented at it, and many of the members were afraid to do anything, because they were sent there simply to reform the Articles of Confederation, and not make a new Constitution of their own. They were afraid—the same as some timid men in Australia might be afraid—of Federation; they were frightened to do anything to alter the existing system. Nothing done by the members of that Convention would have had any good result at all but for the admirable conduct of its President, George Washington. At that very time the different members of the Convention showed a cowardly fear—which sometimes exists, and should not exist in free States—of offending the people they represented.

Sir HENRY PARKES.—I think you will find that Edmund Randolph was the President of that Convention.

Mr. MACROSSAN.—No; George Washington was the President, and the short speech of a line or two which he made turned the fate of the Convention. He said—

"If to please the people we offer what we ourselves disapprove, how can we afterwards defend our work? Let us raise a standard to which the wise and the honest can repair; the event is in the hand of God."

That is what we should do. We should raise a standard which we believe in—that is the standard of a complete Federation—and we may depend upon it that if we do so the people will carry it on to victory. If every man in this Conference will do what he believes inwardly to be his duty, there need be no fear of the result. What would the local legislatures surrender after all? They would surrender a little authority and a little dignity. The people would surrender nothing; and the sacrifice which the local legislatures would make would be fully compensated for by the great gain that would accrue in the union of Australia.

The Conference adjourned at twenty minutes past four o'clock until the following day.

THURSDAY, FEBRUARY 13, 1890.

The public were admitted to the Conference Chamber at half-past 11 o'clock a.m., the PRESIDENT (Mr. D. GILLIES) being in the Chair.

UNION OF THE COLONIES.

Discussion on Sir Henry Parkes' motion in favour of an early union under the Crown of all the Australasian Colonies (adjourned from the previous day) was then resumed.

Sir HENRY PARKES.—Mr. President, I can safely say that I came to this Conference with no desire to even allude particularly to the colony which I represent. I came here not as a resident of New South Wales, but, I trust, in the spirit of an Australian citizen. In submitting the proposition which I had the honour to place before you I did it in a way which I thought could not possibly give any offence, or raise any feeling of acerbity. I even tried to suppress my own passionate yearnings in many respects. I endeavoured to be calm and circumspect, and I thought I tried to keep well to the subject in hand. Probably I ought not to feel any surprise at the debate taking a wider range than I anticipated. It seemed to me, however, that as we contemplated the calling together of a Convention to consider the real matters attaching to the formation of a Constitution, we had little to do outside that simple question. Therefore I cannot admit that the resolution which I placed before you was in any sense bald, or of a merely abstract character. Nor can I admit that I would have been justified in going one step further than I went. As the correspondence which led to this Conference will show, we are not here to deal with doctrines, but to say whether we can or cannot assent in the name of the free peoples of this continent to steps being taken in order to weld them together. If I am not surprised at other delegates having, as I think, departed from what I expected to be the business of the Conference, I am, nevertheless, surprised that I should have been personally treated with, I might say, rudeness; nor can I conceive what offence I have given unless it be that I am the oldest servant of the Australian people. I am equally unable to imagine anything more personally offensive than for a gentleman to tell another to his face that although making certain professions there is strong reason for believing that he is not sincere. To me no deeper offence could be offered. But I have had to encounter another thing which gave me a sort of fear that I was to be overwhelmed. In fact Mr. Playford's behaviour reminded me—I think the allusion most appropriate—of the fable of "The Wolf and the Lamb," for he appeared determined to pick some kind of quarrel with me; why, I do not know. I had not disturbed the running waters, so I can only conceive the position to be that I am the lamb with whom the South Australian wolf is trying to quarrel on account of some imaginary act which I have never committed. What did he tell me? He ventured, and I must say I think it was a piece of presumption, to lecture me on my sentiment of loyalty—on my want of loyalty. He undertook, indeed, to challenge my loyalty to my Sovereign. Why, sir, the fact is that I seized the earliest opportunity, after arriving in Melbourne—at the banquet given by yourself—to express my opinion that the colonies should not, as a matter of common wisdom, think of separating from what I took leave to call the grand old mother country. I am not a man, Mr. President, much accustomed to repeat a thing which I have once tried to say plainly, and though I may have failed last Thursday night to give expression to my feelings of loyalty in the delicate way and with the peculiar kind of eloquence in which the honorable gentleman would have expressed his, I am quite sure that I made my true meaning sufficiently clear. I really don't know how any true subject of Her Majesty could have said more. Certainly, I don't know how he could have said more becomingly. Because my notion of loyalty is not a lip service. My sense of loyalty is a steady consistent adherence to the principles of the institutions under which we live, and a devoted homage to the Sovereign who uses her position to preserve and strengthen the constitutional life of the nation. That is my idea of loyalty, and I have acted up to it at all times, and under all circumstances, throughout my life. Then the honorable gentleman said he had a command to satisfy the people of South Australia on one or two things concerning my public conduct. Sir, I take the liberty of doubting that he had the command of any ten men in South Australia to do any such impertinent thing. If I have ever been well received in any Australian colony I have been well received in South Australia whenever I have visited it, and I have no reason whatever to suppose that there is any urgent inquiry there as to what I may have done or not done, or that he had any mission of the kind he mentioned. He wanted to be in a position, forsooth, to satisfy the people of South Australia as to my conduct with respect to the Federal Council, and he instanced the undoubted fact that I framed the first Federal Council Bill. That is an undoubted fact, but he might have gone further. If he had given himself the trouble of referring back to the year 1867 he would have found that then, at my instance, a law was introduced to and passed by the New South Wales Parliament to establish a Federal Council, and that that law is at this moment on the New South Wales Statute Book. It is a fact that, twenty-three years ago, the legislature of the Colony I have the honour to represent carried an Act to constitute a Federal Council for the purposes of considering the vexed question of postal communication, and if the other colonies, or any of them, had copied our example we could have met at the present moment under that law without any preliminary conference whatever, with authority to adjust all questions arising in regard to mail communication. Again, it is quite true that in the Conference of 1881, I, being one of its members, a bill was framed by me which was undoubtedly the basis of the present Federal Council Act. But when I did that I took care to leave on record my reasons for the step. I will read the resolutions on the subject which I brought forward. I am not quite sure, nor could I ascertain without searching through the papers, whether I actually submitted them or not, but that is not a material point. Here are the resolutions:—

"1. That the time is not come for the construction of a Federal Constitution with an Australian Federal Parliament.

"2. That the time is come when a number of matters of much concern to all the colonies might be dealt with more effectively by some federal authority than by the colonies separately."

I can imagine some member of the Conference, Sir James Lee Steere, for example, stating that this just fits the case. But I will go on:—

"3. That an organization which would lead men to think in the direction of Federation and accustom the public mind to federal ideas would be the best preparation for the foundation of a Federal Government.

" The bill has been prepared to carry out the idea of a mixed body, partly legislative and partly administrative. Care has been taken throughout to give effective power to the proposed Federal Council within prescribed limits without impairing the authority of the colonies represented in that body.

" No attempt has been made to constitute the proposed Council on any historical model, but the object has been to meet the circumstances of the present Australian situation, while paving the way to a complete federal organization hereafter."

Pursuant to this resolution a Bill was drafted, so that it will be observed that even at that time, nearly ten years ago, I sought to give strength to the Federal Council. Then came the Convention of 1883. I have, however, a pretty distinct recollection that the first movement towards that Convention was not to favour Federation at all, but to support the annexation of the Island of New Guinea. The correspondence which led to that Convention will show that throughout the earlier stages of the affair the idea was simply to back up the action of the Queensland Government in taking possession of New Guinea in Her Majesty's name. I have good reason to recollect this part of the case, for although I was not in office at the time a very influential resident of Queensland, who occupies at this moment a very high position there, appealed to me to write a letter to the Queensland Government offering them whatever support might be supposed to attach to my influence, which I did. I wrote at once, approving, with some qualification, of the policy of the act which had been committed. Another thing is that the Convention of 1883 met in December, I having, in the previous July, quitted the shores of Australia on my way to visit America and England, so that the introduction of the Federation question took place after I had left the continent. In truth, I had up to then heard nothing about it. But if I were permitted to say all that is within my knowledge, I could tell this Conference, and I would especially like to tell the representatives of Queensland, that I exerted whatever influence I had in London to forward what I understood to be the main object of that Convention. For example, I had a long correspondence with a very powerful member of the British Government, the Lord Chancellor, and I telegraphed to Sir Alexander Stuart (what became of my telegram I do not know) informing him that if he would abstain from seeking to mop up all the islands of the Pacific, and simply ask to obtain the control of New Guinea, I believe he would succeed. I believe now that he would have succeeded, and that the flag of England alone would now be floating over the portion of New Guinea which was then free for occupation. The member of the British Government with whom I had the long correspondence was the Earl of Selborne, who was understood at the time to be the Minister most opposed to what had been done in Queensland, and he took chiefly one ground, namely, that of affording protection to the native inhabitants concerned, fearing that a misuse would be made of the occupation of the island in order to flood the neighbouring market with cheap labour. I think that what I have said will show that I was no hindrance to the proceedings—so far as I know them—intended to be introduced at the Convention. Mr. Playford asked how it was that, having prepared the measure which subsequently became the Federal Council Act, I was not prepared to advise the Parliament of New South Wales to authorize the Colony to join that body. Sir, I stated the reason why as early as I could, as soon as I had, after my return to the Colony, an opportunity of doing so, and I have repeatedly said the same thing since. Upon reflection, and after further examination of the great and complex question before me, I became satisfied that the body proposed to be created under my bill would never succeed, and, of course, having become satisfied that it would never succeed, I was not foolish enough to persevere with the business, although I had in a measure originated it. Is it fitting that a man who had become convinced by further inquiry and reflection, and by a more close examination of authorities, that something he had proposed was not the right thing to meet what had to be met, should still, for the sake of identifying himself with the subject, persevere with his proposition? Certainly such a course is not one I would follow, and I seized the earliest opportunity of stating to the world that I had become convinced that the Federal Council scheme would never succeed. One of the reasons for the stand I took will, I think, commend itself to every person, however much or little he may be acquainted with the principles of government—every person who is capable of examination and reflection. It was that a body so appointed and so limited in number and authority, and consequently so powerless to acquire prestige, as the Federal Council necessarily is, could never work in harmony in the face of any display of hostile feeling on the part of any of the great parliaments of the continent. Take the case of New South Wales. Our parliament consists, with its two houses, of more than 200 members. Is it likely that a legislative body of that sort would submit to the least movement on the part of the Federal Council in disaccord with its own views on any great question—a question of national magnitude? When such a movement came to be reviewed by that parliament, or by any other Australian parliament holding anything like the same position, what might not be expected? No body designed for the government of men is worthy the support of any rational being if it is not so formed that it will endure conflict, not only in times of peace but also in times of pressure and emergency. Why its very purpose must be, on occasions, to breast the storm—to control the elements—not simply in days of calm and peace, but in days of trial and national agony. Therefore, having become convinced that the Federal Council scheme would not succeed, although I had myself framed the measure under which it was constituted, I, like a sensible man, decided to advocate it no longer. I was not to be swayed in the matter by any such reason as that contained in the fact that the paternity of the body in question was ascribable to me. At the same time I was not the leading spirit in opposition to it. Be it remembered that I did not return to the Colony of New South Wales until the end of August, 1884, the Convention having been held, as I have mentioned, the preceding December. I was absent at the time, and never raised my voice in the business. In fact I could not by any possibility have exerted any influence with regard to it until the end of August, 1884. Moreover, I did not even write a letter to a newspaper, or express my views in public, until, the time having arrived for me to do so, I gave utterance to them in my place in parliament, stating them as I have stated them to this Conference; and I do not see how I could have followed any other course, and still held, as I hope I am allowed to hold, the position of a consistent, rational man. Well, that is the explanation on the subject I have to give to the honorable gentleman who raised the question, and I may state to Sir James Lee Steere also that I hope he will accept it without my taking up the time of the Conference by answering him in particular on this point. Mr. Playford also told us that I had been false to some promise in regard to the exclusion of Chinese. But I may say for myself that I thought I had been singularly conspicuous in my resolute opposition to the introduction of Chinese; for at the very time the Conference the honorable gentleman alluded to sat in Sydney there was before the Legislative Council of New South Wales a bill introduced by me, which had been carried by an immense majority through the Legislative Assembly of New South Wales, and which was a severer measure in the direction of exclusion than any other law on the subject in these colonies. What gave some umbrage was the fact that I declined to withdraw that bill because the

Conference was sitting. I declined to do so because, for one reason, I had already gone through the toil and unpleasantness of passing it through the Legislative Assembly. Some of my friends, who held more moderate views on the question than I did, also thought that the Bill ought to be taken back, but I and my colleagues thought otherwise. We had had great trouble and labour in the matter, and had been successful so far, and we did not feel justified in throwing away what we had accomplished, the outcome being that the measure became law soon after the meeting of the Conference. Of course the Emperor of China could most reasonably object to what I had done, but I do not know that Mr. Playford represents His Imperial Majesty. How any Australian Colony could complain of my taking securer steps than any it had taken in order to effect the common purpose in view I cannot understand. Remember, it is not two years since this Chinese Conference sat, and that what I undertook—I and my honorable colleague, Mr. J. F. Burns—to do was that as soon as any two other colonies adopted the model bill agreed to at the Conference, we would take measures to bring our Act of Parliament into accord with theirs. Well, I have not done that, but inasmuch as my law is more effective than the others, or, at all events, quite as effective, I don't see that much can be complained of, except, as I have said before, by the Emperor of China. He has good grounds for complaint against us. All that we in New South Wales need to do is to repeal the section imposing a poll-tax of £100 on each Chinese entering our ports, and we intend to do that. We have not done it already because we have been overtaxed with other work, which we thought ought not to be interrupted in order to amend the Chinese Act. Under these circumstances I fail to see how we have committed any breach of faith with the other colonies. If the case had stood as Mr. Playford had placed it before the Conference, complaint might have been made that we had agreed to introduce a bill and had failed to introduce it. But, as a matter of fact, all we have to do is to weaken the Act we have passed by making it less drastic, not more so—by making it less effective for the work in view, not more so. I have now explained my most reprehensible conduct on these two important questions, and I do not fear that the explanation, whether satisfactory or not to my friends here, will be at all unsatisfactory to my constituents, the people of New South Wales. I also heard a remarkable doctrine from Mr. Playford, to which, as I have been drawn into this thing, I will make some allusion. He told us that this cause of Federation is a thing that has arisen from what he called the "statesmen" of Australia. Now, I don't know quite what they are. When I have heard persons talk of "statesmen," I could generally utter a sort of secret prayer that I might never be included in the category. The honorable gentleman says this movement has arisen with the statesmen, and that no movement or measure can succeed unless it arises with the people. A little later he stated that the people "drove" the statesmen. Well, all through my life, and all through my reading, I have heard, in connection with the English nation, and the great nations that have sprung up from her, of "the leaders of the people." The expression has been "the people and their leaders." Now, however, I hear, for the first time, of the statesmen and their drivers. I don't understand this strange doctrine, and I venture to say, in contradiction of it, that there has not been one great movement for the benefit of mankind that did not in the first instance arise in some pregnant far-seeing human mind. A great thought has been communicated to other minds; it has been propagated by contact with other minds; and not until the real leaders of the people have become seised of it have the people themselves been roused to its truth, its importance, its grandeur, and its necessity to their welfare. That has been the history of every great movement known to England—of every great movement in the world. If we waited until the many, or any considerable number, originated the movement although it might be talked of often, it would be a long time before it came to light and success. I don't think I need offer any apology to the honorable gentleman from South Australia after his fierce attack on me. I really thought at the time, looking at him, that I had something to fear. And I must assure Mr. Playford that I cannot accept him as an interpreter of my loyalty, and that I have no fear that the time will ever come when I shall need him as an apologist for it. Now, I have a word or two to say to the honorable gentleman who represents Western Australia. I can make great allowances for the youth and inexperience of Mr. Playford, but I can make none for Sir James Lee Steere. He comes before us as a superior personage, and he ought to set us an example, which I for one should be extremely glad to follow. I cannot but take exception to what that honorable gentleman has stated. The honorable gentleman leaped up and at once committed what I think was an insult to every one of us—certainly it was not a compliment. These are the honorable gentleman's very first words:—

"I cannot hope that any effort of oratory or rhetoric on my part will be sufficiently great to assist the imagination of members of this Conference, because my mind is eminently a practical one, and I have little imagination in my constitution. I think, if I may say so without offence, that the debate that has hitherto taken place has had rather too much of an academic character, and has been a little too full of sentiment. We should now take the more practical view of the question."

Well, I shall show you in a moment or two what the practical view of the question is. But Sir James Lee Steere was not satisfied with this assumption of superior importance, but he went on to question my sincerity; and, not satisfied with that, he questioned the sincerity of the people of New South Wales. One purpose for my waiting for or seeking to get permission to speak this morning, was in order that I might obtain the official report of the proceedings of the Conference, from which I purpose quoting. Sir James Lee Steere said:—

"It is a very happy omen indeed that in discussing this question we have with us representatives of New South Wales, because, whether it is true or not, there has been an impression throughout the Australian colonies that the cause of Federation has been delayed in consequence of New South Wales refusing to take any part in the Federal Council. I am very glad indeed to see the representatives of New South Wales present now; because I hope that before this discussion ceases either one or the other of those representatives will give us their reasons for having hitherto refused to join that body."

Then he went on to say that though I had professed myself in favour of Federation for five-and-twenty years, there was good reason to doubt my sincerity, and good reason to doubt the sincerity of the people of New South Wales who supported me. Then, a little further on, he used these words in continuing his address :—

"I shall welcome most gladly any scheme that may be devised to enable us to federate, if only for certain purposes. If we only federate for the purpose of defence it will be well to have had a Conference for that. Mr. Deakin remarked that it was all very well to ridicule the idea of the colonies being attacked by a foreign foe, but I do not see anything ridiculous in the idea. A day may come when England is at war, and our coasts may be ravaged by hostile cruisers, or attempts be made to land a foreign force on our shores. It is absolutely necessary that we should be prepared with a federal defence force. For that reason alone, if for no other, I shall be glad to see Federation accomplished in some form."

Here, Mr. President, comes in the practical operation of this gentleman's practical mind. The colonies, unitedly, have 31,000 men for defence purposes. Western Australia herself has 600 men, and no doubt it would be a most practical solution of the difficulty for the colonies, with their tens of thousands, to join with the 600 for the defence of one of the longest portions of the sea-coast of Australasia. That, certainly, is a very practical question. But that, I think, is not the way in which we shall arrive at any safe conclusion on the main question of uniting the whole of the colonies. With regard to my own course I have explained why I could not join a Federal Council, which, before t received the stamp of Imperial legality, I had come to the opinion would never work for the benefit of the Australian colonies. I have been spoken of as formulating—which I have not done—a Constitution for these colonies similar to that of Canada. I venture to say that I have never alluded to the Canadian Constitution in any way that would justify the inference that I have any intention, so far as I may have the power, of copying it. I only alluded to it once, and that was in my letter to Mr. Gillies, which opened the correspondence on this subject. Since then I have never alluded, except by way of illustration, to the Dominion Government, either in speech or in writing. This is what I said in my letter of October 30th, 1889 :—

"The scheme of Federal Government, it is assumed, would necessarily follow close upon the type of the Dominion Government of Canada."

Of course there must be some indication of the form it might take, and I go on to explicitly explain, fortunately for me, what I meant by that allusion :—

"It would provide for the appointment of a Governor-General, for the creation of an Australian Privy Council, and a Parliament consisting of a Senate and House of Commons."

But I added these words :—

"In the work of the Convention, no doubt, the rich stores of political knowledge which were collected by the framers of the Constitution of the United States would be largely resorted to, as well as the vast accumulations of learning on cognate subjects since that time."

I, therefore, simply indicated that what I wanted, and what believe the people of New South Wales want, is a thoroughly organized Federal Government, consisting of a Governor-General, to represent the Sovereign; of a Privy Council, which, at a later period, I explained should include the creation of a judiciary; and a Parliament, consisting of an Upper Chamber and a House of Commons. I went on to explain that, in constructing this form of government, we should resort to all stores of learning which were open to us, and, though the sentence is a short one, it is sufficiently explicit to show what I mean. I then went on to point out, and I am glad I did so, because it saves me from much misrepresentation now, that we did not want a Federal Government alone for the purposes of defence, but for many other, and, to my mind, many higher purposes. My words are these :—

"Although a great and pressing military question has brought to the surface the design of a Federal Government at the present juncture, the work of a national character which such a government could, in the interest of all the Colonies, most beneficially and effectively undertake, would include the noblest objects of peaceful and orderly progress; and every year the field of its beneficent operations would be rapidly expanding."

I thus showed clearly enough what I meant, as far as it can be stated in a letter of this kind, and in the few words I used on the only occasion when I alluded to the Dominion of Canada at all. I think I have a right to complain of Sir James Lee Steere, as an educated gentleman, being a little disingenuous with me. I will point out what I mean: The honorable gentleman quoted two or three words used by the Premier of Queensland, but he did not quote the context which explained what Mr. Morehead meant. He quoted the words that, in the judgment of the Queensland Government, a Dominion Parliament would be more advantageously brought about by a process of development than by an act of displacement—and he stopped there. But Mr. Morehead did not stop there, and I am going to read what he said, in the name of Queensland:—

"As, however, previous communications and the reports of your public speeches have led me to the conclusion that your concurrence on this point is not to be looked for at present, and as this Government are exceedingly anxious that there should be no action or abstention from action on their part which would tend to render abortive any legitimate effort towards the establishment of a Federal Constitution, it becomes desirable to adopt some course which will neither imply disregard to your objection to the character of the Federal Council, nor prevent the governments represented thereon from availing themselves, for consultative purposes, of the machinery provided by the Council, in order to facilitate whatever further steps may be deemed necessary to bring about a complete federation of the Australasian Colonies."

I am perfectly satisfied with what the Government of Queensland said to the Government of New South Wales in this correspondence, and I think their conduct was not only straightforward and intelligible, but, in a manner, generous. I have had no complaint or doubt about Queensland from that time to the present, and certainly I could have none after listening to the really practical speech delivered last night by Mr. Macrossan. That honorable gentleman grasped the true points of this delicate, difficult, and urgent question, with a knowledge, a tact, and a forcible application of that knowledge, and the principles of government, which I only wish I could equal. The object of this Conference, I was going to point out, is expressed in a few words by yourself, Mr. President. In your letter, addressed to myself, of the 13th of November, you, after expressing doubt as to whether my proposal was the best, admitted that it was very desirable that the whole question should be considered. You then say :—

"To ensure that consideration I would suggest to you that, instead of going through the form of the Parliaments appointing representatives to a Convention, it should be accepted as sufficient if the representatives of the various colonies at the Federal Council were to meet yourself and representatives from New South Wales to discuss and, if deemed necessary, to devise and report upon an adequate scheme of Federal Government."

From that time, or from the date upon which I accepted this proposal, I have regarded this Conference as essentially a consultative and preparatory body, to consider whether it were advisable to take further steps towards ascertaining the verdict of the Australian Colonies on the one great question. And, as I have already said, up to this present hour I have adhered to that regard of its character, and if I have broken through the restraint which I desire to place upon myself, it has been, to say the least of it, thoughtlessly provoked. Now, the honorable gentleman was pleased to characterize the resolution I submitted as a bald resolution. I cannot see its baldness. Another honorable gentleman characterized it as an abstract resolution. I contend it is nothing of the kind. An abstract resolution would be something partaking of this form : " It would be highly to the advantage of the Australian Colonies to have their coasts securely defended." That would be an abstract resolution, and, I think, a very good model of one. But this resolution of mine states all the facts which are necessary at this stage. So far from being abstract, it is very definite, very precise indeed, and it asks you to assent to a number of facts as proved truths, and proved truths with a practical bearing upon the condition of these colonies at the present time. It seems to me that unless we can believe that, we ought not to carry this resolution. The resolution says—

"That in the opinion of this Conference, the best interests and the present and future prosperity of the Australasian Colonies will be promoted by an early union under the Crown."

Nothing could be more definite; nothing could be more expressive. The resolution goes on to recognise the valuable services of the members of the Convention which founded the Federal Council; for in the light of the resolutions which I submitted to the Conference of 1881, that Council has been of great service to Australia. I will quote the words of my resolution, proposed two years before the Convention of 1883 met. The third of my resolutions stated—

"That an organization which would lead men to think in the direction of Federation, and accustom the public mind to federal ideas, would be the best preparation for the foundation of a Federal Government."

I readily admit that members of the Convention of 1883, and the Federal Council itself, have rendered important service in the light of the resolutions which I submitted in 1881, in directing attention to a question, in accustoming men to the federal idea, and in a variety of ways leading on to the great end which every thoughtful man in the whole of these colonies has kept in view—the complete Federation, at some time or other, of Australasia in one great nation. This resolution goes on to state that the time has now come for this higher act, and it declares to what, in the four grandest elements of national life, we had arrived at that time—in population, in wealth, in the result of a wise use of the energy, mental and physical of the population, and in our application to the grand work of discovering what we ourselves possess in the resources of the country, and in our power to govern. These, I contend, are the four great elements of nationl life—numbers, the proper application of the strength of those numbers, the wealth arising from their co-operative action, and their capacity to manage their own affairs. And this resolution declares that all these grand conditions exist. Then the resolution goes on to say that no Government should be sought to be established as a central authority without due regard to the just claims of the several colonies. To call a motion of that sort abstract is simply a misuse of terms. If it had said more, as was pointed out by several gentlemen present, it would have been a mistake. It said enough, and on that broad resolution any structure whatever can be founded which the judgment of Australia may approve, and which the creative powers of Australia may call into existence. The Attorney-General for Tasmania, whom I am very glad to have met here for the first time, alluded somewhat more elaborately than I did to the warning which the attempts at government in the United States hold out to us. I am anxious to state the case more definitely, and with the clearest accuracy that I am master of, because it seems to me that the early years of the existence of the United States supplies sounder lessons for us in this work than are to be found in the mother country or any other part of the world. Lest I should be mistaken, I am not going to speak of the advantages of the American organization. I am not going to speak upon the results that have followed that great organization. I am only going to allude to the process by which the American Constitution came into existence, as exemplified in a more forcible way than anything in the wide world can exemplify, the danger of these colonies going on longer in their separate condition. I say fearlessly that any person who really advocates the separation of these colonies—the continuance of that separation—can be no other than an enemy to Australian welfare; and I think I can prove conclusively, from the highest witnesses that history can produce, that the attempt to go on in that way in America is the most awful warning to us. I do not withdraw the adjective, I say the most "awful" warning. As I am anxious to be quite clear, I shall state five great events which mark the foundation of the present Great Republic. The first blood was shed at Lexington in April, 1775. A party, I think of some 800 English soldiers, who were stationed in Boston, went out to the village of Concord to capture some munitions of war in possession of the American colonists. At Lexington they came upon a party of the patriotic colonists, and killed some eighteen of them. They did not get the munitions of war, because the Americans were on the alert and carried them to a place of safety, and the 800 English soldiers had to return to their quarters in Boston. But the hardy old Puritans—and here we were amongst Puritans, but not throughout the struggle—waylaid them at every yard as they had to make their way back through the forest, and of the 800 only 500 reached their quarters in Boston. They were shot down like dogs in revenge for the first blood they had shed. This is the first great event in this rebellion. On the 4th July, 1776, the Declaration of Independence was approved. This, you will observe, was a considerable time after the blood-shedding at Lexington, because we never should forget, and no Englishman ought for a moment to forget, that there never were a people more loyal to the Throne of England than those Americans who were driven into rebellion by such practical men as Lord North and George III. They endured pains and penalties without number; they endured pains and penalties which can never be properly described, rather than forsake the standard of England, and it was only by the blundering—the wholly incredible blundering—of such men as George III and Lord North (and they were practical men) that the American Colonies were lost to Great Britain. It is worth while pausing to consider for a moment that when this Declaration of Independence was agreed to the delegates to the Convention were split up by the most incredible dislikes, antipathies, and attempts to undermine each other's influence. Though they all assembled with halters round their necks, and every man Jack of them would have been hanged if they had not succeeded in their object, they could hardly keep their hands from each other's throats. I mention these things as a fair warning for Australia. I only want to state the facts that the Declaration of Independence was agreed to in July, 1776; that the articles of federation and perpetual union were adopted on the 15th November, 1777; and that the Independence of the United States was acknowledged by England on the 20th January, 1783. The event that led, as you no doubt all know, to the close of the war was the battle of York Town, and the 8,000 English troops coming before Washington and laying down their arms, or the complete outgeneralling of Lord Cornwallis by that great soldier George Washington. The Constitution of the United States became the supreme law of the land by the ninth State required to give it validity signing it on the 21st June, 1778. So it will be seen that the Articles of Confederation did not come into force until one year four months and eleven days after the Declaration of Independence. During that time there was hardly any government, notwithstanding that Washington had to contend against the experienced troops of England. The Constitution came into force just ten years and seven months after the Articles of Confederation, or five years and five months after the close of the war. For five years, therefore, during which this young country was in the throes of a terrible war, the people were carrying on the conflict under the government of separate States with separate sovereignties. For five years afterwards they carried on their peaceful operations under the separate government of these sovereign States. If it was necessary, I could bring before you hundreds of witnesses of the highest standing to show the disastrous effects of that temporary government of the disunited States; but I shall only bring one —the one man without whose marvellous skill as a soldier, without whose unequalled rectitude as a man and a great citizen, and without whose discernment and whose power of resource, which never failed him, the United States would never have accomplished their independence, and without whose wise counsel, whose great example, and whose commanding influence in peaceful times, they would have broken down—George Washington. All through the awful time that he was fighting against the Crown of England for the independence of the United States hardly a day passed over his weary head without bitter complaints from him of his want of support. I will not, however, quote from the scores and scores of his letters complaining of the disorganized state of the Government under the Articles of Confederation during the war, but I will come to the time of peace. The disorganization, the feebleness, the inadequacy of the Government for any rational purpose was so great that the prophets of evil, the marplots—and they are always too plentiful all over the world—were pointing out with sinful jubilation that the States would soon break down, and that they could not hold out much longer; and it is said that the old king revelled in the anticipation of the collapse of this young Republic. But I will come now to the opinions of George Washington after peace was proclaimed—after the independence for which he had fought so well, setting an example which can never be excelled—and whose independence he, and he alone, won. In 1784, a year after the independence of America was acknowledged by the Crown of England, he writes thus to one of his compatriots:—

"The want of energy in the Federal Government; the pulling of one State and parts of States against another; and the commotions among the eastern people"—

They had broken out into riot and actual rebellion in several places.

—"have sunk our national character much below par, and have brought our politics and credit to the brink of a precipice. A step or two more must plunge us into inextricable ruin. Liberality, justice, and unanimity in those States which do not appear to have drunk so deep of the cup of folly, may yet retrieve our affairs, but no time is to be lost in essaying the reparation of them."

He writes to another friend thus:—

"However delicate the revision of the federal system may appear, it is a work of indispensable necessity. The present constitution is inadequate; the superstructure is tottering to its foundation, and, without help, must bury us in its ruins."

That was after ten years of Government by a cluster of separate States. Again, writing to Edmund Randolph, on the occasion of his appointment to the head of the Congress, he says:—

"Dear Sir,—It gave me great pleasure to hear that the voice of the country had been directed to you as chief magistrate of this commonwealth, and that you had accepted the appointment."

Of course no one will confound this with any appointment to the Presidency, which did not come into force till some years afterwards. The letter proceeds:

"Our affairs seem to be drawing to an awful crisis. It is necessary, therefore, that the abilities of every man should be drawn into action in a public line, to rescue them, if possible, from impending ruin. As no one seems more fully impressed with the necessity of adopting such measures than yourself, so none is better qualified to be entrusted with the reins of Government."

Here, then, I bring one great witness out of hundreds to show, not simply the inadequacy, but the impossibility of governing the people by a number of authorities, and it seems to me that this one case supplies a warning to us not to attempt anything that would disorganize authority and separate the powers which are always most wanted at a time when it is most difficult to obtain them—which are always of most value to the citizens governed at a time which allows of no processes to bring them into existence. If they do not exist already, the country that trusts to such helps as those is lost; and Washington saw clearly enough, from an experience which no other man living had obtained, that America would have been lost had it not been for the wise counsels which led to the adoption at last of the present Constitution and Union Government under it, which now rules between 60,000,000 and 70,000,000 of free subjects. I will endeavour to state as briefly as I can, and, of course, with as much force as I can, the great objects of a Central Australian Government. I omitted entirely some of those objects in my opening speech, because I had really been in a condition in which I could give attention to nothing up to the morning on which I spoke. I would willingly have left the Conference that day for the mere purpose of rest, and it is no wonder to myself that I lost sight of some of the more important of those objects. Two of the most important, from a practical point of view, relate to the Asiatic races and to the islands of the Pacific. No one, I presume, will doubt the principle of growth in the Australian people. What we are to-day is nothing to what we shall be this day twelve months, and if men could go away beyond the reach of the telegraph and post office for ten years, and then return, they would hardly believe that the Australia of the year 1900, was the same country as the Australia of 1890. The elements of growth among us are simply marvellous, and they will go on in an increasing ratio as time progresses. Who knows what troubles may arise in relation to those countless millions of inferior members of the human family who are within easy sail of these shores? Who knows what will take place in the next decade in the empire of China? There are many strong evidences that the thin end of the wedge of change has been driven into that empire, which remained in seclusion for centuries and centuries; and looking to the weak organization of the governing powers, who knows what new forms of socialism may not split up the empire of China with its 400,000,000 men and women? Who knows what form the policy of that vast empire may assume, and who would dare to foreshadow how intimately it may concern the free peoples of this country? I spoke just now of the efforts of New South Wales to restrict the tide of Chinese emigration. I hope I shall be permitted to state here what I have often stated in other places, in order that there may be no misunderstanding as to what my view on this point is. I am not one of those, as I have repeatedly declared elsewhere, who regard the Chinese people with any feeling of loathing. I am not one of those who wish to look down upon them as a people who are in their habits particularly inferior to us. On the contrary, I believe them on the whole to be a law-abiding, industrious, frugal, and peaceable people. I have never opposed the Chinese on any ground derogatory to their character as members of a civilized community, but I have opposed their entrance into Australia, because I believe it is my highest duty and the highest duty of every person who has imagination in his composition to do so. I believe it to be the duty of every one to endeavour to preserve these Australian lands which were acquired according to the rights of nations, for a people modelled on the type of the British nation; and it is on that ground, and on that ground alone, that I have opposed the introduction of the Chinese. I wish to refer to the question now in a much higher light. I cannot lose sight of the fact that these people number upwards of 400,000,000, that they are a hardy race, that they are an adventurous race, and, what is of more importance to us, that they are an imitative race. What we can do they will try to do, and they will, with greater or less success, accomplish it. It is said that Napoleon I, who certainly, in the qualities of statesmanship, was amongst the giants of the world, once expressed his opinion that it was only necessary for the Chinese to acquire European arts, especially the art of shipbuilding, in order to conquer the world. The saying, whether correctly attributed to Napoleon or not, conveys the truth that there are elements of power in this nation, because there is no power except in the number of human minds and human organisms. It is population alone which gives the foundation of power in every structure of government under the sun. And I say again, it is in the highest degree necessary, and it may be necessary to the security, to the integrity, and to the honor of Australia, that there should be a central power to do what is wise and fitting the occasion in regard to these multitudes of Asiatics. Turning from that field to the field of the South Sea Islands, I have no doubt whatever in my mind that if there had been a central government in Australia—if Australia could have spoken with one voice in the year 1883, New Guinea would have belonged to Australia.

Sir SAMUEL GRIFFITH.—Hear, hear.

Sir HENRY PARKES.—I have no doubt whatever of it, and I do not think that any person with a mind accustomed to the contemplation of events, or at all acquainted with Australian history, can doubt it. We know what has followed. As was pointed out by my colleague (Mr. McMillan) with great force and accuracy yesterday, those great armed powers of Europe which are shut in from the sea are not only wanting more earth for their multitudes to live upon, but are wanting the earth which fronts the ocean in any part of the world. I am treading somewhat on dangerous ground, and I do not care to pursue this idea, but we all know what has occurred. We know the tortuous ways in which persons who have had to negotiate with England have acted, and with what marvellous tenacity they hold to any authority in the Southern Seas. Now, Australia ought to be mistress of the Southern Seas. The trade, the commerce, and the intercourse of those groups of rich islands ought to centre in our ports, and with these advantages we ought to hold the mastery of the hemisphere. That is our destiny, and it will come. But why should we not let it come with the least pains and penalties, with the least delays, and with the least possible loss of time and opportunities. These are two very great objects which can only be properly attained, properly promoted, by a Federal Government. I think I agree in the main with Mr. Macrossan's view as to the necessity of giving power, all the power necessary, to this government, if we assent to create it. I also agree with Mr. Playford, and it affords me unspeakable happiness to do so, that it will be the duty of the Convention, if it is called into existence, to jealously watch the rights and privileges of the provincial governments. I agree entirely, and I have as much interest in it—as a citizen of New South Wales—as any of the members of the Conference, I agree entirely, I say, in not stripping the colonial governments of any power which they can hold, consistently with due power being given to the government which represents them all. But there are even higher objects than these waiting to be achieved by an Australian government, a government that can appear everywhere as representing the whole people, a government to which the doors of every court will be thrown open, and before which no nation would appear except with respect and proper appreciation of its present and future importance. There is the national credit, which has been alluded to already, and I will only pass it by with one word, that the credit of Australia under the powers of a Federal Government would, I think, be second to none—certainly it would be second to none excepting England. She would stand amongst the best before the world. Is that no light object? Is that no object in the direct material interest of Australia? There is a higher object still—the object of a national influence. What influence have these detached colonies? It is surprising that they have so much; but the influence of the proudest—we will say Victoria—is nothing to the influence of an Australian nation, an Australian Government. She would be able to influence the destinies of civilized men in all parts of the world. It cannot for a moment be doubted that there is another object scarcely less than this—and I hope Sir J. Lee Steere will not consider that I am merely dealing with imaginary things—there is the object of exercising national power in the community of nations all over the world. Who can doubt that our national power would be incalculably increased by its being exercised by one strong intelligent head? And there is, highest of all, the object of national honor. Why should not the name of an Australian be equal to that of a Briton? Why should not the name of an Australian sailor be equal to that of a British sailor? Why should not the name of an Australian citizen be equal to that of the citizen of the proudest country under the sun? All those grand objects would be promoted by a national organization. But there is something more. Make yourselves a united people, appear before the world as one, and the dream of going "home" would die away. We should create an Australian home—our rich men would find avenues for the employment of their talents, and for the expenditure of their superfluous fortunes on the spot—the Governor-General of Australia would be able to hold a court that would be as attractive as that of the monarchs of the old world, which is not a light thing to be passed over as a mere matter of sentiment. We know what was said by a wise minister to a European potentate who declined to do some trivial thing on the ground that it was only a ceremony. "My liege," said the Minister. "you are only a ceremony." He knew how much the world is moved by the forms, by the ceremonies, and by the social influences which are brought to bear, and which are inseparable from a high state of civilization. We should have "home" within our own shores; "home" with all the lofty ideals for the mere socially ambitious. We should have avenues of employment for the most gifted among our sons, and there would be no object of ambition superior to what could be presented to them on the spot which gave them birth. For some

P

years past I have enjoyed the acquaintance of a man who is perhaps the highest student of the materials of history living in our country. A few years ago I was introduced to Mr. Lecky by Lord Tennyson. I have had frequent opportunities of enjoying his conversation under his own roof, and I am in correspondence with him now. On Tuesday last, I received a letter from Mr. Lecky on the Federation of the Australian Colonies, and I don't think it out of place—and I am quite sure that, if it were possible, I should have his permission—to read it to the Conference. He writes to me on the occasion of my sending him the Federation papers, and his letter is dated December 28, 1889. It is as follows:—

"DEAR SIR HENRY,—I have been reading, with great interest, the papers you were kind enough to send me. Your great work seems marching steadily to its consummation. If a federal system such as you propose, had existed in the American Colonies ——"

Let me say here, that if there is a man living who has ransacked the archives for the materials of American and English history, it is Mr. Lecky. He knows, probably, more than any other Englishman about the events which led to the loss to Great Britain of the American Colonies. He writes:—

"If a federal system such as you propose had existed in the American Colonies in the last century, it is probable that their quarrel with England would have been avoided."

I have already pointed out, what history points out, how anxious the whole of the great men who founded the American Union were to avoid a separation. There never was a more loyal subject of the British Crown than George Washington, and there was not one of the great men who had a hand in framing the Constitution who would not gladly have allowed the country to remain a part of the Empire. Mr. Lecky proceeded—

"The only wish of Grenville was, that they should have an army for their own protection."

Let me pause here. In what was considered to be a most propitious change of Ministry, under the leadership of Lord Grenville, the object was not to endanger the connection, not to tyrannize over the American Colonies—but, on the authority of this great historian, that the American Colonies should have an army for their own protection. They could not, however, agree to give it sanction, on account of the awful dismemberment arising from the existence of so many separate governments.

"The only wish of Grenville was that they should have an army for their own protection; but there was then no single body which could represent them all, and it was the extreme difficulty of obtaining the concurrence of a great number of separate legislatures that induced him to adopt his fatal plan of taxing them by means of the British Parliament."

We now have it, on the authority of Mr. Lecky, than whom there can be no better, that Lord Grenville's object was not to tax the American people, and he would not have done so if he could have got the assent of any single body to the formation of an army, or if he could have avoided the chaotic cavillings of the thirteen separate legislatures, and induced them to tax themselves. Mr. Lecky further states:—

"If America had then been constituted as Australia would be upon your plan, no difficulty would have arisen, and it is totally certain that British taxation would never have been proposed."

I do not know whether the word "totally" is a correct rendering or not. In conclusion, Mr. Lecky says:—

"You seem to be engaged in a work of unity and conciliation, the most appropriate and noblest employment of old age.
"Believe me, dear Sir Henry Parkes, with best wishes,
"Faithfully yours,
"W. E. H. LECKY."

Something has been said by several honorable gentlemen, and especially in those model addresses which were delivered by the delegates from New Zealand, in both of which the highest tone of the gentleman was preserved with the resolute determination of the citizen—perhaps overmuch said, about loyalty. As I observed just now, I do not think that I need any witness to my loyalty; but I cannot shut my eyes to the fact that the future is in the hands of the all-wise God. It is impossible to forecast what the march of events may bring forth—it is very unlikely, indeed, that I shall live to see them—but I trust I am gifted with sufficient foresight to contemplate in some measure what may occur. It may be—because the greatest events are often sent on their sliding-plane of operation by the most trivial circumstances—that the Australian people may not always live under the English flag. I pray God they may. I believe they can have no higher destiny. A religious poet says—

> "Prayer is the soul's sincere desire,
> Uttered or unexpressed,
> The motion of a hidden fire,
> That trembles in the breast."

My whole being trembles with an unuttered prayer of that kind, that the whole of the British possessions may remain for ever forming parts of one beneficent Empire such as the world has never seen. I can see no permanent obstacles to such a grand consummation; I see no reason why the Australias should not become a Federal Dominion, a result which we are all, I hope, now trying to bring about. The North American Colonies will, I think, become more completely a Federal Dominion by some reform of their present Constitution. Our South African possessions may, with great care—and great care will be necessary—become also a united cluster of States; and I can see no reason on earth why this comparatively great independent congeries of States should not unite with the Mother-country in forming an Empire such as has never yet been formed, and which would carry our language, our laws, our social habits, our literature, our great stores of science, to all parts of the habitable globe. My prayer is that wise counsels and unforeseen beneficent influences may bring this about. But it may be otherwise; it may be, as many very respectable and reputable citizens dream, that we shall form a nation by ourselves. But whatever is the future destiny of Australia—whether it is the grand destiny of forming part of this new Empire that ought to rule, in the interests of peace, the whole world, or whether it becomes a separate nationality—what we are attempting to do now is commended by wisdom, commended by foresight, commended by every principle of national morals, and will be equally beneficial to the people whatever course events may take. I trust that this Conference will lead to a better understanding. I deny that I have been the means of any disturbance. Whatever quarrels may have taken place, New South Wales has never been the aggressor. I say that very deliberately. If a Conference assembled, as it did assemble, and certain members of that Conference, including the representatives of New Zealand, went behind the back of the Conference, and voted in their own interests on what they were to consider in the interest of all the colonies, New South Wales had no part in it; she was the victim. If a tax, which to my mind is the most barbarous that we could conceive, is levied upon the live stock of the country—upon the food supplies of the people—we are not the authors of it. If there is not free intercourse across the river Murray we are not to blame. We established free intercourse between South Australia, Victoria, and New South Wales at a cost to our taxpayers of £60,000 per annum—it existed for some time; it was at length abrogated, but not by New South Wales. A few months hence it will be thirty-six years since I was elected to the legislature of New South Wales. I am not going to state these few facts for the purpose of enabling anyone to write my biography, but for another purpose. Since then I have been elected to that legislature considerably over thirty times. I have passed through more than thirty contested elections, I have been at the head of five administrations, and I have sat in every parliament, and voted, with one exception, on every great question. Now I am going to state why I gave you these facts. In no parliament, in no public meeting, in no group of my fellow-citizens, in no intercourse with any personal friend, has the word "retaliation" ever fallen from my lips. Retaliation between nations is an abomination to me; and whatever provocation the colony of New South Wales has had, I have held this doctrine to my angry fellow-colonists who have appealed to me time after time, that nothing would induce me ever to give my adherence to the wicked principle of retaliation. One Christian people has no moral right to retaliate upon another, unless they desire to set the world by the ears. Where does such a policy as that lead to? For the most part our markets have been thrown open to all of you. I believe with my colleague that New South Wales could better than any of the other colonies endure to live alone; and I believe that if any of the colonies have an interest higher than the rest in this question of Federation it is the smaller colonies. I ask, with every respect, how would it be possible for Western Australia to remain outside a federation of the colonies? I live in a Sydney suburb, which is separated from the city by one of the arms of Port Jackson; and this Sydney suburb contains more than two-thirds of the population of all Western Australia. Its 30,000 inhabitants, however, send only four members to our parliament, whereas the 44,000 in Western Australia have a parliament of their own, with the incalculable advantage of Sir James Lee Steere as its president. Surely the great colonies—great in population, great in wealth—have less interest in Federation than the smaller colonies. I think we could defend our ports a little better than Western Australia could defend hers if a time arose for defence; I think that from our resources, our position, the undoubted skill and enterprise of our people, we are as well able to take care of ourselves as are the people of Western Australia. But all through these negotiations I have not only said that we are willing to come into a Federal Dominion with the smallest colonies, but I have said that we seek no advantage for ourselves; we do not wish to make any condition whatever; we are prepared to trust to the wisdom, to the honour, and to the justice of a Federal Parliament, and to commit all our interests to it. That is our position, and unless we are willing to trust to a Federal Parliament, I cannot understand how we can hope to federate in any way which will be worthy of the name. As I did not wish, in the first place, even to mention the name of New South Wales, I am still, if possible, more unwilling to introduce the subject of its fiscal policy. I have no fear of the policy of New South Wales being reversed. I have confidence that that policy will gain strength in the next appeal to the people, and I tell this Conference that, whether we federate or not, I shall not abate one jot of my efforts to promote the noble policy of freedom for the exertions of civilized men. I only mention my determination, as a citizen of New South Wales, to still promote our own policy, first, that there may be no misunderstanding in the matter, and, secondly, to show the genuineness of my professions. We are told that we shall be overwhelmed in the Federal Parliament by those who favour the opposite policy. Even if that fact could be demonstrated to me it would in no way turn my course in seeking to build up in these colonies a Federal Dominion. I would still vote for the same policy ; and, though the first wave of parliamentary authority might be against it, I should have no less confidence in its ultimate triumph, believing as I do that it is based on principles which are eternal—the principles of justice, of freedom, and of human brotherhood—of the ultimate ascendancy of which I have no fear. That in no way intimidates me, or qualifies my desire to enter into a Federal Government. I have thought it necessary, after what has been said, to speak thus plainly. I should have been perfectly willing, as I said at the opening of my speech, to have left the name of New South Wales out altogether, but other gentlemen were not willing to take that course. I have stated my views very briefly on those points which have been introduced into the discussion. But the main object for which, representing New South Wales, I stand here, is to say that we desire to enter upon this work of Federation without making any condition to the advantages of ourselves, without any stipulation whatever, with a perfect preparedness to leave the proposed convention free to devise its own scheme, and if a central parliament comes into existence, with a perfect reliance upon its justice, upon its wisdom, and upon its honour. I think I know the people of New South Wales sufficiently to speak in their name ; and I think I can answer for it that an overwhelming majority of my countrymen in that colony will approve of the grand step being taken of uniting all the colonies under one form of beneficent Government, and under one national flag. Of course I must trust to honorable gentlemen not inferring that when I talk of a national flag I mean anything that is not perfectly in accord with the flag of England, I only mean a flag to represent the whole of the people within the shores of Australia. I came here with my mind quite untrammelled, quite unbiassed, anxious to join the other colonies, and it is my most firm belief that if we arrive at this great end of forming an Australian Dominion, we shall do the grandest work that is possible to our hands and to our generation. Even if honorable gentlemen doubt that this end can be attained now—and I do not doubt it—there can be no doubt it will be attained in a short time. The great living principle of Federation has seized the hearts of the Australian people, and it will warm their nature, take deeper root, and have more splendid attraction as events disclose themselves. And whether we are a federated people within the next two years, as we may be and ought to be, or not, we shall be a federated people within the next decade, if not much sooner. I pray God that this event will come about by the wisest counsels, that it will not be delayed, and that it will be crowned with every kind of happiness for the United Colonies.

The PRESIDENT.—Gentlemen of the Conference: As a member of the Conference, I desire to take this opportunity of addressing myself to the important question which has been under our consideration for the past few days. I congratulate Sir Henry Parkes on his second powerful and eloquent speech in which he has dealt with the great issues before us, and, I venture to think, dealt with them satisfactorily. There was only one part of the address he has just delivered, however, which I make bold to say might perhaps have been better left out, namely, his references to some of the statements made by members of the Conference. I am quite certain that those statements were not made with any intention of creating any ill-feeling in the Conference, much less with a view of embittering this discussion, and I regret that my honorable friend, Sir Henry Parkes, should have thought that the observations made by Mr. Playford and Sir James Lee Steere were of such a character as to call for serious comment. I noticed that Mr. Playford was a little warm while he was speaking, but his observations certainly did not convey to my mind any idea of intentional affront. Under these circumstances, and seeing that the deliberations of the Conference have been so well conducted, with such excellent taste and judgment, as well as with great ability, it might perhaps have been better if the observations of Sir Henry Parkes to which I have referred had remained unsaid. No doubt on a point of that kind every man is entitled to consider his own case, and as Sir Henry Parkes thought proper to believe or think that the statements made by Mr. Playford and Sir James Lee Steere improperly reflected upon him, undoubtedly he was perfectly justified in resenting them under the circumstances. There was one other point in which I think Sir Henry Parkes was scarcely fair—I do not mean to say that he was intentionally unfair—but having taken the views he has advocated for a number of years and pressed them so forcibly, I think he was not altogether fair in his remarks with regard to the Federal Council. May I be permitted to draw attention to the fact that his observations appear to me to be scarcely consistent with a portion of the resolution which he has submitted to this Conference? A portion of that resolution gives great credit to the founders of the Federal Council for the good work they have done; but if the Federal Council is, in his judgment, wholly useless, then a part of his resolution is inconsistent with his own opinions.

Sir HENRY PARKES.—I certainly did not say the Federal Council is useless.

The PRESIDENT.—I understood the honorable gentleman to convey the idea that from the very time he heard of the formation of the Federal Council the reason he did not urge New South Wales to join it was that he believed its works would be useless, and that it would be utterly impossible for the Council to do any good at all. And the honorable gentleman made a comparison between its numerical smallness and the large legislature of New South Wales, to the effect that inasmuch as the Federal Council was a small and the legislature of New South Wales was a large body it was wholly out of the question that the legislature of New South Wales could think of remitting any question to the Federal Council, because they could not allow 200 members of parliament in New South Wales to be overruled by a handful of men in the Federal Council. Now, I venture to submit that that is hardly putting the question in its proper light, and I desire to make one or two observations upon that point, with a view of justifying not only the existence of the Federal Council, but the work it has been enabled to do. It is well known, and has been set forth by Sir Samuel Griffith and other members of the Conference, that the Federal Council was originally established to do work which no one Colony could do for itself, to legislate upon subjects in which all the colonies in the group were interested, and upon which it was desirable that legislation should take place, but upon which none of the colonies was able to legislate alone. The necessity for a legislative body like the Federal Council has been shown over and over again. A number of Intercolonial Conferences have been held from time to time, but in nine cases out of ten in which they came to agreement on the questions remitted to them for consideration, as to the lines upon which each Colony should legislate by itself, from one cause or another the majority of the subjects on which agreements were arrived at were never legislated upon at all. Changes of governments, changes of situations and circumstances, intervened to prevent local legislation on many of the subjects in reference to which the basis of legislation had been laid down by the representatives of the different colonies in the Conferences to which I have alluded. I dare say it was not the deliberate intention of any of the governments represented at any one of those Conferences not to legislate on the subjects in question, but changes of government, or other circumstances over which they had no control, often occurred to prevent such legislation, and the agreements between the representatives of the colonies came to naught, notwithstanding that it was a patent fact to all Australia that uniform legislation was absolutely necessary on important questions on which there was great confusion, and in reference to which it was impossible for each colony to legislate separately on its own lines. The desire in everybody's mind was that there might be created a body which should have the power to legislate upon subjects in reference to which the representatives of all the colonies were agreed, but upon which the colonies could not legislate in their local parliaments. That was the origin of the Federal Council, and notwithstanding the number of gentlemen occupying seats in the legislature of New South Wales, and the number of gentlemen occupying seats in the legislatures of the other colonies, I venture to think that it would be in no way disparaging to them to remit any subject they might think proper to remit to the consideration of the Federal Council; nor would it be derogatory to them if the Federal Council should come to conclusions on the subject, and give legislative shape to those conclusions. As a matter of fact the Federal Council has legislated in a variety of ways on important matters, and, I believe, wholly to the satisfaction of the colonies represented, and I submit to Sir Henry Parkes that the only reason why the Federal Council has not been of greater value is simply owing to the fact that the whole of the Australian continent was not represented in that council. Had the whole of this vast continent been represented, I am confident that the Federal council would have been able to do work which would have met with the approval of all the Australian Colonies. The Federal Council is a legislative body, and has no administrative power, and it was never contemplated from the first that it should have administrative power, unless great changes were made in its Constitution which might bring that about, but I venture to think that the powers of the present Federal Council, if all the colonies of Australia were represented in it, are such as would enable the Council to do great and good work for the people of this continent. As I have said, notwithstanding its restrictions, the Federal Council has already done good and valuable work, and the only reason it has not been able to do still more is because one of the principal colonies of Australasia has not been able to see its way to join the council. Of course the Federal Council would not require to do work which each of the colonies is able to do for itself. Passing on to the subject under the consideration of this Conference, I may be permitted to say that the importance of our meeting here on the present occasion cannot be over valued. We have heard many eloquent speeches dealing with both the sentimental and the practical sides of this great question, many of the speeches, such as large portions of the speeches of Sir Henry Parkes, dealing with the bright and noble aspect of the question, and forecasting to some extent the great future that is awaiting Australasia. I am confident there is no one who has paid the slightest attention to the increase of population in these colonies, to the increase of their wealth and resources, and, as Sir Henry Parkes has pointed out, their capacity for self-government, but will be ready to admit that Australia has within itself all the elements of a successful and prosperous national life, and that the colonies ought to be quite prepared to adopt the policy of creating a Federal Constitution and a Federal Government. Well, we have met here on this occasion for the purpose of endeavouring to come to a conclusion among ourselves, after full discussion, as to whether the time is ripe for creating that Federal Constitution, and I now propose to consider very briefly how far our discussion has advanced the proposals which have been submitted to us. Have we been in a position to come to the conclusion that we can well establish a Federal Constitution, consisting of a Federal Parliament and Federal Government? I think the course we have pursued in having a meeting of this kind has turned out to be a wise one, as I believe that if we and the other colonies had accepted the proposal made by Sir Henry Parkes in the first instance, for each of the parliaments of this continent to appoint delegates to a Convention for the purpose of setting forth the principles of a Federal Constitution, and, in fact, drafting a Federal Constitution, there would have been very little hope of those parliaments appointing delegates to that Convention within any reasonable time. We have had an opportunity, however, of discussing this question on the present occasion, and exchanging opinions, not as to what the future Federal Constitution should be, but with the object of determining in our own minds whether we believe the time is ripe for Federation, and whether the views of the people of this continent are so far advanced that they are prepared by their representatives in Parliament to send delegates for the purpose of considering this great question of a Federal Constitution. Now, I believe that in all the references which have been made to the desirability of framing this Constitution, while there is no doubt whatever that Sir Henry Parkes clearly indicated that it should consist of a Governor-General, two Houses of Parliament, and a Federal Government no doubt responsible to the Federal Parliament; and while it is quite true that this is the main principle in the Constitution of the Canadian Dominion, yet I nevertheless agree with Sir Henry Parkes that it would not necessarily follow that the whole of the provisions contained in the Constitution of the Canadian Dominion should be inserted in our Federal Constitution. In fact in a communication I addressed to Sir Henry Parkes at an earlier stage, I expressed these views, I think, quite clearly. In my letter, dated 12th August, 1889, I stated :—

"I gather from your letters, especially from the last one, that your proposal is to create a Federal Parliament of Australia, consisting of two Houses with an Executive Federal Government, constitutionally responsible to the Federal Parliament, the Crown, no doubt, being represented by a Governor-General. This, of course, would be a Federation on the same lines as the Dominion of Canada. Whether the parliament so created would, in other respects, be the same as that of the Dominion would depend on the powers granted to it and those reserved to the local parliaments."

So that it was clearly indicated, as far back as August last year, that while it would be quite possible to agree to a Federal Constitution on the same lines as that of the Canadian Dominion, yet at the same time it did not follow that the whole of the provisions should be copied from the Dominion Constitution, because, as has been recognized throughout this discussion, the great difference which might lie between the two would consist in the powers which would be given to the Federal Parliament and the powers which would be retained by the local governments. I confess that when the proposal was lately made by Sir Henry Parkes to meet for the purpose of discussing this question, I did not in any way feel over-confident of our success. I can quite conceive that while you may get tens of thousands of men to agree that a grand federation of these colonies must come sooner or later, it is a totally different thing to be able to arrive at a satisfactory answer to the question as to whether the time is ripe now, and as to what the character of the Federal Constitution ought to be; and that we may be no nearer a practical settlement, even if we arrive at the conclusion that the time will come when we shall have a Federated Australia, or even if we resolve that the time is ripe for considering the question. I think, therefore, that it would not be out of place if I should endeavour to collect generally the views of honorable members who have addressed themselves to this subject, in order to see how far we have been able, up to the present, to come to some understanding. To start with, it has been acknowledged on all sides, even by the representatives of South Australia and of Western Australia, who, perhaps, are least strong for a great Federal Constitution, that we ought to have a Federal Parliament; and Mr. Playford expressed himself very strongly indeed that the time will come when a Federal Parliament will be established in Australia. His language was, " Sooner or later it will be established." Now, the first thing that suggests itself to one's mind is this: Does that mean that he is prepared, and others with him, to take steps for the purpose of inducing the various parliaments of Australia to appoint delegates to a Convention for the purpose of laying down the principles upon which that Constitution is to be based.

Mr. PLAYFORD.—Undoubtedly.

The PRESIDENT.—Then the question arises: On what is that Federal Constitution to be based? What form shall it take?

I venture to think that that will be a question that will ultimately present the greatest difficulties. That we should federate is agreed. That we should federate as soon as possible is also agreed. But what is not agreed upon, and that which we cannot possibly now determine, is the exact terms upon which we should federate. Now, there is no one who is more anxious to see a great Federation—a Federation complete in the largest sense—than I am; but I confess that I see great difficulties—not insuperable, but great difficulties—in the way of bringing about this Federation, and I am very much afraid that even when delegates are appointed to the Convention our troubles will only have just begun. I have no doubt whatever that upon a number of important general principles we shall be able to agree, but at the same time I think it will be a great mistake if we underestimate the difficulties that lie immediately before us. Those difficulties are not few; they are numerous, and at the same time they are great. Taking even the various views which have been expressed by members of this Conference on the question of our tariffs—of the Customs duties—I am afraid it is only too obvious that there will be great difficulty in coming to an agreement. But I say that, although there may be great difficulties in being able to come to an agreement, that is no reason why we should not attempt to overcome those difficulties and arrive at some common understanding. And when we meet, as I hope we shall shortly meet, in the Convention, I believe we shall be able, in thrashing out the whole of these questions, to come to a solution that will be satisfactory to the whole of our parliaments. In fact, on the subject of the tariff, I feel perfectly confident that, even if we are not able at once to level the barriers between the colonies so far as Customs duties are concerned, we shall be able to arrive at some modification which will be satisfactory to all, and that modification may be a very reasonable one. It is quite possible that South Australia may not be prepared to agree to the abolition at once of the whole of the Customs duties between the colonies; but if she is not, surely it will be possible to make some provision by which the time may be postponed for bringing that about, but in which a time shall nevertheless be definitely fixed when the abolition shall take place. A few years one way or other is nothing in the life of a great nation, and if only we are able to find a solution that will effectually overcome the difficulties and give us such a Federal Constitution, we will not require to reopen the question at any future time. After all, the important question which will have to be considered by the various parliaments is: Is the time ripe for Federation? But I think they should also consider this other question. If we are not in a position to enter into the consideration of that great question now, and lay down the lines upon which our Constitution is to be based, when are we likely to be able to take up the subject more advantageously? A number of the members of this Conference have clearly indicated that the present time is as good as any other time, and that the future, so far as we know, may present even greater difficulties than does the present. I think that might be used as an argument to introduce the various parliaments to send delegates to the Convention. It might be well to point out that while at present we have peace and quiet generally, and on the whole there exists a friendily spirit among the colonies, it is impossible to tell, if we put off the creation of this Federal Parliament, at what period in the future the time will be more appropriate for the consideration of the question. The financial question will be one of very great difficulty, but I believe it can be solved, and if the Parliaments come to a determination that Federation shall be brought about in the best way possible, I believe that all difficulties will speedily vanish. At the same time I think it would be a great mistake for members who vote for this resolution to come to the conclusion that the carrying of this resolution really settles everything. It settles only one great thing, and that is very important—that the time is ripe for the federation of the Australian Colonies. Having settled that question, we should all feel bound to make every possible effort to induce our respective Parliaments to appoint delegates who will be in a position to consider, not only the general principles, but also the details of the great measure which we will be called upon to submit. Now, a number of the members of the Conference have discussed at some length the question as to what the nature of the Federation should be. Should it be like the Dominion of Canada, or should it take in some of the provisions of the Constitution of the United States. I have no doubt in my own mind but that we shall find the Canadian Constitution is about the best basis that we can select. Whatever modifications we may make in that Constitution—whether we shall grant the same powers to the Federal Parliament as does the Constitution of the Canadian Dominion, or whether we shall allow the local governments to retain larger powers than the local parliaments have made under the Dominion Constitution—will, no doubt, be a matter for earnest consideration. But I venture to think that, simply to create a Federal Parliament with little or no powers—that is to say, only such powers as the local parliaments cannot exercise—would be a great mistake. I believe that we can leave to the local parliaments vast powers, giving them the whole internal administration, and everything required to secure the progress and prosperity of their respective colonies, and at the same time be in a position to grant great and varied powers to the new Federal Parliaments which we shall bring into existence. I have always felt, however, that as we shall then be in a position to discuss these matters in detail, the less this Conference goes into detail perhaps the better, lest views may now be expressed by honorable members which may hamper them in dealing with the subject afterwards. Under these circumstances I felt, before coming to this Conference at all, that it might be better that some general resolution such as this should be submitted, and that there would be much more likelihood of its being successful than if it were to submit a series of resolutions on which we proposed to lay the basis of the new Constitution. One important consideration which, I think, ought to weigh with us is this, that, in order to make the Convention a success, the various Parliaments, in appointing their delegates, ought to leave their hands untied and untrammelled. The consideration of the various

Q

difficult and important questions, and the working of them out, in my judgment renders it indispensably necessary that resolutions ought not, in the interests of the whole country, to be passed by any Parliament tying the hands of its delegates either in one direction or another. If their hands were tied on one or two important questions, the result would be that they could scarcely give us the benefit of their valuable advice when we were discussing those questions. I have always felt that had there been very serious difference of opinion at this Conference, a great responsibility would rest upon all the members if they refused even to submit to their various parliaments the proposal to consider a new Constitution. If two or three colonies stood apart, and declined to join in our movement, the chances are that that movement might not be successful. But there is every probability, if all the members of the Conference are prepared to make a recommendation to their several parliaments, that those parliaments will undertake to seriously consider it. If, on the other hand, there is any one representative who declines to ask the consent of his parliament to the appointment of delegates to a Convention, it would be extremely unfortunate, and a very great responsibility for any delegate to undertake. However great the difficulties I saw before me, I would feel that I undertook a great responsibility if I undertook not to recommend to our parliament the appointment of delegates to a convention simply because of those difficulties. Difficulties are made to be overcome, and I think there is something of the true ring in the words put into Richelieu's mouth when he said, "There is no such word as fail." If we have a good work before us there is no doubt whatever that we ought to be strengthened rather than weakened by what are known as difficulties. Mr. Playford, in speaking on this subject, intimated, as an objection, that this movement had not sprung from the people. Surely the honorable gentleman will go with me in saying that, whether a movement springs from the people or not, so long as it be a good and a wise movement, and one to promote their interests, we should not think of objecting to it. Whatever the interests of these colonies are, I think they can best be promoted by union, and though for many years there may be difficuties in dealing with some subjects, these difficulties will and can be overcome, simply because experience has shown that they have been overcome elsewhere. What has been done elsewhere ought not to be too difficult for us to do. All we have to do in approaching this question is to approach it in a determined spirit, first believing that the movement is a good one, and then putting our shoulder to the wheel in order to carry it through. I think we have great reason to be encouraged by what we know to be the opinion of a great portion of the civilized world in regard to this movement. England recognizes that if we are a federated people, if we are united, if we have a Federal Parliament with a general government, a power will be created on this Continent, which, in the future, will be of the greatest value to the Imperial Government and the whole of the Empire. Feeling that the creation of a great power like this will not only strengthen ourselves, but at the same time strengthen all those belonging to us, they recognize that it is a matter of the utmost importance that we should, at any rate, take the first step in recommending our several parliaments to appoint delegates to a Convention to frame a Federal Constitution. I feel perfectly convinced that if we do that, and are prepared to being the same spirit to bear on the movement as was done in British North America, where men of all parties met together for the purpose of subordinating their difficulties, and placing them as a sacrifice on the altar of their country, Federation will be accomplished at a very early date. Seeing the unanimity which to so large an extent prevails amongst us at the present time, I feel confident that the people of these colonies, knowing that the members of the Conference have their interest at heart, will support the Convention in any recommendations it may make. The Convention will have an opportunity of presenting its conclusions to the various parliaments, and I have no doubt whatever that these conclusions, being based on reason as well as justice, will commend themselves to their good judgment. The interests of the colonies ought to prevail before any individual interest. Yet it is not difficult to see that individual interests will be pressed to the front. I am confident that those interests will require to be considered, and, whatever may happen, justice ought to be done. The colonies united have a great future before them, but, disunited, they will never be able to accomplish the great end to which they ought to look forward. I feel pleased indeed that we have had such a successful discussion, and I have been extremely pleased at what I conceive to be the moderate view of the majority of honorable gentlemen present. It indicates, I think, a great future, and a great future before these colonies means more than we can at present understand. Should a Federal Parliament be created, and a Federal Government formed, they will be able to do work which the colonies, disunited, would never be able to do. As has been frequently pointed out, had we had a Federal Parliament in the past, the work that parliament would have been able to do would have been great indeed—far greater than has been yet accomplished. I trust that the remaining resolutions which are to be submitted will be discussed in the same spirit as the resolution now before the Conference, and which has been supported on all sides. To those who have taken a prominent part in the idea of a Federated Australia—many of them outside this Chamber—the conclusions we arrive at will be deemed of great importance. The good wishes of the whole of the community will be with us in our movement, and whatever difficulties may arise in the future, will be solved by consideration of mutual interest, and, if necessary, compromise.

Mr. PLAYFORD.—I think I have an opportunity now, if I choose to avail myself of it, of replying to what has fallen from Sir Henry Parkes to-day, in regard to a speech I made upon this question a short time ago. But I intend to adopt that honorable gentleman's precept, not his practice. The honorable gentleman's precept was that he did not believe in nor did he practice retaliation. I do not on the present occasion intend to resort to retaliation, and I shall, therefore, leave all that he has said in regard to myself unanswered, leaving it to the good sense of the people who have taken an interest in what has been done here to judge whether the attack upon me was warranted by the facts of the case or not.

On the motion of Sir HENRY PARKES, his proposition was amended by the substitution of the words "Australian" and "Australia" for the words "Australasian" and "Australasia," as they occurred in the resolution.

The motion, as amended, was then adopted.

Captain RUSSELL.—Mr. President, I feel sure that I shall only be consulting the wishes of the Conference if I merely formally move the following proposition, which appears on the notice-paper in my name:—

"That to the Union of the Australian Colonies contemplated by the foregoing resolution, the remoter Australasian Colonies shall be entitled to admission at such times and on such conditions as may be hereafter agreed upon."

It is, in fact, a corollary to the resolution just passed. I understand that the members of the Conference are good enough to consider that at such a time as the remoter colonies shall feel the influence of that centripetal force which will draw them all into contact—believing that a day will come in which that force will make itself felt—they ought to be then admitted into the Union, and that therefore it would be a great pity if they should have no voice in the Convention which will assemble to discuss the question. With that feeling, and with the belief that New Zealand will send delegates to the Convention, as well as that the remoter Australasian Colonies will take part in the Union, I submit that it is desirable that they should have some say in the formation of the Constitution under which they will eventually be governed. After the exhaustive debate we have had it would be merely traversing ground twice turned over to say anything further on the subject.

Sir JOHN HALL seconded the motion.

The proposition was agreed to.

NATIONAL CONVENTION.

Mr. DEAKIN.—Sir, I beg to move,—

"That the members of the Conference should take such steps as may be necessary to induce the Legislatures of their respective colonies to appoint delegates to a National Australasian Convention, empowered to consider and report upon an adequate scheme for a Federal Constitution,"

with one alteration. I propose to insert after the word "National" the word "Australasian," an amendment which will perhaps meet the view just expressed by Captain Russell. By introducing the word "Australasian," it will be made perfectly plain that it is the desire of this Conference that the representatives of the remoter Australasian Colonies should take part in the Convention as well as the representatives of the colonies of the Australian continent. The adoption of a Convention as the means of promulgating a Constitution has the sanction of experience, both in the United States and Canada. The Convention which assembled in the United States deliberated with closed doors, and after some length of time presented a Constitution to the country which was not considered by the country itself, but which was considered by Conventions nominated specially for that purpose, so that, in the instance of the United States, a Convention was twice introduced, and the adoption of the Constitution as well as its drafting was by Convention only. In Canada a Convention also sat for a considerable period, and brought forward as its result seventy-two resolutions embodying its recommendations, which, having been approved by the local parliaments, were sent straight to the Imperial Legislature, and received the sanction of the Queen without having been submitted to the people of Canada. I take it that by universal consent in these Colonies no Constitution will be sought to be obtained without the direct consent of the whole of the people of Australasia. The method to be followed may possibly be the submission of the scheme which this Convention drafts in the first instance to the local parliaments, and then to the country at the succeeding general election. Let me now, in passing, suggest that while this course of procedure has all the sanction of precedent, and while possibly it may be the course which will most commend itself to the judgment of the parliaments of this country, it is not necessarily the only means by which the finding of that Convention might be tested at the bar of public opinion. In the work on the "American Commonwealth," by the Right Honorable Professor Bryce, which I have already alluded to, he points out that the practice of obtaining not only an indirect verdict of the people at a general election, but the practice of obtaining a direct verdict of the people on questions submitted to them, is growing in favour in both the old and the new world. At the same time he calls attention to the difficulties which surround a question which is sought to be decided at a general election. At page 72 of the second volume of the work I have referred to, Professor Bryce says—

"A general election, although in form a choice of particular persons as members, has now practically become an expression of popular opinion on the two or three leading measures then propounded and discussed by the party leaders, as well as a vote of confidence or no-confidence in the Ministry of the day. It is, in substance, a vote upon those measures; although, of course, a vote only on their general principles, and not, like the Swiss Referendum, upon the Statute which the Legislature has passed. Even, therefore, in a country which clings to and founds itself upon the absolute supremacy of its representative chamber, the notion of a direct appeal to the people has made progress."

And a few pages further on he points out that Professor Goldwin Smith deplores the want of an arrangement in the Canadian Dominion by which direct issues may be submitted to the people. For the consideration of the Conference—not because it is a matter upon which it can arrive at any conclusion, but in order that thought may be stimulated by the contemplation of alternative methods—I desire to call attention to the fact that there are innumerable precedents in the United States for the submission of constitutional amendments direct to the people. I ask whether, under certain circumstances, some of our colonies may not prefer to adopt this method. In the United States each of the several States has a Constitution, which is as much to its citizens as that of the United States is to the whole people.

Those Constitutions, during the present century, have been amended and reamended. In every case a Convention has been called to consider whether amendment was necessary. The Convention has drafted the proposed amendments—in some cases amounting to the establishment of a new Constitution—and these have then been submitted directly to the vote of the whole body of the people of the State concerned. The simple "aye" or "no" of the majority of the electors has accepted or rejected them. That has been done on scores of occasions, and in almost every State of the Union. One of the notable features of this system is that the people, having once exercised this power, have sought to use it again and again, not merely in constitutional amendments but in other matters, and have thus proved their appreciation of such powers. We cannot but recollect that, although the verdict of a general election may be decisive, it is a verdict which is obtained at some cost, both to the main question submitted and to the minor issues submitted with it at the election. Let us presume that a Convention has agreed to propose a certain definite Constitution, which has been considered and approved by the several parliaments, and that they desire to obtain the judgment of the people of each colony upon it at the next general election. How can the verdict of the people be sought upon this question, and this question alone? Is it not inevitable that it must be associated with issues as to the fate of the Ministry of the day, issues as to the principal proposals of that Ministry, and issues as to local proposals which may seem to be of more moment to certain constituencies? The question of the acceptance or rejection of the Constitution must be confused at a general election with personal issues, with political issues, with platform issues. Is it not certain that the verdict must be more or less confused by the introduction of these conflicting issues, so that it is just possible that in some colonies, owing to the confusion, an apparent verdict might be given against the Constitution, while, if that issue had been submitted alone, the public would readily have endorsed it. It is also perfectly possible that while there may be other grave issues which the people desire to pronounce upon, yet, feeling themselves to be federalists in the first place, they will vote for men who approve of the Constitution, without regard to the principles which they profess in any other connection. And if we suppose that in any or several of the colonies the Federal Constitution is happily carried by a majority of the representatives, yet those representatives may be men who remain in the House dealing with important local issues upon which they do not represent the feelings of their constituents. It is therefore clear that, if remitted to a general election, the proposed Constitution must suffer, or, if it does not, that local interests must suffer. If our union depends upon general elections, the parliaments returned to federate may be parliaments out of touch with the popular sentiment of the several colonies on matters of vital importance to their people. I will content myself with this simple reference to a question the solution of which lies with the several parliaments themselves. The resolution now being moved is purposely left vague as to details. It simply recommends that a National Australasian Convention should be appointed. It does not presume to suggest any particular method by means of which the members of the Convention should be selected; this and all other details it leaves to parliament. I re-echo the fervent hope expressed by our President, that the parliaments of Australasia, in appointing their delegates, will see fit to leave them absolutely uncommitted on any point or points of policy—that they will select the best men available, whether from political circles or outside them—men whose judgment, whose ability, whose knowledge of political affairs, whose experience of the world, and whose aspirations they are acquainted with, and in whom they have confidence, and that, having chosen them, they will not tie their hands upon any particular matters, but leave them untrammelled to give the best verdict which their conscience and judgment can attain to. I would repeat, if I were not afraid of enfeebling it, the eloquent appeal of Washington to the delegates to the American Convention, that they should not choose any but the best proposal, and thus, unfurling a standard they could proudly defend, leave the issue in higher hands. It must be remembered that the proposed Convention can impose no statute upon any colony or parliament. If the best men of Australasia frame a Constitution for a Federal Dominion which any colony is unable to accept, that colony will reject it, and remain outside the Union as long as it may desire to do so. Consequently, there is no risk in sending delegates absolutely free to the Convention. I am perfectly certain that in the Convention any of the delegates who are trammelled—if there should be any who are trammelled—will meet their associates with a feeling of inferiority, and that the restrictions imposed upon them will be a serious bar to those minor concessions which must be made if the meeting is to be a success. Whatever the Convention may accomplish, we may be sure of this, that the finding will not be exactly what any one person, party, or colony may desire ; compromises will have to be effected, and it is therefore essential that the delegates should be free to do that which they find to be best both in the interests of their own constituents and in the interests of the whole people. The task which lies before the Convention is not that of creating a new Constitution. Any assemblage meeting with the design of shaping out of the inner consciousness of its members some novel form of government, which might appear to be theoretically perfect, would fail to do any useful or practical work. It is scarcely necessary to remind honorable gentlemen that the Constitutions to which attention has been most directed in this Conference have assumed their present form by gradual growth, and have not been, in a mechanical sense, the work of human hands. The British Constitution itself, to which all students of constitutional history have turned with so much admiration, is essentially a growth and not a creation. That Government which has been supposed by some persons to be an artificial creation and not a natural growth—the Government of the United States—is a closely-allied offshoot from the British Constitution. The differences introduced were in each case founded on precedents in the State Governments, except indeed in the instance of the separation of the legislative, judicial, and executive authorities, which plan was obviously taken from the reigning school of French thinkers. Mr. Alexander Johnston, in an elaborate article which some time ago appeared in the *New Princeton Review*, shows that each and every provision of the American Constitution is to be found in some of the Constitutions of the several States prior to the formation of the Union, with the exception of that providing for the election of President, the one proposal which has not fulfilled the intention of its founders. In their essence the principles of popular government in the United States are closely allied to those of the mother country. In the same manner the Constitution which the North American Provinces adopted was obtained wholly and solely from practical experience, either of the English Constitution or of the working of their colonial Constitutions. With you, Mr. President, I think that if we have regard to the fact that the United States Constitution separates the legislative, judicial, and executive authorities, and that it does not allow of the presence of responsible Ministers in the Legislative Chamber, the chief model of our Federal Constitution, in relation to its form, will be taken from the North American Provinces; that we, like them, will have a Governor-General and two Chambers of representatives; that there will be Ministers present in those Chambers who will introduce legislation, and be responsible to parliament for their administration of the affairs of the country. We have had so much experience of the working of such governments, that there is no doubt that the proposals of the coming Convention will follow the lines on which we have gained our present development of free institutions. With regard to the first and popular Chamber, I presume that it will be as directly representative of the people as the British House of Commons, or the Assemblies of these colonies. With regard to the second Chamber, there are different circumstances to be taken into consideration. If we look at the Upper Houses of these colonies, we shall find that they differ considerably. While some of them are composed of nominee members, others are elected; and the question of the form the Upper House of the future Dominion of Australia shall take is one of the problems on which the minds of the members of the Convention will be most exercised. I trust that they will recollect that in the two colonies which have Upper Houses elected by a more or less restricted franchise of the people, a feeling prevails that these bodies are not sufficiently amenable to public opinion. A strong desire exists that the Upper Chambers should be brought into more close relation with the electors, and thus with the Chamber which represents the whole body of the people. We need not attempt to forecast the course the Convention may take with regard to the conditions under which the Federal and Colonial Legislatures shall exercise their several powers. The cardinal distinction between the United States and Canada is that in the United States the central government has its powers limited, while in Canada the provincial legislatures have their powers limited; and it appears to me that the model of the United States, preserving State rights with the most jealous caution, is that most likely to commend itself to the people of these colonies. And, Sir, confident that the Convention will bring to the consideration of this question all the knowledge and experience of government which we have been enabled to obtain in these colonies, I trust it may not neglect the very valuable criticism of Professor Goldwin Smith, as applied to the Canadian Dominion Government. Let us hope that it will provide the elastic remedy for any errors which may creep into the scheme as first adopted, which is so useful in each of the State Constitutions of the American Republic. It is but reasonable that the people of these colonies should be enabled, when necessary, to revise the Constitution under which they live without the disorganization of their local parliaments, or in other words, that when the need for an amendment of the Federal Constitution arises (as it has arisen repeatedly in regard to the Constitution of the United States, without any sufficient means for the distinctly affirmed will of the people to secure the amendment it desires) we shall possess the power of obtaining a direct reference of the issue to the electors independently of all other issues, and without affecting their choice of representatives. The ablest jurists in the United States consider the great difficulty of amending their Constitution to be a serious defect; but they find no such defect in their State Constitutions, where a safety-valve has been provided in the appeal to the people; and recognising this, I trust that the members of the Convention will shape the Constitution they propose for an Australian Dominion in such a way as will not only allow it to answer to the needs and necessities of our time, but render it capable of answering to all our future needs, sufficiently pliant to adapt itself to the course of circumstances, related to our national characteristics and capacities so that it may unfold with their unfoldment, expand with our expansion, and develop with our destiny. They can only accomplish this by making, in all things, the nation the sole judge and the sole arbiter of legal forms which may confine but should sustain our national life.

Sir JOHN HALL.—Mr. President, I am very pleased that the alteration suggested by the last speaker in the terms of his resolution enables the New Zealand delegates to support it, and therefore I have much pleasure in seconding the motion. I understand that Mr. Deakin proposes it shall read that the colonies are to be requested to appoint delegates to a National Australasian Convention. I will only say I am glad of the opportunity of expressing the appreciation, which I feel sure will be shared by my fellow-colonists, of the consideration which this Conference has shown, in the amendments that have been agreed to on the suggestion of Captain Russell, to the position of the remoter Australasian Colonies. I feel strongly that great consideration has been shown to us, and I believe that it will bear good fruit. It will give evidence to the residents in the remoter Australasian Colonies that in this Convention to which they are asked to send delegates their interests will receive full and fair consideration. I will not follow Mr.

Deakin in his speculations as to what the proceedings of this Conference may be. I agree with him in regard to the terms on which delegates should be appointed to this extent, that they should not be absolutely fettered, but don't let us go to the other extreme; don't let us request that they shall be appointed without full information as to the wishes and aspirations of the people they represent. That would be going to another extreme, and I am afraid that if we did that, if full consideration were not shown to the feelings of the people of the several colonies, it might perhaps tend to make the deliberations of the Convention much less successful than they otherwise would be. I was very glad to hear the honorable member suggest that provision should be included in the new Federal Constitution for such amendments of it as experience might from time to time show to be required. That will enable us not only to admit such colonies as may be willing to join, but also to include such subjects as it may be desirable to include within the province of the Dominion Parliament. I say, let us do what we can. If we cannot include all the colonies at once, don't let us despair; let us include those who will join, trusting to the forces which I am sure will make themselves felt on those who remain outside the Dominion, to come in as soon as they can. And if we cannot at once include all those subjects which an individual entertaining a high sense of the value of local government would grant should be included, let us at all events secure the inclusion of those subjects upon which nearly all will agree a Dominion Parliament should legislate, trusting to the working of the Constitution to show whether further powers should be granted hereafter to the Dominion Parliament, by the means which Mr. Deakin has just suggested. In this way, I think, we shall lay the foundation of a power which will ensure such an organization of the forces possessed by the British race in these seas as will bring about the fulfilment of that great destiny which I am sure is in store for us.

Mr. PLAYFORD.—Mr. President, it appears to me that there are two points which ought to be considered in connection with this resolution, namely, when shall the members of the Convention meet, and where shall they meet? It may be said that we should leave those questions to the different legislatures of the different colonies, but I think the legislatures will look to us for some little indication at all events of our views as to when and where the Convention shall meet. Therefore I will move the addition to the resolution of the words "to meet in Hobart some time early in 1891." I do not want to go into the questions raised by Mr. Deakin, who was followed by Sir John Hall, because I think they are so much like "the flowers that bloom in the spring, tra la," and have "nothing to do with the case." I don't say this offensively, and I hope Mr. Deakin will not call me a wolf afterwards, but really the question we have to consider, as members of the Conference, is, in the words of the resolution, the desirability of taking such steps as may be necessary to induce the legislatures of their respective colonies to appoint delegates to a National Australasian Convention. And if we are going to discuss the whole question of Federation over again, we may be here until this day month. Therefore I don't propose to go into it, but I do think that we should indicate where and when we desire the Convention to meet. I fix upon early in 1891, because it is the most convenient period of the year for the delegates of the various Australasian Colonies to meet. They will mostly be members of the legislatures, and the respective parliaments will no doubt be out of session at the beginning of the year, and as that is the hottest season, and the Convention will have a considerable amount of work to do, I think it is extremely desirable to fix upon Hobart as the place of meeting, because that is about the coolest of the colonies in the summer months, and the delegates would get on much better there than in any other part of Australia. Melbourne has this year lost all her credit for having a decently cool climate, and has got the reputation of being considerably hotter than Adelaide.

Sir HENRY PARKES.—Why not suggest Auckland as the place of meeting?

Mr. PLAYFORD.—The New Zealand delegates have said that their colony cannot see its way to join the Federation, and I am sure that Auckland is very warm.

Sir JOHN HALL.—Say Wellington, then.

Mr. PLAYFORD.—Auckland would be about the very warmest spot we could possibly fix upon. It is true that Mount Eden is close at hand, but we should not be able to get to Mount Eden. I think it is highly desirable we should fix upon a time for the Convention, otherwise the question may be postponed for another year, and that will mean until two years hence. The question of Federation is under the consideration of the people of the different colonies, and we should " strike while the iron is hot."

Mr. BIRD.—Mr. President, I rise with very much pleasure to support the proposed addition to the resolution now before us. I think the fact that we have in Hobart about the coolest locality that can be found in the Australasian Colonies in the summer months, is of itself sufficient to justify the choice of that city for the place of meeting for the Federation Convention. I fancy I detect an incredulous smile on the faces of some honorable members, no doubt in view of the fact that we have had some weather in Hobart this summer almost equal in intensity of heat to the weather we have recently experienced here, but I can assure them that such heat is quite exceptional, and certainly there is not the continuity of it that we have had to endure of late in Melbourne. Gratified though we have been by the superabundant hospitality we have enjoyed, I am sure we would not like to spend five or six weeks in such weather as we have experienced during our present sojourn in Melbourne, and the Convention would probably occupy that length of time. As to the time of meeting, I agree with Mr. Playford that early next year is the latest period to which we should defer the assemblage of the Convention, in view of the public interest that has been awakened by the discussions at this Conference.

Sir JOHN HALL.—Mr. President, may I suggest to Mr. Playford that in putting before us two distinct propositions in one amendment, he is placing the members of the Conference in a difficulty. The time and the place of meeting are two distinct subjects. If the honorable member will divide his proposition I shall be prepared to vote for meeting early in 1891.

Sir HENRY PARKES.—Or earlier.

Sir JOHN HALL.—Or earlier, if practicable.

Sir HENRY PARKES.—And as to the place of meeting, say Lord Howe Island.

Sir JOHN HALL.—I am not prepared to vote for the place of meeting at the present time.

Mr. PLAYFORD.—I am quite prepared to divide the amendment. The time and the place are two distinct questions.

Mr. McMILLAN.—Why fix the place now?

Mr. PLAYFORD.—We can leave the place out if you like, or we can make it the top of the Blue Mountains.

Sir HENRY PARKES.—Why not the crown of Mont Blanc, if you want a really cool place?

The PRESIDENT.—If agreeable to honorable members, I will divide the amendment. The first part fixes upon the place at which it is proposed the Convention should meet, namely, in Hobart.

Sir HENRY PARKES.—Mr. President, before you put the question to the Conference I would suggest that the place of meeting should not be included in the resolution. So many circumstances may arise to determine that point, that I think it would be very unwise for this Conference to come to any binding decision with respect to it. It would probably be a much wiser course to appoint some Minister of the Crown—yourself, Sir—as convener, with power to name the time and place of meeting.

Sir SAMUEL GRIFFITH.—Sir, the time and place of meeting are distinct questions, but they may be mutually interdependent. We cannot tell when all the Parliaments will have appointed their delegates, we cannot foresee what delays may occur—I hope they may not be many—but a number of incidents might occur to prevent the holding of the Convention at a time and place appointed nearly twelve months beforehand. All of us who have had parliamentary experience know how absolutely impossible it is to fix even six months in advance when and where a Conference or Convention shall meet. If the Convention is to be held in January, then Hobart is the best possible place to meet, but some of the parliaments may be in session in January. The place is dependent on the time of meeting, and the time is dependent on the place. In 1883 a committee was appointed to supervise the resolutions of the Convention, and Mr. Service, as the prime mover, was appointed convener, and authorized to take the necessary steps, which is really the only practical way. Supposing some important parliament is prevented from coming to a conclusion to appoint delegates, it would not be desirable to hold the Convention without them. Some parliaments may appoint delegates with particular restrictions, or decide that it is not desirable to move further without a reconsideration of the matter, and so on.

Mr. PLAYFORD.—Unless you fix a time you leave the door open to all sorts of things, and, naturally, the opportunity will then be seized by some to defeat the object in view, and any number of years may pass before we will get a Convention. If, however, we state definitely that the Convention ought to meet early next year, some effort will be made to carry out the arrangement. Ministers will tell their parliaments—"If you delay that will simply mean that nothing will be done." All the different colonial legislatures will meet before January next, so that there will be ample time to appoint delegates. Asking the various parliaments to sanction a Convention, and getting them to appoint delegates, are two very different things. If it is the wish of the Conference, I will excise the words relating to the Convention meeting at Hobart. It would strengthen the hands of the governments concerned if the time was definitely fixed for early in 1891.

The PRESIDENT.—It is often very difficult, on an occasion like this, to satisfactorily fix either place or time. I suggest that the various parliaments should be simply asked to appoint delegates to the Convention, leaving the time and place of meeting to be decided upon subsequently, after consultation between the governments interested. If the matter is so left, and I have the honor to be one to communicate with other governments on the matter, I shall be very happy to give every possible assistance. No doubt, as Sir Samuel Griffith has pointed out, there will be, in several instances, a number of difficulties in the way, but I think every effort will be made to overcome them. Unquestionably the proper season for meeting will be early in the year.

Mr. PLAYFORD.—I still consider that the Conference ought to express the opinion that the Convention should be held early next year. We need not be particular as to the month or day. My judgment tells me that that will be a wise course to follow, in order to get the delegates elected before the close of this year.

Mr. CLARK.—I think the views of both Mr. Playford and the President would be met if after the word " appoint," and before the word " delegates," in Mr. Deakin's motion, the words " during the present year" were inserted.

Mr. PLAYFORD.—I ask leave to withdraw my amendment in favour of that just suggested by Mr. Clark.

Mr. Playford's amendment was withdrawn.

Mr. CLARK.—I now beg to move the amendment I have indicated.

The amendment was agreed to, and the original motion was amended accordingly.

Sir SAMUEL GRIFFITH.—Sir, before the amended motion is put, I would like to offer a few remarks on the general question.

I came here with the view of getting information, for the sake of both myself and the colony I have the honor to represent, upon the real present attitude of the people of this continent on the question of Federation. I came here with an inquiring mind, for I confess I had great doubts on many points—doubts to which I gave expression the other day. At the same time I was perfectly clear about what it was desirable to attain to if we could attain to it. I am now, however, very glad to say that during the discussion a great deal of light has been thrown on the subject, and the uncertainty I felt has been almost entirely removed. One great doubt was as to whether fiscal difficulties would prevent Federation. I was under the impression that the idea of asking the several colonies to break down their respective Customs barriers was an utterly impracticable one; still, I thought that obstacle was not sufficient to prevent Federation for other purposes. But the arguments I have listened to have shown me that my fears were groundless—that the obstacle was one which need not be feared. It has been very clearly pointed out that any discussion between delegates to a Convention appointed with limited powers will be attended with great inconvenience. I see no reason why the representatives of the various colonies should not, with the most perfect confidence, ask their parliaments to confer plenary powers on their delegates. I am satisfied, if that is done, that those delegates will be able to use such arguments, derived from discussions at this Conference, as will overcome all opposition. I am glad to acknowledge that it is the discussion which has taken place which has brought about that change in my mind, for I certainly came here under a different impression. There can be no doubt that the Convention should meet as soon as possible. I am satisfied that the fiscal difficulties can be overcome by a Convention. Many ways have been suggested, and many more may be suggested. I am perfectly convinced, however, that those difficulties can be overcome, and that the Convention will be able to make arrangements which will be satisfactory to the whole of the colonies. I have previously doubted whether it will be necessary to suggest a limitation of the powers of the Convention, but now I have no doubt whatever upon that subject, and I can cordially approve of the proposition in the form it is now before the Conference.

The motion was then agreed to in the following amended form :—

"That the members of the Conference should take such steps as may be necessary to induce the Legislatures of their respective colonies to appoint, during the present year, delegates to a National Australasian Convention, empowered to consider and report upon an adequate scheme for a Federal Constitution."

Mr. DEAKIN moved :—

"That the Convention should consist of seven members from each of the self-governing colonies, and four members from each of the Crown colonies."

He said :—Here again, I wish to make a slight amendment, by inserting, after the word "of" in the first line of the motion, and after "and" in the second line, the words "not more than." The understanding which has been evolved in the course of the previous discussion is that, as the delegates will vote by colonies, it will be immaterial what number of delegates any particular colony sends to the Convention. At the same time it will be considered essential that some maximum number should be mentioned, in order that there might be a limitation upon an undue attendance from one or more of the colonies. The number seven suggested itself, but I know of no reason why honorable gentlemen should not alter that maximum as they may deem fit.

Mr. McMILLAN seconded the motion.

Sir JOHN HALL: I cannot allow one remark of the proposer of this motion to pass without some challenge. Mr. Deakin said it was understood that the Convention would vote by colonies. I do not know where that understanding was arrived at, and I would suggest that such an understanding must land us in practical difficulties when the Convention meets. Where there are only two representatives from a colony it will be quite easy, upon simple propositions, such as those which have been before this Conference, to agree how the vote of that colony shall be given. But if complicated questions of detail arise, it may be very difficult for the representatives of a colony to agree as to how their vote shall be given. I would submit for the consideration of honorable gentlemen whether that is not a serious consideration, and whether the question as to how the votes should be given—by colonies or individuals—should not be left to the Convention itself. With reference to the numbers of the representatives of the self-governing colonies, it seems to me that six would be a more convenient number than seven. An arrangement of this kind would allow two representatives to be appointed by the upper branch of the legislature, and four by the lower branch. A seventh representative will come in something after the fashion of the fifth wheel of a coach.

Mr. DEAKIN: I desired to point out that the matter cannot be left to the Convention. The question must be settled before the Convention assembles, otherwise the Conference will require to fix the number of representatives each colony must send. Whilst I fully admit the difficulty to which attention has been called, I would point out that it has been the practice, in cases of this kind, where an equality in voting has existed among the representatives of a colony—say, three taking one side and three the other—for the senior member to have a casting vote. One advantage in having seven representatives would be found in the fact that a casting vote would not be required. A difficulty which suggests itself is, that some of the colonies may not desire to send so many as six representatives; if we vote by colonies this will be immaterial. By the time the Convention is held Western Australia may be a self-governing colony, and if the meeting takes place at Hobart that colony may not desire to send the number suggested.

Sir SAMUEL GRIFFITH: It seems to me to be impossible to fix the number. My opinion is that upon more important matters the voting will have to be by colonies, as it was in Canada and United States, and as it has been in Australasia in previous important conferences. Mr. Macrossan informs me that the difficulty as to an even number of votes is not an insuperable one, because the practice in America has been that where the delegates of the States are equally divided in number no vote is recorded. Upon minor matters no doubt the Convention would decide to allow the majority to rule, but on great questions of principle the colonies must vote as colonies.

Mr. McMILLAN: The Convention will make its own rules.

The amendment was agreed to, and the motion was then carried in the following form :—

"That the Convention should consist of not more than seven members from each of the self-governing colonies, and not more than four members from each of the Crown colonies."

FEDERAL COUNCIL.

Mr. DEAKIN moved :—

"That as some time must elapse before a Federal Constitution can be adopted, and as it is desirable that the colonies should at once take united action to provide for military defence, and for effective co-operation in other matters of common concern, it is advisable that the Federal Council should be employed for such purposes so far as its powers will permit, and with such an extension of its powers as may be decided upon, and that all the colonies should be represented on the Council."

He said, in moving this resolution I wish to explain to the representatives of New South Wales and New Zealand, why it seemed desirable that there should be an opportunity afforded of considering this question before the proceedings of the Conference closed. Those honorable gentlemen will recognize that there is no attempt, either patent or latent, to in any way coerce them. Such coercion is absolutely impossible, and it is frankly recognized as impossible and also as undesirable. The passage of a resolution to compel any colony to enter the Federal Council against its will would be most injurious. No union could be satisfactory or profitable to those associated in it unless it was entered into with a free will, and with a cordial desire to obtain the objects of the union. It is therefore under no mistaken apprehension of what even the carriage of this resolution would involve that I venture to place it upon the notice paper, but I placed it there being sure that the relation of the Federal Council to the proposed Federated Parliament would certainly assert itself during this debate, while there would be no means of testing the general feeling in regard to what that relation should be unless we had a substantive motion of this kind dealt with. The proposition is submitted to give those members of the Conference who desire it an opportunity of stating to the representatives of the great colonies outside the Council why they belong to the Federal Council, why they intend to continue to belong to it, and why they cherish an ambition that the other colonies should also join it. The occasion for the assembling of this Conference alters in many ways the position of all the colonies in regard to that Council. I hope that it will alter entirely the attitude of New South Wales and New Zealand. For my own part, I can perfectly well understand that men whose minds have been filled by the vision of a Federated Australasia, with a General Parliament and an Executive Government, may well feel disposed to consider that the Council is a body too imperfect to meet their desires. But now that, happily, the representatives of Australasia have fallen into line, have passed the motion submitted by Sir Henry Parkes in favour of a Federal Union, and a further consequent resolution, pledging us to endeavour to induce our legislatures to appoint delegates to a Convention to frame a Constitution, and a new era in Australasian history having thus been heralded, I think the members of the Conference must confess that the circumstances are so changed as to present this issue to them in an entirely different aspect to that in which it has hitherto appeared. I say this, not because an apologetic tone requires to be adopted in regard to the Federal Council. As one in no way concerned in the formation of that body, I am myself satisfied that if the thing remained to do again it ought to be done, that it was a thoroughly wise procedure to form the Council, and that it has accomplished a great and good work in the federal cause. But with regard to the representatives of the two great colonies who stood out of the Federal Council, I ask them if, prior to the assembling of this present Conference, they regarded the Federal Council as being too incomplete to justify their adhesion to it, will they not now consider that, pending the passage of a measure which will give Federal Australasia its legislature and executive, there is room which can well be filled by the Council— that it can do work for them in the interim which ought to be done, and which they cannot do for themselves. If the representatives I refer to will take that view, they will not find themselves in any conflict on the general question with members of the Federal Council. It has always been regarded as a temporary and tentative body, and its authors and members have always accepted as an axiom the doctrine that it was to be employed only until we could find some body more powerful than itself to take its place. The very resolution on which it was founded, passed in the Convention of 1883, ran as follows:—

"That this Convention, recognizing that the time has not yet arrived at which a complete Federal Union of the Australasian Colonies can be attained, but considering that there are many matters of general interest with respect to which united action would be advantageous, adopts the accompanying draft Bill for the Constitution of a Federal Council, as defining the matters upon which, in its opinion, such united action is both desirable and practicable at the present time, and as embodying the provisions best adapted to secure that object, so far as it is now capable of attainment."

Three times over in that resolution it is indicated that, in the opinion of the founders, the Council was intended only to have a temporary existence, until a Federal Union could be established. Then, no later than the commencement of last session, resolutions were carried in favour of an alteration of the Constitution of the Council. Those resolutions increased the number of representatives—to thirty or thirty-four members if New Zealand and New South Wales joined—and provided that each colony should determine whether its representatives should be nominee, elective, or representative. By proposing this increase in the number of members one of the chief objections Sir Henry Parkes has raised is removed, because the proposal is to increase the Federal Council until it forms a body nearly as large as our Upper House. And this extension of the numbers of the Council was only proposed as a step preliminary to asking for increased powers for that body, so as to make it more useful and authoritative than at present. Even in doing this the Council was true to its traditions, and recognized that it was still a temporary and tentative body. A resolution passed at the last meeting of the Council says—

"The Committee (on the Constitution of the Council) desire to add that they recognize that further amendments of the Constitution of the Council will from time to time become necessary, until complete Parliamentary Federation is eventually obtained; but they consider that a substantial advance towards that end will be made if effect be given to the foregoing recommendations."

So that, even when recommending an increase in the number of members, the Council repeated its cardinal doctrine. Mr. Kingston, the South Australian representative, who took an active part in bringing forward this amendment, was only deterred from submitting a further resolution by the feeling that the Council ought to adopt this proposal for an increase of its members before any further step was taken. He, however, gave notice of the following resolution, which, though not adopted, was generally approved by the Council:—

"That, in the opinion of this Council, it is desirable that, after the Constitution of the Council shall have been amended by the increase of the number of its members, the Council shall, on behalf of the colonies represented, consider the question of Australasian Parliamentary Federation, with a view to making recommendations thereon to the local legislatures."

So that, if the Federal Council had obtained the increase it sought, it might at this very time be considering the question this Conference is now considering. Thus the members and authors of the Federal Council, so far from being opponents of Australasian Federation, are its warmest supporters; and they have never taken any step, from the beginning, without recording the fact that the work they were doing was only work introductory to the establishment of a complete Federal Parliament.

Without quoting further, I think that what I have cited should be sufficient to prove to the representatives of the two colonies who remain outside the Council that if they, having endorsed the resolutions which this Conference has carried in favour of Federation, should now enter the Federal Council they will not enter a body with which they will be out of sympathy or a body which is deaf to their appeals for Federation, but one which has proved itself to be loyal to the cause we are assembled here to advance. They will not find that members of the Council desire to maintain it at the expense of a higher organization, or that they are desirous of clinging to their dignity when they see an opportunity of making way for a greater power. With the exception of the representatives of two of the colonies represented here to-day, every member of this Conference is a member of the Federal Council, and the cordiality with which we have endorsed the proposal for a Federal Parliament is a proof that if the motion had been submitted in the Federal Council they would have endorsed it with the same heartiness. Under these circumstances the representatives of the Australasian Colonies can have nothing to fear for Federation from association with the Council, and nothing to dread in the way of its antagonism. They may now not unreasonably ask: "What advantages would arise from our becoming members of a Council which will shortly be absorbed in the greater Australasian Parliament?" The answer is that, first of all, the earliest possible time at which an Australasian Parliament could assemble for the transaction of business would probably be about two years. In the uncertain course of political affairs this interregnum may be extended to three or even four years. It might take a still longer period than that, but it is certain that we have to face a period of two years without any federal authority; and the question I would like to put to the representatives of these colonies is, whether they consider that during these two, three, or four years, as the case may be, there is not good work to be done in connection with the Federal Council? I would say, in anticipation of objection, that if it be urged that the colonies which now stand aloof might, in joining the Federal Council, lead some of the members of the group to waver in their energy as regards Federation, those colonies could join, as South Australia did, for a definite term of years. It is perfectly possible for both the colonies in question to fix the time for which they would give the Federal Council its trial, supposing that the Federal Parliament did not come into existence. As to the results to be obtained by their entrance into the Council I will not weary the Conference with citations from the Federal Council Act, but I will quote the list of questions which the Council is enabled to deal with, with which none of the parliaments it represents can deal with in the same manner, while it is highly desirable that they should be dealt with. These questions are:—Relations of Australia with the Islands of the Pacific, prevention of the influx of criminals, fisheries in Australasian waters beyond territorial limits, the service of civil process of the courts of any colony within Her Majesty's possessions in Australasia out of the jurisdiction of the colony in which it is issued, the enforcement of judgments of courts of law of any colony beyond the limits of the colony, the enforcement of criminal process beyond the limits of the colony in which it is issued and the extradition of offenders, the custody of offenders on board ships belonging to Her Majesty's Colonial Governments beyond territorial limits, and any matter which, at the request of the legislatures of the colonies, Her Majesty, by Order in Council, shall think fit to refer to the Council. These are the matters with which the Council has authority to deal. Surely it cannot be said that nothing could be done under any of those heads during the next few years which would not be well worth doing in the interests of the different colonies. For instance if we dealt with the purely legal questions—such as the enforcement of civil and criminal process and of judgments, the law relating to companies, and the estates of lunatics, on all of which matters our legal procedure is at present in an unsatisfactory condition—surely we would have done something worth doing. In addition to that, power is given to the several legislatures to refer questions to the Federal Council, and upon these the Federal Council may legislate. Foremost among the many questions which the Imperial Government has allowed to be referred to the Federal Council is that of general defence. Sir Samuel Griffith, in the course of his first speech, drew attention to the anomalies which would exist if the forces engaged under the laws of the different colonies were sought to be employed in colonies other than their own. At the present time the militia of Victoria would be beyond the control of our law directly they crossed the River Murray, and the militia of New South Wales are in exactly the same position if they enter our territory. Discipline would, of course, be impossible under these circumstances. Again, the resolution to which, under the guidance of Sir Henry Parkes, we have assented, affirms that the time has arrived in which a Federal Executive and a Federal Legislature are necessary. The occasion for calling this Conference and coming to such a resolution was the report of Major-General Edwards on the state of our defences. This very question is capable of being dealt with, though in a partial manner yet to a most valuable extent, under the provisions of the Federal Council Act. It is true that there cannot be a Federal Army such as a Federal Government could establish and maintain, nor is that desirable under the present Council. But what the Federal Council could do would be to pass a law making the militias of the various colonies one force, capable of acting anywhere, by making them amenable to discipline when outside the colony in which they were enlisted. If we recognise the imminence of the danger to which we may be exposed during the next few years, none of us, I am sure, will say that this is not a work that is well worth doing. And who can tell that the need for this general defence may not occur before the Parliament of Australasia is called into existence? I will point, in conclusion, to two other provisions of the Federal Council Act which are not without importance. Section 16 gives the governments of any two or more of the colonies power, upon an address of the legislatures of such colonies, to refer for the consideration and determination of the Council any questions relating to those colonies or their relations with one another, when the Council shall have authority to consider and determine by Act of Council the matter so referred to it. There are matters of intercolonial agreement, or requiring intercolonial agreement, and which are at present matters of comparative disagreement, which might be on their way to settlement before we have a Federated Australia; and if the interested parties think proper they could refer these questions to the Council, and thus obtain at once the assistance of a body capable of solving and settling them. That, I think, is a power of extreme practical value. Another power is given which is of less practical value, but not of less importance, in section 29, which authorizes the Federal Council to make such representations or recommendations to Her Majesty as it may think fit with respect to any matters of general Australasian interest, or to the relations of Her Majesty's possessions in Australasia with the possessions of foreign powers. No one could have spoken more sympathetically or powerfully than Sir Henry Parkes did when he referred to the threatened influx of Asiatics into Australia, or to the possible domination of the Pacific Islands by foreign powers. We may not obtain notice of any intended action on the part of foreign powers in time to constitute a Federal Parliament to deal with such questions, and we may, at any moment, find ourselves by their action plunged into a serious crisis. The powers given to the Federal Council are all I think useful, are all such powers as we might require to exercise in the interest of Australasia during the next few years; and yet they are all powers that we shall be unable to exercise with full strength and authority unless all the colonies of Australasia join us. If New Zealand and New South Wales could see their way at the present juncture to make their entrance into the Federal Council, the number of members could be increased, its powers, if they were considered to be insufficient, could be enlarged, and we should at all events have in an incomplete form an Australasian Union which would enable us to cope with many difficulties which may confront us at any moment, and with which at present we are unable to cope. The question we put to the delegates from these colonies is: What possible reason can there be for refraining to join hands even in this small work of Federation now, especially as we have agreed to join hands in the larger work that lies before us. We are all of one mind in regard to the constitution of a Dominion Parliament and Executive for Australasia, and surely the greater includes the less. We are of one mind in regard to the desirability of facilitating commercial intercourse between the colonies as much as possible, of giving to the citizens of all the colonies similar laws, of providing for our united defence, and of being able to forestall foreign aggression by making, in a constitutional manner, proper representations to Her Majesty. These powers are now within our reach; and we ask with surprise, why we should allow them to lie idle because we see greater powers promised in the future? I will consent to stand second to none in respect to the ardour of my desire for the creation of a Federal Parliament, and I yield to none in the loyalty of allegiance which I promise to such a body. But I have an equal loyalty to the Federal Council as it exists to day, because, after all, it is our only federal institution, our only accomplished union. It has done useful work, and it may do more useful work. Why should we despise the day of small things, especially when those small things may at any moment become of the largest and last importance to us. It might become of vital moment to Australasia that the colonies should speak with one voice on some instant question of foreign policy, or pass some drastic law for the protection of our shores such as the Federal Council Act empowers us to pass. Why should we not receive the assurance of the representatives of New South Wales and New Zealand that they will do what in them lies to join us in such tasks, as they are prepared to join us in establishing an Australian Dominion? We know they cannot bind their parliaments, but if they would only seek to induce their parliaments to enter temporarily into the Federal Council, and wed with us from to-day, instead of putting off our marriage for two or three years, they would give striking evidence of the strength of the federal spirit. I trust that the expressions which have fallen from them as to their ardour for the federal cause in general will be repeated with reference to this particular federal cause, and that we will be able to welcome at the next meeting of the Federal Council representatives from all Australasia. If that were so, the one reason for the partial character of the success achieved by the Federal Council would be removed; its great and immediate success would be assured, and it would become a body that would win the gratitude of the people of Australasia by the practical work it would do for them without delay, while it would not fail them in the day and hour of their need, if a time of peril should arise within the next two or three years.

Dr. COCKBURN seconded the motion.

Mr. McMILLAN.—Mr. President, after the very great harmony and unanimity which has occurred throughout the proceedings of the Conference, it is a matter of great regret to the delegates of New South Wales that they cannot agree to the motion. Certainly if anything could have led us away from our allegiance to what we believe to be the opinion of our own people, it would have been the charming eloquence of our friend in whom the Church has certainly lost an extraordinary light, for if ever eloquence was fitted to convert the sinner from the error of his ways, that eloquence belongs to the Chief Secretary of Victoria. But the fact is we are absolutely powerless. The Federal Council has existed for the last five years, and during the whole of that period, by every proof that we can obtain— the utterances of public men, the sentiments of public meetings, the expressions of opinion in the best papers of the colony—we have reason to believe that if our colony were polled to-morrow a large majority would be against entering the Federal Council. Consequently, Sir, as representatives of the people, and as owing our authority to the people, we must bow to that opinion, whether it be reasonable or not. But apart even from that view of the case, it seems to me that if this motion were carried we would be open to the very grave charge of putting forward a lesser issue and shadowing the larger one to be put before the colonies as the result of this Conference; and popular opinion might be inclined to say that instead of the first resolution being the principal one proposed in the Conference, the last resolution was the real thing which the members of the Conference had in view. I don't think, Sir, as far as New South Wales is concerned, that she will be a block to an early decision of this Federation question. I believe that in the shortest time mentioned for the commencement of the Convention's operations New South Wales will be ready to take her part in the proceedings. There is no doubt that the question of military defence, as brought before the colonies by General Edwards, presents a great and a real danger, and in the present state of affairs in Europe it is impossible to say that certain contingencies may not occur; but as representatives of the people of New South Wales, and feeling certain that public opinion, by a large majority, is against any idea of our entering the Federal Council, we must absolutely decline to vote for this resolution.

Captain RUSSELL.—Sir, I regret that I must come to the same conclusion as Mr. McMillan. There are several reasons why I arrive at that conclusion. First of all, and possibly when that is enunciated you will say it is unnecessary for me to go any further, this question was not relegated to us as delegates, and therefore we have no power to deal with it; secondly, the question has not been raised in our colony, that is to say, the people of New Zealand have not for years considered this matter; but I believe that, if there was to be any test of public feeling on the subject, public opinion in New Zealand would be found rather adverse to than in favour of our joining the Federal Council. I say that with regret, because personally and individually I think there might be much to gain if we were able to join. All the matters that have been so ably alluded to by Mr. Deakin, and many other subjects besides those, might come before the Federal Council, and even supposing New Zealand should not join ultimately in the great Federal Union of

s

Australia, still she would gain enormously by having laws passed affecting criminals and great social questions which might be dealt with by the Federal Council in such a manner as to be very beneficial to the people of Australasia. But, unfortunately, we are not in a position to join the Federal Council. It is an open question, however, whether in the cause of Federal Union it would be wise to give increased powers to the Federal Council. It may be very true to say it is absurd that a lesser power shall not be granted to these colonies which are anxious to assume far greater powers; but we must bear in mind that, in passing through life, we continually find people, after taking a smaller quantity, satisfying themselves with that smaller quantity, and not going on to take possession of the larger quantity which was within their reach. Take in illustration a simple every-day incident that has, no doubt, very frequently come under the notice of honorable members. A man builds a house of wood, with small rooms and of insignificant appearance—a shanty, in fact—intending however, to erect a very much bigger house in two or three years. Time passes by, the years roll on, but the man and his family are still to be found living in the shanty he first put up, and not in the palatial place with which his earlier dreams blessed them. So it may be with the Federal Council. If all the colonies of Australasia are satisfied to go into the shanty of the Federal Council, is it not possible they may never get into the palatial mansion of a Dominion Parliament? That is a good reason why New South Wales should not join the Federal Council. I say all this with sincere regret, because I do feel that we in New Zealand, at any rate, would have much to gain by joining the Federal Council; and I promise the members of this Conference that on my return to my own colony I will endeavour to bring the matter before the people of New Zealand, and that it shall be submitted to my government, who will give the subject their calm and careful consideration before the next session of parliament.

Mr. MACROSSAN.—Mr. President, taking into consideration the views of the representatives of New South Wales and

New Zealand, and the fact that there will be no meeting of the Federal Council this year, I think it would be as well if Mr. Deakin were to withdraw his resolution. It has too much the appearance of trying to coerce New South Wales and New Zealand to join the Federal Council. We are all very anxious they should join, but if they don't see their way to do so I think we should not put forth any effort that would have the appearance of seeking to force them to join.

Mr. CLARK.—Sir, I also concur in the opinion expressed by my honorable friend, Mr. Macrossan, that Mr. Deakin would take a wise course in withdrawing his motion. Although we know that the honorable gentleman has no such intention whatever, his resolution might, in the eyes of some persons, have the appearance of being an attempt to compel New South Wales and New Zealand to come into the Federal Council. I have very much felt the smallness of that Council as an obstacle in the way of its usefulness. An increase of its members by the addition of four representatives from two such important colonies would undoubtedly impart new life and new vigour to the Council, enabling it to do very much better work in the future than it has done in the past; but notwithstanding the advantage which I see would accrue from the entrance of New South Wales and New Zealand into the Council until the larger federation is established, I yet believe that there is a good deal of weight in the arguments submitted by Captain Russell, that if the whole of the colonies are once represented in the Federal Council, particularly with increased powers and increased representation, there might be a tendency to remain content with that kind of federation for an indefinite time; and I should be very sorry indeed, as a member of this Conference, to have been a party to such an undesirable result. But it is not that argument which particularly influences me at the present time; I am influenced still more by a desire to avoid anything like an attempt to compel New South Wales and New Zealand to join the Federal Council.

Mr. DEAKIN.—Mr. President, it would, as I have already said, be perfectly idle for the members of the Federal Council to have cherished any intention of compelling any colony to join the Council, simply because they have no power to compel any one to join, or to influence the other colonies in any degree, unless they are fortunate enough to be able to influence them by argument.

Sir HENRY PARKES.—Sir, if Mr. Deakin would kindly allow me, before he replies, I desire to say that I should be extremely sorry, on the part of New South Wales, if any feeling could possibly exist that we thought for a single instant that there was any intent to compel us to join the Federal Council. That would be impracticable, because we could not be compelled; but I should be very sorry if any one supposed that we entertained any such illiberal view as that there was any design even to induce us to take that step. On the contrary, I for one believe that Mr. Deakin has submitted this motion in the very best of good faith. We do not complain on that score for a moment, nor are we so purblind to the actual state of things as to suspect any desire to induce us, by reason of our being amongst the parties to such a resolution, to join the Federal Council. Our position has been pretty fairly stated by my honorable colleague, Mr. McMillan; but I would like to call attention to my own individual position. If honorable members accept my explanation that I had convinced myself, before I was called upon to take any step in consequence of the Convention of 1883, that the Federal Council scheme, instead of being a promoter of Federation, would be a stumbling block in the way of Federation, I don't see how it can possibly be expected that I, as an individual, could consent to urge New South Wales to enter the Federal Council now. That appears to have been frankly recognized by the government of Queensland in the quotation which I made from Mr. Morehead's despatch. If I could by any means be brought to see the matter in the same light as Mr. Deakin does, I should be disposed to submit the case to our parliament; but my conviction is in strict accord with that of Mr. McMillan. I might suffer by submitting the case to parliament, but I could never induce the parliament of New South Wales to assent to it. From some cause or causes, not in any marked degree through my influence, the parliament and people of New South Wales are opposed to the Federal Council. Those who paid any attention to my explanation would see that I could not have had much to do with influencing this state of feeling in New South Wales. I explained that for fully eight months after the Convention sat, in 1883, I was out of the colony. I was a member of parliament at the time, because, although I had tendered my resignation, my constituents would not accept it during my absence; but soon after my return I saw what appeared to me a sufficient reason for resigning my seat, and I placed myself outside parliament, I think, for the remainder of that year, so that I could have had personally very little to do with influencing public opinion on this question. And I have seldom spoken of the Federal Council since, unless on occasions when I have been compelled to speak of it, so that the opinion in New South Wales has crystallized against the Federal Council from other influences than mine. One of those influences has been the steady and powerful conduct of the public Press in opposition to it. Any one who has read the leading papers of New South Wales must know that the best of them—those which carry most weight—have been consistently, and with singular ability, opposed to the Federal Council, and the result is that the public opinion of New South Wales is so confirmed that it would be impossible for that colony to join the Federal Council. There is the real objection to the motion proposed by Mr. Deakin, and it was forcibly, though somewhat humorously, embodied in Captain Russell's figure. It is a most dangerous proceeding, if a people is aiming at some great object, to set up some smaller object in the interval. It is very likely, by the operation of the laws which influence human nature, more or less to exclude from sight the larger object, and it is certain to weaken the effort for the attainment of the larger object. That is a valid argument, based on grounds with which we are all acquainted; but apart from that argument or any other argument, what I stated in a letter addressed to Mr. Gillies I repeat now, that no man and no party of New South Wales could induce parliament to consent to enter the Federal Council. I say that, I hope, in the best spirit possible, and only with a desire to state what I believe to be the truth.

Mr. DEAKIN.—As my arguments do not appear to have made any impression on the minds of the representatives of New South Wales or New Zealand, I can only conclude that they will not have any greater weight with the parliaments they represent. I, therefore, accept the suggestion thrown out by Mr. Macrossan and Mr. Clark, although I entirely differ from them in conceiving it possible that such a resolution as this could be supposed to be intended to coerce or compel a consent. But, in order that there may be no resolution affirmed by the Conference which is not unanimously carried, I will withdraw the motion.

Sir HENRY PARKES.—In order to satisfy my friends in Victoria and the other colonies, I undertake, in good faith, to consult my colleagues in Cabinet on the question which has been raised by this resolution; and I will undertake more than that, namely, to consult leading men in opposition to the government, as well as leading men in support of the government on the same subject. More than that I cannot undertake.

The motion was withdrawn.

Sir HENRY PARKES.—May I ask if that concludes the business of the Conference?

The PRESIDENT.—It will be necessary to embody the whole of the resolutions in an Address to Her Majesty, through His Excellency the Governor and the Secretary of State for the Colonies. It will, therefore, be necessary for the Conference to meet to-morrow, at eleven o'clock, for the purpose of transacting that business, as well as to dispose of some other formal business which may arise.

ADDRESS TO THE QUEEN.

Sir HENRY PARKES.—Mr. President, you will recollect. I think, that at our first interview on my arrival in Melbourne, I suggested to you the propriety of this Conference adopting a humble and dutiful Address to Her Majesty, expressive of our loyalty as members of the Conference representing all the colonies. You replied to me that if anything of the kind were done it would be more becoming at the close of our proceedings, and I have no doubt whatever that your view is a correct one. I should like now to elicit from you, and from the Conference through you, whether, in the judgment of my fellow representatives, the action would be a proper one to take. It will be noticed, from the telegrams which have appeared in the press, that the Imperial Government has made our sitting a matter of sufficient importance to include in Her Majesty's Speech, and it seems to me that it would be in no way going out of our proper line of conduct for us to close our proceedings with such an Address. If that is the view of other members of the Conference, I should be very happy to undertake, if they wish it, to move such an Address to-morrow.

The PRESIDENT.—Does the honorable gentleman desire to indicate that the Address which he speaks of would require to be separated from the one which will embody the resolutions which have been adopted?

Sir HENRY PARKES.—I think it would be better for the Address to be separate. Upon important occasions, Englishmen acting in public life very frequently take advantage of those occasions to renew the expression of their loyalty to the throne and person of Her Majesty, and it seems to me this is a question of sufficient magnitude for that course to be taken.

The PRESIDENT.—The matter is one which can be settled to-morrow. If there is no objection, the honorable gentleman will, I understand, prepare the Address he refers to.

Mr. PLAYFORD.—I think that perhaps the best way to approach Her Majesty would be first by a short telegram; then we could send on the more formal matter in ordinary course. A telegram might state briefly the results arrived at by the Conference, and express our devotion to Her Majesty's throne and person. I think that would be very appropriate.

Sir HENRY PARKES.—If we do this thing it will be best to do it in the most formal way we can. A preliminary communication could be sent by telegram, and the remaining matter would follow in proper form. The address in these cases usually communicates to the Secretary of State what has been done, and I do not think that a communication of that sort in any way renders the other address unnecessary. I presume that we ought to adopt some form of address to be transmitted through His Excellency the Governor of Victoria to the Secretary of State; but an address of that kind would be quite different from the address to the Queen which I suggest. It would be a very becoming and graceful act, at the closing of this Conference, to adopt an address direct to Her Majesty.

Sir SAMUEL GRIFFITH.—At the close of the Convention of 1883 it was resolved that copies of the proceedings of that body should be forwarded to the Secretary of State. I understand Sir Henry Parkes to propose that besides that an address shall be forwarded to the Queen, informing Her Majesty of the proceedings of the Conference, and expressing whatever the members of the Conference may desire to express in it.

Sir HENRY PARKES.—Precisely.

The Conference adjourned at twenty minutes to six o'clock p.m. until eleven o'clock a.m. the following day.

FRIDAY, FEBRUARY 14, 1890.

The Public were admitted to the Conference Chamber at a quarter to Noon, the PRESIDENT (Mr. D. GILLIES) being in the Chair.

ADDRESS TO THE QUEEN.

Sir JOHN HALL moved the adoption of the following address:—

"TO THE QUEEN'S MOST EXCELLENT MAJESTY.

"MAY IT PLEASE YOUR MAJESTY—

"We, Your Majesty's loyal and dutiful subjects, the Members of the Conference assembled in Melbourne to consider the question of creating for Australasia one Federal Government, and representing the Australasian Colonies, desire to approach Your Most Gracious Majesty with renewed expressions of our devoted attachment to your Majesty's throne and person.

"On behalf of Your Majesty's subjects throughout Australasia, we beg to express the fervent hope that Your Majesty's life may be long spared to reign over a prosperous and happy people.

"We most respectfully inform Your Majesty, that, after mature deliberation, we have unanimously agreed to the following resolutions:—

"1. That, in the opinion of this Conference, the best interests and the present and future prosperity of the Australian Colonies will be promoted by an early union under the Crown, and, while fully recognising the valuable services of the Members of the Convention of 1883 in founding the Federal Council, it declares its opinion that the seven years which have since elapsed have developed the national life of Australia in population, in wealth, in the discovery of resources, and in self-governing capacity, to an extent which justifies the higher act, at all times contemplated, of the union of these colonies, under one Legislative and Executive Government, on principles just to the several colonies.

"2. That to the union of the Australian Colonies contemplated by the foregoing resolution, the remoter Australasian Colonies shall be entitled to admission at such times and on such conditions as may be hereafter agreed upon.

"3. That the members of the Conference shall take such steps as may be necessary to induce the Legislatures of their respective colonies to appoint, during the present year, delegates to a National Australasian Convention, empowered to consider and report upon an adequate scheme for a Federal Constitution.

"4. That the Convention should consist of not more than seven members from each of the self-governing colonies, and not more than four members from each of the Crown Colonies."

He said—Mr. President, I have great honor in moving that this respectful address be presented to Her Majesty the Queen, assuring Her Majesty of the devoted loyalty of her subjects in Australasia, as represented at this Conference, and respectfully conveying to Her Majesty the result of our deliberations. I think we may take it as a happy augury for the success of our great undertaking, that it has been held at a time which afforded an opportunity to Her Majesty to express to the Imperial Parliament her deep interest in the work in which we are engaged. The words used by Her Majesty in opening the Imperial Parliament were, no doubt, words chosen by Her Majesty's Ministers, but honorable gentlemen who know, not only the deep and sincere interest which Her Majesty takes in the welfare of all her subjects, and which I may say has been the strength and glory of the Throne in our day, and who also know the special interest which Her Majesty has always manifested in the welfare and prosperity of her colonial dominions, will not doubt that it will afford Her Majesty much gratification to receive the resolutions at which we have arrived, and that anything which it is in her power to do to further this great undertaking, and to secure the establishment of a great Australian, or even Australasian, Nation, under the Crown of Great Britain, will be done. With these few words I beg to move that the address to Her Majesty, which I have placed in the President's hands, be now adopted by this Conference.

Dr. COCKBURN.—Sir, I beg to second the adoption of this address of loyalty to the Queen's Most Excellent Majesty, which has been so ably moved by Sir John Hall. I think that our fervid expressions of loyalty cannot come at a better time from any body of men than from this Conference, which has assembled to debate the most momentous question of the day, as far as Australasia is concerned. And the expressions of loyalty to which Sir John Hall has given utterance, which are placed on record by this address, will go further than anything else possibly can go to remove all misapprehension as to the views of members of this Conference, and the Parliaments and people they represent, in advocating the union of the Australasian Colonies. It is not to be feared that the union of the Australasian Colonies will in any way remove any of those jewels which at present adorn the Imperial Crown, but we hope that by that union a jewel of unprecedented lustre will be added to the traditions of the Crown of the British Empire.

The motion was agreed to, and the address was unanimously adopted.

Sir JOHN HALL moved—

"That the President do sign the foregoing address on behalf of the Conference, and present the same to His Excellency the Governor of Victoria, with a respectful request that he will be pleased to transmit such address to Her Majesty's Principal Secretary of State for the Colonies, for presentation to Her Most Gracious Majesty."

The motion was seconded by Dr. COCKBURN, and agreed to.

OFFICIAL RECORD OF PROCEEDINGS AND DEBATES.

Sir SAMUEL GRIFFITH moved—

"That the President forward copies of the Report of the Proceedings and Debates of the Conference to His Excellency the Governor of Victoria for transmission to the Right Honorable the Principal Secretary of State for the Colonies."

The motion was seconded by Mr. DEAKIN, and agreed to.

Mr. DEAKIN moved—

"That the President forward copies of the Report of the Proceedings and Debates of the Conference to the representatives of the colonies at this Conference, for presentation to their respective Parliaments, and for general distribution."

The motion was seconded by Mr. PLAYFORD, and agreed to.

It was further directed by the Conference that the Official Record of its Proceedings should be signed by the PRESIDENT and SECRETARY to the Conference; and also that the communications addressed to the Conference from various persons and public bodies should, inasmuch as the conference could not deal with them, be returned by the SECRETARY to the senders.

CONVENER OF THE CONVENTION.

Mr. CLARK moved—

"That the Premier of Victoria be requested to act as Convener of the National Australasian Convention of Delegates to be appointed by the several Legislatures of the Australasian Colonies, and to arrange, upon consultation with the Premiers of the other colonies, the time and place of the meeting of the Convention."

The motion was seconded by Mr. PLAYFORD, and agreed to.

VOTE OF THANKS.

Sir HENRY PARKES moved—

"That the thanks of the Conference be given to the Honorable Duncan Gillies for the services rendered by him as President of the Conference."

He said—I am quite sure that we are all prepared to testify to the courtesy, the dignity, and the efficiency with which you, Mr. President, have filled the Chair. I do not think I need say anything to support the motion which I have been asked to move beyond the few words I have uttered.

Mr. MACROSSAN seconded the motion.

The PRESIDENT.—Before I submit the motion, I may be permitted to say that very few things could give me greater pleasure. I do not refer to presiding at this Conference, or to sitting in the Chair, because I confess that the position of sitting in the Chair, and occupying the position of President or Chairman, does not afford me much personal pleasure. My positions elsewhere have not been such as to afford me that amount of comfort in occupying the Chair which I probably would have felt if I had been sitting simply as a member of the Conference. Nevertheless, I think it was my duty to accept the position in the first instance, as it was offered to me so graciously. What has given me special pleasure has been the result of the Conference, and though I admitted yesterday that when it was first suggested I did not feel such great confidence as I knew other gentlemen felt in the probable prospects, it has nevertheless given me all the more gratification that the deliberations of the Conference have been more successful than I originally contemplated. I can only say that if we can get anything like a similar unanimity elsewhere, when the time of the real struggle comes, nothing will afford my colleague and myself more satisfaction than that great result. Personally, I have to thank honorable members for their great consideration whilst I have been in the Chair, and I have only to say that the duties of the President, under the circumstances, have been extremely light, and the work performed has been exceedingly pleasant.

The motion was agreed to.

Dr. COCKBURN moved—

"That the thanks of the Conference be given to Mr. George Henry Jenkins for the services rendered by him as Secretary to the Conference."

He said:—I think it is the desire of every member of the Conference, before parting, to place on record their appreciation of the manner in which the Secretary's duties have been fulfilled. Mr. Jenkins not only enjoys the confidence of every member of the legislature with which he has been so long associated, but he also possesses what I may say is an Australasian reputation as a constitutional authority. I am sure I am only expressing the views of the members of the Conference when I say that his assistance to us has been of a marked character, and that, as individuals, we have reason to thank him for the way in which he has looked after our comfort.

Sir J. LEE STEERE.—I have very much pleasure in seconding the vote of thanks to Mr. Jenkins as Secretary of this Conference. I have known Mr. Jenkins now for some few years, and I think I have gathered that his great characteristic is loyalty and devotion to parliamentary government, and respect and esteem towards those gentlemen who occupy positions—as I do—as Speakers or Presidents of the different legislatures of these colonies. Although some disparaging remarks were made yesterday with reference to the body over which I have the honor to preside, I think its principal defect is one which will every day grow less and less. I gathered from the observations made yesterday that its principal defect was that it was in its early youth—that it was a body elected by a small population, insignificant in itself, and presided over by a gentleman almost as insignificant. These are defects which every day will cure. The youth which now exists will, we expect, very shortly be manhood; and I hope it will then take its place among other Australian Colonies without it being considered any disparagement that it should do so. I have reason to think that it will be satisfactory to our Secretary to know that a person occupying the position which I do, and which he, at any rate respects, has risen to second the vote of thanks proposed by Dr. Cockburn. As Dr. Cockburn has said, Mr. Jenkins, besides being Clerk of the Legislative Assembly of this colony, has an Australian, or an Australasian, reputation; and I am quite certain that the character which he has gained in this colony, and in the other colonies of Australia, for his ability as the Clerk of the Legislative Assembly of this colony, has been well exemplified in the duties which he has performed for this Conference. I know, from the position I occupy, how much of the smooth working of deliberative assemblies is the result of the manner in which those duties are performed by the Clerk of the Legislature. We are all of us assured by the manner in which Mr. Jenkins has performed the duties of Secretary that those duties could not have been more efficiently performed by anybody else. The comfort and convenience of the members has been most carefully studied by him, and we shall go away with the most gratifying remembrances of the attention which has been paid to us by him.

The motion was agreed to.

The PRESIDENT.—Gentlemen, I think I may, on behalf of Mr. Jenkins, take the liberty of thanking you for the way in which you have shown your appreciation of his services.

ADJOURNMENT.

Mr. DEAKIN moved,—That the Conference do now adjourn.
The motion was agreed to.
The Conference then (thirty-five minutes past noon) adjourned *sine die.*

PUBLIC OPINION

OF

ENGLAND

AS EXPRESSED BY THE PUBLIC JOURNALS.

PUBLIC OPINION OF ENGLAND

AS EXPRESSED BY THE PUBLIC JOURNALS.

Birmingham Post—
February 5th, 1890.

THE Conference which was arranged to be held in Melbourne to-day is, I am told, the outcome of a strong feeling in favour of an Australian Federation which has existed in the minds of many of the foremost Antipodean statesmen for many years. Sir Henry Parkes, the Premier of New South Wales, gave the movement a decided impetus by his letter to the various colonial Premiers, which formed the subject of so much discussion here a short time ago. I hear that there is every probability of Sir Henry consenting on behalf of his Government to forego the free-trade policy in New South Wales, if by so doing he can bring about a partial solution of the federation problem. Many hard words were said when he refused to identify himself with the Federal Council, but it will hardly be denied that he is thoroughly in earnest in his federation ideas when he consents to give up a policy to which he had held so tenaciously until now. The questions of amalgamating the public debts and of central railway management are also to be discussed, and the result of the Conference is being looked forward to with much interest in colonial circles.

Glasgow Mail—
February 6th, 1890.

FEDERALISM is in the air. It is an old idea, though it was long scouted as impracticable on any large scale. Cherished by a few far-thoughted patriots, their faith caused them to be branded with the stigma of visionary dreamers. Now, all has changed. The notion that federation is possible, and would be advantageous, is widely diffused. The influences

Glasgow Mail—*continued.*

that make in its favour, whether as a sentiment or a policy, are many and strong. The thought is becoming compactly solidified. It will by-and-bye be transmuted into fact. What has been done in the United States and in Canada will speedily be accomplished in Australia, while, after that, the circle will widen. In Australia things are in advance. To-day, not for the first time, a Conference on the subject will begin its sittings in Melbourne. Its composition surpasses in width, in power, in freedom, in earnest, unconstrained, deliberate sympathy with the object in view all its predecessors. Every colony of the group is represented, and for the most part the marked diversities of thought in each. The delegates are:—From New South Wales, Sir Henry Parkes and Hon. W. McMillan; Victoria, Hons. Duncan Gillies and A. Deakin; South Australia, Hons. D. Cockburn and T. Playford; Queensland, Hon. J. Macrossan and Sir T. W. Griffith; New Zealand, Hon. Captain Russell and Sir J. Hall; Tasmania, Hons. A. J. Clarke and B. S. Bird; West Australia, Hon. Sir James Lee-Steere; and Fiji, Sir J. Hurston. That is a strong Council. If its members can reach a positive agreement it will carry an enormous weight. The two most remarkable men in the body, possibly the two ablest, stand farthest apart. They are the Premiers of New South Wales and of Victoria. Both have had very eventful careers. Both were working men. Sir Henry Parkes was a mechanic in England, began colonial life by selling toys, an occupation which he varied by inditing poetry, and for long years has been, with only brief intervals, the supreme ruler of the Colony, is accustomed to revolve great thoughts, has an extraordinary gift of copious and lofty eloquence, and is noted as the most ardent champion of such a union as shall not be absolutely incorporative. Mr. Gillies is a Scot. In early days he was a gold-digger. He ruled his mates by dint of hard-headed reason, uttered in brief though incisive speech. They combined to make him a Member of Parliament, and to give him a modest stipend. Their confidence in him was fully vindicated. He is now an old hand in public life, is admittedly the best master of Parliamentary practice as well as the ablest debater in the Legislative Assembly, where he heads the Conservative or, as they call themselves, the Constitutional party, to which he has been all along attached. A correspondence he had with Sir Henry Parkes originated the present Conference. Sir Henry, of course, put forward his wide and high views. Mr. Gillies was mainly concerned about united action for

Glasgow Mail—*continued.*

defence; but he concluded with this cannily suggestive remark: "The creation of a Federal Government must be the work of years, but the Federal Council, although devoid of executive authority, could act straightway if all the colonies agreed." Why should they not agree, and that as regards larger and more intimate interests than military defence? It is surely palpable that the Australasian colonies have everything to gain, nothing to lose by federation. The conditions of success exist. They are connected by situation, by history, by ties alike of origin and descent. Of course there are difficulties in the way, not only as regards arrangements for organizing a fleet and an army but as regards the vexed question of tariffs and the choice of a capital. Still, these are not so formidable as the difficulties which beset Canada and were surmounted. Federation would really be the cheapest, as well as the wisest, defence of Australia. It would be the most effective method of keeping her intact, and perpetuating that alliance which more than half a century since Lord John Russell petrified a French agent of King Louis Philippe by announcing. The French Minister had been instructed to sound the ready and intrepid little man, and put the question, "How much of the Australian Continent do you really claim?" The cool response, which fairly flabbergasted the querist, was. "Why, the whole." A well-timed article by Sir Charles Duffy has appeared dealing with the subjects of retention and unity. Sir Charles, it may be recalled, was the ablest and wisest, though not the most eloquent, of the Young Ireland party well-nigh half a century since. He was persecuted as a rebel and a "Separatist." but remains a great champion of federal unity. He knows Australia, where, though with different leanings. he filled the post of Premier, which Mr. Gillies now holds, and repeatedly presided over conferences convened for a like purpose with that now met at Melbourne. They did much to ripen opinion on the subject. Sir Charles thinks Sir Henry Parkes has borne too prominent a part in intercolonial disputes to succeed in piloting the measure through; but as to its reasonableness and value he has no misgiving. There may be a touch of ancient jealousy in the remark that Sir Henry is as ill-fitted for such a task as Mr. Chamberlain to arbitrate on differences betwixt Home Rulers, or Mr. Spurgeon to compose the controversies betwixt Ritualists and Evangelicals in the Anglican Church. There is sense, however, in his suggestion, that two men such as Lords Roseberry and Carnarvon, provided with a resolution

Glasgow Mail—*continued.*

of Parliament that federation is of high importance to the Empire, should be sent out to advise and mediate. The result, he thinks, would be a speedy and signal success, linking together in bonds without bondage six States with wider territories, a better climate, more natural wealth than half-a-dozen great kingdoms in Europe. Never, he declares, since human history began has so noble an opportunity been treated with more ignorant and perilous insensibility. Contrariwise he affirms that "Westminister has been illuminated, a *Te Deum* sung in St. Paul's, statues and columns erected all over the country to commemorate events of less importance to the United Kingdom than the easy victory of gathering under one Government the colonies of the Pacific." To like purpose, though more sedately, writes Sir Charles Dilke in that very able and painstaking book, "Problems of Greater Britain," in solid and durable worth the most important contribution ever made to literature dealing with our colonies. Surely Australian Federation will be an event of the near future, the beginning of a new and increasingly prosperous epoch. Related questions, if not settled before, will then take the form of Cobden's question, What next? and next? and that question will have to be answered despite Lord Salisbury's alarmist prophecy that seriously to consider it would be to throw "the Constitution into the melting pot." Has it not been there before, and come out vastly improved?

Manchester Courier—

February 7th, 1890.

THE Conference which met yesterday in Melbourne, to discuss the proposed federation of Australia, is an event of more than ordinary importance. It is to be hoped that the union of the various colonies will be the result, and that the Dominion of Australia will thus spring into existence. As Sir Gavan Duffy has pointed out in his article in this month's *Contemporary*, the matter has been under discussion at intervals for about thirty years. In the first place the Home Government, strange to say, were not in sympathy with the movement, and, later on, the jealousies of the colonies and of their leaders, have formed the obstacles in the way. That the present condition of things has outgrown its usefulness, in many respects, has been apparent for several years, and there is no doubt that this feeling led to the formation of the Federal Council in 1885. This body

Manchester Courier—*continued.*

received the adhesion of all the colonies one after another, excepting New South Wales, but, having no executive power, little or nothing has resulted from its organization, and it has only been regarded as a step in the direction of that complete federation which should be a union for the general good of the community, in every sense of the word. Sir Henry Parkes has certainly given the movement its present impetus, but it must not be forgotten that the same gentleman has, up to his period of federal activity, been the great difficulty in the way. The wonder is that the practical common sense of the Australians has not pressed the matter to a conclusion before, and the only explanation is the inter-colonial jealousy already alluded to. There are not so many obstacles to overcome as was the case with Canada, for the colonies are more or less connected with railways, and there is no race difficulty. The settlement of the question seems, therefore, to be one of detail rather than of principle. The tariff is not likely to give rise to much discussion. New South Wales is the only Free-trade colony, and Sir Henry Parkes has already said that he will not let this stand in the way, as all the other colonies are more or less Protectionist. In any case, federation will lead to the abolition of the intercolonial Customs tariffs, and will give Free-trade over all the continent of Australia, although there will in all probability be a tariff against all outside countries, including Great Britain. It will be curious to see if any proposal is made to place the mother country in a preferential position in this respect. Many people maintain, and there is some force in the contention, that any such arrangement would be a matter of purely domestic policy, and would not be contrary to the spirit of any of our commercial treaties. As to the colonial debts, they would no doubt be assumed by the new Government, who in the future would arrange all the borrowings for federal purposes, the liabilities for principal and interest becoming a first charge upon the revenue of the country. It is the case that some of the colonies have borrowed more heavily than others, and a limit would therefore have to be fixed, as was done in Canada, to represent the debt allowed to each, the federal authorities paying interest on any balances that might remain to the credit of the provinces, and the provinces paying to the Federal Treasury interest on any debit balance in excess of the fixed limit. In all probability the railways would remain in the hands of the provinces for the present, the revenues being paid to the Dominion Treasury, or they

Manchester Courier—*continued.*

might be transferred to the new authority, as representing the principal asset against the liabilities of the country. No doubt it would be possible to arrange for the lines to be placed on the same gauge, in order that the usefulness of the through line from Adelaide to Brisbane might in this way be increased. The defences of the Colonies would be a matter for the "Dominion," and its policy in that and many other subjects would no doubt be discussed in the new Parliament. To fix the composition of the new and of the provincial legislatures, to define their respective powers, and to fix upon a new capital may cause considerable discussion, as also the question of the amount of subsidy to be allowed to each of the provinces towards their expenses out of the general revenue; but if the delegates meet with a sincere desire to arrive at a solution of the question, the settlement of these details should not be difficult. That great advantages would follow the federation of Australia is generally admitted. It would enable the united colony to speak with one voice on any questions that affected its interests; and, among other things, would lead to the development of its trade and commerce, and of the immense area of land, and the manifold resources, to be found in the different colonies. But more than all this, it would be another step in the direction of the closer union of the different parts of the empire. With a federated Canada, and a federated Australia, South Africa might not be long in following suit, and such a state of things would be a practical step in the direction of what is known as Imperial Federation. Let us hope that the delegates of the different colonies will meet each other in this Conference with the full determination to settle a basis on which the federation may be organized. Local jealousies must be dropped for the good of the country and the Empire, and there must be a readiness shown on all sides to adapt the condition of things to the situation, and not to insist upon a too rigid maintenance of existing rights and powers. It will express the feeling of the country if the Queen's Speech contains some reference to the interest with which the mother country is watching the efforts of her sons in the East, to weld into one strong band of union that important group of colonies which their energy, industry, and enterprise have brought to its present state of vigour. The cry of "United we Stand" will be received with much gratification in every part of the Empire; and "Advance Australia" will then have a significance it has never possessed before.

Daily Chronicle—
February 7th, 1890.

YESTERDAY the Australian Federation Conference met for business. They appointed a chairman, and "greatly daring dined." At the banquet they drank the toast of "United Australasia" with wild enthusiasm—and that, too, though it was seconded by Sir Henry Parkes. Sir Henry has been all his life a promoter of the federal idea; but it is not generally known in this country that he is not liked by the other colonies because he has arrogated for New South Wales, in so far as he was able, a position of imperious dominance over the younger settlements, and most of all because he recently introduced a measure to change the name of New South Wales to "Australia." It was this imprudent proposal that has done much to intensify the ill-feeling that exists between Sydney and Melbourne. However, they seem at last to be able to unite in furthering a policy of federation—an idea that would have been carried many years ago but for the obstruction and hostility of Lord John Russell. It is easy to see why common action cannot be taken on the basis of intercolonial federation. The Conservative or "National" party in Australia detest the idea of Imperial Federation, for they think it is in some way or other connected through Lord Rosebery with the intrigues of the Irish Home Rulers. The Australian Conservatives are also for the most part Separatists, and think that federation will lead to a declaration of independence whenever England is involved in war. The Australian Liberals who have the Irish Home Rulers attached to them now pretty well monopolize the idea of Imperial Federation. But they too can work with the Conservative democracy in getting intercolonial federation, because they also imagine it will bring about closer union with England, and therefore a more copious shower of titles and decorations on their politicians and millionaires. Australian politics form a most interesting study just now.

St. James' Gazette—
February 8th, 1890.

IN a burst of noble eloquence, Sir Henry Parkes has been describing at Melbourne the vision of his mind's eye—the Australian Nation of a near future, four millions of people,

St. James' Gazette—*continued.*

all of British origin, united to the soil by ties of birth, parentage, friendship, and love ; the rapid disappearance of all local jealousies ; each of the colonies hastening to merge its separate entity in the greater unity of an Australian dominion. In common justice to Sir Henry Parkes we must commend him for the great renunciation which he is prepared to make in the cause of a United Australia. It is pretty certain, when a Federal Capital has been selected and a Federal Premier is appointed, that the Capital will not be Sydney, and the Premier will not be Sir Henry Parkes, although he *is* called by his admirers the Grand Old Man of Australia.

Pall Mall Gazette—
February 8th, 1890.

"THE question of a common tariff," said Sir Henry Parkes at the "Federation Banquet" at Melbourne, on Thursday, "is a mere trifle as compared with the question of national existence." This may or may not be an important statement, according as Sir Henry meant it. If it was a mere pious opinion about what ought to be, it was worth no more than the expression of any other lofty sentiment. But if the Premier of New South Wales meant it to give the key-note of his own future policy, then it was a very important pronouncement. For it would mean that he was prepared to compromise on the question of Free-trade, by agreeing with the other colonies on a common tariff as against the extra-Australasian world.

There was one phrase in the same speech which is likely to become classical. "It was a wise dispensation," he said, "that each colony should have worked out its own salvation separately ;" but, he added, the time for union had now come :—

> The crimson thread of kinship ran through all.

The "crimson thread" of Sir Henry Parkes will be as often quoted as the "silver streak" of Mr. Gladstone.

The Economist—

February 8th, 1890.

It has been said that finance lies at the root of all political questions, a proposition which is aptly illustrated whenever Australasian political questions come to the front. The Australasian Federation Conference which assembled in Melbourne on Thursday is a case in point. Ever since 1886 there has existed a Federal Council of Australasia, which has been in session thrice at Hobart, in Tasmania, and has done nothing, mainly because it has possessed no power to levy taxes, or to vote moneys, and has not the wherewithal to enforce its decrees. New South Wales and New Zealand have held aloof from that Council Chamber because it was a powerless body, subject to the dictation of the various Australian Ministries, and not rising superior to local influences; and this Council has consequently become, for all practical purposes, a dead letter. Now, Sir Henry Parkes, that dictatorial veteran of innumerable New South Wales Ministries, has suddenly told his fellow-colonists that the time is ripe for, not a sham, but a real federation, and he, in the face of the somewhat cold reception his proposals at first met with in Victoria, has been enabled to assemble the seven colonies together for the discussion of a question which, while it is of chief interest to the colonists themselves, is, nevertheless, one we cannot regard as other than of moment to the Empire at large. From the standpoint of this country there can be no doubt that an equitable arrangement for federating Australia, or Australasia, will be as warmly assisted and endorsed as was the establishment of the Dominion of Canada over twenty years ago; and it will be so assisted from this side, even though it is quite possible British commerce may as a result be subjected to more searching imposts than it is subjected to at present in Australasian ports. We think it right to point out that the British manufacturer undoubtedly has little to gain, and something to lose, by a Dominion of Australasia. At present, some of the colonies—Victoria and New Zealand standing first amongst the number—are very strongly "protected," while New South Wales justly boasts of her Free-trade policy and her readiness to buy in the cheapest market. But the fact remains that the colonies are divided against themselves, and give no special trading facilities to one another. If, however, they become united, they will at once grow from a number of small communities into one big one, and this will give increased facilities for internal

The Economist—*continued.*

manufacture on cheap terms, and increased powers of consumption for such Australian-made goods. If the colonies were to adopt the Free-trade views of New South Wales—and we trust they may do so—these increased powers would be counterbalanced by the tariff inducements afforded to our manufacturers to ship to Australasian markets; but we cannot disguise from ourselves the possibility that in a country where the working-man's vote is paramount a considerable measure of protection may be the policy of an Australasian Dominion, and this would not be to the advantage of our home manufacturers. It was so in the case of the Canadian Dominion, where federation has acted to the disadvantage of British commerce. Whatever good offices, then, the mother-country may render in assisting in the establishment of a united Australasia must certainly be regarded as disinterested.

But from an Australasian standpoint there is much to be gained by unity. The difference between a series of disjointed, jealous, and oftentimes antagonistic colonies and a united whole is as the difference between a number of disconnected bodies of men, and the same under proper training and control as a disciplined army. Few can have failed to observe how frequently these colonies, both in Australasia and through their representatives here, have been found pulling in different directions, and that not in regard to comparatively small questions only. Larger ones, like our dominion over the Pacific Islands, have been dealt with in similar fashion, and to one colony can generally be set the task of answering another. Such being the political condition of these colonies, Major-General Edwards was appointed, on the application of certain of their number, to proceed from Hong Kong to Australia, Tasmania, and New Zealand, and there to report upon the condition of their defences and military organization. Sir Henry Parkes at first did not fully see the force of General Edwards' visit; but before it was over he modified his views considerably. The report of General Edwards lies before us, and from out a large number of questions discussed therein we extract the following:—

Before the completion of the railways which unite Adelaide, Melbourne, Sydney, and Brisbane, it was impossible for the colonies to co-operate for defence; and this is not even now possible, on account of their different organizations, and because the colonies cannot employ their forces outside their own borders.

Combined action for defence would be more economical and far more effective than the present system of purely local defence. Suppose,

The Economist—*continued.*

for instance, an enemy captured Newcastle in New South Wales, the joint action of the colonies would at once supply a powerful force to retake it. The fact that 30,000 or 40,000 men could be rapidly concentrated to oppose an attack upon any of the chief cities would deter an enemy from attempting such an enterprise; and this can be accomplished by means of a common system of organization, and without materially increasing the present state of the forces. It would also prevent the unseemly scares which take place whenever the relations of the mother-country with a foreign Power are somewhat strained; the mere fracture of the cable between Darwin and Batavia, which recently took place, was sufficient to cause uneasiness throughout all the colonies, and in Victoria preparations were actually made to resist an attack.

My proposals, briefly summarized, are as follows:—

1. Federation of the forces.
2. An officer of the rank of Lieutenant-General to be appointed, to advise and inspect in peace, and command in war.
3. A uniform system of organization and armament, and a common Defence Act.
4. Amalgamation of the Permanent Forces into a "Fortress Corps."
5. A Federal Military College for the education of the officers.
6. The extension of the Rifle Clubs.
7. A uniform gauge for the railways.
8. A federal Small-arm Manufactory, Gun Wharf, and Ordnance Store.

If the Australian Colonies had to rely at any time solely on their own resources they would offer such a rich and tempting prize that they would certainly be called upon to fight for their independence and isolated as Australia would be, without a proper supply of arms and ammunition—with forces which cannot at present be considered efficient in comparison with any moderately-trained army, and without any cohesion or power of combination for mutual defence among th. different colonies—its position would be one of great danger. Looking to the state of affairs in Europe, and to the fact that it is the unforeseen which happens in war, the defence forces should at once be placed on a proper footing; but this is, however, quite impossible without a federation of the forces of the different colonies.

Immediately after the issue of this weighty report, Sir Henry Parkes sounded the Queensland Ministry upon the question of defence, and returning to New South Wales, he, early in October, addressed a formal communication to the Premiers of the other colonies, suggesting a Conference to consider General Edwards' report, and the consequences to which it would give rise. He said that it would be impossible to organize and mobilize their respective forces, except under a system of Federal Government. That was the first step. His proposals provided for the appointment of a Governor-General, a Privy Council, a Federal Court of Appeal, and a

The Economist—*continued.*

Federal Parliament, consisting of a Senate and House of Commons, thus closely following the Canadian precedent. At first there was hesitation, and the Victorian premier did not think that the time was ripe for the complete federation which Sir Henry Parkes advocated. Queensland, however, gave the scheme less cold water; and it is worthy of remark that all the Governors went out of their way warmly to advocate the cause of federation. The result is, the Conference which assembled this week at Melbourne. What are its prospects? It will have before it a most weighty document—General Edwards' report—and the support of a large number of enlightened Australians in favour of federation. But to arrange for the establishment of a Dominion of Australia (New Zealand, it appears, will not, under any circumstances, join yet awhile) will be a very difficult task. We do not know whether Sir Henry Parkes is right in saying that the forces of the different colonies could not be mobilized without federation. It is said that Victoria will make counter-proposals to the effect that the naval and military forces of Australia shall be federated under a supreme command, while fiscally the colonies shall maintain their present independence. But this would be a troublesome and partial arrangement, and to establish the railways upon a common gauge by such means would be practically impossible. To adopt the 4 ft. 8½ in. gauge of New South Wales would involve all the other colonies in millions of expenditure; to adopt the Victorian 5 ft. 6 in. gauge would be yet more costly; to adopt the Queensland metre gauge is not to be thought of. To act upon General Edwards' suggestion in this point alone has been estimated to involve the outlay of £10,000,000 or more, and this could only be provided at federal expense. But riverine navigation and water conservation are likewise subjects calling loudly for federal control. The great stumbling-blocks in the way of this federation undoubtedly appear to be the tariffs and the debt. Probably it would be possible to defer the question of amalgamating the debts of the different colonies for a time, though it would have to come; but to effectively federate while retaining the present hostile tariffs would be simply impossible. Australian statesmen have not hitherto shown themselves sufficiently accommodating towards each others interests to render the prospects of the Conference at all promising. But for their own good, for their own strength and future development, this country will watch the progress of the discussions with great interest. We cannot, more-

The Economist—*continued.*

over, forget that there is nearly as much British as there is Australian capital embarked in those colonies, and everything which tends to enhance the value of Australasian investments and increase the stablity of that great and growing offshoot of the Empire is a direct concern of ours.

Daily News—
February 8th, 1890.

THE proceedings at the Melbourne banquet in honor of Australasian Federation were marked by the enthusiasm which is the most essential element of the success of the movement. Only sentiment can give the colonists an impulse to union, though a sense of interest will, of course, tend to make the union binding. The speech of Sir Henry Parkes, which we report to-day, will sufficiently explain the nature of the step which the colonists contemplate. They form at present a number of Governments perfectly independent of each other, though they are united under the British Crown. The proposal now is to keep this tie of loyalty as strong as ever, but to unite the colonies one with the other by a common tariff, a common scheme of defence, and other arrangements of the same nature. Strictly speaking, the colonists are bound to none of these proposals in advance. They are simply in conference as to the possibility of union, and these methods are before them as suggestions. But as there can be no effective unity with hostile tariffs and seperate fleets and land forces, a rejection of these propositions would involve the defeat of the whole scheme. There seems little likelihood of this, and it is hardly to be doubted that, whether Australasians federate or no with the Empire, they will federate among themselves. That will be a great step gained, for at any rate it makes a nation. Now or never is the time for the attempt ; in another quarter of a century of such astonishing prosperity as Australasia has hitherto enjoyed the growth of vested interests might keep these great communities apart for ever, and make one of the most magnificent conceptions of Empire which the world has yet known no better than as a dream.

Liverpool Mercury—

February 8th, 1890

AUSTRALIAN federation is now in a fair way of realization. Difficulties that rise up when a great problem is first considered are only there for statesmen to overcome. For this we have the word of Mr. Gladstone, who has contrived more solutions than any other public man. The Intercolonial Conference opened at Melbourne on Thursday. It was not continued on Friday, in consequence of the indisposition of Sir Henry Parkes, Premier of New South Wales, but will be resumed on Monday. As we pointed out a fortnight ago, in anticipation of this auspicious gathering in the capital of Victoria, the goodwill of New South Wales is of good omen. This Colony, as represented by its older statesmen, was formerly opposed to the idea of federation, and now that it has come in to line with the rest the principal obstacle is removed. We must not assume, however, that the path to federation is perfectly clear even yet. At a banquet which took place on Thursday night, the Hon. James Service said the chief question was a uniformity of tariffs. One of the inevitable consequences of the system which has hitherto prevailed is that each Colony, looking solely to its own particular interests, has had a distinct tariff. The protectionist spirit, if once in the ascendant, leads to these curious developments. The very best thing the Colonies could have done was to throw their ports open to all the world; but they imagined that imposts upon goods received would nourish their native industries, and hence each section of territory constructed its tariff with a single regard to its individual conditions. Not content with fighting the other continents, they became impressed with the necessity of fighting each other as well. Therefore the Hon. James Service was well advised when he referred to the tariff question as having a direct bearing on the aims of the Conference. He said there could be no national unity as long as one Colony levied hostile duties against the other. Nothing of the kind is done in Canada. When taunted with encouraging protection, the citizens of the United States make the retort that theirs is the only absolutely free-trade country in the world, inasmuch as the exchange between about forty different States, each supreme in its own affairs, is free from every description of duty. Federation implies a uniformity of system in this respect at least. If the Australians admit the advisableness of joining together and building up a nation out of a group of independent

Liverpool Mercury—*continued.*

Colonies, they must make up their minds to revise their fiscal arrangements, as these affect each of the parties to the proposed compact. For the sake of Australian integrity it is desirable that a union should be brought about, as in Canada. These young countries need to coalesce their strength in these days of enormous armaments, and they can only do so efficiently by first concluding a treaty which will practically mould them into one. This movement, as Sir H. Parkes observed, is not in any sense inimical to the Imperial link. As children grow they should learn how to take care of themselves, without for a moment contemplating a repudiation of the control of the parent. Indeed the Imperial tie presses so lightly upon Australia and Canada that there is no motive for shaking it off. Sir Henry Parkes knows this very well, and would rather maintain a connection which, while costing nothing, is a guarantee of potent protection. Australasians and Canadians, with all their vigour, represent small nations in the calculations of statesmen, and neither, left to their own resources, could successfully resist a power of the first class. But beneath the broad shield of Britain they pursue their avocations in security, and are not called upon to make a larger sacrifice than is involved in assisting in their own defence. We thoroughly agree with Sir Henry Parkes that they would be unworthy to occupy their beauteous land if they were incapable of welding their separated fragments into a nation. Sir C. Gavan Duffy describes the Premier of New South Wales as "a poet who has visions of a great empire planted on the coasts of the Pacific." This does not appear to be the general opinion of Australians. Sir Gavan Duffy himself is a poet of more distinction than Sir Henry Parkes, and yet he has done admirable service as a working statesman beneath the Southern Cross. He writes upon Australian Federation from the statesman's point of view, and with an authority that no one will gainsay. His demand is that the mother-country should intervene in this matter. That will be time enough when the representatives of the colonies have failed, which does not now appear probable. We are bound to recognize the difficulties that have to be surmounted, but we are willing to believe that Australian public life has produced sufficient ability for the work. Let us see the end of this Conference before we venture upon the conclusion that Sir C. Gavan Duffy understands the situation more clearly than those who are in the midst of it.

u

Leeds Mercury—

February 8th, 1890.

The Conference now sitting at Melbourne for the consideration of the subject of Australasian federation and federal defence, seems to have opened its work under very favourable auspices. This morning we publish a telegraphic summary of the principal speeches delivered at the banquet given on Thursday evening by Mr. Gillies, Premier of Victoria, to the Governor of that colony and the delegates to the Australasian Conference. The toast of "A United Australia" was proposed by Mr. Service, a former Premier of Victoria, and replied to by Sir Henry Parkes, Premier of New South Wales, who, as all our readers are aware, has been prominently instrumental in bringing the question to its present position. This fact was recognized by the reception accorded to Sir Henry on Thursday evening, when the whole company rose from their seats and cheered him enthusiastically. It is pointed out in an interesting article in the current number of the *Contemporary Review* by Sir Charles Gavan Duffy that more than thirty years ago Sir Henry Parkes was favourable to action in the direction of federation among the Australian colonies, although his own colony, New South Wales, defeated the project of holding a Conference at that time to consider the subject. Down to last year New South Wales remained the obstacle in the way of the development of closer relations among the Australasian colonies, and refused to take part in the Federal Council which was appointed under an Act passed in 1885 by the Imperial Parliament, with a view to giving the colonies opportunities for joint action with respect to the prevention of the influx of criminals, patent laws, copyright, mutual recognition of marriage laws, and also general defences. As our readers are aware, Sir Henry Parkes, as explained in recent despatches to the Premier of Victoria, has regarded the constitution of the Federal Council as essentially inadequate for promoting the realization of effective unity among the Australasian colonies. But he has advocated, and at last with, as we may presume, the main body of public opinion in New South Wales behind him, the adoption of measures which would make Intercolonial Federation in Australasia a reality. There is little doubt that he will urge in the present Conference the organization of an Australian unity something after the fashion of the Canadian Dominion, with a Federal Legislature and a Federal Executive. We sincerely hope that

Leeds Mercury—*continued.*

some such scheme will be realized. It need not be disguised that some of the sentiment in support of it in some of the Australian colonies is associated at present with a coolness towards the mother-country and a concentration of aspiration upon the future grandeur of Australia. But if we may judge from what has happened in Canada, the consolidation of the Australasian colonies into one great dominion will be likely to tend not to the quickening of Separatist feeling but to the development of an increased sense of the dignity of Imperial citizenship and of the material advantages of the Imperial connection. In his speech on Thursday night Sir Henry Parkes spoke warmly in deprecation of the idea that the Australians, in the movement, at the head of which he has placed himself, are seeking for any separation from the British Empire. He urged also, as we are glad to see, that tariff questions, specially difficult as they are of arrangement among the Australian colonies, should not be allowed to interfere with the realization of a project aiming at national unity and national security, and he stated that "New South Wales was prepared to go into this National union without making any bargain and without stipulating for any advantage whatever, but waiting on the good faith and justice of a Federal Parliament." If the Australasian Conference is prosecuted in the spirit of these declarations its success is assured, and will be heartily welcomed by every Englishman. And in our belief the intercolonial union which it bids fair to bring about will be eminently conducive to the advancement of the still greater cause of the effective consolidation of the Empire as a whole.

Birmingham Post—

February 8th, 1890.

The Conference which is now being held at Melbourne will, there can be little doubt, form another step towards Australian, or even to Australasian, Federation. New South Wales and New Zealand, which have held aloof from the Federal Council, are both taking part in the new movement in favour of a closer and more effective union of the various colonies. Indeed, it is due to the initiation of Sir Henry Parkes that the present form of agitation has been adopted, and the speech which he delivered last night at Melbourne

Birmingham Post—*continued.*

affords ample evidence of the enthusiasm with which he now supports the project. When the proposals for the holding of such a conference were propounded, Mr. Gillies, who is the Prime Minister of the colony of Victoria, argued strongly in favour of referring the discussion in the first instance to the Federal Council, and it is not easy to understand why this course was not adopted. For the Council is the result of the deliberations of the Australians themselves. It is a constitutionally-formed body, with not only deliberative but legislative functions. These powers did not, of course, amount to effective federation, but they formed a starting-point from which it might have been thought that a further departure might have been taken. It would surely have been a wise economy of force to have accepted the progress which had already been made, and to have completed a structure actually commenced. However, agreement about processes is not to stand in the way of combined action, and Mr. Gillies has so far given way with regard to making use of the Federal Council that he has taken the chair at the conference which is to go into the whole question of an Australasian Federation. On the part of New South Wales a still more important concession will have to be made, or, indeed, has already been accomplished. The great reason which has hitherto prevented the premier Colony from active union with her neighbours has been the fact that she alone has adopted a free-trade policy, all the other colonies being more or less protectionist. Now, no federation could be really effective which did not involve the power of raising joint funds for federal purposes either from Customs or excise duties. But if neighbouring colonies do not agree on the main question of free-trade or protection no such common action would be possible, since not only what may be called foreign, but intercolonial commerce would be adopted. It is now said that New South Wales is prepared to abandon her free-trade policy as the price of securing such a complete federation as her Premier and her legislature alike seem to desire. Sir Henry Parkes, indeed, last night announced that New South Wales was prepared to enter the Union absolutely without any preliminary stipulation. The case with regard to New Zealand is quite as remarkable. She has all along declined to send representatives to the Federal Council, and seemed to have some sound reasons for her refusal. The distance alone which separates her from Australia will always place difficulties in the way, and it is probable that with regard to the matter of defence the same

Birmingham Post—*continued.*

circumstance will constitute a serious obstacle to joint action. As respects the objects for which these concessions are being made, and towards which these efforts are being directed, it may be useful to see what are those provisions of the Federal Councils Act which are now held to be inadequate. The Act was passed in 1885, and its preamble declares that "it is expedient to constitute a Federal Council of Australasia for the purpose of dealing with such matters of common Australasian interest in respect of which united action is desirable as can be dealt with without interfering with the management of the internal affairs of the several colonies by their respective legislatures." In the first place it has to be noticed that it is optional with any colony whether or not it will send representatives to the Federal Council. This permissive character destroys its effective operation, for two of the most important of the Colonies have, as we have seen, hitherto declined to send representatives. There are some few subjects on which the Council has the power of original and independent legislation. Of these the chief are the prevention of the influx of criminals, the fisheries in Australasian waters, the enforcement of the law by service of process beyond the Colony in which it issues, and as to extradition. These things are interesting, but they are by no means in the first rank of political importance. On the subjects which do take that position the power of the Council is of a purely permissive and very limited character. Nearly all the legislation which can be described as of a national as apart from a purely local kind is withheld from the initial or imperative action of the Council. With regard to general defence, quarantine, patents of invention and discovery, copyright, bills of exchange and promissory-notes, uniformity of weights and measures, recognition in other colonies of marriage or divorce, naturalization of aliens, intercolonial status of corporation and joint-stock companies, the Council can only act when the special matter is referred to it by the Legislatures of two or more colonies, and its legislation can only affect the particular colonies by whom it has been invited, or such others as may afterwards choose to adopt it. Whilst one or more colonies stood apart from the Council anything worthy of the name of federation was under these conditions impossible. The question whether such a constitution was to be regarded as efficient and final was scarcely arguable, but it might nevertheless have been taken as a beginning from which further progress could conveniently be made. In

Birmingham Post—*continued.*

looking over the list of subjects on which the action of the Federal Council is permissive and restricted it will be seen that many of them are such as can never be properly dealt with from a common centre unless the status of independent colonies is merged in that of members of a federation. It is only a national Parliament and a national Executive that could obtain or exercise absolute authority with regard to them. Of this character is the subject of national defence, which has received by far the greatest amount of attention, or at least of discussion, from the advocates of federation. A scheme for military federation has been discussed, and it is only natural that the colonists should be anxious to provide for the absolute security of their country from attack, and that by means of forces which shall not be subject to removal, and shall be clear of the very possibility of use for political purposes. Here, again, it does not seem possible for separate and independent colonies to organize and control proper military forces. Not less prohibitive of joint action by several States is the question of the regulation of commercial policy either between the colonies or with other nations. And this refers not only to the flow of trade itself, but it affects the means of internal communication. The construction and the maintenance of intercolonial railways must to a great extent depend upon the existence of tariffs and the methods of their administration. We should in this country, of course, regard with regret the abandonment of the principle of free-trade by New South Wales, whose experience has hitherto formed a vindication of its wisdom. Yet it is certain that between a free-trade and a protection colony there could be no such close union as is involved in full and complete federation. That those colonies which now adopt protection will alter their policy is too good a thing even to hope for. In this matter England can exercise little if any power. She might, it is true, refuse to permit the constitutional federation which is now being discussed. Such a thing is conceivable, but not practically attainable; but to put limitations as to trade upon the federation when formed would be absolutely impossible. From an English point of view, therefore, no opposition to the course now being advocated is to be expected. The Australasian Colonies accompany all their arguments in favour of federation by declarations of affection for the mother-country and loyalty to the Crown. There is no reason to doubt the sincerity of these sentiments. For the present, at east, the protection of England is necessary for the colonies.

Birmingham Post—*continued*.

If the time should arrive when this necessity ceases, there will be no desire to force it upon an unwilling people. It has been shown by the Constitution of the Canadian Federation—the union into a compact and powerful State of colonies which alone were comparatively feeble—that there is no jealousy here of the growth of colonial power and independence. The same thing was manifested by the passing of that very Federal Council Act which is now found to be insufficient. It has been declared by those colonies which have refused to enter the Council that the Act was hastily passed, without full consideration of the subject with which it dealt. This, however, must be admitted, that the movement for its adoption was initiated in Australia, and that the Colonial Office here thought it was acting in accordance with colonial wishes when it was brought forward. Whether or not a scheme of federation so extensive as that proposed will turn out to be workable, some writers—amongst them Sir Charles Dilke, who has thoroughly studied the question—think that New Zealand will not ultimately accept a position which will be looked upon by some of her people as one of partial dependence upon Australia. Others think that in Australia itself local jealousies may impede the adoption of a complete scheme. These, however, are matters which the Australasians must settle for themselves. On our part we have only to welcome any proposals which can be proved to promise increased prosperity to the country and contentment to its people.

Birmingham Gazette

February 8th, 1890.

Australasian questions bid fair to attract a considerable amount of attention this year. A Conference is now in progress at Victoria on the question of federation for purposes of defence, and upon the decision which it arrives at a great deal depends. Since General Edwards reported to the Home Government on the necessity of some more efficient system, it has become evident that the matter could not for any length of time be neglected. At present the Australasian Colonies are practically defenceless. They have a naval force which the Imperial Government are about to augment into a powerful and permanent squadron. They have small land forces in the several colonies, but there is

Birmingham Gazette—*continued.*

no facility for concentrating these at any given point in the event of danger. But for their common speech the several colonies—Queensland, Victoria, New South Wales, and South Australia—are as separate and distinct as any similar number of nations on the Continent of Europe. General Edwards recommended the formation of a Supreme Federal Council which should have the control of the whole of the defensive forces of Australasia. Difficulties have been found in acting upon this suggestion, and the Conference has met at Melbourne for the purpose of overcoming them. That it will do so we have full confidence, for where there's a will there's a way, and the colonists cannot be lacking in willingness to protect themselves from all outside danger. It may be said that Australia runs little risk of interference, but that is not at all certain. If England were engaged in a war with any of the great European Powers, our navy would be required for the defence of our own shores and the protection of our commerce. It is not at all improbable that the enemy might determine to deliver a blow at some of the far distant and unprotected outworks of our Empire. It is the duty of the Australians to prepare for such a danger. We guarantee them against the wanton attacks to which they might be subjected from jealous Powers if they were wholly independent, and in return they must prepare to look after their own defence when the Imperial forces are engaged nearer home. Closely associated with this question is one which will come under the attention of Parliament early in the session. The Western Australians number 45,000, and they wish to be made the responsible governors of a territory 1,060,000 square miles in extent. On the face of it the demand seems preposterous. A population so small that if it were confined to an English borough it would not entitle it to rank as an urban county asks for governing power over an area about nine times as great as that of Great Britain and Ireland combined. The question has been asked whether it is wise for the Imperial Government to give up its direct control over such tracts of country, and that will no doubt form the basis of discussion in the House of Commons. The *pros* and *cons* are pretty evenly divided. The Western Australians point out that much of this territory is mere barren waste land, which for want of irrigation is not at all likely to develop a population in the future. They point out also that thirty years ago Queensland, with its area of 668,224 square miles, was handed over to a population of 27,000 people, which has

Birmingham Gazette—*continued.*

now grown to about 320,000. Would Responsible Government give a like impetus to Western Australia? If it did, of course, the present demand would be in a measure justified. Yet there are, it seems to us, many points of view from which the matter should be considered. We do not yet see the end of State efforts to relieve the pressure of population in Great Britain, but clearly if at any future time it were resolved to attempt a bold scheme of State-aided emigration it would be an enormous advantage for the Imperial Government to have tracts of country under its undisputed authority upon which settlements could be founded. It may be said that the land difficulty could never arise while we have 3,520,000 square miles of territory in America with a population of less than six millions. But the colonies which have been granted "Home Rule" do not show all the anxiety they might do to encourage emigrants of the class who would be assisted under any State scheme. The Trade Unions of Australia send delegates to this country to spread gloomy accounts amongst English working-men as to the position of artisans in the colonies, so as to discourage emigration, and to bolster up their own monopolies. If the Imperial Government were attempting any relief of population it might find such influences as these brought to bear upon the Colonial Legislatures, and creating obstacles of a formidable character. That is only one view to take, and other arguments might be used. There would be very little harm in advising the Western Australians to wait for a time, or, if they must have a Government, at any rate it should be confined to a less ambitious area. We have every possible desire to see the colonies prospering, but they should be used so as to give the very best possible assistance to the mother-country in all things, and we cannot now be so prodigal in alienating Crown territories as it was safe to be half a century ago.

Glasgow Mail—

February 8th, 1890.

Sir Henry Parkes, the New South Wales Premier, is indisposed to-day. The second sitting of the Australasian Conference has, therefore, been adjourned until Monday next. At the banquet given last night by the Hon. Duncan Gillies to Lord Hopetoun and the delegates to the Australasian Con-

Glasgow Mail—*continued.*

ference, the Hon. James Service, in proposing the toast of "A United Australia," upheld the work done by the Federal Convention of 1883, at which the constitution of the Federal Council was drafted. He contended that the Council was prevented from being successful owing to the abstention of New South Wales. Now, however, all the colonies were inclined to enter into union. He did not wish to magnify the difficulties in the way, but the chief obstacle was the question of a uniform tariff, as no national unity was possible with hostile tariffs. If found impossible at the present time to arrive at the final goal of their wish for a complete union, the question should be discussed carefully and thoroughly whether some other course could not be adopted to bring the colonies into perfect harmony with each other. Sir Henry Parkes, in rising to respond, received a splendid ovation, the whole company rising from their seats. The New South Wales Premier commenced by eulogising Mr. Service's speech, which he described as being worthy of their country and of their cause The creation of national unity was an event which could never recur. There were four millions of people, all of British origin, united to the soil by ties of birth, parentage, friendship, and love. If they were incapable of making a nation they were hardly fit to occupy their bounteous country. It was a wise dispensation that the colonies of Victoria and Queensland should spring into existence and work out their own prosperity independently of New South Wales, but the time had arrived when they were no longer isolated. The crimson thread of kinship ran through all. Was there a man living in Australia who said that it would be an advantage to remain separated? No sane man would say so. If this was admitted, then it followed that at some time or other they must unite as one great Australasian people. No advantage could arise from delay, and the difficulties would be greater as the years went on. If this reasoning was correct, continued Sir Henry, the colonies had now arrived at the hour when they were fully justified by all the laws regulating the growth of free communities in uniting under one Government and one flag. This implied no separation from the Empire, nor the creation of a separate political organization. All free communities, he said, must have a political head. And what head could be more attractive, more ennobling, or more consonant with the true principles of liberty than the sovereign, who, during her beneficent reign, had seen more improvements for the amelioration of the human race than ever sovereign saw in

Glasgow Mail—*continued.*

the world's history. It should not go forth for a moment that in seeking complete authority over their own affairs they were seeking any separation from the great Empire. New South Wales was prepared to go into this national union without making any bargain, and without stipulating for any advantage whatever, but waiting in the good faith and justice of a Federal Parliament. Small questions ought not to be considered at the present time, and should not deter them from attaining the great consummation in view. Sir Henry Parkes, in conclusion, said that he believed the people of Australia had already made up their minds to be united, and no hand on earth was strong enough to keep them asunder. The speech throughout was loudly applauded, and Sir Henry Parkes resumed his seat amid prolonged cheers. The company present subsequently sang the National Anthem.

Daily Chronicle—

February 8th, 1890.

In another column we publish a fuller report than we were able to publish yesterday of the speeches which were delivered at the "Federation" banquet in Melbourne by Mr. Service and Sir Henry Parkes respectively. Few speeches, in our opinion, could be more worthy of the careful attention of politicians at Home than those utterances of two of the foremost statesmen of Australasia. Mr. Service is not a member of the Conference, but as a former Premier of Victoria, and the real author of the Federal Council, it was peculiarly fitting that he should be entrusted with the duty of proposing the toast of "A United Australasia." It was equally fitting that Sir Henry Parkes, the "Grand Old Man" of New South Wales, should respond to that toast. The Premier of New South Wales has adopted this policy of federating the British possessions in the South Pacific with an enthusiasm that knows no bounds. It was at his suggestion that the present Conference was summoned, and he is more fortunate than Mr. Service was seven years ago, when only a portion of the Australasian Colonies sent representatives to the Convention. In dealing with this subject two or three weeks ago, we stated that the premier colony of New South Wales "held aloof" from the previous Conference. On the following day our statement

Daily Chronicle—*continued.*

was traversed by a communication emanating from an authoritative source. But from two other sources equally authoritative confirmation of our view has been forthcoming. Sir William Robinson, the late Governor of South Australia, and Governor-Designate of Western Australia, used our actual phraseology when explaining to an interviewer what had occurred in 1883. New South Wales, he said, had then "held aloof." At the banquet given by the Premier of Victoria the other night, Mr. Service naturally referred to the Convention of 1883 when speaking on the subject of "A United Australasia"; and, according to the report which we publish to-day, he upheld the work done by that Convention, but contended that the Federal Council "was prevented from being successful owing to the abstention of New South Wales." Our view is, therefore, sustained, not only by one of the ablest and most experienced of Australasian Governors, but by the author of the Federal Council himself. The author of the communication which represented our former statement to be incorrect does not think that New South Wales "held aloof" from the movement of which Mr. Service was the guiding spirit in 1883; but Sir William Robinson says distinctly that she did, while Mr. Service himself declares in the presence of Sir Henry Parkes that "the Council was prevented from being successful owing to the abstention of New South Wales." We think, therefore, that the public will now consider us justified in having described the premier colony as holding aloof from the positive movement which took place seven years ago. The point is worth explanation as it is historically interesting; but, fortunately, the march of events and the growth of opinion have deprived it of any practical importance.

Mr. Service did not seem to be moved by the same enthusiasm as Sir Henry Parkes, although he is not less devoted to the principle of federation. Indeed Mr. Service not only approves of the federation of the Australasian Colonies, but desires imperial federation as well. But he recognizes the difficulties in the way of even creating an Australasian Dominion, and prudently suggests that if everything cannot be done at once, it will be advisable to go as far as is practicable, leaving the work of completion to be accomplished in the future. He sees, as we pointed out recently, that the chief obstacle to complete federation is the question of a uniform tariff, and he declares that hostile tariffs are incompatible with national unity. We are glad

Daily Chronicle—*continued.*

to find, however, that Sir Henry Parkes was not abashed by this " lion in the path." With characteristic enthusiasm he urged that such "subordinate questions" as fiscal systems should be sunk in face of the ennobling policy which the Conference is intended to promote—a policy which is nothing less than that of creating a nation. The question of a common tariff, says the veteran Premier of New South Wales, is "a mere trifle" as compared with the question of national existence. But he urges, in the true spirit of statesmanship, that the various colonies should be willing and prepared to deal with each other on the basis of compromise. New South Wales, as is well known, favours freetrade, while it is equally well known that Victoria is wedded to protection. Yet Sir Henry Parkes declares that the former is prepared to "go into this national union without making any bargain and without stipulating for any advantage whatever, but trusting in the good faith and justice of a Federal Parliament." If all the colonies do this success may be more completely attained now than Mr. Service is disposed to expect. That, however, is clearly the way in which the great question of federation should be approached. Sir Henry Parkes believes that the people of Australia have resolved to be united, and he also believes that no hand on earth is strong enough to keep them asunder. If they have really formed this resolution they will soon surmount the obstacles involved in those " small questions" which Sir Henry Parkes thrusts aside as unworthy to be considered until the " great consummation" at which he is aiming has been achieved. It is interesting to observe that this strong advocacy of Australasian federation is associated with an almost passionate devotion to the empire and loyalty to the Crown. If our statesmen at home can only be induced to adopt what may be called a reciprocal policy, we shall be confident of preserving the unity of the empire. The policy of unification has, however, more to hope for from colonial than from " imperial" statesmen. With the exception of Lord Rosebery and Lord Carnarvon both of whom are unfortunately out of office at the present time—there is hardly a statesman of the first rank at home who gives encouragement to the magnificent aspirations of the colonies. It is quite time that this policy of negation should be abandoned.

Bradford Observer—

February 10*th*, 1890.

AUSTRALIA a nation. It is safe to say that this phrase embodies the thought just now uppermost in the mind of every man of British blood dwelling under the Southern Cross. It is the great absorbing topic wherever two or three meet together; it represents the highest reach of patriotic effort, and its influence dominates every estimate of colonial sentiment or interest. But six months ago, and to most outside observers, the formula expressed nothing more than a vague aspiration; a definite idea it certainly could not be called; and few, indeed, could have been induced to consider it as offering any near prospect of taking practical shape. Now it is more than any of these. It is a fixed policy. The aspiration has grown to an idea, and the idea to a set project, with a rapidity almost bewildering to men looking on from a distance. What has been the electric spark which has caused the sympathetic elements thus to flash into almost instantaneous fusion it would be puzzling to decide. But there can be no doubt at all as to the hand which applied it. Sir Henry Parkes it is who slashed a way through every difficulty and obstacle, and the representative men who on Thursday gathered round the council board in Melbourne are the living testimony to the fulness of his success.

Even should the Conference break up without carrying the scheme visibly nearer to completion, the greatness of the achievement will not be materially lessened. To have brought together men of the highest political standing from every quarter, not of Australia, but of Australasia, and in their presence formally to enunciate the far-reaching policy of which the words an Australasian Dominion is the terse embodiment, is in itself enough to set the movement forward to a point from which, until Anglo-Saxon human nature changes, it can never go back. To have done so much towards establishing a new power amongst the nations might alone satisfy one man's ambition. But Sir Henry Parkes is not the man to be so satisfied. His genius is of the dogged sort, and having pushed his work so far, he means to see it through. That he will prevail to the end, as he has prevailed from the beginning, seems to admit of little doubt. The difficulties yet to be encountered are small compared to those his energy has already surmounted. In a scheme so vast, in which (*parti pris, amour propre*) conflicting interests and opinions have to be reconciled or subdued, it is the first step

Bradford Observer—*continued.*

which is difficult. Australasian unity has now advanced many steps beyond the first. The principle has solidified into a watchword for the yet divided nation, and its foremost statesmen are sitting in council to make it a living reality. Having regard to all that this fact implies, we cannot doubt of the issue. Victoria and the other colonies which established the partial federation of 1886 have seen their effort fail through the almost ostentatious refusal of New South Wales to have any share in it. To have convinced the authors of that scheme that their work had been brought to naught, to have reconciled them to their defeat, to have brought them to see the necessity of a new departure, and after barring their previous course, to have led them to strike the new path, is alone a monument to the personal ascendency of the man who has brought it all to pass. What is more important, it is a most hopeful augury for the future. Men who have surrendered so much will hardly hesitate at what remains. Mutual forbearance and concession are alone needed to steer the new policy safe to port. Unless the statesmen now assembled in Melbourne, and the peoples they represent, have lost that constructive genius which has made their race pre-eminent in the world, these qualities will not be wanting.

Indeed, so far as the published utterances of responsible politicians have reached us, they are already assured. Trade relations are the chief difficulty. New South Wales has adopted free-trade; the other colonies are firm on protection. They are protected not only against the outside world, but against one another. Shall the proposed Dominion trade freely within itself, or not? If trading freely within itself, how shall it deal with the outsider? That is the crux of the question; beside it such points as the common capital and the powers of the common Parliament are small. A private statement made by the leader of the Victorian Opposition, and the speech of Sir Henry Parkes to the Conference, clearly indicate the solution. "The protected colonies," says the Opposition leader, "are willing to have free-trade with one another." "New South Wales," says Sir Henry, "will make no stipulation, leaving every question to the new Dominion Parliament." That settles it. The other colonies will purchase union at the price of intercolonial free-trade; New South Wales will purchase it at the price of protection against the outside world. On the part of the latter the sacrifice is great. But the New South Wales people perhaps think that national unity is not dear at the

Bradford Observer—*continued.*

price of protection; and that free-trade for all the colonies would be dearly bought indeed if the cost were national disintegration. In any case we can heartily wish success to the Conference, and wish that its counsels may forge another link in the chain of strong, free nations with which Britain is girdling the earth.

Nottingham Guardian—
February 10*th*, 1890.

IT is too soon as yet to make any prediction respecting the result of the Conference of the Australian colonists, now sitting at Melbourne, because the second sitting only takes place to-day, but all the colonies are now united in the object of the Conference, that is, the framing of a scheme of federation, and where there is harmony of sentiment there ought not to be much difficulty in arriving at amicable conclusions. At a banquet given to the delegates at the Conference the other night, some excellent speeches were delivered, and the general tone of the speeches promises well for the future. Sir Henry Parkes, the Premier of New South Wales, remarked that the creation of national unity was an event which could never recur. They were four millions of people, all of British origin, united to the soil by ties of birth, parentage, friendship, and love. If they were incapable of making a nation, they were hardly fit to occupy their bounteous country. It was a wise dispensation that the colonies of Victoria and Queensland should spring into existence and work out their own prosperity independently of New South Wales, but the time had arrived when they were no longer isolated. The crimson thread of kinship ran through all. Was there a man living in Australasia, continued Sir Henry, who said that it would be an advantage to the whole to remain separated? No sane man would say so. If this was admitted, then it followed that, at some time or other, they must unite as one great Australasian people. No advantage could arise from delay, and the difficulties would be greater as the years went on. If this reasoning was correct, the colonies had now arrived at the time when they were fully justified by all the laws regulating the growth of free communities in uniting under one Government and one flag. This implied no separation from the Empire, nor the creation of a separate

Nottingham Guardian—*continued*.

political organization. All free communities, he said, must have a political head, and what head could be more attractive, more ennobling, or more consonant with the true principles of liberty than the Sovereign who, during her beneficent reign, had seen more improvements for the amelioration of the human race than ever Sovereign saw in the world's history. We think we can safely say that if the delegates at the Conference address themselves to the consideration of the great question they are met to discuss, in the spirit of these remarks, they will not have any difficulty in coming to an understanding, and if this object is attained the delegates will probably lay the foundation of one of the mightiest and most enlightened States the world has yet seen.

Ipswich Times—

February 10th, 1890.

SIR HENRY PARKES, Premier of New South Wales, has just made a declaration which, coupled with the way in which it was received, is of the highest significance in regard to the future position of Australasia. Sir Henry has been somewhat of an obstacle to the federation of these colonies in the past, but he now declares with great vigour that the time has come when it should be done, and when provinces that have so many interests in common should have a common government. It is gratifying also to note that he coupled with this declaration another of renewed attachment to the Empire, declaring that there could be no fitter head of such a federated Australia than the illustrious Sovereign in whose reign the British race had made such progress; after which the National Anthem was sung with great heartiness. All this goes to show that if the Australian Colonies remain in their present mood they will first federate themselves, and then lead the way to that federation of the Empire, towards which, if it is to succeed, the colonies must take the first positive step.

Leicester Post—

February 10th, 1890.

SIR HENRY PARKES, the New South Wales Premier, received a splendid ovation at the banquet given by the Hon. Duncan Gillies to Lord Hopetoun and the delegates of the Austral-

Leicester Post —*continued.*

asian Conference. Replying to the toast of "A United Australasia," Sir Henry Parkes said the creation of national unity was an event which could never recur. They were four millions of people, all of British origin, united to the soil by ties of birth, parentage, friendship, and love. If they were incapable of making a nation, they were hardly fit to occupy their bounteous country. It was a wise dispensation that the colonies of Victoria and Queensland should spring into existence and work out their own prosperity independently of New South Wales, but the time had arrived when they were no longer isolated. The crimson thread of kinship ran through all. Was there a man living in Australasia, continued Sir Henry, who said that it would be an advantage to the whole to remain separated? No sane man would say so. If this was admitted, then it followed that at some time or other they must unite as one great Australasian people. It should not go forth for a moment that in seeking complete authority over their own affairs they were seeking any separation from the great Empire. The question of a common tariff was a mere trifle as compared with the question of national existence. Subordinate questions should be sunk. New South Wales was prepared to go into this national union without making any bargain, and without stipulating for any advantage whatever, but trusting in the good faith and justice of a federal Parliament.

Daily Graphic—

February 10*th*, 1890.

That for certain common purposes, such as, for example, military organization, the Australasian Colonies should find it desirable to establish a Federal Council, we can well understand; but from this purely administrative measure to the ideal question of Australian national existence, on which Sir Henry Parkes dwelt with so much vehemence last Friday, is a very long cry. It is, perhaps, somewhat cruel to analyse closely the post-prandial heroics of a statesman who lives and works in a generous atmosphere, where the diplomatic reservations of the old world have no being; but still this cry for nationality is so exceedingly significant that it should not be passed over in silence. Australia a nation means eventual severance from the mother-country, or it means nothing. The Aus-

Daily Graphic—*continued.*

tralians already have a nationality, inasmuch as they are a branch of the great Anglo-Saxon race, which has created the British Empire. To substitute for this any other national existence of a local kind must represent a disintegrating movement. If it is not a move towards independence it is an attempt to found a subject nationality, and this is a retrograde absurdity which we are sure no Australian contemplates. The practical lesson of Sir Henry Parkes' speech is that there is a rising spirit in Australia which aspires to a prouder activity in the world's affairs. Of this spirit we must take due account. To give it a proper direction, we should push forward the scheme of Imperial Federation, which will bring home to our remotest colony the idea of a common empire.

Times --

February 11th, 1890.

YESTERDAY the Conference convened at Melbourne to consider the subject of Australasian Federation was to have resumed its sittings, which have been interrupted for two days by the indisposition of Sir Henry Parkes, the Premier of New South Wales. Sir Henry Parkes is not only the most commanding figure in Australian politics, but he is the heart and soul of the federation movement. It would therefore be particularly unfortunate for the cause of federation if his illness were to prove serious. Owing to the influence of its Premier, New South Wales has recently taken up a far more advanced position with regard to federation than the rest of the Australasian Colonies. It may be roughly said that the views of the other Ministries are represented by Mr. Duncan Gillies, the Prime Minister of Victoria. Mr. Gillies, although he looks forward to federation with a Federal Parliament and Government in the future, is not sanguine that it will be realized at any early date. For the present, he cautiously limits his ambition to the constitution of a central authority for purposes of defence. He recognizes the necessity, urged by General Edwards in his report upon the Australian defensive system, of uniting the several Australian contingents under the same command, and of organizing and arming them upon a uniform system. He sees the advantage to Australia of possessing a compact fleet, in the place of independent squadrons, and of constructing its land defences in accordance with a comprehensive plan. But he

Times—*continued.*

thinks that federation for the purposes of defence is as much as can be expected to be attained just now. Sir Henry Parkes, on the other hand, will be satisfied with nothing short of federation in full panoply. He points out that even to carry such a scheme of combined defence into effect will require some paramount authority. "Hence this first great federal question," he wrote in his memorable despatch to Mr. Gillies of the 30th of October, "brings us face to face with the imperative necessity for a Federal Government." Why not, asks Sir Henry Parkes, finish the job while the work is on the anvil? Why not follow the example of the North American Colonies, and make a complete constitution? He asks for nothing less than a Governor-General for the whole of Australia, a Federal Ministry, and a Federal Parliament, composed of an Upper and a Lower House. His views are sufficiently mature to allow him to refer to the Canadian and American Constitutions. He does not think it too early to discuss whether the Federal Parliament should be made the residuary legatee of all the powers not specifically given to the provinces, or the provinces of the powers not reserved to the Federal Parliament. From the reception given to Sir Henry Parkes' stirring speech at the banquet on Thursday it might be inferred that his large views evoked a good deal of sympathy even outside his own colony. But it is uncertain how far the enthusiasm he aroused was due to the personality of the man, how far to admiration for his eloquent generalities, and how far to approval of his demand for urgency.

If Sir Henry's ardour persuades the members of the Conference to be as bold as himself, his triumph will be signal. The barriers of sentiment and interest which divide the Australasian Colonies are not easy to throw down. The captious spirit in which colony regards colony is discernible in the very negotiations which have led up to this Conference. Certainly New South Wales cannot be absolved from the common charge. The senior colony stood out of the Federal Council—a deliberative body constituted in 1883 with a view to concerted action for certain limited purposes. Then, when the colony had been converted to federation, it would not recognize the despised Council as a ready-made medium for discussing details. Nothing would do but a brand-new Conference. Happily, Mr. Gillies and the other colonial Premiers did not stand upon their dignity too long. They proposed, and Sir Henry Parkes accepted, a compromise by which the members of the Council, in their

Times—*continued.*

private capacities, were to meet representatives sent by the Government of New South Wales. If we wanted another example of intercolonial perversity, it might be found in Sir Henry Parkes' late proposal to appropriate to his own colony the name of Australia. First, then, the spirit of pure contrariety must be "laid" before anything practical can be achieved by the Conference. But this is far from all. At many points the solid interests of the several colonies are thought to be in conflict. Which colony, for instance, is to supply the new federal capital? The oldest colony, or the richest and most populous? Then it seems improbable that New Zealand, although it may enter the federation for the purposes of common defence, will submit itself in other respects to a central Government sitting 1,200 miles away by sea. But the most formidable lion in the path is undoubtedly the question of the tariff. It may be found possible to erect a central Government which, while possessing powers of taxation, has no control over the tariffs of the different colonies. But Mr. Service, who on Thursday evening proposed the toast, to which Sir Henry Parkes responded, of "a United Australasia," was clearly correct in saying that no national unity was possible without uniform tariffs. Is Victoria ready to lower her tariffs for the sake of *les beaux yeux* of Australian unity? Or is New South Wales prepared to sacrifice her predilections for free trade for the same ideal? Sir Henry Parkes loftily brushes away the tariff question. It is a detail upon which no colony ought to stand out when the making of a nation is at stake. If he means that New South Wales is ready to give way, and if he has rightly gauged the feeling of his colony, *cadit quæstio*. But if he means that the Protectionist colonies also must abate their claims, the immediate prospects of federation are less cheerful. We cannot forget that this difficulty has hitherto acted as a stumbling-block in the way of South African confederation, and that a Conference directed to the specific subject of a customs union has failed to grapple with it successfully.

For these reasons, then, we must not expect too much from the deliberations of the Conference. But even if it is content to provide Australasia with a common army and navy, and to do nothing more beyond affirming its adhesion to the principle of federation, much will have been gained. The various colonies will have become familiarized with the idea of federation, and its complete attainment will become a matter of time and opportunity. It cannot be doubted

Times—*continued.*

that Australian federation must come some day; nor can the mother-country regret the prospect, or wish the consummation delayed a moment. It could not be approached in a spirit of more ardent loyalty to the British connection. The eloquent words of Sir Henry Parkes on this point quite carried away his audience. In one aspect, the federation of the Australasian Colonies would tend to diminish the power of the Home Government; but it would simplify the relations of the mother-country with her colonies. Heavy as is the burden which rests upon the Colonial Office, it would be intolerable if, instead of a Dominion of Canada, it had to deal separately with the seven provinces which now make up the Dominion. This motive alone would dispose the Home Government to welcome a similar work of unification in South Africa and Australasia. Nor are the advocates of Imperial Federation slow to discern the improvement in their position resulting from these successive colonial federations. The alliance of Great Britain and her colonies and dependencies may possibly never emerge from the region of dreamland; but if the magnificent project ever enters upon a practical path, it will find the distance to the goal greatly shortened by the solidification of the colonies into groups. Fewer authorities to settle with, fewer interests to reconcile—this is exactly what Imperial federationists want, and what the silent working of natural forces seems likely to give them.

St. James' Gazette—

February 12*th*, 1890.

At the sitting of the Federation Conference at Melbourne on Monday Sir Henry Parkes moved the following resolution:—" That in the opinion of this Conference the best interests and the present and future prosperity of the Australian Colonies will be promoted by an early union under the Crown, and while fully recognizing the valuable services of the members of the Convention of 1883 in founding the Federal Council, declares its opinion that the seven years which have since elapsed have developed the national life of Australasia in population, wealth, discovery, resources, and self-governing capacity to an extent which

St. James' Gazette—*continued.*
justifies the higher act, at all times contemplated, of the union of the colonies under one Legislative and Executive Government, on principles just to the several colonies." Sir Henry, in a lengthy speech, urged that the federation of the colonies early in their career would economize their resources and substitute national for local interests. In the debate which followed the resolution was generally supported.

Echo—
February 12*th*, 1890.
THE sittings of the Federation Conference at Melbourne were resumed yesterday. Sir Henry Parkes moved a resolution urging an early union under the Crown. Sir Henry, in a lengthy speech, urged that the federation of the colonies early in their career would economize their resources and substitute national for local interests. " All the elements of national life are present," he proceeded, " whether in their population, their industrial productions, or their military strength, and together amply justify the creation of that national unanimity which is alone necessary to ensure the accomplishment of the scheme." The Hon. A. Deakin (Victoria) formally seconded the motion, which was supported by Sir S. W. Griffith (Queensland), who declared that the time had arrived for a completer federation. It was impossible for the individual Parliaments to adequately legislate in matters of defence. Federation even without fiscal union would be better than none, and he would be disappointed if the Conference failed to lay the foundation of a strong Federal Government. The Hon. A. Deakin, in an eloquent speech supporting the motion, said that Australia would sooner or later be forced to unite, and the difficulties would be increased by delay. The people of Victoria were only in favour of federation, to accomplish which they were prepared to make sacrifices. The Victorian delegates, he added, were prepared to work side by side with the other members of the Conference. Mr. Deakin dwelt upon the importance of Australians possessing one centre of national life, and said the establishment of a Federal Parliament and executive must be determined by a properly authorized national convention.

Liverpool Post—
February 12th, 1890.

FROM the report of the Australian Federation Conference just to hand, it is pretty evident that a good many obstacles must be surmounted before the project becomes a *fait accompli*. Everything points to a federation of the Antipodean colonies as the ultimate and inevitable outcome of the circumstances under which they are placed. In the possible event of an invasion by any foreign Power an isolated colony like New Zealand, for instance, would be helpless in the grip of her Titanic foe, and eager to accept any terms of peace, long before the mother country could send succour and deliverance. It is undeniable that any surrender by an Antipodean colony, whatever the considerations by which it might be extorted, would not be for a moment binding upon the Imperial Government. Nevertheless the situation created would be extremely awkward for all parties, and on the whole it is a satisfactory sign to see the leaders of Australian opinion endeavouring to create an alliance for defensive purposes sufficient at least to keep a hostile force in play until Imperial reinforcements can be brought upon the scene. From an Imperial standpoint it must be admitted that painful reflections are associated with this exhibition of forethought on the part of England's Antipodean offshoots. When once the scheme becomes an accomplished fact —as it inevitably will sooner or later— the parental control which has hitherto been patiently submitted to will begin to chafe and gall. The right of independent action will be insisted upon whenever a difference of opinion arises upon any point of supreme importance to Antipodean interests, and an impartial survey of the circumstances must result in the admission that sturdy races such as the Australian colonies have produced are likely to know better what is good for them than any Colonial Department sitting in London. The annexation of New Guinea by Queensland was an ambitious step, but certainly not deserving of the icy derision and prompt repudiation with which it was received by Lord Derby. It need not have received overt sanction all the same. The tacit acquiescence of the Colonial Office in the policy of Queensland would have given the Imperial Government the rights of first possession over the whole island, whereas the wily Germans, taking occasion by the hand, adroitly slipped in and established a claim to something like one-half of the vast island continent. The Australian Federation Conference is now discussing its

Liverpool Post—*continued.*

programme in the comprehensive resolution which has been put before it by Sir Henry Parkes, viz.:—"That in the opinion of this Conference the best interests and the present and future prosperity of the Australian colonies will be promoted by an early union under the Crown, and, while fully recognizing the valuable services of the members of the Convention of 1883 in founding the Federal Council, declares its opinion that the seven years which have since elapsed have developed the national life of Australasia in population, wealth, discovery, resources, and self-governing capacity to an extent which justifies the higher act, at all times contemplated, of the union of the colonies under one Legislative and Executive Government, on principles just to the several colonies." It is impossible, of course, to discuss such a project as the resolution implies without bringing to the surface numerous intercolonial jealousies. Victoria, for instance, regards herself as the destined centre of the federated colonies, and her premier City of Melbourne as the capital. Sydney is not inclined to lightly yield her own important claims, and so the project meantime hangs fire. Similar difficulties have been conquered, however, on a far larger scale in the case of the German Empire, and on a hardly inferior one in that of the Argentine Republic. In Australia it is only a matter of time and the common stimulus of any danger which may present itself more strongly than at present.

Liverpool Mercury—

February 12th, 1890.

There are no features of particular interest in the Queen's Speech which did not duly appear in the forecast. These important documents are no longer shrouded in secrecy until divulged to Parliament. Her Majesty commences by referring, in a mild manner, to the dispute with Portugal, then passes on to the slave trade conference at Brussels, the commercial convention with Egypt, the adjustment of some pressing fiscal difficulties with Bulgaria, and the agreement arrived at provisionally with Germany and the United States with respect to the government of Samoa. This latter instrument only awaits the ratification of the Senate to become absolute. We then learn that an inquiry is being

Liverpool Mercury—*continued.*

instituted in Swaziland, which is independent territory, with a view to the removal of disorders between the aborigines and the white settlers. The Queen is prepared favourably to consider any practical measure for federating the Australian colonies, and she awaits with "lively interest" the result of the conference assembled at Melbourne. This conference will probably not be conclusive, for no statesman except Sir Henry Parkes believes in the feasibility of creating an Australasian Dominion immediately; but it will certainly mark at least the beginning of a great movement destined to go on to fruition. After an allusion to the Estimates, which "have been drawn with a due regard to economy," the Speech turns to the affairs of Ireland, and devotes the longest paragraph to an exposition of Ministerial intentions towards that country. Mr. Balfour's juggling in recent proclamations with the apparent severity of the Coercion Act had a definite purpose, now revealed. It enabled him, because a number of districts were relieved from the pressure of certain sections, to have a statement inserted in the Speech to the effect that he has found it possible to govern more mildly by reason of the falling off in agrarian crime. This is throwing dust in the public eyes. That which was given with one hand was taken away with another. Some areas were freed from a part of their burden, and concurrently in a dozen counties there were fresh ones imposed. As to agrarian crime there has notoriously been very little of it to repress, and 99 per cent. of the cases heard by the removable magistrates have had nothing to do with crime of any description. The right honorable gentleman had the opening of Parliament in view when he instructed his law officers to make a show of diminishing the stringency of coercion. We have the testimony of Mr. John Morley for the fact that the commission was fulfilled in such a way as to baffle anybody except a skilled lawyer in tracing out its precise effects. The Chief Secretary's motive in meeting Parliament with a boast of success in Ireland is obvious enough. Irish legislation had become imperative, and the Minister desired the House and the country to believe that, as a consequence of his policy, some large concessions may now be safely made. There are three bills specially mentioned—one for increasing the number of occupying owners, another for an extension of the principles of local self-government, and a third for improving the material condition of the population in the poorer districts. All three are promised during the present session. Local self-government

Liverpool Mercury—*continued.*

is not put forward as a scheme contemplated in the future, which was the course anticipated, but as a project already prepared and to be introduced this year. But there is a significant qualification which we have foreshadowed for two years past. The principles to be applied are those which have been adopted in England and Scotland, " so far as they are applicable" to Ireland. The genuine Tory spirit is here. It is unchanged and unchangeable. Because the tactics of the Government, and its hopes in the country, render inevitable some kind of gratification of the Irish demand for fuller local control, a Bill must be brought in sooner or later; but it is an article of the Tory creed that the sister island ought not to have similar institutions to those of Great Britain, and therefore such measure as may be forthcoming will be strewn with disabilities and inequalities throughout its constitution. We shall await its appearance with much interest. Other Bills to be submitted will provide for the cheaper transfer of land, for the better levying and redeeming of tithes, for improving private Bill legislation required for Scotland, for the more efficacious winding-up of insolvent, limited companies, for ascertaining the liability of employers in cases of accident, or consolidating and amending the laws relating to public health in the metropolis, and for the promotion of the comfort of troops in barracks. Taking the programme as a whole, it is of formidable dimensions, although there is not a word in it about district councils for England and Wales, or the breakfast table duties, or free education. Mr. Goschen will enjoy an unusually fat surplus, but what he is going to do with the money he has yet to disclose.

Manchester Guardian—

February 12*th,* 1890.

The Government will, the Queen's Speech informs us, await with lively interest the result of the Conference now being held to discuss the important question of the Federation of the Australian Colonies, and will regard with favour any well considered measure tending towards that object. The Conference, at which all the colonies are represented, met at Melbourne on the 6th, and its serious discussions are to begin this week. Already on the evening of the 6th, at a

Manchester Guardian—*continued.*

banquet given by Mr. Duncan Gillies, the Premier of Victoria, speeches which may be looked upon as the opening speeches of the Conference were made, and Sir Henry Parkes on one side and Mr. James Service on the other stated what may be shortly described as the two views of Federation in Australia. Mr. Service contended that the Federal Council created in 1883 is the real germ of Australasian Federation, that it has only been rendered unsuccessful hitherto by the abstention of New South Wales, and that since New South Wales is now in favour of Federation there can be no serious obstacle other than the Customs tariff. Mr. Service was not confident of overcoming the difficulties in the way of establishing a uniform Customs tariff, and is apparently prepared, if this difficulty prove insurmountable, to accept some other means of bringing the colonies into harmony with one another. This may be called the moderate colonial view of a subject which is one of first interest to the Australian continent. Sir Henry Parkes, the Premier of New South Wales—who has made himself responsible hitherto for the abstention of his colony, not on the ground of opposition to the principle of Federation but because he held that the Federal Council, possessing no executive power, hindered rather than helped the triumph of the principle by satisfying the people of Australia with a sham,—is inclined now to accept no compromise, and to be content with no half-hearted measure. Is there a man living in Australia, he asks, who thinks that it would be an advantage to remain separate ? Not one. This being so, the question of protection and free-trade as between the colonies must sink into insignificance. It becomes a mere trifle as compared with national existence, and Sir Henry expressed his confident belief that the time has now come when the colonies are fully justified by all the laws regulating the growth of free communities in uniting under one Government and one flag, that the people of Australia have made up their mind to do it, and that no hand on earth is now strong enough to keep them asunder. It will be very interesting to see whether the practical difficulties in the path of union or the national feeling in favour of it will prove the stronger. It is also interesting and suggestive of many interesting parallels to find that the national party of Australia is eloquent in protest against separation from the Empire.

Evening News—
February 12th, 1890.

The illness of Sir Henry Parkes, the apostle of the federation idea in Australia, is naturally causing some uneasiness among his friends and admirers in the colonies. The old Premier is now seventy-five years of age, and during the half century he has spent in New South Wales, hard, wearing work has continuously been his portion. Like many of the men who now hold prominent public positions in the colonies, in the early part of his colonial career the future Federationist had to work hard with his hands for a living, and he is in no way ashamed of the fact that for a considerable time he worked as a dock labourer in Sydney. He afterwards kept a tobacco-shop in Hunter-street in that city, a place which under him became quite a rendezvous for the rollicking politicians of the early days of the colony. It was in writing rhythmic skits on passing public events that the future "Grand Old Man" of New South Wales first began to develop his literary attributes, and in 1849—ten years after his arrival in Port Jackson—he founded the *Empire*, a daily newspaper which exercised a considerable amount of influence during its existence. In 1854 he was elected to the old Legislative Council, and a couple of years later was returned to the Assembly as one of the first representatives of Sydney under the new constitution granted to the colony.

Should anything unfortunately deprive the Federation Conference of the assistance of Sir Henry Parkes during its present sitting, the onus of the initiative part of the work will to a great extent fall upon the shoulders of Mr. Duncan Gillies, the Premier of Victoria. Like Sir Henry, Mr. Gillies had to do hard work in his early colonial days, and he was following the cheerful avocation of a gold-miner on the Ballarat fields when that golden spot was honoured with the presence of the present Prime Minister of England. Some local historians indeed go so far as to say that the globe-trotting Lord Robert Cecil was a digger himself during his sojourn on the Ballarat fields, but this is not authenticated.

Advertiser—
February 13th, 1890.

The Conference which has assembled in Melbourne for the purpose of discussing proposals to bring about the early establishment of a Federal Parliament and Government of

Advertiser —*continued.*

Australia, on the lines of the Canadian Dominion, has opened auspiciously. The science of political gastronomy, it will be seen, has penetrated to the Antipodes. It is as true there as here that a little dinner "offers human life and human nature under very favourable circumstances." Therefore the Victorian statesmen were well advised in inaugurating the proceedings, which we may hope will result in the consolidation of a great Australian nation, under mellowing influences which are almost invariably irresistible to people of British descent. Before the issues have been thoroughly threshed out it will be found that the advocates of federation will require all their tact and discretion to make the movement "march." Not that popular opinion is hostile to national unity—quite the contrary is the case—but public opinion has to be satisfied that the difficulties of the situation have been met in a practical and businesslike manner. Under the glamour of political after-dinner oratory obstacles often vanish away, but only to reappear in a very solid form when sober judgment resumes her sway. Therefore we do not regard the cause of Australian national unity as won because Sir Henry Parkes achieved a rhetorical triumph and could airily refer to one of the greatest obstacles to harmonious action as "a mere trifle" compared with the question of national existence.

The Hon. James Service, the founder of the Australasian Federal Council, is a statesman of a very different type to the Premier of New South Wales. Calmer, less emotional, more readily accessible to reason, he cannot disguise his conviction that the chief obstacle to federation is the difficulty of arranging a uniform tariff; to his mind no national unity is possible with hostile tariffs. To many minds the most hopeful view that seems possible is that the fiscal barriers which one colony now raises against its neighbour may be abolished in favour of intercolonial free-trade, with high protective duties against the outside world. But how will the mother-country like this treatment? If that be the result of federation, would not those who assert that "the British manufacturer has little to gain and something to lose by a Dominion of Australasia" be very correct? Hitherto the parent colony of the group, which proudly boasts itself the richest and most populous member of the brilliant galaxy, has not adopted the selfish policy of exclusion which Victoria, New Zealand, and in a measure the other colonies have enforced against the mother-country and all other "foreigners." Sir Henry Parkes is right in inculcating

Advertiser—*continued.*

in season and out of season that protection would do New South Wales no benefit but would suck her blood and impose fetters upon her trade. But what hope is there that he will be strong enough to superimpose a free-trade policy upon colonies which for years have evinced a stronger and stronger inclination to plunge headlong into the wildest vagaries of protection? It is all very well for him to talk of "the crimson thread of kinship;" but experience does not confirm his belief that the colonies will cheerfully make material sacrifices in order to accelerate the advent of their national existence. The Australian working man is a staunch believer in protection; and, in the communities where the democratic vote sways the destinies of all, it is impossible to successfully combat the fiscal heresies to which he is so devoutly attached. It is ominous that already the Premier of South Australia has declared that the fiscal question is of more importance than even that of defence. The enormous public debts of the several colonies constitute another serious impediment to to easy federation. Collectively the Australasian colonies have borrowed, say, £160,000,000 from the mother country. It need not be questioned that they have expended the money judiciously. But is this immense liability to be assumed by the Dominion, or to remain a State or provincial responsibility? This question will provoke not a few heartburnings. It will not be settled as easily as in the case of Canada. It has never been the policy of the North American group of colonies to contract liabilities with the levity, or, to be lenient, shall we say enterprise, that the Australian provinces have displayed. The result is that while the average indebtedness per head in Australasia is about £45, that of each Canadian is not much more than £9 9s. If we estimate the total indebtedness of the Empire at about 1,132 millions sterling, Australasia is responsible for one-seventh of the whole. This may be a great fact, but does it make for federation?

So far it may be thought we have not approached the federation problem in a very sanguine spirit. It is, however, not from any desire to minimise the advantages that may nay, must—result from the colonies putting off the juvenile garb of provincialism for the more virile garments of federation. Sir Henry Parkes is confident that the moment is ripe for making the crucial change, and it cannot be denied that the colonies are now confronted with work of a national character, which can only be satisfactorily accomplished by a great and all-sufficient Federal Government. They have for years past made brave but spasmodic attempts to provide for

Advertiser—*continued.*

their own defence, while relying upon the mother-country to secure their commerce against attack. Millions have been lavished upon all sorts of wild defence schemes, but the result is that in the year 1890 Victoria is really the only colony which can confront the dangers of foreign invasion with anything approaching equanimity. And yet the colonies possess really formidable means of repelling attack. They could muster 40,000 well-armed, well-trained soldiers if facilities for concentration existed; but owing to different organizations, to the fact that the colonies cannot employ their forces outside their own borders, and to the unfortunate want of uniformity of gauge for their railways, anything like effective co-operation for defence purposes is at present impossible. Australasian statesmen have not been blind to this state of things, but so long as peace prevailed they were content to put off until "a more convenient season" the arduous task of grappling with the difficulty. It was left to General Edwards to bring home to them the conviction that the evils could only be met by federal action, and that the matter was one of national magnitude and significance. Sir Henry Parkes was the first to rise to the occasion. Brought face to face with this great federal question, he recognized at once the imperative necessity for Federal Government. Mr. Duncan Gillies, the Victorian Premier, was scarcely less eager. He objects to the colonies remaining "a concourse of disintegrated atoms," and is quite prepared to subordinate individual preferences in order to obtain the united action essential to conserve the national interests of Australia. It largely rests with these two statesmen to promote or to delay the federal movement. If they are really willing to subordinate their individual preferences they may plant a tree which, in the glowing language of Sir Henry Parkes, will rapidly grow in the rich colonial soil until "it overshadows with its protective and glorious branches the whole of the Australian people." Lord Palmerston once declared that "a united Italy" was "a geographical impossibility." The jeer was speedily shown to be without foundation. We trust that those who disbelieve in the speedy advent of "a united Australasia" will be confounded with equal celerity, and that a new nation will spring up under the Southern Cross, and there develop "a freedom, a civilization, and a pure and beneficent morality" as perfect as the parent State has achieved in the northern hemisphere.

Belfast News Letter—

February 13th, 1890.

The gracious reference in the Queen's speech to the federation of the Australian colonies is sure to attract the approbation of patriotic citizens. It is evident from the language employed that the advisers of the Crown are favourably disposed to this very important question, which is opportunely and ably dealt with by Sir Charles Gavan Duffy, in the current number of the *Contemporary Review*. Most people are thoroughly tired of parochial politics—of the endless squabbles about matters for the more part personal, and in which the great body of the population of the United Kingdom cannot be reasonably supposed to take any interest. The integrity of the British Empire ought to be the dominant idea of all parties; and this integrity will be best maintained by uniting the various parts of the Queen's dominions by a well-defined legislative bond cementing the colonies to the mother-country. Sir Charles Gavan Duffy knows Australia, and he ardently advocates federation, which his experience enables him to describe as affecting British interests more seriously than any question keeping ambassadors at Berlin or Paris or other European capitals. Difficulties, no doubt, are in the way; but it is the duty of statesmen to overcome difficulties. "If the British taxpayer cannot look sacrifice cheerfully in the face for adequate ends, if the British statesman cannot draw all the scattered or discontented fragments of the empire into one confederacy at any present cost, a penalty little dreamed of will have to be paid by-and-bye for their incapacity or neglect." Thoughtful men, who have studied the subject, assure us that, sooner or later, we must have Imperial Federation or Imperial disintegration. The first step in the right direction is to draw the colonies into closer relations among themselves, as in the case of the Dominion of Canada, and we hope will be the case in Australasia. Why should local jealousies be permitted to interrupt the instincts of patriotism? The days are gone when political leaders would be heard if they spoke of the colonies as of no importance. More than forty years have elapsed since the Privy Council, reporting on Australian affairs, recommended that one of the Governors should be appointed Governor-General, with authority to convene a General Assembly of Australia in any part of her Majesty's Australian possessions whenever the need arose. A Federal Union of the colonies might then have occurred; but Lord John Russell thought the time for such a change had not

Belfast News Letter—*continued.*

arrived. In 1857 the Legislative Assembly of Victoria appointed a Select Committee to consider this business, and the result was favourable to the change. The Committee reported that the common interest suffered, and would continue to suffer, while competing tariffs, naturalization laws, land systems, rival schemes of immigration, ocean postage, and other alienating influences existed. Therefore federation was strongly urged, one of the advantages being the power to promptly call new states into existence throughout the immense territory, to meet the demands of increased population, thus enabling each State to apply itself to the special industry its position and resources render most profitable. The difficulties were not overlooked, and they were to be left to a Conference of Delegates from the respective colonies. Shortly after this movement in Australia, a meeting of Australians, presided over by Mr. Wentworth, to whose statesmanlike qualities a high compliment is paid, was held in London, and it was agreed to present a memorial to the Colonial Secretary, asking for a Permissive Act to be passed by the Imperial Parliament, empowering the Australian Colonies to confederate in the manner most convenient and agreeable to themselves. The Colonial Minister replied, assigning the initiative to the colonies, after which he would be happy to co-operate in obtaining the sanction of Parliament for any measure the memorialists desired. The prospect was fairly bright. The Upper House in all the colonies, and the Legislative Assembly in all but one, were ready to act. Nevertheless, party feeling and petty jealousies prevailed, and the efforts were abortive. Three years later the question was again taken up by the Victorian Parliament, a Select Committee was appointed; but no report appeared. South Australia, Tasmania, and Queensland were willing to make the experiment; but New South Wales objected. In 1870 a Royal Commission was appointed under letters patent from the Crown to inquire into the subject. The time was suitable; for Von Moltke was marching to Paris, and the colonists might naturally begin to think of the defenceless condition of their homes. On this occasion a report was produced; and the Commissioners alluded to the relations between the mother-country and the colonies as eminently insecure and intrinsically unfair, liable to give way on the first emergency. "The British Colonies," they said, "from which Imperial troops have been wholly withdrawn, present the unprecedented phenomenon of responsibility without either corresponding

Belfast News Letter—*continued.*

authority or adequate protection. They are as liable to all the hazards of war as the United Kingdom; but they can influence the commencement or continuance of war no more than they can control the movements of the solar system; and they have no certain assurance of that aid against an enemy upon which integral portions of the United Kingdom can confidently reckon." The description is true; and the conditions cannot be regarded as durable unless some change occurs to secure mutual responsibility. The English Liberals had treated the colonies badly. They spoke and acted as if the United Kingdom would be better without them; and they ordered the Colonial Governments to provide for the defence of their countries, or they might do as they pleased. Indeed, few would have been surprised if there had been a general revolt in the colonies. Exponents of Canadian opinion declared, if they could not negotiate successfully in Westminister in summer, they would negotiate at Washington in autumn; and Sir Charles Gavan Duffy says the Australians were beginning to contemplate a measure of independent statesmanship almost as decisive. The Report of the Royal Commission recommended the passage of a Permissive Act by the Imperial Parliament, authorizing the Queen to call into existence, by proclamation, a Federal Union of any two or more of the colonies as soon as Acts had been passed in their respective Legislatures. Still, the proposals failed. A dozen years had not ripened the question for action. On the contrary, new difficulties appeared, and the desire for federation had declined. Twelve years more elapsed, and the question was again revived. France meditated sending her criminals to the New Hebrides; and it was rumoured that Germany intended to seize New Guinea, the portal of the Pacific, and a necessary part of the defence of the future Australian Empire. Then a Conference of colonial delegates was held. Application was made in London for a Permissive Act, to afford power to the colonists to create a Colonial Council for joint action. The Council, however, became practically useless, New South Wales and South Australia refusing to join. The latter has since joined, and Australian colonies are brought so much nearer federation. We may expect to see the difficulty altogether removed when the present conference has concluded, and the question passes from local into Imperial hands. Sir Charles Gavan Duffy says the only hope of success is when Australian Federation is made an Imperial question.

Dumfries Standard—
February 13*th*, 1890.

There has been much talk of late in reference to Colonial Federation. I see from cablegrams that some of the London papers have been discussing the subject, and are evidently favourable to the movement. The recent discussion in the colonies on this question has been brought about by General Edwards' report and Sir Henry Parkes' action. As I have previously stated, General Edwards was appointed by the Imperial Government to inspect the military forces of the colonies, and to recommend any improvements that he considered necessary. His report, which was recently issued, may be summarised as follows: Federation of the forces; an officer of the rank of Lieutenant-General to be appointed to advise and inspect in peace and command in war; a uniform system of organization and armament; a common defence Act; amalgamation of the permanent forces into a fortress corps; a federal military college for education of officers; the extension of the rifle clubs; a uniform gauge for the railways; a federal small arm manufactory and ordnance store. Following this report, the somewhat erratic Premier of New South Wales paid a visit to Brisbane to consult with the Government of Queensland on the matter. He does not appear to have met with much encouragement there. Sir Henry then issued a lengthy manifesto, in which he advocated strongly the formation of an Australian Dominion, much after the Canadian style. This document, I believe, was wired to London. There does not appear to be any objection to meet Sir Henry's wish so far, and hold a consultation, but the other colonies feel it would be absurd to ignore entirely the Federal Council which at present exists. New South Wales has been the block to any real federation in times past, and there is a certain amount of mistrust in anything she now says. Sir Henry Parkes is very fond of show, and cannot play second fiddle to anyone. Unless he takes the lead and gets all the glory he will do nothing. All that is wanted at present is for New South Wales to join the Federal Council, and it seems more than likely a real federated Australia would very shortly become an accomplished fact. The other colonies will make the Council a stepping stone to something better, but they will not fling it aside as Sir Henry suggests. It will be years before what he wants can be brought about, and it would be remarkably foolish for the other colonies to throw aside the amount of federation they have acquired for something which may be obtained in the distant future. Everything

Dumfries Standard—*continued.*

points to a real federation as suggested by Sir Henry Parkes, but it will not be accomplished till after much discussion and a decidedly stronger feeling amongst colonists in its favour. The want of fiscal unity and many other things must receive attention and a certain settlement before it is possible to attempt a federation as they have in Canada. The suggestions of General Edwards are by no means new. They have been prominently brought before the Australian public over and over again by editors of newspapers and by our political men in and out of Parliament. If New South Wales and Victoria could only get rid of the wretched jealousy which abounds in each of these colonies it would be a more certain step to federation than anything which has yet been done. I shall keep you informed from time to time as to the progress being made towards the real federation of what will undoubtedly in years to come be one of the strongest commonwealths in the world—"The Dominion of Australasia."

Globe—

February 14th, 1890.

THE unanimous adoption of Sir Henry Parkes' motion by the Federation Conference affords one more proof that the idea of a central government is making steady progress. Of course, there is all the difference in the world between an abstract resolution and a concrete scheme. Had any definite plan of federation been placed before the Conference, it is certain that very strong antagonisms would have become manifest. During the discussion some delegates advocated the adoption of the United States system; others gave preference to that of Canada; others, again, thought it would be best to borrow from both. The New Zealand representatives also evinced some doubtfulness as to whether the proposed fusion of the land forces would be of much advantage to their colony. As a matter of course, the vital tariff question obtruded itself from time to time, and in such shapes as to indicate that this stumbling-block to federation remains almost as formidable as ever. But while in disagreement on details, the delegates showed, both in their speeches and by their final vote, that Australasia fully recognizes the necessity of closer union. It now only remains, therefore, for Antipodean statesmanship to enter into the practical work of drafting a scheme for submission to the National Convention. This must be more or less in

Globe—*continued.*

.the nature of compromise; some sacrifice will have to be made by every colony. If, for instance, the protectionist group made it a *sine qua non* that the Federal Government should adopt their fiscal policy, the free-trade settlements would be sure to reply with an emphatic *non possumus*. At the final meeting of the Conference, the New South Wales and Tasmanian delegates took up the position that federation would be worthless unless it brought with it free-trade. But Victoria and the other protectionist colonies would never subscribe to that programme, although they might, perhaps, be induced to approach it by concessions to their fiscal views. The most hopeful feature of the situation is that the delegates have been able to handle in a temperate manner a number of prickly questions which a few years ago could not even have been approached in conference.

Evening News Post—
February 14*th*, 1890.

The Australasian Federation Conference when yesterday it unanimously adopted Sir Henry Parkes' motion for the union of the Australian Colonies under one Government came to a decision which may have far-reaching results. The question of intercolonial customs dues has hitherto been the great difficulty in the way of a settlement, and the assembled representatives were pretty well agreed that no scheme of union would be satisfactory which did not deal with, and if possible abolish, border dues. It must be taken, therefore, though up to the present the telegrams are silent on the point, that some settlement of this thorny subject has been arrived at. If so, we have nothing but congratulations for the delegates. A federal authority for Australia, strong enough to command the respect, and, where necessary, the obedience, of the local legislatures, would be highly beneficial both to the colonists and the mother-country. It would stand on a sounder basis than exists at present, would have far greater financial resources than the local legislatures, and would be able to give powerful impetus to the general development of the colonies. It would be a gain to England to have to deal with one central authority rather than with a number of possibly discordant bodies, and many incidental advantages, such, possibly, as the formation of a federal navy for the defence of the Australian coasts, may be reaped in the near future.

Pall Mall Gazette—
February 14th, 1890.

THE unanimous acceptance of Sir Henry Parkes' resolution by the Australasian delegates at Melbourne yesterday is a landmark in the evolution of that federated Empire of the English-speaking folk which promises to be the most important birth of the coming time. The resolution which has thus been unanimously affirmed, declares that "in the opinion of this Conference," at which all the Australasian Colonies were represented, "the best interests and the present and future prosperity of the Australasian Colonies will be promoted by an early union under the Crown." This union, it goes on to declare, "is the union of the colonies under one Legislative and Executive Government on principles just to the several colonies." The principles favoured by the Conference as just to the several colonies were those of the American Republic rather than those of the Canadian Dominion; and they included intercolonial free-trade, with a protectionist barrier against all imports from without.

St. James' Gazette—
February 14th, 1890.

BY accepting without a dissentient vote the somewhat abstract resolution moved by Sir Henry Parkes, the delegates at Melbourne have taken the first step towards Australian Federation. But to agree upon a general principle is by no means the same thing as to draft a definite scheme which shall be supported by the legislatures and the peoples of the different colonies. It would appear that the question is eminently one upon which the constituencies must be consulted before they are pledged by their representatives. The three points which are supposed to stand in the way of United Australasia are as follows:—

1. The choice of a Federal Capital. (This may be settled by selecting an inconspicuous Season City, and thereby avoiding colonial jealousies.)
2. The contributions to be required from the different colonies towards the common Army and Navy. (This would be mainly a matter of account.)
3. The abolition, or at least the rearrangement, of intercolonial Customs.

It is on the last of these points that the main difficulty may be expected to arise.

Glasgow Herald —

February 14th, 1890.

WHETHER any practical result will immediately follow the holding of the Federation Conference which, on the initiative of the Premier of New South Wales, has been sitting at Melbourne for some days, may perhaps be doubted. On the surface, the federation of the Australian Colonies under a single Legislature and Executive seems to be a perfectly simple and natural arrangement. With the exception of New Zealand—for Tasmania can scarcely be considered an exception—they are all conterminous. They have a common language and common creeds; their peoples are all of the same stock, and have brought with them from the mother-country the same political and social ideas. Their Constitutions are virtually identical; and in all of them, as Sir Charles Dilke has very ably shown in his "Problems of Greater Britain," the organic questions which have to be confronted in every modern community have hitherto followed pretty much the same lines of solution. To colonies so situated, a form of federation which would leave reasonable freedom of action to each local legislature would offer very great advantages. It would at once remove all necessity for inland Customs barriers. It would secure joint action on questions such as the establishment of improved telegraphic and steamship communication with the old world, where joint action would mean both economy and success. It would immensely facilitate the execution of those measures of self-defence of which the necessity has been recognized by almost all the individual colonies, and it would give to the voice of Australia on such external grievances as the continued transportation of French habitual criminals to New Caledonia a potency which it does not at present possess. Last, but perhaps not least in the eyes of practical men, a federal guarantee would enable the colonies to borrow money in the Home market on still easier terms than exist at present for the execution of those public works, such as railways and irrigation schemes, which are needed to develop the enormous resources of the great island continent.

All these considerations have been recognized within the past few years by many of the Australian leaders of thought, and though there has not, perhaps, been a distinct manifestation of public opinion in favour of federation in any of the colonies, the tendency of the general feeling is believed by acute observers to be distinctly in that direction. The mere fact that, as we have already had occasion to note, Sir Henry

Glasgow Herald—*continued.*

Parkes has been the chief promoter of the Conference now being held, and that it was he who on Monday submitted a resolution declaring it to be the opinion of the delegates that "the best interests and the present and future prosperity of the Australian Colonies will be promoted by an early union under the Crown," is very significant of such a tendency; because until very recently New South Wales, and Sir Henry Parkes as its most influential politician, has shown a good deal of hostility to the federation movement, and the colony is not even at the present time represented on the existing Federal Council. The real, though unavowed, reason for this attitude is the intense jealousy of the younger colony of Victoria, which has always been a potent factor in New South Wales politics; and the recognition of this jealousy naturally leads to a consideration of the practical difficulties which will have to be overcome before a real Australian or Australasian Federation becomes an accomplished fact. These difficulties are neither few nor small. If the colonies have many common interests, there are also several questions on which they do not by any means see eye to eye. On the delicate matter of the protection of native industries, for instance, there is among them considerable diversity of practice. Victoria is out-and-out protectionist; New South Wales is at present—though she may not long remain so—as strongly free-trade; while in South Australia and Queensland protection is professedly only adopted for revenue purposes. It may be acknowledged, however, that the party which advocates thorough-going protection is gaining the upper hand all over the Australian Continent, and also in New Zealand, and that divergencies of practice on that account would not, perhaps, be likely to stand long in the way of a Federal Union. But there is another aspect of the problem. Federation, while insuring a general identity of fiscal policy in regard to all extra-Australian products, would also imply free trade between the colonies themselves, and it is by no means certain that such an arrangement would be acceptable to any of them except Victoria. The manufactures of that colony have, in consequence of the long prevalence of a protective policy there, become so largely developed that the industrial producers of the other colonies entertain serious apprehensions of the consequence of unrestricted Victorian competition.

There was more than one reference to this subject in the speeches delivered—all of them by prominent and representative men—at Monday's and Tuesday's sittings of the

Glasgow Herald—*continued.*

Melbourne Conference. Sir Samuel Griffith, speaking on behalf of Queensland, where he has long been the recognized head of the Liberal party, hinted that the question of tariffs might be left to be dealt with, even after the federation, by each colony according to its own discretion. "Federation without fiscal union would," he said, "be better than none." Mr. Playford, the influential ex-Premier of Queensland,[*] where he is familiarly known as "King Tom," did not chime in with this suggestion. He held that the fiscal question was more important than that of defence. But Mr. Deakin, of Victoria—perhaps the most eloquent, as he is certainly one of the ablest, of Australian statesmen—seemed to agree with Sir Samuel Griffith. He spoke of the possibility of the continuance of the present tariff arrangements "for a period of years after federation was established." This is surely a somewhat Utopian view. The existence of Customs barriers between the different colonies is at present one of the great causes of friction between them, and there can scarcely be real union among them until such a state of things is ended. A great question like that of Australian Federation cannot, however, be dealt with all at once. Not even the most sanguine promoters of the present Conference can have expected that it would be able to do more than bring the project fairly before the various colonies, and Mr. Deakin expressly said that the general principles, as well as the details, of the scheme must be left to be settled by a properly-authorized National Convention. When such a convention is assembled it is assumed that the Federal Union of Australia —with or without New Zealand, which stands in a different position from the other colonies, and in which its representative, Captain Russell, said on Tuesday the idea of federation had scarcely taken root—will be in a fair way for early realization. That such a union will be entitled to the support and hearty assent of the mother-country may be taken for granted. Whether it will help forward the achievement of the still vaster project of Imperial Federation which is cherished by many men of all shades of political opinion here at Home is perhaps questionable. Most of the Australians have a feeling of warm attachment to the old country; they would do nothing to sever the ties which still bind them to her, and if necessary they would doubtless come forward, as some have already done, in her defence. But they have a good deal of confidence in their own strength, and no lack of determination to manage their own affairs in their own way,

---

[*] Should be South Australia.

Glasgow Herald—continued.

as was made abundantly evident at the time of the colonial refusal to permit Chinese immigration in 1888. Their notion of what the future connection with Britain ought to be is that of an alliance, as close and warm as possible, but on equal terms; and whatever be the future of Imperial Federation in the large sense, it seems not altogether impossible that the accomplishment of Australian unity will tend to the realization of this ideal.

Newcastle Leader—
February 14th, 1890.

FEDERATION is in the air. It is a common subject of everyday talk. But to different men it means very different things. When the word "Federation" is used in the hearing of the working-man trades unionist the auditor pricks his ears and thinks of some great national union, embracing all the societies and branches of his trade in one common and united effort for the enforcement of higher wages or shorter hours of labour. To the manufacturer or merchant the word suggests a national combination of capitalists for the purpose of protecting the national industries from the ruinous demands of the sons of toil in times of commercial activity. But the term is at least as familiar in the political as it is in the industrial sphere, and here again it has two significations. There is a Colonial and there is an Imperial Federation. Both projects are closely related, and to a certain extent interdependent. The one is generally regarded as the necessary forerunner of the other. Yet both can and must be considered from separate and independent standpoints before any practical result can be achieved.

Colonial Federation is not entirely a new question. It has been with us before, and it has accomplished great results. In North America it has produced a Canadian Dominion, stretching from ocean to ocean, embracing several provinces, and while linking them together on the United States principle of one out of many, still retaining the connection with the British Imperial Government. In South Africa it has created a Cape Colony, and promises to create at no distant date a South African Dominion, fashioned very largely on the Canadian model. The particular development of the idea which for the present is uppermost in the public mind has Australia for its sphere of operations. A Conference is now being held at Melbourne for the discussion of

Newcastle Leader—*continued.*

the question of the federation of the Australian Colonies. Adverting to this Conference, the Queen's speech delivered at the opening of the Imperial Parliament this week contained words of the most gracious encouragement. Her Majesty was made say:—"Any well-considered measure which, by bringing these great colonies into closer union, will increase their welfare and strength will receive my favourable consideration." Judging from an article by Sir Gavan Duffy, published at the beginning of the month, these words, friendly and stimulating though they be, must be considered to fall short of the necessities of the situation. According to Sir Gavan Duffy, the Home or Imperial Government must take the lead before any definite result can be attained. He writes in a kindly way of Sir Henry Parkes, who is the chief inspirer of the present movement, and the leading spirit in the Conference. But he has no faith in Sir Henry's ability to carry a federation scheme, or (in view of former intercolonial contests and still existing prejudices) even in his suitability as the leading promoter of such a scheme. Certainly, whatever may be Sir Henry Parkes' qualifications or disqualifications as a leader of Australian Union, the proceedings at the Conference seems to justify Sir Gavan Duffy's view as to the unpreparedness of the Colonial Governments for federation. The general benevolence of the delegates from the different colonies towards the federation idea or principle happily cannot be disputed. The members all seem agreed that union is necessary and unavoidable; but they are not by any means agreed as to the conditions or extent of federation. Most of them seem disposed to fashion the new dominion on the Canadian model; but the moment a practical proposal for the realization of this ideal is suggested, questions arise as to the extent of the federation, as to whether or not New Zealand should be included in the Australian Dominion, as to the organization of a common army, as to the adoption of a common commercial policy, and as to the division of authority between the Provincial, the Dominion, and the Imperial Legislatures and Government. So far as the telegraphed summaries of the speeches delivered at the Conference indicate, the delegates seem convinced that Australian Federation is inevitable, and is likely to prove advantageous, but the time for its realization has not yet come; and just because this feeling prevails, the Home Government or Legislature will hesitate to take the lead or apply the compulsion suggested by Sir Gavan Duffy.

Times—

February 15th, 1890.

At yesterday's sitting of the Federation Conference, Sir Henry Parkes, replying to various speeches delivered at the previous sittings, declared that he came to the Conference in the spirit of an Australian citizen. He denied that his resolution was in any way bald or abstract. On the contrary, it was definite and decisive. Sir Henry proceeded to reply to the suspicions expressed as to his loyalty and sincerity, and declared with some warmth that he had done much in the past to advance the cause of federation. He had been unable to support the Federal Council because it was so limited, both in numbers and authority, and lacked the prestige necessary to insure its working in harmony with the Australian Parliaments. The Council, however, had done good service by accustoming the people to federal ideas. Sir Henry described the events which led to the creation and constitution of the United States, which he said were full of examples for Australia. Among the great objects requiring central government, two of the most important related—first, to the Asiatic races, because it was impossible to foresee what political or social changes might take place in China and how they might affect Australia; and, secondly, to the Pacific Islands, because Australia should be mistress of the Southern seas. A Federal Government should represent the whole people and command the respect of every nation. He proceeded to describe in eloquent terms the possibilities of Australia in regard to national influence, power, and honour. The Court of the Governor-General would be as attractive as any in the world. He left the proposed Convention free to devise a scheme of federation, and had the fullest confidence in its justice and honour. It was impossible to predict what the march of events might be, but he prayed God that Australia might always remain under the British flag. He hoped that all groups in the colonies might continue to form part of this magnificent empire.

The Hon. Duncan Gillies, in putting the resolution, said that he felt confident that the Conference would prove of great value, and defended the Federal Council, which he declared had legislated in various ways to advance the colonies represented. Its incomplete success was due to the fact that all the colonies had not joined the Council. The Conference tended to demonstrate the thorough necessity for federation in its largest sense. The time was ripe for union, and delay might cause obstacles. He would leave the

Times—*continued.*

proposed Convention to determine the lines of federation. Mr. Gillies admitted that there were weighty difficulties in the way, but difficulties were made to be overcome, and would be overcome. He believed the Convention would arrive at a solution satisfactory to all the Parliaments. The Constitution of Canada was the best basis for Australia, but with the necessary modification regarding the tariff. He said he felt confident that, even if the Convention were unable at once to level the Customs barriers, it would be able to arrive at a modification satisfactory to all. The Federal Parliament should have great and efficient powers, without, however, impairing those of the local Legislatures. The colonies should not tie the hands of their delegates to the Convention, and the delegates would have to approach the question in a determined spirit. The Convention would create a power of the greatest value for the whole Empire. The colonies united had a great future before them, but disunited could never accomplish their aim. In conclusion, Mr. Gillies congratulated the Conference on the manner in which the debate had been conducted.

The resolution was then unanimously adopted, declaring that the time had come for the union of the Australian colonies under one Government.

A motion brought forward by Captain Russell, New Zealand, providing for the admission into the union of the more remote Australasian colonies at such times and under such conditions as might hereafter be agreed upon, was next put and carried.

The Hon. A. Deakin, Victoria, then moved, and the Conference adopted, the following motions, after a brief discussion:—

(1) That members of the Conference should take the steps necessary to induce the Legislatures of their respective colonies to appoint, during the present year, delegates to a national Australasian Convention empowered to consider and report upon an adequate scheme for the Federal Constitution.

(2) That this Convention should consist of not more than seven members from each self-governing colony and not more than four from each Crown colony.

Another motion brought forward by Mr. Deakin, suggesting that all the colonies should take immediate united action to provide for military defence and co-operation in other matters, and stating that it was advisable to employ the Federal Council for such purposes, pending the estab-

Times—*continued.*

lishment of a Federal Constitution, was, after a brief debate, withdrawn, Sir Henry Parkes urging the inability of New South Wales to join the Council. He promised, however, to consult his colleagues and the leaders of the Opposition on the matter.

The Conference then adjourned.

When the Conference re-assembled to-day, Sir John Hall. New Zealand, moved, and the Hon. Dr. Cockburn, South Australia, seconded, and the Conference unanimously adopted, the following address to the Queen :—

We, your Majesty's loyal and dutiful subjects, members of a Conference assembled at Melbourne to consider the question of creating for Australasia one Federal Government, and representing the Australasian colonies, desire to approach your most gracious Majesty with renewed expressions of our devoted attachment to your Majesty's throne and person. On behalf of your Majesty's subjects throughout Australasia, we beg to express our fervent hope that your Majesty's life may be long spared to reign over a prosperous and happy people. We most respectfully inform your Majesty that, after mature deliberation, we have unanimously agreed to the following resolutions.

(Here follow the resolutions quoted above, proposed respectively by Sir Henry Parkes, Captain Russell, the Hon. A. Deakin, and Sir John Hall.)

The Conference then resolved that the Premier of Victoria should be empowered to convene a Convention, which will probably meet early next year.

Votes of thanks to Mr. Gillies, the President, and to Mr. G. H. Jenkins, the Secretary of the Conference, having been adopted, the Conference closed.

Standard—

February 15th, 1890.

The Conference convened at Melbourne to consider the question of Australasian Federation, brought its deliberations to a satisfactory close yesterday by passing a series of resolutions favourable to the formation of a union between the English communities of the Pacific. The rapidity and unanimity with which the business of the Conference was despatched are, we trust, of happy augury. The members held their first sitting on the 6th inst., and after placing Mr. Gillies, the Premier of Victoria, in the chair, they proceeded to the discussion of the resolution proposed by Sir Henry Parkes, the veteran statesman of New South Wales.

Standard—*continued*.

This resolution, which was agreed to without dissent on Thursday, declared that "the time had come for a union of the Australian colonies under one Government." When this proposition had received the assent of all the assembled delegates, it had to be determined what means should be adopted to bring about the desired result. Accordingly, Mr. Deakin, of Victoria, next moved that the members of the Conference "should take the steps necessary to induce the Legislatures of their respective colonies to appoint during the present year delegates to a national Australasian Convention." To this body, which is to be empowered to consider and report upon an adequate scheme of Federation, not more than seven members are to be sent from each self governing, and not more than four from each Crown colony, Further, it was proposed by Captain Russell, of New Zealand, and carried without opposition, that the more remote Australasian colonies should be admitted to the Union "at such times and under such conditions as might hereafter be agreed on." After passing these resolutions, the Conference, with a proper regard for the importance of the work on which they had been engaged, embodied them in an address to the Queen, in which they express their loyalty to the throne, and inform Her Majesty of the momentous step which they have taken towards uniting the English-speaking communities of Australia under a single Government. Finally, the Conference empowered the Premier of Victoria to summon the Federal Convention at an early period next year. Bearing in mind the prophecies that have been so freely indulged in as to the impossibility of getting the Australian colonies to take common action in regard to Federation, the smooth working of the Conference must be regarded with no ordinary feelings of satisfaction. Doubtless, the graver difficulties connected with the proposal have not yet been met, or rather, have been postponed for the consideration of the Convention, and it is there that old grievances and jealousies will have to be overcome. Still, the fact remains that all the Australian colonies, as well as Tasmania and New Zealand, stand pledged to union, and that New South Wales and Victoria have given a public proof that the sense of kinship is stronger than any petty feelings of local antagonism.

When the Convention meets at the beginning of next year, it is more than probable that a strong popular feeling in favour of union will have been developed throughout the island continent. If this should prove to be the case, and

Standard—*continued.*

if the delegates find themselves supported in their work by an unmistakable mandate from the public opinion of Australia, their efforts will be enormously facilitated. To bring their work to perfection, the members sent to Melbourne next year must feel that there is something more behind them than a mere general acquiescence in the notion of Federation. The closest interest and attention from all their fellow-countrymen will be required to ensure a strong foundation for the fabric they are called upon to build. That they will obtain it we do not doubt for a moment. The people of Australia are already beginning to show that they fully appreciate the importance of the subject, while the fact that the leading statesmen of Victoria and New South Wales are deeply in earnest on the question is a guarantee that they will leave no effort untried to educate public opinion in their respective communities. The chief obstacle to a successful termination of the labours of the Convention is, of course, the existence of hostile tariffs, and a second, although comparatively trifling one, is the difficulty of determining the claims of the various colonies to include the Federal Capital within their boundaries. The first of these is undoubtedly a matter of great gravity. As was pointed out at the Conference, federation and the maintenance by the various provinces of the new Dominion of tariffs hostile to each other are incompatible. If there is to be a union, there must be free-trade within its boundaries. Let us trust that when the fiscal conditions of the problem come to be discussed at close quarters, it will be possible to arrange a *modus vivendi*. If New South Wales and Victoria are really set upon accomplishing the work of federation, they will manage to agree upon a compromise which will contain concessions to both free-traders and protectionists. As for the question of a capital, it surely ought not to prove a stumbling clock. Naturally enough, neither Melbourne nor Sydney would be content to see the other chosen, and Brisbane, Adelaide, and Perth are out of the question. It will, however, be easy to find a piece of neutral ground fit to become the Washington or the Ottawa of the federation. Sir Henry Parkes has suggested Albury as a suitable spot, and we see no reason to doubt that the choice would be a wise one. The town stands on the Murray River, at the point where the railway which connects Sydney and Melbourne crosses the boundary between the two colonies. If a district of some hundred square miles on either side of the river were carved out, similar to the district of Columbia on

Standard—*continued.*

the Potomac, and subject only to the Federal Government, the problem would be solved. Neither of the great rivals could claim to own the capital, and their sister colonies would surely acquiesce in a choice which has so many geographical reasons to recommend it. No other spot on the continent would be so generally accessible to a majority of the inhabitants of Australasia.

There were not a few indications at the Conference that a severe struggle will rage in the Convention as to whether the Constitution of Canada or that of the United States shall be taken as a model. Though we have not the slightest desire to appear to instruct the Australians in regard to their own business, we very much trust that in the end their preference will lean towards that of the Dominion. When the Australians have actually to choose which system they will adopt, we cannot doubt that they will see the advantage of concentration in regard to military defence, and of a common system of criminal jurisprudence. In one or two points, no doubt, the Constitution of the United States is to be preferred to that of Canada. The Upper House of Congress, owing to the fact that it represents the States in their corporate capacity, has a weight and influence secured by no other Second Chamber in the world. The Senate of Canada, being a nominated body, has little authority, and it finds it impossible to prevent the powers it nominally enjoys falling into disuse. Possibly the Australians may decide for a single Chamber. If, however, they incline to the system in operation in most of the self-governing communities of the world, it is probable that they will in this matter follow the precedent of the Constitution of the United States rather than that of the "British North American Act." There is another point of great importance in which they will do well to imitate the founders of the American Union. The members of the Convention which drafted the Constitution of the United States, in obedience to a happy instinct, resolved to hold their deliberations in secret. We have it on the authority of the chief actors in that memorable gathering that, had they omitted to take this course, it would have been utterly impossible for them to have come to a working agreement. In the task of founding the Great Republic, men were often led to change their attitude from day to day, and, as they gained experience and learnt the lessons of Constitutional and political wisdom, to completely alter their previous opinions. This they could not have done had they been exposed to a running fire of irresponsible criticism.

Standard—*continued.*

Just as no Cabinet could live for twenty-four hours if its deliberations were made public, so it is impossible for a constituent body to sit except with closed doors. When the fabric is completed, it must be submitted, to the decision of the electors. To suffer the web of compromise spun each anxious day to be torn to pieces in the newspapers the next morning would be to render the task hopeless. When the knots have all been tied securely, but not till then, will it be fit to stand the test of popular approval. To the men who will meet next year at Melbourne will be entrusted duties as momentous as have ever been undertaken by Englishmen. The fate of a continent now inhabited by four millions of people, and destined some day, perhaps, to contain a population as great as that of Europe, will be in their hands; for on a successful grappling with the task of federation depends the whole future of Australasia. The prayer of all English-speaking men will be that they may use their opportunity wisely, and that, remembering " the crimson thread of kinship," they will use the Federation of the Southern Cross to strengthen the unity of the British race.

The Saturday Review—
February 15th, 1890.

Imperial federation is a great idea, which Englishmen in all parts of the world would gladly see pass into achievement, and which many are striving to make good. But the difficulties of carrying it out were always visible to those who, with some knowledge of the different condition of things in different parts of the Empire, had imagination enough to view the project now with Canadian, now with Australian, now with South African eyes—looking to the diverse interests of the various colonies, and considering them as they must necessarily be considered " on the spot." Not that any such survey compels a reasonable mind to give up the idea. Imperial Federation would bring with it advantages so great, and its accomplishment would be so extremely gratifying to that perfectly wholesome sentiment, British pride in domination, that it would not be abandoned if the difficulties that stand in the way of it were more stubborn than they really are. Nevertheless, it is quite evident by this time that Imperial Federation is not to be accomplished out of hand. No plan yet conceived has brought the project nearer to

The Saturday Review—*continued.*

attainment; but it should not be very difficult to avoid all approach to the contrary thing in the colonies, and all provocation to it at home, till the common misfortune threatens which is more likely than anything else to do the business. Something else may be done, which we may presently mention. Meanwhile we have to welcome a movement in Australasia which, whether it means Colonial Federation first and last, or whether it can be regarded as not that alone, but also as a step towards Imperial Federation, must be applauded.

A conference is sitting at Melbourne with intent to bring about a federation of the Australasian Colonies as speedily as may seem convenient. Proposals for union have been debated before; but nothing could be made of them at the time, on account (mainly) of the very warm jealousies between New South Wales and Victoria. Not that more substantial obstacles were absent. Federation cannot work well without fiscal union; and the difficulties of arranging a common tariff were supposed to be insuperable. Now, however, the jealousies seem to have softened very considerably, if they have not melted away altogether; and if we may judge from the Conference speeches so far as they have been reported while we write, federation with or without fiscal union is the desire of nearly all the delegates—certainly of the more important; the tariffs difficulty has taken a lower place in the estimation of most; and the main question is whether measures should not be immediately set afoot to confederate Australasia. New South Wales has been the most obstructive colony hitherto; but it was Sir Henry Parkes who, at Melbourne, moved that, "in the opinion of this Conference, the best interests and the present and future prosperity of the Australian Colonies will be promoted by an early union under the Crown"; and that the development of "the national life of Australasia in population, wealth, discovery, resources, and governing capacity" warrants the union of the colonies under one legislature and Executive Government. Sir Henry Parkes had already spoken strongly in favour of uniting under one Government and one flag, "though it should not go forth for one moment that, in seeking complete authority over our own affairs, we are seeking any separation from the great Empire." The Victorian delegates spoke vigorously in the same sense. The Queensland delegate said that he would be disappointed if the Conference failed to lay the foundation of a strong Federal Government. The Tasmanians were represented as

The Saturday Review—*continued*.

so anxious for federation that they would rather have partial union than none. The delegate from Western Australia could only complain of Sir Henry Parkes's motion as being "somewhat too abstract"; he moved that the Conference should lay down the lines of federation. The representative of distant New Zealand doubted whether the time had come for union, though he saw no real difficulty about it, and was sure it would be established before long. More hesitating was the South Australian delegate, who thought federation should not be forced; but the reports leave no doubt that the predominant feeling predominates strongly. This is more clearly seen from the tone that was generally taken when the fiscal difficulty was dealt with. It is obviously a disturbing one for the Victorian delegates. They acknowledge that there can be no complete federation with hostile tariffs, but have made up their minds that a sufficiently effective union ("for which the people of Victoria are prepared to make sacrifices") can be established without a uniform fiscal system. "Let us have federation with or without fiscal union," cries the Queenslander, echoing the general opinion. As for the once-obstructive New South Wales, its Prime Minister is reported to have said that "the question of a common tariff was a mere trifle as compared with the question of national existence: subordinate questions should be sunk."

From all this it would appear that Australasian Federation has become a common desire, which there is a general eagerness to satisfy. Most of its advocates at the Conference are known to be thorough men of business, as well as resolute politicians. It must be supposed that they have well considered the ways and means, and believe that no differences of a forbidding character are likely to arise. Nevertheless, we may still doubt whether the federation project will proceed at once to accomplishment; but not that the men whose business it is to think for these Southern colonies, and whose judgment is trusted most by the various Australian communities, believe themselves to be under strong compulsion to federate as soon as may be. And we can well understand why. These colonies are growing richer, they are becoming a more tempting prize, every day. They see fleets upon the seas that are not British, and are aware that, at their present rate of growth, these fleets will become far more formidable ten years hence, or even five; while another powerful navy is coming into existence. This when new fields of enterprise are opening out for Australian commerce,

The Saturday Review—*continued*.

and while the Australians see, in what they regard as their own waters, an aggressive competition at work which the Home Government rather permits than hinders. We may think the Australians unreasonable on that point; but, reasonable or unreasonable, that is their view. "Defence," "the defences," "the question of national existence"—the constant recurrence of words and phrases like these in the Conference debates testifies to the fundamental purpose of federation; while the present readiness to sink all minor questions of tariffs and the rest, shows how importunate that purpose is felt to be. Defence—and ability to command a greater degree of attention from the Government at home. When we read that Mr. Deakin, a remarkably eloquent Victorian, "referred to the question of the New Hebrides, Samoa, and other places in the Pacific, and said that the voice of Australia should be heard as one by the Imperial Government," we recall certain disappointments and grievances which were bitterly resented in the colonies lately, and understand his meaning at once. It is beyond all doubt true that, in seeking federation, the Australian Colonies are "not seeking separation from the great Empire," as Sir Henry Parkes put it. But we shall find when we get full reports of the Conference speeches that one very substantial part of the design is that which Mr. Deakin spoke of. The Australians propose that, when any further questions of New Guinea, the New Hebrides, Samoa, and other places in the Pacific do arise Australasia shall be able to speak with one voice to the Imperial Government. Remonstrance from this colony to-day, from that to-morrow, from others hardly at all, is found to be of small effect, or none. It will be a different thing when an Australian Union speaks by the mouth of a Federal Government; and it is even thought, perhaps, that it will not speak with less effect if the Union has some sort of naval and military equipment wherewith to help itself. That, we shall probably find, is the mother-motive of the movement, and we must allow that it is a reasonable motive by ourselves supplied. Moreover, it is true in any case that the time has come when the Australians should lay the foundations of what, with courage and good luck, will become a great maritime power in the Pacific; and though it is possible to suspect in the federation movement an intention to prepare for separation from the mother-country, it is as reasonable to hope that Imperial Federation will be advanced when Australasia has become compacted under a Union Government and a Union Executive. That conse-

The Saturday Review—continued.

quence, however, must depend very much upon ourselves; and the something that we can do is, not to repeat our very unimperial conduct in "the question of the New Hebrides, Samoa, and other places in the Pacific," and to strengthen the fleets of the Empire in every sea.

St. James' Gazette.
February 15th, 1890.

THE meeting of the Australasian Conference at Melbourne has beyond all doubt materially forwarded the formation of a federation of our colonies in the Southern Seas. The work is not yet done, and the actual execution of it may be found to present serious difficulties; but, as the Hon. Duncan Gillies observed, difficulties are made to be overcome. If only the will is not wanting, they can be mastered. In this case there seems every sign that the various colonies represented at Melbourne are genuinely anxious to be consolidated into a Dominion on the Canadian or some other model. They have committed themselves to the attempt to form the federation, and next year we shall see them at work. The fiscal question will call for the display of all the ingenuity they can devote to it, and may even test their willingness to make mutual concessions pretty severely. Still there is no obstacle in the path which good will and good management cannot turn.

The colonists are well aware that whatever plan they may adopt will be most favourably received in this country. They have just been assured in the Queen's Speech that their effort to federate has Her Majesty's hearty approval, and these words were no idle form. Indeed, the immediate cause of this Conference at Melbourne is alone enough to earn it the most hearty approval of the mother-country. The colonial leaders have been induced to again take the work of federation in hand, by the pressure of that public opinion which calls for a strenuous combined effort to provide for the defence of Australasia as a part of the Empire. It was the extreme difficulty of combining their naval and military resources without also establishing a common administration which has urged them all to set about forming a Federal Bond. This of itself would be enough to secure our sympathy for the attempt. We hardly need Sir Henry Parkes' loyal speech to assure us that the object of the

St. James' Gazette—*continued.*

colonies is the common good of the Empire, and that their spirit is excellent. The facts of the case confirm Sir Henry's words and our own hopes. It is a fact of which colonial politicians are perfectly well aware that any scheme of defence which they can adopt must largely depend for its efficiency on the general support of the Empire. The scattered Australasian Colonies, and the vast territory of Australia, must for some generations remain open to attacks by a Great Power. They are too thinly inhabited as yet to be able to provide the forces on sea and land which would be required to repel a resolute invasion conducted with the resources at the disposal of a Great Power. Even 50,000 well-organized militia—and Australia with its present population can hardly provide a larger mobile force than that—combined with a squadron of half a dozen cruisers and a few coast-defence turret-ships, could not guarantee its immense seaboard. Germany, France, Russia, or even Italy, could always land an armament in, say, Western Australia or Queensland long before the colonial forces could be concentrated on the menaced spot. Nobody supposes that the colonies could be conquered by any of these Powers, or even two of them combined. But to resist a conquest is one thing; to avert disintegration, and prevent a well-armed enemy from landing in some distant and thinly-inhabited region is another. From this last danger Australia, and all Australasia indeed, must look to be defended by the mother-country. One power, and one only, can guarantee them, and that is the navy which is strong enough to command the sea routes. For that reason it is the interest of the colonies to take care that their Federation and its attendant scheme of military defence form a coherent part of the general organization of the Empire. A local combination, a local army formed within the Empire and animated by a spirit of manly intelligent loyalty, are the objects at which the colonies are aiming. The speeches of Sir Henry Parkes, Mr. Duncan Gillies, and others leave no doubt on that point. The speakers have, we feel sure, the firm support of their fellow-colonists. For such objects, sought in such a spirit, we have, and can have, only the most hearty approval. These things are done in the interest of all of us. As long as that community of interest endures and is intelligently recognized the unity of the Empire is in no danger. Take that community of interest away and there is no guarantee for it.

Pall Mall Gazette—
February 15th, 1890.

Having agreed unanimously to Sir Henry Parkes' resolution in favour of Australian Federation, the Melbourne Conference yesterday proceeded, also unanimously, to move an address to the Queen expressing their "devoted attachment to your Majesty's throne." This is as it should be, and is an earnest, we will hope and believe, of what will always be. "Deakin's Dream," as his opponents called it at the last Victorian election, will only be half fulfilled unless the federation of Australia within her own borders leads to the continuance and the confirmation of her connection with the mother-country.

Daily News—
February 15th, 1890.

The movement for the federation of the Australasian Colonies has made an important step in the Conference which was brought to a close at Melbourne yesterday. Whether the inevitable rivalry of the capitals will ever allow of the adoption in the Southern Seas of such a union as has been formed by Canada is still somewhat in doubt. There are unusual difficulties in the way. Australasia is scattered. There are a thousand miles of sea between Sydney and New Zealand. There are great tariff differences, moreover, which will be very hard to overcome, though the President, Mr. Gillies, expressed his confident hope that even if the proposed Convention were not able to level the Customs barriers, it would be able to arrive at a modification satisfactory to all. The proposed Convention is one which the Prime Minister of Victoria was empowered to call by resolution passed yesterday, and which it is understood he will invite to meet early next year. Meanwhile the subject will be exhaustively discussed in all the colonies, and it may be hoped that out of the intercolonial debate some agreement may come. The scheme for federation is one which we in the Old Country can but regard with the fullest sympathy. We believe with Mr. Duncan Gillies that an Australasian Convention would create a power which would be of great value for the whole Empire. English Liberals at least will watch with the greatest interest the progress of the discussion in the colonies, with the earnest wish that those great communities, founded on the full development of liberal principles, may constitute themselves, as they desire, the paramount power in the southern hemisphere.

Post—
February 15th, 1890.

The curtain has fallen upon the first act in the drama of Australasian Federation. For more than a week the Conference of representatives of the Australian Colonies convened for the purpose of considering a scheme of federation and federal defence has been sitting in Melbourne, and on Thursday it adopted a resolution proposed by Sir Henry Parkes, the Premier of New South Wales, affirming the principle of federal union. The idea is no new one; the difficulty which has existed has been the discovery of the means of giving practical effect to it. A federation to be thoroughly useful must be complete, and the central authority must be supreme over the federated colonies so long, of course, as the exercise of its powers does not bring it into conflict with the Imperial authority. To the strengthening of an opinion of this sort in the Australasian Colonies there can be very little doubt that the valuable report of General Edwards on the defences of those colonies materially contributed. The idea of a union for defensive purposes became popular, and was carefully considered; and it was speedily recognized that a distant approximation brought about with such an object would be not only incomplete but might easily become awkward in its results. It required to be made intimate. The result was the Conference which met last week. On paper, the abstract resolution proposed at the Conference by Sir Henry Parkes has not advanced the cause of Australasian Federation in the smallest degree. It simply affirmed a proposition at which no one was likely to cavil—that the development of Australia "justifies the higher act, at all times contemplated, of the union of the colonies under one Legislative and Executive Government on principles just to the several colonies." But the fact that such a statement was formally and unanimously accepted, and that the representatives of the various colonies showed in the main a strong desire to make certain concessions in order to give practical effect to it, is in itself a long step on the road towards federation. There are difficulties in the way, no doubt, and the debate at the Conference served to bring some of them into prominence. This is a decided advantage, for the advocates of federation now know exactly what obstacles stand before them. It is clear that whilst the principle of union was unanimously accepted, there exists considerable difference of opinion as to the methods by which it should be carried out. There are advocates for a development of the Federal

Post—*continued.*

Council, and there are those who would prefer to see an entirely new and differently constituted body. Some of the representatives, too, were in favour of a limited federation if obstacles stood in the way of a more complete union, whilst there seems to have been considerable difference of opinion as to the system of federation which ought to be adopted. Suggestions were not lacking in favour of an imitation of the method pursued in the United States, whilst some representatives advocated a union on the plan in force in the Canadian Dominion, and others desired to combine the best features of both methods. Amid such diversities of opinion there was abundant room for argument, and when, to the points to which we have already referred, are added the difficulties created by hostile tariffs, it is evident that the path of Australasian Federation is yet far from being smooth. New South Wales and Tasmania are adherents of free-trade; Victoria is strongly protectionist; and South Australia has increased her Customs duties for the purpose of guarding her nascent industries against the competition of Victoria. Under such circumstances there must necessarily be a very serious conflict of interests, and it is somewhat hard to conceive of a federated Australia whilst the various components of the federation are engaged in a war of tariffs with one another. This is one of the practical details which has to be dealt with now that the principle has been formally adopted by the various colonies. Dr. Cockburn, the Premier of South Australia, declared that he anticipated the consummation of Australian union, though it might not come immediately. When it does come it must carry with it the adhesion of the remaining Australasian colonies. Meanwhile it would be well if Australasians in general would recognize the truth of the statement of Mr. J. M. Macrossan, that what local legislators might lose the people of federated Australia would gain. An Australasian has at the present moment two outlets for his patriotic feelings. He has his loyalty towards the British Empire and his love for his own colony. It would be well if the latter could be merged in an attachment to a United Australasia. In this country an Englishman has none the less regard for England as a whole because he happens to have been born in Yorkshire on the one hand or in Devonshire on the other, and though the cases are not, we admit, an exact parallel, it would augur well for the future if a similar spirit should grow up in Australasia. There was considerable common sense in the statement of Mr. Deakin, the

Post—*continued.*

Premier of Victoria, that Australia would sooner or later be forced to unite, and the difficulties would only be increased by delay. At any rate, the ball has now been set fairly rolling, and it rests with our Australasian fellow-subjects themselves to keep it moving until the end is achieved.

Statist—

February 15*th*, 1890.

If we were tempted to indulge sanguine hopes as to the result of the Conference of delegates which has been discussing in Melbourne this week the question of the federation of the Australian colonies, the recollection of previous unsuccessful efforts to achieve that desirable end could hardly fail to cool our enthusiasm. More than thirty years ago the Melbourne Chamber of Commerce passed a resolution advocating the assimilation of Australian tariffs. This initial step towards the fiscal unification of Australia, however, led to nothing, although communications on the subject were opened between four colonies. In the long interval down to the present, resolutions have been passed by the Parliaments of New Zealand and Tasmania, in support of the same object, but without awakening the least sympathetic response either in the neighbouring colonies, or in Downing-street. Representatives of several Colonial Chambers of Commerce and Manufactures have assembled on different occasions in recent years, and affirmed the principle of intercolonial federation on the basis of a Customs Union and a uniform tariff; but these gatherings only ended in talk. The first Conference which gave a real impulse to the federal cause and bore any permanent fruit was held in Sydney in 1883. It was attended by Parliamentary delegates from a majority of the colonies. It led to the passing of an Act by the Victorian Legislature for intercolonial federation, an attempt on the part of Victoria to conclude a reciprocity treaty with Tasmania, and the actual establishment of the Federal Council. For the last few years the latter body, which comprises delegates from all the colonies except New South Wales, has met annually for the transaction of intercolonial business at Hobart Town; but the great drawback to its efficiency is that its decisions are not binding on the colonies unless ratified by the Colonial Parliaments by which it is recognized. The notable circumstance connected with the latest movement to promote federation is that it has been brought about by the politician who encouraged his

Statist—*continued.*

colony to stand aloof from the Federal Council. We refer to Sir Henry Parkes, the Premier of the parent colony.

Being a free-trader and a shrewd tactician, Sir Henry cannot shut his eyes to the rising tide of protectionist agitation in New South Wales, which almost threatens the very existence of the party he so ably represents. The manufacturers and working men of that colony have been accustomed to look with envy on the rapid industrial progress of Victoria, which, rightly or wrongly, they persist in ascribing to protection. Accordingly, they cherish a desire to raise tariff barriers sufficiently high to exclude Victorian products from their own territory and foster home manufactures. Sir Henry Parkes, with meritorious foresight, sees in the spread of protectionism in New South Wales not only the downfall of his own party, but ultimate disaster to a group of protective colonies, whose tariffs will inevitably stimulate local production until not only are local wants supplied, but there is a glut of local production which can find no outlet in adjacent markets, owing to prohibitory fiscal barriers bristling in every direction. But whatever be Sir Henry Parkes' motives, and without criticising too narrowly his previous attitude towards the federal movement, we do not hesitate to say that he deserves the thanks of the Empire for urging forward proposals eminently conducive to the extinction of existing mutual jealousies, and vitally affecting the development of Australian resources, the judicious and economical administration of the colonies themselves, and their permanent consolidation in a prosperous nationality. The beneficial tendency of Intercolonial Federation has long been demonstrated beyond question. As regards the United States and Canada, the rapid progress of these communities dates from their union, respectively, under Federal Governments. When the basis of Australian Federation is perfected, it is probable that the main features of the Canadian Dominion will be adapted to the requirements of our fellow-subjects in the South Pacific. A Federal Parliament would legislate upon matters of intercolonial and national concerns, such as customs, defence, and Imperial relations. The provinces would, of course, retain self-government, subject to federal conditions. Through provincial Legislative Assemblies and Councils, laws would be framed relating to civil rights, property, municipal institutions, prisons, asylums, and so forth. Whether or not education, railways, land, and mining systems of administration in the separate provinces shall be left in the hands of colonial Parliaments, or

Statist—*continued.*

centralised in the federal authority, are details which can alone be settled by the National Convention by which the scheme of federation is matured. There would also be a federal justiciary, by which appeals from provincial courts would be tried. Obviously, the most difficult of all points to adjust, however, will be the federal customs tariff, despite the comparatively trifling importance which Sir Henry Parkes seems to attach to it. It can hardly be supposed that New South Wales and Tasmania will meekly accept the present high fiscal imposts of Victoria as applicable to goods imported from countries beyond the federated colonies after the persistent bitterness with which the two former have not unnaturally regarded these imposts. Nor is it likely, on the other hand, that Victoria will assent, without dispute, to external commerce being subject to a free-trade tariff. But we are not without hope that even this grave difficulty will yield when threshed out in friendly debate.

Perhaps the most striking result of federation will consist of the enormous saving which will be effected in the administration of Government. It is simply preposterous that £40,000 per annum should be expended on the salaries of Australian Governors alone, for ruling a collective population not much exceeding half the population of London, that the Ministers of a single colony numbering but little over a million should receive over £10,000 a year, and that payments to members in the Legislative Assembly of the same colony, with incidental costs incurred by that section of the Parliament, should amount to £30,000 a year. Governmental expenditure in other colonies is no less lavish in proportion to their revenue and population. Another £30,000 a year is consumed in supporting the Agents-General and their staffs against a single official of that class representing the Canadian Dominion, with a salary not exceeding that of the Agent-General for Victoria. Under the present *régime* the annual rate of public expenditure ranges in Australasia from £4 6s. 4d. to £10 12s. 3d. per head of population, as contrasting with £2 10s. 3d. in England and £1 14s. per head in Canada. The restriction now placed on struggling inventors, who have now to pay for taking out patents in seven different colonies, would be removed by federation, to the advantage of the whole Australian community, and a wave of prosperity would result from the inauguration of inter-colonial free-trade—an indissoluble adjunct of federation—surpassing all anticipation.

Investors' Guardian—

February 15th, 1890.

Our readers have already been informed of the meeting of delegates from the various Australian Colonies, at the capital of Victoria, for the purpose of discussing the question of confederation. At the sitting on the 11th of this month, Sir Henry Parkes moved the following resolution: "That in the opinion of this Conference, the best interests, and the present and future prosperity of the Australian Colonies will be promoted by an early union under the Crown, and, while fully recognizing the valuable services of the members of the Convention of 1883, in founding the Federal Council, declares its opinion that the seven years which have since elapsed, have developed the national life of Australasia in population, wealth, discovery, resources, and self-governing capacity to an extent which justifies the higher act, at all times contemplated, of the union of the Colonies under one Legislative and Executive Government, on principles just to the several colonies." From a Melbourne telegram of Thursday last, we learn that this resolution was carried by the unanimous vote of the assembled delegates, and, consequently, there is before the world the installation of an Australian "Dominion," which, there cannot be a shadow of doubt, will be second only in importance to that of Canada, while fully equal to that vast territory in loyalty to the Crown. It is earnestly to be desired as was shadowed in the address of Sir Henry Parkes, that this federation will not only economize and strengthen these resources, but will merge local into national interests.

Some considerable time must elapse before a properly authorized National Convention can be appointed to discuss the terms, as between the various provinces, and for the subsequent necessary confirmation by the various legislatures. But if the difficulties which will then arise be met with fairness and conciliation, so that the whole of the colonies enter with heart and soul into the confederation, it is certain that the movement cannot fail to be of great benefit to all of them, and we look at this strengthening of the colonies as a matter for congratulation to the mother-country. The tie which binds us is one of affectionate relationship cemented by mutual self-interest. We are proud of the manly growth and vigour of our offspring, whose younger and more tender bloom we have always been ready to foster and protect. Australia on her part, has not been slow to acknowledge or to reciprocate the services we

Investors' Guardian—*continued.*

rendered, as instanced by the promptitude with which she voluntarily sent the finest of her stalwart sons to our aid at the time of the Egyptian War.

Therefore we heartily sympathize with this movement, as marking a new departure in the history of the Empire; it should be the first step in advance towards the consolidation of British and Colonial interests, enabling both to present a firmer front against all foreign antagonism, and enhancing our mutual commerce and prosperity by facilitating a freer exchange of our various productions.

Star—

February 15th, 1890.

Everybody who wishes well to the Australian Colonies will rejoice in the unanimous adoption of the resolution in favour of federation by the Conference convened for the preliminary discussion of the question. It is only a preliminary proceeding, to be sure; but where you have a will in these matters a way very soon follows; and nothing has been more remarkable about the Conference, so far as its proceedings have been reported over here, than the hearty goodwill with which the idea of federation has been received, even where there have been differences over details.

The result of the Conference is to commit the Colonies—including New Zealand—to Federal Union "under the Crown," and, of course, our Imperial Federationist friends are jubilant over the result. We should advise them, however, not to make too much of it. It is a noteworthy point that the drift of opinion at the Conference was in favour of federation on the United States rather than the Canadian line. That alone ought to remind us that some of the most ardent federationists in Australia openly avow the "United States of Australia" to be the ideal they have in view. Conservative Sir Henry Parkes himself is opposed to Imperial Federation, and among Australian Radicals the only countenance given to the idea does not go further than a pious opinion that an *independent* Australia may some day join the United States of America and the old United Kingdom in a federation of the English-speaking States. That day is not in sight yet.

Daily Graphic—
February 15th, 1890.

In his last speech at the above Conference, Sir Henry Parkes laid stress upon a point which will yet obtain much more importance. On urging the necessity of central government, he remarked that "it was impossible to foresee what political or social changes might take place in China, and how they might affect Australia." What requires no foreknowledge is the fact that the Chinese are quick to learn the mechanical arts, that they are industrious to a degree, that already they have much capital invested in concerns outside their own country, and that, conceivably, there will be a time when they will enter into the world's competitions on equal terms with white men. The same may be said about India. We are educating all the native races on Western models, and they are beginning to travel. What China and India may yet do no prophet may pretend to tell. The tolerance of cosmopolitanism is on the side of the weak, whose chief weapon is cunning. Perhaps it may be reserved for the Anglo-Saxon breed to fetch and carry for the races it has trained.

Birmingham Gazette—
February 15th, 1890.

Amid the hubbub of home affairs, scarcely a due amount of attention is being bestowed upon the important Conference now sitting at Melbourne. That Conference has been called together to consider the question of Australasian defence, and for the last few days it has been engaged in the discussion of a motion made by Sir Henry Parkes, the Prime Minister of New South Wales, that the time has now come for the union of the Australian colonies under one Government. This important, we may almost say revolutionary resolution, has been carried unanimously, and thus the first great step has been taken in a reform which may have momentous consequences upon the future of Australasia. Naturally there have been various opinions expressed in the course of the discussion. Some of the speakers maintain that the idea of federation has scarcely yet taken root; others went into careful details as to how much of the Canadian and how much of the American form of union should be adopted. It is hardly necessary to consider these points in detail at

Birmingham Gazette—*continued.*
this stage. The wisest course will undoubtedly be to graft upon one stem the best features of the great federations which have been tried by other countries. If the Australasians fail to make a model Constitution it will not be for want of materials upon which to design it. The great central fact is that after a prolonged and anxious discussion the step has been resolved upon. We congratulate the colonies upon the fact that they have shown a disposition to sink local interests to some extent in order to attain the common good. Since General Edwards presented the report, in which he pointed out that the defensive service could only be made effective under some system of federal control, the clear-headed statesmen of the colonies have been asking each other the question,—Why take any half-measure ? It would have been possible to establish a Federal Council, charged only with the control of the defensive service; but there has long been a feeling in the several colonies that it would be an immense gain to have some Court of Appeal which would be independent of local influences, and that this could only grow out of a Federal Government. There is a widespread recognition also of the hurtful effects of the border tariffs. Whatever views may be entertained as to external commerce, the general opinion favours free-trade amongst the Australasian colonies. This, again, could be best secured under a Federal Government. And thus it has come about that a unanimous resolution has been passed in favour of embarking upon an effort "to rise to a higher level of national life, which would give the Australasian Colonies a larger space before the eyes of the world, and would in a hundred ways promote their united power and prosperity." Believing that it is to the interests of the colonies to federate, we see no reason for indulging in any gloomy forecasts of the effect their action may have upon the relations with the mother-country. For the present they fully recognize the advantages of the tie. Australasia has an area of 3,256,117 square miles, and Canada an area of 3,520,000. They are thus almost identical in extent, and although the proximity of Canada to this country has enabled it to increase its population more rapidly, there is no reason why the future of "the Southern Empire" should not be quite as prosperous as that of our magnificent possession on the American Continent.

Chronicle—

February 15th, 1890.

Seldom has a more momentous resolution been passed by any deliberative or consultative body than that which has just been passed by the Conference of Australasian representatives in Melbourne. Those representatives of all the Australasian colonies have unanimously agreed to the resolution of Sir Henry Parkes in favour of the federation of those colonies, and we may be confident that the various populations will ratify the decision of the Conference. It is reasonable, therefore, to assume that the creation of an Australasian Dominion will be accomplished in the near future, and the mother-country will watch with sympathetic solicitude over the birth of what may be termed a new English nation. Mr. Gillies, the Prime Minister of Victoria, admits that there are serious difficulties in the way of accomplishing the object which the Conference has in view, but he insists, as we have often done, that such difficulties are made to be overcome. The Australasian colonies have an example which they can imitate. Mr. Gillies declares that the Constitution of Canada is the best basis on which the Australasian Dominion can be built, but with " the necessary modification regarding the tariff." Into these details, however, it is not our purpose to enter at present. The great thing is to have the people of Australasia giving formal expression, through their accredited representatives, to a desire for federation, and taking measures for the speedy realization of that wish. With this important object kept steadily in view all difficulties will ultimately disappear. A Convention is to be held later on for the purpose of carrying out the decisions of the Conference. That Convention, Mr. Gillies asserts, will " create a power of the greatest value for the whole Empire," and Sir Henry Parkes prays that Australia may always remain under the British flag. What is wanted, however, is judicious statesmanship at Home, as well as at the Antipodes. Everything seems to be ready to the hands of our statesmen. Will they prove themselves worthy of their position ? It need not be difficult to utilize the passionate spirit of loyalty to the Crown and the British connection, which has just been exhibited in Melbourne, in order to cement the various parts of the Empire in a common union. The course which ought to be taken is so patent that it would only seem possible to miss it by accident. Ordinary sagacity and prudence may now prevent the possibility of ultimate disintegration.

Chronicle—*continued.*

The Earl of Belmore, who was formerly Governor of New South Wales, intends to ask the Secretary of State for the Colonies on Monday, whether there is any correspondence in the Colonial Office on the subject of Australian federation which may be laid before the House of Lords without public inconvenience. It is not unlikely that an interesting debate on the subject may take place. Besides Lord Stanley of Preston, the Governor-General of Canada, there are six members of the House of Lords, including Lord Knutsford, who have held the office of Secretary of State for the Colonies. Lords Grey, Granville, Carnarvon, Kimberley, and Derby have presided over the Colonial Department, and three of them have had a second tenure of office.

Mr. Gladstone, in writing to a correspondent lately, made the following guarded statement in respect to Australian federation:—" I have written to Sir H. Parkes. It appeared to me that the steps taken by him as to the movement were judicious, but I have not such a knowledge of the case as alone could justify the utterance of an opinion meant to be conveyed to the public. I do not doubt that the citizens of Australasia will work their way to just conclusions."

Lord Derby, writing to a correspondent on the 7th instant, says:—" The movement in favour of the federation of the Australian Colonies among themselves seems to me one eminently deserving of support. If it can be effected, the Australians will feel themselves to be members of a powerful and important State. They will have free-trade at least with one another, which is better than not having it at all; and their relations with the Colonial Office will be rendered easier, since any difference between the various colonies as to what they wish the mother-country to be will be settled by the decision of the majority. I believe you will find a practically unanimous agreement in this country in favour of intercolonial federation. It has succeeded in Canada, where the difficulties to be overcome were much greater, and it will succeed in Australia if the feeling in its favour shall be (as I hope and expect) strong enough to overbear the petty local jealousies which statesmen make it their object to suppress, but which politicians find it to their advantage to trade upon."

Inquirer—

February 15th, 1890.

An important speech was made last week at Melbourne by Sir Henry Parkes, the New South Wales Premier, in connection with the sittings of the Australian Conference. It will be remembered that in 1883, when the constitution of a Federal Council was drafted, the abstention of New South Wales was fatal to the success of the scheme. New South Wales no longer holds aloof, though there are difficulties in the way of federation in connection with the question of tariffs—difficulties, however, which it is the object of the Conference to surmount. At a banquet given to the delegates, Sir Henry, in response to the toast of "A United Australasia," said that no advantage would arise from delay, which would only increase the difficulties. The colonies had now arrived at the time when they were fully justified by all the laws regulating the growth of free communities in uniting under one Government and one flag. This implies no separation from the Empire, nor the creation of a separate political organization, and it should not go forth for a moment that in seeking complete authority over their own affairs they were seeking any separation from the great Empire. New South Wales was prepared to go into this national union without making any bargain, and without stipulating for any advantage whatever, but trusting in the good faith and justice of a Federal Parliament. In concluding his speech, which was throughout loudly applauded, Sir Henry Parkes said that he believed that the people of Australia had already made up their minds to be united, and no hand on earth was strong enough to keep them asunder. The passage in the Queen's speech referring to this question lends additional interest to this speech. We do not anticipate a repetition of the blunder made rather more than a century ago in America, or rather more that fifty years ago in Canada.

Telegraph—

February 17th, 1890.

In the words of the President of the Conference the Australasian Colonies seem "ripe for union." The facts show full justification for the erection under the Southern Cross of what will be in effect a new nationality. Australia alone has a population of three millions—the figure which our

Telegraph—*continued.*

North American Colonies reached when they issued their Declaration of Independence. Adding New Zealand, Tasmania, and other smaller islands, the United States of Australasia would start with four millions of people. In other respects they are far beyond the thirteen Colonies of America when they "set up for themselves" in 1782. The mineral wealth of the new State has been proved already; since 1851 the gold produced has been equal to more than a third of our National Debt, and there is every reason to believe that the treasures of the soil are far from being exhausted. Australia's imports are worth fifty millions a year; its exports, mainly wool, frozen meat, and gold, nearly as much. The united public debts of all the Colonies amount to the very serious total of one hundred millions; though the burden assumes its true proportions if we consider that it has not been spent in "gunpowder and glory," but in the making of railways and other useful works. Probably the interest payable on this borrowed capital would be diminished if, as a result of federation, all the States became jointly answerable for each. The political necessity for a closer bond is partly due to the difficulties of physical alliance. Australia is a large island or continent with central deserts and a colonised coast. There are no transcontinental railways, as in America; every delegate who joined in the Conference came by sea in a coasting steamer. This characteristic of the new land makes common naval defence absolutely essential to safety. Were a foreign foe to attack South Australia it would be necessary for New South Wales and Victoria, the nearest Colonies, to send assistance by sea. Short cuts by land across the waste expanse may be eventually developed, but at present the new nation will be in fact a fringe of States along the coast of a vast expanse of central uninhabited territory. The detached positions of New Zealand, twelve hundred miles off, and of Tasmania, New Guinea, and many other islands, indicate that above all things the new nation must be a naval power. The maritime provinces of our other great Dominion, Canada, do not contain a fourth of her population; Australasia will practically be all maritime States. The Sea-Queen's daughter will be a Sea-Princess herself.

Nothing is more remarkable, though it is little noticed, than the readiness of successive home Governments to promote, even to push on, the union of isolated Colonies, so as to form larger and stronger States. The short-sighted statesmen of the eighteenth century would have scouted

Telegraph—*continued.*

high treason and conspiracy in the efforts which the public men of the present day directly encourage and promote. The explanation is that, whether our distant possessions remain separated or agree upon federation, we have long since wisely given up all idea of ruling them from Downing-street. There are still questions that crop up, chiefly relating to the international interests of the colonies, and sometimes arising out of diverse laws of marriage and divorce. But there is reason to believe that naval defence will be to a great extent simplified, if not solved, by the rise of one great dominion in the place of several isolated colonies. A new State, with large territories and revenue, will be quite able to bear the chief, if not the sole, burden of its own protection. It may be said if Australasia, under its new regime, has its own Militia, its own Navy, and its own tariffs hostile to our goods, what difference will there be between it and a State in those seas entirely independent of Great Britain? Why should we retain a barren sceptre and a titular rule? Why keep the responsibility for defence when we have not the privilege of control? The reply is very simple. So long as the Australians prefer the sovereignty of the Queen it certainly is not for the mother-country to cast them off. We receive with gladness proofs that love of the old institutions and the old land are still cherished "by the long wash of Australasian seas." Nor are the associations purely sentimental. While the Queen is still Sovereign of Canada and Australasia, her ships in case of war will find coal, comfort, and sympathy in scores of harbours on the Atlantic and the Pacific that will be sternly shut against the fleets of her enemies. The voluntary despatch of a New South Wales contingent to the Soudan also indicates possibilities of future willing help. Nothing in the history of England's relations with her colonies is more remarkable than the enthusiasm with which this service was offered, and it cannot be doubted that the same disposition to fly to the assistance of the mother-country in case of necessity will be shown again. True, the aid thus given would not be, in the event of a European war, of great value from a military point of view; but in one of those "little wars" in which we are engaged from time to time it might prove a service not to be despised, while in any case it could not fail to have considerable moral weight. The price for this advantage is our ultimate responsibility for the defence of the colonies. That burden, however, will be an easy task if we retain command of the seas; if we lose it

Telegraph—*continued.*

we shall suffer much more through home want than through colonial losses. In fact it seems to us that under the new system the losses and gains will be on both sides fairly balanced. Australia, like Canada, will remain part of a great Empire, involved remotely and indirectly in our quarrels, it is true, but exposed to no serious danger. Her new fleet can protect her coasts against a mere surprise, and to meet any more elaborate attack she will have the broad shield of Britain. For us the responsibility of defence is balanced by the retention of friendly harbours in distant seas. Were Canada and Australia independent States they would have to issue, in case of war between England and another Power, declarations of neutrality, and our ships would receive exactly the treatment accorded to the other belligerent. This would be an enormous disadvantage to a Power that depends, as we do, so extensively on food from abroad and on the security of our widespread commerce. Therefore those who contend that a semi-independent Dominion in the Southern Seas would be the same thing as an independent Australasia forget some of the most salient and significant facts of the situation.

One question touched on in the Conference is of more interest to the colonies themselves than to Great Britain. At present each of the separated States has a fiscal system of its own. New South Wales has adopted and has clung to free-trade; the other colonies have framed their tariffs on the protectionist principle, and endeavour to shut out not only foreign and English goods, but the imports of their own sister communities on the same continent. This goes beyond the United States, which build up a barrier of duties against the world, but have perfect free-trade amongst themselves. It has been asked, if all Australasia came under one supreme Executive and Parliament, would the intercolonial tariffs and custom-houses be still kept up? Or, if they were abolished, would free-trading New South Wales be obliged to raise her tariff against the rest of the world in order to purchase unrestricted intercourse with Victoria, Queensland, and the rest? The probability, it seems to us, is that something like a compromise will eventually be struck out. Sir Henry Parkes, speaking for New South Wales, declares that free trade is secondary to federation. It is also probable that when protection is spread over a wider area and managed by a Federal Parliament the narrow views of the Victorian statesmen will be considerably modified. We must remember that even now

Telegraph—*continued.*

Victoria and the other protectionist colonies take per head of English produce an amount at least tenfold the quantity imported by any foreign customer. It is not likely that, leavened by New South Wales opinion and influence, the new dominion will be more hostile to us in matters of trade than the greater portion of it is now. As to the unsettled questions that vex our Colonial Minister, they will certainly be of easier solution if we have to deal with one Executive and one Parliament, and not with four or five. Whether the few thousand West Australians should have complete control of a vast unoccupied estate is a more thorny topic than if the territory were claimed by four millions of people. There is also a difficulty in the shape of divorce legislation which our Government does not quite approve, and hesitates to endorse; but, if such questions were relegated to a central Australasian Parliament or tribunal, we should be quite ready to abide by the issue. Altogether we see no reason why we should not rejoice at the readiness of our sons beyond the seas to assume as soon as possible the "toga virilis" of politics, the responsibilities and burdens of nationhood.

Advertiser—

February 17th, 1890.

It is just forty years since Mr. William Wentworth, the first Australian worthy of the name of statesman, took the initiatory steps to educate the then lethargic colonial mind up to the idea of an Australian confederacy. He desired to create "a new Britannia in another world," and if he could have had his way would have inserted in the constitution which he was then framing for New South Wales a provision to enable the Australian colonies to federate whenever they considered that the fateful hour had arrived. The then presiding genius at the Colonial Office evidently thought there was no future before the Australian dependencies; at any rate he coldly declined to grant powers to establish a federal union of the colonies, and so facilities for initiating concerted action were long withheld. It is well to recall this antiquarian curiosity of the days when, as Mr. Gladstone once said, the Colonial Office was haunted by a disembodied spirit, known by the title of "Mrs. Mother Country." But a great change has taken place during the last two decades. The narrow tradi-

Advertiser—*continued.*

tions of the past have quite disappeared, and Lord Knutsford and every other British statesman can be safely counted upon to keenly sympathize with the aspirations for unity—the stirring of national life—which have found such eloquent expression at the Federation Conference just held in Melbourne. Sir George Baden-Powell's opportune motion will enable the House of Commons to evince its interest in the efforts which are being made to establish a closer union between the Australian colonies, and to express a hope that the result will conduce to the increased well-being of those great self-governing dependencies, and give additional strength and solidity to the united Empire.

The abstract resolution which the Conference has just adopted without a dissentient voice will have a very far-reaching effect. It probably sounds the knell of the Federal Council of Australasia, which the Hon. James Service, Sir Samuel Griffith, and others established some seven years ago. It says much for the commanding influence which Sir Henry Parkes exercises in colonial politics that he should have so readily succeeded in persuading the other delegates that the Federal Council had served its end, and that it should yield its place to a union of the colonies under one Legislative and Executive Government. When the Conference assembled a very strong party held the opinion that the proposed federation should proceed slowly by a process of evolution, which could be best brought about by widening the powers of the existing machinery and by the admission of New South Wales and New Zealand into the Federal Council. But all that has been changed, and even the Premier of Victoria appears to have caught the prevailing enthusiasm and to have advocated as warmly as his great rival that the time was ripe for union and that delay would only cause obstacles.

> "The fated sky
> Gives us free scope, only doth backward pull
> Our slow designs when we ourselves are dull."

So far everything is satisfactory and eminently encouraging, but the real difficulties have yet to be grappled with. The members of the Conference have, first of all, to persuade the Legislatures of their respective colonies to appoint delegates to a national Australasian Convention to be held early next year, empowered to consider and report upon an adequate scheme for the Federal Constitution. They will probably succeed in this, but the delegates will have a very delicate and difficult task to accomplish. Constitutions

Advertiser—*continued.*

suitable to the requirements of a free self-governing community cannot be evolved with magical celerity, except from the brains of reforming Turkish pachas, and then they are not worth the paper they are written on. It must be noted that a distinct preference has been expressed by some of the delegates for the adoption of features embodied in the constitution of the United States, instead of reproducing the constitution of the Dominion of Canada, modified to suit Australasian peculiarities. The chief difficulty will be to propitiate the local legislatures by entrusting them with wide and important State powers. Any attempt to focus all political power into the Federal Parliament, and to degrade the existing provincial parliaments into enlarged parochial vestries, will arouse a spirit of intense antagonism. But no doubt this mistake will be avoided. There are many other rocks ahead, but, as one of the delegates bravely declared, difficulties are made to be conquered. Some of the most serious problems we have already indicated, but none of them are insoluble if only they are approached in the spirit which so far has animated the originators of the movement. The native-born Australians, who now constitute a distinct majority in the colonies, will have to be reckoned with. Many of these ardent young politicians are Australians even before they are Englishmen. Intensely proud of their rich and prosperous country they are almost inclined to resent the ties which bind them to the mother-country. It is idle to deny that a national or separatist party exists, and it includes in its ranks men of high position and influence. It was the knowledge that this sentiment prevailed that impelled Mr. Service to declare some years ago that " he wanted federation, and he wanted it now." We do not desire to create the impression that at present the national party is supreme, or even commands a majority amongst native-born Australians. The steps that are being taken to broaden the issues of public life may probably stay the development of the separatist spirit. We trust that this will be the case, but the force to which we have referred cannot be safely ignored, and it constitutes one of the lions in the path of Imperial federation. Meanwhile, it is eminently gratifying to Englishmen to observe the loyal haste which the Conference exhibited to acquaint her Majesty, amid many expressions of devoted attachment to her throne and person, with the result of their deliberations last week. The announcement will certainly be received with a degree of gratification which will only be increased when some

Advertiser—*continued.*

heaven-sent statesman is able to proclaim that all the components parts of Great and Greater Britain have been blended " in one harmonious, loyal, and lasting federation." In that case the federation of the Canadian and Australasian dominions would be but

> " Happy prologues to the swelling theme
> Of an Imperial act."

The Globe and Traveller—
February 17th, 1890.

It cannot be alleged against the Melbourne Conference that it has broken up without doing anything but talk. The important resolutions passed at the final sitting represent a considerable amount of good work well done. It is unanimously affirmed that Australasia has pressing need for a centralized Government to direct her foreign affairs, administer her fighting forces, and exercise control in other matters which affect the whole of the colonies in a greater or less degree. The little bickerings about the Federal Council, which at one time threatened to produce inharmonious relations between New South Wales and Victoria, may now be relegated to the limbo of obsolete controversies. Sir Henry Parkes admits that the Council did good service by accustoming the popular mind to the idea of federation, and although Mr. Duncan Gillies makes a somewhat larger claim for his pet project, the two Premiers are practically at one in giving honorable burial to the defunct body. Stronger still is their agreement on the proposition that the time has come when Australasia must have a concrete foreign policy, directed by a single head. Aspiring as she does to become " Mistress of the Southern Seas," as Sir Henry Parkes puts it, her statesmen recognize the imperativeness of joint action to accomplish that splendid but perilous destiny. Nor is it in the Pacific alone that these colonies perceive the likelihood of political complications and embarrassment. The measures to which they have been compelled to resort for the restriction of Chinese immigration are deeply resented at Pekin, and were it not for the cordial relations between the Chinese and English Governments, Celestial reprisals would probably have taken place before now. In a word, Australasia, having reached the *status* of a great and growing

The Globe and Traveller—*continued.*

nation, naturally desires to exercise proportionate power in the outside world; but this she can never hope to achieve so long as the fatal system of separatism militates against united action. Perhaps some English politicians may learn a lesson from this, not without application to the United Kingdom. Australasia has experimented with separatism, and finds it so wanting that all her leading statesmen are cudgelling their brains for some method which would produce closer union.

Very wisely, the Conference has devolved on a Convention to be assembled early next year the task of framing a concrete scheme of federation. Neither the Federal Council nor the Conference had any mandate to undertake that difficult work, nor would it have been prudent, in a matter of such vital consequence, to proceed without mature deliberation. Before the Convention assembles there will be ample time for the Governments of the several colonies to draft plans suitable to the wishes and requirements of their respective populations. This being accomplished, their delegates will attend the Convention with full authority to act within the prescribed lines, and it will at once become apparent whether any divergent views are absolutely irreconcilable. We do not believe that this is at all likely to happen. Now that there is unanimous agreement among the colonies as to the necessity of a supreme Government, difficulties of detail will be surmounted, we confidently anticipate, by reasonable compromise. The eternal tariff question still remains the chief embarrassment, but even here there are abundant signs of a more accommodating disposition. It might even be possible at the outset to dispense with a Customs' Union, postponing any decision on that point until further experience had proved whether fiscal freedom was compatible with federal rule. The important matter is to get a Central Government established, with power to control foreign policy, and with exclusive command over the naval and military forces of all the colonies. Were that done, free-trade and protection would, no doubt, somehow come to terms, unless it happened that each found that it could go on its own way without causing embarrassment to the Federal Government. The spirit of enthusiastic loyalty to the mother-country which was displayed at the Conference may not be relished, perhaps, by those who have been seeking to turn the Australasian mind against England, for political purposes of their own; but more patriotic Englishmen will cordially reciprocate the fervent wish expressed by Sir Henry Parkes

The Globe and Traveller—*continued.*

and others that "Australia may always remain under the British flag, and continue to form part of this magnificent Empire." The Queen has no more loyal subjects in the world than those who own her sway in the South Pacific.

Reynold's Newspaper—
February 17*th*, 1890.

THE result of the deliberations of the Federation Conference at Melbourne is in every way satisfactory, and Sir Henry Parkes, who is one of the originators and the leading spirit of the movement, must be proud of the issue of so many years' effort. The proceedings are, of course, only initiative, but the spirit of the delegates would seem to assure the ultimate success of the proposal to bring about a union between all the English-speaking communities in the South Pacific in alliance with the mother-country. A convention is to meet next year, and by that time the public feeling in the various colonies will have been tested. That the scheme abounds with difficulties which the Conference wisely left open, has not deterred the representatives of all the Australian colonies, as well as New Zealand and Tasmania, from pledging themselves to the scheme. These difficulties include the present tariff arrangements and the delicate question as to which town should become the central capital of the United States of the Southern Ocean, or whether, as was done in the United States of America, a new town should be built, which would be the seat of the Government. But no doubt these will all be met by concessions on all sides, as it is evident that there could be no real federation if the hostile tariffs of the various colonies were not abrogated. The other ticklish question is as to whether the new constitution is to be devised on the lines of that of the United States or of Canada. The feeling of the delegates seems to incline to the system existing in the States. The meeting next year will be one of momentous interest to all Englishmen. The future of 4,000,000 of our kith and kin, and these the most progressive and prosperous, will depend upon the decision taken; and it is the earnest wish and hope of all men that it may be one that will strengthen the bonds that bind the English-speaking races, not as subjects of the Crown, but as men and brothers of the Anglo-Saxon race.

Observer—

February 17th, 1890.

It is difficult to say whether the Melbourne Conference, so far as it has gone, indicates an early consummation of Australian Federation or otherwise. Sir Henry Parkes' motion, that an early union of the colonies under one Legislative and Executive Government would promote their best interests, has been adopted unanimously, but it is clear from the debate that some of the delegates look upon this as merely expressing the conviction that such a union will be desirable some day. It is already apparent, too, that there exists a considerable divergence of views as to essentials and non-essentials, Tasmania, for instance, holding intercolonial free-trade to be a *sine qua non,* while Victoria considers that the various tariffs might be maintained for a period of years after federation was establised. Then the kind, or rather the degree, of federation which is desirable affords another ground for difference. Some would work on the lines of the existing Federal Council, others would retain for each Colony an independence analogous to State sovereignty as it existed in the American Constitution previous to the War of Secession, while others would have federation after the Canadian type. Whatever be the outcome of the present Conference, it cannot fail to further the cause of Australian unity, for the debates must make plain to the people of the various colonies the essential solidarity of Australasian interests.

Liverpool Mercury—

February 17th, 1890.

Nothing but satisfaction can be felt at the result of the Federation Conference which has closed at Melbourne, after a week's deliberation. It was brought together to consider whether federation could not be promoted by a common disposition in the various colonies, because the initial step was obviously to ascertain, by free and candid interchange of opinions, if the people were ripe for a serious movement. This is the earliest occasion upon which it has been possible to elicit so favourable an expression of feeling. A Federal Council was established in 1883, and has certainly helped by its existence and its measures of legislation to pave the way for more complete machinery; but New South

Liverpool Mercury—*continued*.

Wales, one of the most important sections of the continent, would not join the council, and therefore deprived the arrangement of some force. We may date the fresh departure from the moment when the necessities of defence impressed themselves strongly upon the colonial mind. With the enormous material interests growing up on every side, the concurrent development of warlike force in Europe, and the desire of England's great rivals to seek openings everywhere for trade and settlement, it had become imperitive that the Australasian Governments should make a united effort to guard their own households and possessions from attack. It was soon perceived that this could not be effectively done by independent and isolated action. In order to achieve success there must be a firm union of some kind, and none appeared to answer the requirements except federation. And now the principle of federation is unanimously affirmed. The resolution passed affirms that "the best interests and the present and future prosperity of the Australasian Colonies will be promoted by an early union under the Crown;" which object is more specially described as a coalition "under one legislative and executive government, on principles just to the several colonies." It was not intended to proceed further with the first effort; nor, indeed, was progress beyond this point feasible. The path is strewn with difficulties which can be only slowly removed. Sir Henry Parkes, who has taken up federation so enthusiastically, was opposed to the plan of the Federal Council. He considered that it did not proceed far enough, and would not attract the prestige it would need to be effective. But he confesses that it has done the good service of accustoming the people to federal ideas, and he looks forward, especially after the issues of the Melbourne Conference, to a rapid ripening of public opinion. It is the first step only that costs, says a French proverb, and no doubt the gravest obstacle has been overcome by inducing the colonies to decide in favour of a system essentially reproducing that of Canada. However, the making of a federal constitution is no easy matter, and it is complicated here by a war of tariffs. The Canadians do not levy duties against each other, nor do the States of the American Republic. We have always held that protection is nonsensical and injurious, and protectionists themselves begin to realize the folly and the inconvenience of it when they are in such a situation as our Australian friends. Inter-state tariffs would not be tolerated for an instant in America either

Liverpool Mercury—*continued.*

north or south of the St. Lawrence, and yet they would be just as sensible as the tariffs which the Australian colonies have set up against each other as well as the rest of the world. They are not even agreed as to protection itself; for while New South Wales and Tasmania have open ports, some of the other colonies are far more stringent than others. The 'Premier of Victoria is hopeful that, even though the Customs barriers should continue to exist for a time, a modification may be found to which all parties can agree. It is evident that he sees the inconsistency of federation and Customs barriers, and we have no doubt the people at large will see the same truth with a little experience. The moment there is a federation and a supreme government, the populations become practically one, with identical interests, amongst whom the tariffs now existing would be absurd in the extreme. Hence we confidently anticipate a reign of internal free-trade at least as soon as a union shall have been achieved under a federal constitution. Before the termination of the Conference, a resolution was passed urging the various Legislatures to appoint delegates to a National Australasian Convention empowered to consider and report upon an adequate scheme. This Convention will be summoned by the Premier of Victoria, probably before another year has elapsed, and in the meantime the whole question will be so fully discussed in all its bearings that the Convention will probably have to linger rather over details than general plans.

Manchester Examiner—

February 17th, 1890.

AUSTRALIA leads the way in the direction of federation. The Conference which has been sitting at Melbourne broke up last Friday with the declaration that the time has come for the union of the Australian colonies under one Government, and unanimously resolved that the Legislatures of the several colonies should be requested to appoint delegates to a National Australasian Convention, empowered to consider and report upon a scheme for the Federal Constitution, which will probably meet early next year. When it is remembered that not six years have elapsed since, under the presidency of the late Mr. W. E. Forster, the first con-

Manchester Examiner—*continued.*

ference to consider the question of how best to bring about the Federation of the British Empire was held in London, it must be admitted that what was at that time a dream of the few has rapidly become the hope and anticipation of the many. The step now taken by Australia, if the wish so warmly expressed by her leading representative men is realized, cannot but tend to pave the way to the attainment of the ultimate goal of Imperial Federation. The one Imperial Parliament of the United Kingdom will have a much easier task in dealing with this great question when Australia is enabled to speak with one voice. When the minor and local differences that at present occupy the attention of the colonies are composed, and the difficulties—not lightly to be estimated—which for the moment lie in the way are overcome, the hour may be at hand when the one Parliament of Australia will be found concerting measures with the Parliaments of Great Britain and Canada to bring about federation on a still larger and more extended scale. According to Sir Charles Dilke, the *crux* of Imperial Federation lies in the tariff question, but surely, important as are all questions relating to trade, they are not the only, much less the chief, ones that concern the welfare and greatness of a people. This little island of ours made her mark in the world's history in other fields than those of trade and commerce. Her children, scattered far and wide, are justly proud of their part in the great heritage of England's fame; they will not willingly drift away from their mother-country on a mere matter of tariffs.

Edinburgh Scottish Leader—

February 17th, 1890.

THE unanimous adoption, by the Federation Conference which has been sitting at Melbourne for several days, of a resolution in favour of the early union of all the Australasian colonies under the Crown, with a Central Federal Executive and Legislature, is an event of the very greatest importance. The Conference was thoroughly representative, including the most influential political leaders of all the colonies; and though some time must elapse before the federation scheme can be matured, there is no longer room for doubt of the

Edinburgh Scottish Leader—*continued.*

complete and early success of the movement initiated by Sir Henry Parkes. Now that the business has been taken in hand in good earnest—for the Conference did not separate until after taking the preliminary measures for the holding of a national Australasian Convention to consider the drawing up of a Federal Constitution—it will, as a matter of course, receive the support of the Home Government; because its accomplishment will undoubtedly be for the benefit of the colonies themselves, and will in certain directions materially diminish the anxieties and cares of the Colonial Office. A united Australia can take upon herself the due share of responsibility for her own defence. She will at once become by far the strongest power in the South Pacific, and her voice will be much more potent than those of the separate colonies in preventing the intrusion of undesirable elements within her legitimate sphere of influence. The question as to whether Australasian Federation is or is not destined to prove a half-way house to the yet vaster project of Imperial Federation is one on which there is room for wide difference of opinion. The Australians themselves do not appear to have any very definite ideas on the subject. On the whole, they appear very well contented—as, indeed, they can afford to be—with the present relations between them and the mother-country. Save in one or two of the colonies, there is no party or section of politicians which openly advocates the severance of the ties; and at the Federation Conference a very loyal address to the Queen was unanimously adopted. At the same time it is quite certain that the colonies will insist on being left, in all essentials, to manage their own affairs in their own way. It is worthy of remark that while the Australians are preparing for union, they are resolved that it shall be on a distinctly federal basis, and no point was more frequently or strenuously insisted upon at the Melbourne Conference than the necessity of leaving ample liberty of action to the local Legislatures. The colonists are, in short, what the Liberals are here at home at once Home Rulers and unionists. They appreciate the truth which seems not to have dawned as yet upon our sham-Unionists, that there can be no real union without local self-government of the various connected States.

Glasgow Mail—

February 17th, 1890.

The cause of Australian Federation has been greatly advanced by the Conference which has just concluded its sittings at Melbourne. All the Australian colonies were represented at the Conference, and the delegates have unanimously adopted a resolution in favour of federation. It is rather curious that this step should have been taken at the instance of New South Wales. When the existing Federal Council was established, New South Wales was the one colony that held aloof. Its politicians thought that the constitution and powers of the Council were insufficient for the ends to be attained. This has proved to be the case; but, whatever its powers, the Council could not have had any great measure of success so long as an important colony declined to recognize its authority. Sir Henry Parkes, the leading statesman of New South Wales, aimed at the institution of something higher than a Council that could do little more than make recommendations to the Governments and Parliaments of the various colonies. He wanted a genuine union for common purposes, and especially in order that Australia might present a united front to the possible enemies of the British Empire; for each colony has its defensive forces, both by land and sea, and, in the event of war, these could not act in concert unless there were a recognized central authority to direct their operations. It was Sir Henry Parkes who brought about the Conference, and his views have been accepted. He said that what Australia required was a Federal Government that should represent the whole people, and command the respect of every nation. It would be interesting to know what Lord Salisbury thinks of this statement. In the Queen's speech he has committed himself to approval of Australian federation; but he can hardly have counted upon United Australia claiming a place of influence among the nations of the world. It may seem to him to be very like treason; but he cannot help himself. Australia is too far away for the exercise of Mr. Balfour's system of repressing—or attempting to repress—natural aspirations. Had that system been tried Australia would probably long ere this have been an independent country. The coercion which produced the United States of America would have produced the United States of Australia. Had Ireland had Home Rule, like the Australian colonies, her loyalty would have been as irreproachable as theirs. After all, the federa-

Glasgow Mail—*continued.*

tion which they propose is only a development of Home Rule. It is not what Lord Salisbury calls consolidation. Each colony is to retain its full right of self-government—its own Parliament, and its own executive. Sir Henry Parkes said, at the Conference, that the Federal Parliament must have great and efficient powers, but that the powers of the local Legislatures must remain unimpaired. Without this condition there could be no union of the colonies. The Conference resolved to summon a Convention, which will probably meet early next year, to take practical steps towards uniting them under a Federal Government. We view the proposal with unmixed satisfaction. By strengthening a part of the Empire it will strengthen the whole. It is in accord with the best political tendency of our time, and it will afford a further example of that which will prove to be the true democratic Government of the future—Home Rule, crowned with federation.

Leeds Mercury—

February 17*th*, 1890.

THE general course and the issue of the deliberations of the Melbourne Conference upon the question of Australian Federation cannot fail to be regarded with very cordial satisfaction throughout the British Empire. Differences of opinion have been manifested as to the constitutional lines on which Australian Federation should proceed, as to the treatment of the tariff question, and as to the probability of reaching a practical solution of the various difficulties connected with the whole subject at an early date. All this, however, was perfectly natural; indeed it would have been unnatural and of no good augury for the movement of which the Melbourne Conference has been the first fruits if there had been any general refusal or neglect on the part of its members to recognize that the aspirations at present indulged after a federal union of the Australian colonies could only be realized after a large amount of philosophic thought and practical contrivance on the part of statesmen, and after a general manifestation on the part of the colonists concerned of their readiness to sacrifice prejudices and sectional interests for the general good. To have overlooked these aspects of the subject would have argued the presence of an unreasoning impulse which would be only too likely

Leeds Mercury—*continued.*

to spend itself in declamation and to prove itself unequal to the treatment of the complicated problems which Australian Federation involves. Happily, it has been otherwise with the Melbourne Conference. The difficulties of the problem have been acknowledged, but they have been treated with a due regard for proportion. Serious as they undoubtedly are, it has been recognized that they are not of such a character as to justify their being allowed to prevent the vigorous prosecution of a movement for the establishment of true Australian unity. The resolution which was moved on Monday by Sir Henry Parkes declared that the development of the national life of Australasia in population, wealth, discovery, resources, and self-governing capacity, in recent years, justified the union of the colonies under one legislative and executive Government under the British Crown; and on Thursday this resolution was unanimously passed. Resolutions were adopted providing for the appointment by the Legislatures of the several colonies during the present year of delegates to a national Australasian Convention empowered to consider and report upon an adequate scheme for the Federal Constitution. Crowning the whole work of the Conference came an address, unanimously adopted, to the Queen, expressing the devoted attachment of the Australasian Colonies to Her Majesty's throne and person, and respectfully laying before Her Majesty the resolutions agreed to on the subject of federation.

It has been thought that behind the movement for Australian Federation there lay a certain amount of feeling of a separatist tendency in regard to the British Empire. It is certain that no indications of any such feeling are afforded by the telegraphic reports of the deliberations of the Melbourne Conference. That does not prove by any means that the sentiment in question, wherever it has existed in Australia, has disappeared; but it does, in our opinion, afford a strong presumption that the realization of the Federation idea in Australia, which will most certainly be to the advantage of our fellow-subjects in that part of the world, not only need not prejudice, but may distinctly tend to promote the advancement of the federation idea throughout the Empire. Australians will increasingly recognize that Englishmen at home rejoice in every development of Australian institutions which tend to aid the material prosperity and civic elevation of the great English-speaking communities of the Southern Seas. And, recog-

Leeds Mercury—*continued.*

nizing this, they will, we may reasonably hope, be growingly disposed towards the fuller realization of that vaster unity in which it is open to them to play a great and indeed splendid part. It is also beyond question that many of the difficulties in the way of Imperial Federation will be materially lessened when we have to deal with an Australian, as we have now to deal with a Canadian Dominion, instead of individual colonies whose several sentiments it may take a long time to collect and adjust. We are glad to hear that in the course of next month Mr. G. R. Parkin will again visit Yorkshire, where he has already received invitations from several important towns to address meetings on the subject of Imperial Federation, and we trust that the very valuable opportunity thus afforded of acquiring knowledge upon a subject of paramount national importance will be made full use of in various parts of this great country.

Leeds Yorkshire Post—
February 17th, 1890.

THE close of the Conference on the Federation of the Australasian Colonies which has been sitting at Melbourne, and the resolutions unanimously adopted by the delegates, have a special interest and significance for politicians in the mother-country at the present crisis of our history. It is in no carping spirit, but simply by way of illustration of the general tendency of political ideas and parties, that we refer to the fact that to Liberal statesmen of the last generation no better or wiser mode of dealing with our great dependencies suggested itself than that of "cutting the painter" and letting them drift off alone on any course that their fortunes might work out for them. They were almost invited to avail themselves of their power to sever the ties which bound them to the British Empire. Wiser counsels happily prevailed, and the address of the Conference to the Queen at the close of its session is at once a rebuke to the timorous and short-sighted views of the political party which was then supreme at the seat of Empire, and an evidence of the strength of the attachment which binds the remote members of the English body politic to the head. The unanimous decision of the delegates at Melbourne, representing, as they did, the mind and will of the people of the Australasian States, is curiously in contrast with the idea to

Leeds Yorkshire Post—*continued.*

which the same political party are now striving to give effect in the United Kingdom. While the constituencies at home are being urged to seek refuge from passing troubles by repealing the Acts of Union with Ireland and Scotland, the people of the vigorous young States in the Southern Hemisphere have with more statesmanlike instinct resolved to consolidate their strength by closer union. The Legislatures of the several colonies will probably take steps during the present year to appoint delegates to a "National Australasian Convention empowered to consider and report upon an adequate scheme for a Federal Constitution." The subject has not been approached in any hasty temper or without a full perception of the difficulties that have to be faced in any scheme of construction. Sir Henry Parkes was fully justified in his assertion that the federal principle has grown steadily and naturally in the mind of the colonial public. The advantages of the proposed union have been weighed against the prejudices that will have to be overcome in an exhaustive course of discussion, and the conclusion seems to have been arrived at that the difficulties arising from hostile tariffs are not insuperable. The great point to be settled in the first stages of the movement was the general advisability of closer union. When all parties are agreed upon that essential preliminary, the methods by which local jealousies may be allayed will not be far to seek. A people who have already shown so much political sagacity and foresight will not be disposed to reject reasonable concessions to both free-traders and protectionists, and the question of the Federal Capital of the new dominion will probably be solved in the same way as it was solved by the United States—by the creation of a small neutral territory in a central position readily accessible from all parts of the Union.

The step thus taken in the Melbourne Conference goes far towards preparing the way for that larger scheme of Imperial Federation which has of late occupied the minds of statesmen in this country whose opinions are entitled to great consideration. Lord Roseberry, who is an advocate for the repeal of the Union with Ireland, would nevertheless consolidate the Empire by a Federal Union with the Colonial dependencies. At present, however, the idea of Imperial Federation has not emerged from the region of sentiment in a form that might bring it within the scope of practical politics. The statesmen of the United Kingdom and of the colonies are inviting each other to put a definite scheme of federation into shape, but neither seems disposed to take the

Leeds Yorkshire Post—*continued.*

first step. Something is gained, however, by such a discussion of the subject as that which has brought the people of the Australasian Colonies to such a conclusion as has now been arrived at by the Melbourne Conference. The public mind is made familiar with the idea, and it begins to be seen what can and what cannot be done in the direction of an Imperial Federation. In the first place there seems to be a general recognition of the fact that the existing institutions of the United Kingdom could not be made the basis of the wider scheme. The House of Commons is too large as it is for the speedy despatch of business, and to double its numbers by the addition of colonial representatives would be to make it altogether unworkable. The inefficiency of the House of Commons for all the work that is heaped upon it has necessitated the removal of much of the business to the County Councils, and to replace this by a host of Imperial questions would be to charge the Lower House with functions for which its constitution altogether unfits it. The idea of representative government in the form in which it is familiar to us for an Imperial Federation must therefore be abandoned as impracticable. The House of Lords with some modifications might serve as the basis for a deliberative assembly, and perhaps Lord Rosebery may have some such idea in his mind when he advocates what he deems to be the reform of the Upper House. But probably the plan most generally accepted by those who have taken the trouble to think the matter out is that of an Imperial Council to advise Her Majesty, the members of which would be nominated in certain proportions by the British and Colonial Governments. A very important question would at once arise as to such membership depending upon the fluctuating balance of popular feeling at home and abroad. But if their tenure were made independent of party conflict the gain in the direction of stability would more than counterbalance any shock that might be given to popular ideas on the subject of the present scramble for office, and would tend to prepare the public mind for that further strengthening of the Executive which is becoming year by year a matter of more pressing necessity for the safety of the Empire. We could not expect the Colonial Governments to send delegates to a Federal Council the whole constitution and policy of which was liable to be overthrown at any moment by some gust of feeling on a merely insular question. Imperial politics would have to be kept distinct from local politics, either of the United Kingdom or of the colonies.

Leeds Yorkshire Post—*continued.*

The idea of an Imperial Federation forms the justification to the minds of many Home Rulers of their action in support of the repeal of the Union and the disruption of the United Kingdom. Mr. Gladstone's first scheme for Home Rule contemplated a direct step in this direction by the proposal to exclude Irish members from the Imperial Parliament and treat the island as a Crown colony; but it reserved, for the sake of the safety and welfare of Great Britain, certain rights and powers over the independent action of the proposed Irish Government to which no self-governing colony had been called upon to submit. His crude idea was rejected by the good sense of the constituencies, and then he turned round and advocated the retention of the Irish members in the Imperial Parliament, while giving the proposed Irish Legislature the full control of "purely Irish affairs." To the present hour neither Mr. Gladstone nor anybody else has been able to define where a line can be drawn between Irish affairs and National affairs, and nobody now knows whether the Home Rule scheme that is so loudly contended for is to place Ireland in the position of an independent State or of something lower than a self-governing colony. Separatists who have honestly tried to think the matter out have come to the perfectly logical conclusion that a federal union with Ireland would involve a similar arrangement with regard to Scotland, and even with Wales. If Ireland were represented in proportion to population in a federal union with Great Britain she would be as far off from independence as ever. Even if Scotland should consent to a disruption of her profitable fusion with England, the proportional representation of England would outweigh that of both Scotland and Ireland together, and, therefore, England would have to be broken up into federal provinces. The federal union with Ireland, in fact, involves the throwing of the British Constitution into the melting-pot for the sake of trying the hazardous experiment whether it would be the stronger for being recast in a different mould. The process which the colonists of Australia are now proceeding to adopt is the opposite to this. They do not propose to separate that which is already united, but to combine in one compact whole what is now disjoined; and if the advocates of Imperial Federation are sincere in their desires and efforts, it would be well for them to take into consideration what the Colonial Governments and people may have to say to a scheme of disruption which would entirely alter the status of one essential party to the proposed federation.

Bristol Times—
February 17th, 1890.

In the House of Lords to-night Lord Norton will ask for papers on the subject of Australian Federation. The matter will simply be raised as a question of the convenience of the public service; and it is not likely that any discussion will be raised upon it; but the subject is one of deep interest to all Englishmen. The great Continent in the Southern Seas has evidently such a momentous destiny before it that anything which touches the well-being of its people is of vital importance. England is fast becoming one huge workshop, dependent on other countries for her food supply. Every year a portion of her population must leave her or starve. Australia is growing up under the most favourable conditions for affording relief. The distance between England and Australia has now been made so short, by the splendid improvements in navigation, that there is little fear of any movement which would make Australians cease to be Englishmen in name. For many centuries to come, as far as it is safe to prophesy, and probably as long as the world may last, Australia will continue to be a Southern Britain, its pulse of life regulated by the heart-beating in London. Yet there is a certain local patriotism in Australia which finds expression in such resolutions as that of Sir Henry Parkes, passed unanimously at the Melbourne Conference. The resolution was to the effect that an early union of the colonies, under one legislative and executive government, would promote their best interests. It is true that this is only an abstract expression of opinion; but there is no reason why it should not be regarded as the basis of future action. If the colonies can so far lay aside their jealousies as to declare, even academically, in favour of union, they may be expected some day to find a *modus vivendi* which will enable them to work out their future in concert. Long before Australian federation was heard of, or thought of, it used to be the fashion to speak colloquially of Australia as a whole. Thus, a Queensland colonist hailing from Victoria would describe himself, or be described, as coming from the "Melbourne side." If he came from New South Wales he would be from the "Sydney side"; and so on through the list of the various colonies. It will be remembered that, not long ago, great offence was given by the proposal, seriously made, to change the name of New South Wales to "Australia." The sovereigns issued from the Mint at Sydney, which are slightly more valuable than those coined in

Bristol Times—*continued.*

England, have always borne the inscription "Australia," but that is a mere matter of detail. Difficulties in the way of federation present themselves in the shape of tariffs. Then there are questions of distance. Perhaps this consideration might tend to keep New Zealand out of the federation for a while. There are also conflicting proposals as to the form which a Federal Union should take. It is clear, indeed, that the discussion has only reached its threshold. But it is something that the threshold should have been reached.

Bristol Western Daily Press—
February 17th, 1890.

UNANIMITY awaited the vote at the Federation Conference in Melbourne on the resolution that the time has come for the union of the Australian colonies under one government. The discussion has been conducted with combined energy and eloquence, and there can be no doubt that, although a few points may suggest themselves as by no means easy of solution, the opinion of the Hon. Duncan Gillies is that of Australians in general on this subject, that difficulties were made to be overcome, and will be overcome. The respective colonies have to approach each other on the question of tariffs, and it will also be necessary to decide upon a capital where the Federal Parliament would meet to legislate. For this purpose the neutralization of a piece of land on the Murray River, at Albury, has been suggested. In the construction of the scheme of federation the Constitutions of Canada and of the United States could be freely referred to, at the same time that the Australian requirements would probably evolve provisions not contemplated by either. The definite progress made at this Conference arouses high expectations as to the National Australasian Convention to be called together by the Premier of Victoria, probably early next year, to consider and report as to the proposed Federal Constitution. It is well worthy of attention in this country that, while the Conference adopted a loyal address to the Queen, the excellent reply of Sir Henry Parkes to previous speeches closed with these significant sentences:— "It was impossible to predict what the march of events might be, but he prayed God that Australia might always remain under the British Flag. He hoped that all groups in the colonies might continue to form part of this magnificent Empire."

Newcastle Journal—

February 17th, 1890.

The die has at length been cast as regards Australian Federation, and the most puzzling rubicon that yet seems to divide its various colonies will no doubt be ultimately crossed. A resolution has been unanimously adopted declaring that the time has come for the union of the Australian colonies under one Government. There is no time, Sir Henry Parkes thinks, like the present for giving formal expression to the union that is acknowledged and valued by all the colonies. Union has been still further developing while the delegates of the Federation Conference were freely discussing its advantages so far as it has been realized, the desirability of making it closer, and above all of making known to all the world that Australia is now one great nation, just as Germany is one as an empire, Italy one as a kingdom, that its colonies are in deed and name united by a similar bond to that which has knit together under the British Crown the mighty provinces of Canada, and has made of the wide-stretching States of the other half of North America something like a huge empire under the form of a Democratic Republic. The Federation Conference, like the Federal Council, was, in fact, the evidence of the progress of federating forces, of the vitality, energy, and spread of federal ideas in Australia. The Melbourne meeting is the response to the first Colonial Conference in London, the natural result of a gradual drawing together of the colonies to each other, which dates really from the day that they began to desire closer union with the mother-country. The address to the Queen is the enthusiastic recognition of the touch of nature, the unity of origin, that dictated the warm reception of the delegates to the London Conference. It conveys to Her Majesty a warm expression of devoted attachment to her throne and person, as the fittest preamble to the resolutions by which they have solemnly placed on record their desire to create one Federal Government not only for Australia, but for Australasia, as soon as it shall be possible to adjust the details of the connection for mutual defence, all the Australian colonies have at length declared it is desirable to establish in connection with the Empire and its other colonies throughout the world. More than this could not have been done by the Conference, and less would have been but another name for frustration and failure.

The path of the Conference was not to be sought or found in any set of propositions or in any polemic strife over

Newcastle Journal—*continued.*

separate policies, and the problem of harmonizing them into one general system. It was marked out by the drift of events, and that drift was only an indication of the decided "trend" of Australian opinion. The latest event of historic significance was the proposal to place all the naval and military forces of Australia under one authority. Every colony felt that its own defence involved the defence of its neighbouring colonies. Melbourne could not be in safety if Sydney or Brisbane were in peril from attack. Separate forces were, therefore, useless in the face of a powerful foe, and the same impulse of self-preservation that led the colonists to ask aid from the old country in war vessels and armaments, suddenly prompted them to combine their strength, and to devise some means by which it might be wielded on an emergency with that unity, energy, and success that only attends action under one central executive power for the defence of all. But obviously it would be folly to expect useful results from a scheme that did not ensure vital and permanent combination. Of what use would it be, for example, to say that the separate forces were to be summoned if necessary to unite under an emergency commander elected to face a sudden and overwhelming peril? The folly of such a plan is manifest. It would not provide any permanent assurance of safety, as it would merely recognize a danger as probable, without in any efficient manner suggesting a practical method of meeting it beforehand. Nothing, will, in fact, be done to the purpose until the Federal Council be co-extensive in its representation with all the colonies. Not that the Federal Council is the most suitable body to undertake a scheme of federal defence for Australia, far less to form the executive of a system of naval and military administration for Australasia. But no effective step to military and naval unity can be taken, it is clear, until a Federal Council of all the colonies has agreed upon the main lines of a federal army and navy; and such an agreement could hardly be possible until the general resolution adopted at Melbourne had at least been accepted by them as the basis of federal union, to be followed by the draft of a federal constitution.

And this is the meaning of Sir Henry Parkes when he asks the colonies as a whole to affirm that the time has come for the union of the Australian colonies under one government. Unity that is to be an accident of war can never be thorough and efficient; but unity cemented by common interests and aims, common anxieties, hopes and fears in time of peace is just that which can be utilized for common

Newcastle Journal—*continued.*

defence in war. The scheme of united defence has at last awakened even the most torpid politicians in Australia to their real condition in separated communities. Its elaboration has revealed the weakness—as it always has done for ages in such cases—of isolation and independence. In preparing for union as military and naval powers, the colonists have discovered that the preliminaries of defensive union does not exist. There is in that respect to this hour no material out of which a united Australasian army or navy can be constructed. The volunteers are there, the rifles and guns, the war vessels and gunboats, the torpedo defences on the coast—all are there; but there is no United Australia with a Federal Diet, a war secretary, a commander-in-chief, or lord high admiral, to make these forces a terror to the invading foe. In some processes of political development, the order of growth is like the advance in some intellectual and physical inquiries, one of a synthetic character, in which at a certain stage the bold thinker goes far beyond the apparent exigencies of the hour. The greater must, in some exigencies, be accepted, if the lesser is to be obtained. Australia is arrested on its way to taking up an effective position as a military and naval power because it lacks that without which no permanently great and effective military and naval power has ever existed in this world. Federation—a Federal Constitution, a Federal Council—all startle and alarm good souls in Sydney or Melbourne, who hug their colonial independence to their bosom, and delight in showing how much better their fiscal policy, their land policy, or their educational policy is than that of other colonies. But to a Federal Council they must ere long reconcile themselves, and if the vote taken at Melbourne has any historic value, it heralds the inauguration at a national Australasian Convention next year of a Union which will not, on its natal day, seek precedents either in Canada or the United states. When United Australasia, as the eastern development of "Greater Britain" at the Antipodes, "mews its mighty youth," in the Southern Seas, it will make a history all its own; and idle indeed were it to make any feeble attempt to lay down limits or a model for the Dominion that is already in embryo, and seeking a Federal Charter as the first means of being able to warn off any spoilers of its wide domain, a Power in the Far East corresponding to that Imperial Dominion of Canada that guards the other Pacific shore of Greater Britain in the Far West.

Leicester Post—

February 17th, 1890.

WITH the aid of the extensive correspondence which was ordered to be printed by the Legislative Assembly of New South Wales, copies of which have been forwarded to the English press, we are able to estimate the full significance of the telegram we published in our last issue, to the effect that the Federation Conference at Melbourne had unanimously adopted an address for presentation to the Queen expressing loyalty and attachment to the throne, and setting forth a declaration in favour of the union of the Australian Colonies. That was by far the most important item of news that has been given to the people of this country, as well as of the Colonies, for many years; though comparatively few persons at home would at once be able to realize all that it implied. Sir C. Gavan Duffy in his recent article on this subject in the *Contemporary Review*, though he appears to have taken up an unwarrantable position of scepticism as to the possibility of a true union of colonial sentiment, and also as to the likelihood of sympathetic action by the home Government, does not underestimate the vast issues of the question when he says, "The federation of the Australian Colonies concerns British interests closer than any question for which we keep ambassadors at Berlin or Paris." He is right also in declaring that now or never is the time for federation, that the federation of the Empire, in the process of which an Australian union is a necessary anterior step, "if it is postponed until after the next European war, will probably never take place while the world lasts"; but Sir Gavan is proved to be wholly wrong in his belief that the colonists could not overcome the hindrances to their agreement without external assistance, and we believe the events of the next few weeks will also show that he is unjust to the spirit of British politics when he manifests an inclination to adopt the sarcasm that "its keynote is parochial." Undoubtedly intercolonial jealousies have greatly hindered the proposals of the Australian federalists, and indifference of a culpable character has been exhibited at Downing-street years ago, but it never could have been doubtful that the sentiment of unity would dispel the mists of personalities and petty colonial rivalries whenever it became a genuine power; and until it had been strengthened and concentrated it was idle to expect its rays to penetrate the cold shadows of the Colonial Office. The correspondence to which we refer, extending from the 15th October to the 16th December

Leicester Post—*continued.*

of last year, displays in a cheering and most convincing manner the fact that the desire for unity has at length become so strong and general as to completely overcome every merely local difference; and it also shows that the preliminary negotiations have been throughout of such a conciliatory and even fraternal character that the Home Government can no longer have a single doubt upon which to hang another pretext for evasion or delay. For this splendid manifestation of the federal spirit, Sir Henry Parkes is entitled to great honour. His published letters are a remarkable refutation of the statements regarding him made by Sir Gavan Duffy, whose article is thereby put curiously out of date. It may or may not be true that Sir Henry prevented Victoria using the waters of the Murray for the purposes of irrigation, and there may be warrant for asserting that he desired New South Wales to be renamed "Australia," thereby intending to insult the sister colonies; but whatever may have been his mistakes in the past, there can be no doubt that the New South Wales Colonial Secretary, who is rightly styled "the recognized Apostle of Federation," has by his manifest desire to kindle and sustain the sentiment of union, "avoiding subordinate questions coloured by party feeling or collateral issues," made the Melbourne Conference possible, and is largely responsible for the most important decision at which that Conference has unanimously arrived.

The moot question with the Colonies has been the nature of the powers conferred by the Federal Council Act of 1885. That Act, it will be remembered, was the outcome of representations of a Conference of Colonial Delegates at Sydney in 1883, when general alarm was felt at a project on the one hand then believed to be entertained by France of sending her most dangerous criminals to the New Hebrides and other Pacific islands, and, on the other hand, at a design evidently manifested by Germany of seizing New Guinea, the portal of the Pacific. The Act was regarded by Sir Henry Parkes and many others as of little practical value; but Mr. Duncan Gillies, the present Premier for Victoria, and others with him formed what now appears to be an over sanguine estimate of the powers it conferred. One of its provisos was that a Federal Council which it contemplated could be called into existence by the separate resolution of each colony adopting the Act, and sending representatives to the Council. In the result, only one of the colonies—Victoria—accepted the Act forthwith, and only South Aus-

Leicester Post—*continued.*

tralia has since joined. Among the powers to be conferred on the Council was authority to take action in the matter of "general defences," if two or more of the colonies should make a representation regarding it. But this specified authority was curiously huddled amongst such comparatively small matters as quarantine, copyright, weights and measures, recognition of marriage and divorce, &c., &c., and clearly it was not intended that by means of this Act the Australian colonies should be able to co-operate in the way they desired. On the whole, it is fortunate that they took this view of their limitations, or the possibilities of a grave dispute with both France and Germany would at that time have become most alarming. The Act was dangerously equivocal, and might have resulted in giving the proposed Federal Council all the power to quarrel with a great enemy, whilst it left the rest of the nation merely the responsibility of fighting it out. In proof of this jeopardy, we have the letter of Mr. Duncan Gillies in reply to General Edwards' proposed organization of military forces. It is dated so late as October 15, 1889, and in it he says that section 15 of the Act gives the colonies all "needful authority and powers." The Federal Council, he says, "can deal with the whole matter satisfactorily. It can not only consider and devise a practicable scheme, but can embody it in the form of legislative enactment. If the Federal Council be not accepted for this purpose, what else is possible?" New South Wales has, however, rightly held aloof from the entire machinery of the new Council. It either conferred too much power—that is, authority without responsibility—or not enough, for it did not recognize the vital principle of federation. The subject was kept alive, but in a state of suspended animation, until the unexpected but enthusiastically welcomed statement made by Lord Carrington in opening the New South Wales Parliament on November 26 last year. His Lordship stated that the Government had opened negotiations with the other Australian Governments with a view to the several colonies "rising and uniting in the formation of one powerful Australian nation." He added eloquently, "The birth of a nation is an epoch which can have no succeeding parallel, and the national sentiment awakened in the parent colony is a sure presage of the august time which is approaching in her fortunes. There is every prospect of the colonies cordially meeting in consultation on such preliminary steps as may be deemed advisable, and no reason to doubt but that free intercourse will lead to patriotic agree-

Leicester Post—*continued.*

ment." That Lord Carrington has proved a true prophet, the unanimous decision of the Conference at Melbourne shows. It rests with the Government at home to make a response equal to the just expectations of the now united colonies. This we may reasonably expect from the anticipation of what would be required explicitly indicated in the Queen's Speech, and it is likely that in a very short time Australia will merge from the position of a group of ineffective and divided colonies into the power and dignity of national life. It will, we presume, be created by royal proclamation a Dominion like Canada, having, as Sir Henry Parkes anticipated, a Governor-General, a Privy Council, and a Parliament, consisting of a Senate and a House of Commons. Whatever may be the precise character of the new Constitution, however—and we are not sanguine that the present Government will concede the full measure of domestic liberties—there can be little doubt that we are on the eve of a most momentous development of the Imperial problem.

Nottingham Express—

February 17th, 1890.

Among the earliest Bills to be brought before Parliament is one for granting responsible government to Western Australia, which considers that it has now been quite long enough in leading strings. The Bill proposes to hand over to the colony not only the duties of local government, but also the control of its lands, from which a large part of the local revenues has been, and is likely to be, derived. Some discussion may again arise on the question of relinquishing the right of Imperial control over the immense tracts of West Australian land. The principle has now, however, been accepted that the territory is to be divided. A portion is to be reserved for the founding of a future colony, and the remainder will, in the meantime, be reserved for administration by the colony to which it is proposed to grant responsible government. A good deal turns upon whether the division is to be made north and south or east and west. In the latter case the colony will get 400,000 square miles of the territory, whilst the Home Government will reserve 600,000 miles. In the former case, which is said to be preferred by the Australian delegates, the colony get a proportion larger in extent, but evidently less valuable

Nottingham Express—*continued.*

in quality. Whichever alternative as to the line of frontier be adopted, it is a matter of satisfaction that there will be abundance of suitable area left for the energies of our surplus population in the formation of a new colony. Colonists at the antipodes need not be afraid that we shall send them infirm persons or paupers. The population of the mother country continues to increase at a rapid rate, and we are glad to know that a large proportion of the surplusage consists of useful labourers.

Apropos of the same subject, it is interesting to note that a resolution in favour of a union of all the Australian colonies under one Federal Government has been passed by the influential Conference which has just concluded its labours at Melbourne. This movement had its immediate origin in the need for an organization of the Australian forces and the importance of securing some effective plan of combined action of defence. The scheme now approved in principle is the outcome of a meeting of the Federal Council of Australasia with a deputation from the Sydney Government. The members of the Federal Council are representative public men, who possess the confidence of their respective colonies, and who are qualified to discuss the question without any undue usurpation of authority. Although the idea of federation has been approved, four or five years must pass before it can be completed, for there are many difficulties, including those connected with variations in the commercial tariff, to be overcome. No national unity is possible with hostile tariffs. Meantime it is proposed that the members of the recent Conference should take the steps necessary to induce the legislatures of their respective colonies to appoint during the present year delegates to a national Australasian Convention empowered to consider and report upon an adequate scheme for the Federal Constitution. A loyal address to the Queen was adopted, conveying to her Majesty the resolutions adopted, and indicating those hopes of a still greater future for our Australian colonies which have led to their adoption. We have received from the Agent-General's office in London a copy of an important letter on the whole question, addressed by Mr. Gillies, the Premier of Victoria, to Sir Henry Parkes, the Colonial Secretary of New South Wales. In one of his eloquent speeches at the Conference, Sir Henry responded in a more accommodating and favourable spirit than had been expected. He recalled the fact that four millions of people in the Australian colonies are

Nottingham Express—*continued.*

of British origin, united to the soil by ties of birth, parentage, friendship, and love; adding that, if they were incapable of making a nation, they were hardly fit to occupy their bounteous country. The crimson thread of kinship runs through all these colonies, and the time has arrived when they can no longer remain isolated. No one can any longer pretend that it would be an advantage to the whole to remain separated; and no advantage, but the reverse, can arise from delay. Happily the proposed union of the Australian colonies under one Government does not imply any separation from the Empire, or the creation of a separate political organization. In Australia, as in Ireland, Home Rule does not mean separation—a fact upon which Sir Henry Parkes laid special stress in his able speech.

Nottingham Guardian—

February 17*th.* 1890.

The news from Australia respecting the Conference which has been sitting at Melbourne to consider the subject of Australasian Confederation is most encouraging. A proposal made by Sir Henry Parkes, the Prime Minister of New South Wales, to the effect that "the time has come for a union of the Australian colonies under one Government" was carried without a single dissentient, and from beginning to ending the proceedings were characterised by almost perfect unanimity. The Conference then accepted another resolution, proposed by the delegate from Victoria, Mr. Deakin, to the effect that the members of the Conference "should take the steps necessary to induce the Legislatures of their respective Colonies to appoint during the present year delegates to a National Australasian Convention." This Convention is to be composed of seven members from each self-governing colony and four from each Crown colony, and to it will be entrusted the power to frame a working scheme of federation. If the Legislatures of the different colonies accept the proposal, as no doubt they will, the Convention will meet in Melbourne early next year, and we do not think there would be any serious difficulty in framing such a Constitution for the new Australian State as would contain every provision necessary for the future welfare of the country. That there are several difficult points to be settled we cannot deny. The question of a capital is one of them; but this will probably be got over by

Nottingham Guardian—*continued*.

the acceptance of a suggestion informally made by Sir Henry Parkes, that a small place on the Murray River should be selected. It is well situated, easily accessible, and, moreover, it is too small to excite the jealousies of any of the larger towns. Another point is the question of intercolonial free-trade; but we believe that the colonists are quite prepared to accept this, provided they can have a protective tariff against the rest of the world, as, of course, they could have. These are, we believe, the most serious difficulties, although, of course, others may crop up during the deliberations. In regard to the future Constitution, there is, we believe, a disposition to accept that of the United States of America as a model rather than that of Canada, but a better result would probably be attained by a judicious blending of the two. In some particulars the Canadian Constitution is greatly the superior, and the Australian colonists will do well to take what is good from each. It is rather premature, however, to discuss this matter at present. The Convention has to be appointed before deciding what it shall do. The first step has, however, been taken, and the unanimity and despatch with which the preliminary business was completed is a happy augury for the future.

Dundee Advertiser—
February 17th, 1890.

THE movement in favour of Australasian Federation has received an additional stimulus from the Conference which has just been brought to a close at Melbourne. There were representatives from all the Australian colonies, as well as Tasmania and New Zealand. The Conference, on the motion of Sir Henry Parkes, agreed without dissent that "the time had come for a union of the Australian colonies under one Government." This was followed by a resolution to the effect that "members of the Conference should take the steps necessary to induce the Legislatures of their respective colonies to appoint, during the present year, delegates to a National Australasian Convention, empowered to report upon an adequate scheme for the Federal Constitution." An address to the Queen was also adopted, informing Her Majesty of what had been done by the Conference, and assuring her of the "devoted attachment" of the Australian people to her Throne and person. It was finally agreed to empower the Prime Minister of Victoria

Dundee Advertiser—*continued.*

to summon the proposed Convention, which, it is understood, will meet early next year. This is a decided step in advance; but the graver difficulties have yet to be encountered. Something more is needed than a mere vague desire to form a great English-speaking nation in the South Seas. There must be unanimity as to fiscal arrangements. Tariff differences have until now formed a formidable obstacle in the way of a closer union between the colonies. There can be no federation if the colonies are to maintain hostile tariffs as at present. Mr. Duncan Gillies, Premier of Victoria, acknowledges that there are weighty difficulties in the way; but difficulties, in his opinion, were made to be overcome. Mr. Gillies is evidently not very sanguine that the Convention will be able to level the Customs barrier. He anticipates, however, that it would be able to arrive at a modification satisfactory to all. The Constitution of Canada is the model which Mr. Gillies thinks Australia should follow. Sir Henry Parkes seems to think that much may be learned from the events which led to the creation and Constitution of the United States. A common tariff is an essential feature in both Constitutions, and the Australasians must accustom themselves to that idea if the proposed Convention is to bear fruit. This movement will be watched with interest in this country. The federation, if carried out on broad and liberal principles, would unquestionably, as Sir Henry Parkes predicts, make the new Dominion mistress of the Southern Seas, and command the respect of every nation.

Aberdeen Free Press—

February 17th, 1890.

THE proceedings of the Australasian Federation Conference, which were brought to a close in the end of last week, have been characterised by great unanimity and heartiness as regards the main purpose of the Conference. From the manner in which the project was taken up so soon as it was put forward by Sir Henry Parkes with a view to practical action, there could be no doubt that the public mind in the various colonies was well-matured on the question; but the Conference has shown a maturity of opinion and a preparedness for action such as could hardly have been believed to exist. The proceedings of the Conference, in fact, show that the general question has entirely passed beyond the stage

Aberdeen Free Press—*continued.*

of discussion, and that the union of the Australasian Colonies as a single nation under a strong Federal Government is only a matter of time, and of just such time as may be necessary for framing a satisfactory scheme of federation. The chief feature of the Conference has been the testimony borne by the several representatives to the development of a national spirit in Australia, and to the decadence of the provincialism and separatism which have hitherto characterised the colonies, and of which their existing condition is the political expression. Sir Henry Parkes, who has been the leading spirit in the present movement, gave eloquent voice to the new sentiment of Australian nationality in a speech delivered at a banquet on the opening day of the Conference. It was, he said, a wise dispensation that the colonies should so far work out their own prosperity independently of each other, but the time had gone for them being longer isolated. "The crimson thread of kinship ran through all," and no sane man would say that in Australia they should remain longer separated. The colonies were, he went on to say, now called upon by "all the laws regulating the growth of free communities to unite under one Government and one flag." Nothing could be truer or more appropriate to the occasion than this appeal to "the law regulating the growth of free communities." All the world over, this law is to be seen in operation. Wherever there is freedom, progress, and development—in Germany, in Italy, in America, and now in Australia itself—the political forces of the time are making, not for separation, not for provincial autonomy or Home Rule, but for national unity and the building up of great and powerful states.

The chief business of the Conference was the consideration of a resolution submitted by Sir Henry Parkes, declaring that, "in the opinion of the Conference, the best interests and the present and future prosperity of the Australasian colonies will be promoted by an early union under the Crown," and that while recognizing the services of those who founded the Federal Council, the Conference "declares its opinion that the seven years that have since elapsed have developed the national life of Australasia in population, wealth, discovery, resources, and self-governing capacity to an extent which justifies the higher act, at all times contemplated, of the union of the colonies under one Legislature and Executive Government." The true note is here struck. It is the development of the "national life" of Australia that compels the new departure; it is not merely federation

Aberdeen Free Press—*continued.*

that is in view, but "union" and "union under one Legislature and Executive Government." The discussion that took place upon the resolution was in almost perfect harmony with the terms of the resolution itself. By what was proposed, it was urged by Sir Henry Parkes, the colonies would "economise their resources and substitute national for local interests." Mr. A. Deakin (Victoria), who seconded, said his Colony was prepared to make sacrifices for the cause of union, by the partial abandonment, he went on to indicate, of the system of protection which Victoria has hitherto maintained. The great and important thing for Australians, he contended, was that they should possess "one centre of national life." The Federal Government too, he urged, must be a strong Government, exercising all the powers of a Sovereign State, though it need not impair, he significantly added, the efficiency of the "local governments for local ends." Some of the representatives of the smaller colonies appear to have been a little afraid of the policy thus advocated, no doubt seeing that the stronger the central Government the more would these particular colonies suffer in dignity and independence; but their reservations were distinctly overborne by the prevailing voice of the Conference and the vigour with which the speakers for the larger colonies urged the subordination of provincial to national interests. "Whatever Executive was created," said the Hon. W. McMillan, the colleague of Sir Henry Parkes, "must be strong, potent, and acknowledged, otherwise they might find local Legislatures running against its authority"; and those who might regret the loss of provincial independence were comforted by a representative from Queensland, who pointed out that what the local Legislatures might lose, "the people of Australia would gain." The dominant view expressed in the discussion was that embodied in the resolution—that the federation of the colonies should be no mere association of the several Governments for certain purposes of common interest, but the establishment of a new and strong National Government, with large powers both of legislation and administration, and to which all "local" Legislatures and Executives should be distinctly subordinate.

The remaining resolutions were to the effect that steps should be taken without delay to carry the scheme of Australasian Union into effect. It was resolved that the Legislatures of the respective colonies should be asked to appoint, during the present year, delegates to "a National Australasian Convention, empowered to consider and report

Aberdeen Free Press—*continued*.

upon an adequate scheme for the Federal Constitution," and that this Convention should consist of not more than seven members from each self-governing colony, and not more than four from each Crown colony. After what has taken place, there can be no doubt of the several colonial Parliaments falling in with the scheme and making the necessary appointments for the proposed Convention, or of the result of the Convention itself being to carry to a practical issue the policy so distinctly defined and so harmoniously adopted at the Conference just held. There were one or two questions touched upon in the Conference speeches which will fall to be considered at the Convention, with respect to which there may be more or less conflict of opinion. Some of the speakers seemed to think that the Constitution of the Dominion of Canada would form a suitable model for adoption by the Australians, while others pointed with more distinct approbation to that of the United States. There is room for such differences of opinion, and the Australians would presumably do well to keep their minds open, and select for themselves from Canadian, American, or other precedents such provisions as they think best suited to their circumstances. There is doubt, too, as to what New Zealand may do. Lying as it does at a distance of 1,200 miles from Australia, the colony is in a considerably different position from the others as regards the chances of benefit or otherwise from the proposed Union. At the Conference the representatives of the colony naturally reserved for their constituents freedom of action, and suggested the expediency of leaving the matter in such a way that New Zealand could join afterwards if she saw her way. Presumably this will be arranged, as obviously there can be no compulsion employed, and New Zealand is too important a member of the group not to be treated with all due consideration.

Cork Constitution—

February 17*th*, 1890.

ANOTHER step has been made towards Australian Federation. Representatives of the Australian colonies have been in conference for a week, discussing the question at length, and eventually, on the motion of Sir Henry Parkes, the Premier of New South Wales, a resolution was passed affirming the principle of federation. This principle has

Cork Constitution—*continued.*

hitherto been admitted, and is not, therefore, novel; but the Conference has undoubtedly advanced the question, though few of the difficulties which stand in the way of its acceptance have been overcome. The following address to Her Majesty the Queen, proposed by Sir J. Hall, of New Zealand, and seconded by the Hon. Dr. Cockburn, South Australia, was unanimously adopted:—

"We, your Majesty's loyal and dutiful subjects, members of a Conference assembled at Melbourne to consider the question of creating for Australasia one Federal Government, and representing the Australasian colonies, desire to approach your Most Gracious Majesty with renewed expressions of our devoted attachment to your Majesty's Throne and Person. On behalf of your Majesty's subjects throughout Australasia, we beg to express our fervent hope that your Majesty's life may be long spared to reign over a prosperous and happy people. We most respectfully inform your Majesty that after mature deliberation we have unanimously agreed to the following resolutions:—

(1) That members of the Conference should take the steps necessary to induce the Legislatures of their respective colonies to appoint, during the present year, delegates to a national Australasian Convention, empowered to consider and report upon an adequate scheme for the Federal Constitution

(2) That this Convention should consist of not more than seven members from each self-governing colony, and not more than four from each Crown colony."

This prepares the way for further consideration; but no federation can be effective unless complete, and few suggestions have been made to overcome the difficulties which naturally arise. At the Conference the idea of a union for defensive purposes was unquestionably popular, and was carefully considered, but in matters of detail there was a wide difference of opinion. Some are in favour of an imitation of the method pursued in the United States, others advocate a union on the plan of the Canadian Dominion, while not a few support a plan claiming to embrace the best features of both. Then, in addition to these diverse views, must be added the difficulties to be found in hostile tariffs. New South Wales and Tasmania are in favour of free trade while Victoria is protectionist. These conflicting interests have to be reckoned within a complete scheme of federation. Though the question is as yet distant from settlement, it is making progress, and will eventually come to the front, for it is evident that the colonies are anxious to form a federation. The movement is as yet, however, scarcely ripe for the intervention of the Home Government, who, no doubt, will be ready for the demand when it has been formulated on a sound basis.

Dundee Courier—

February 18th, 1890.

YESTERDAY, in the House of Lords, the Earl of Belmore put a question on the subject of Australian Federation, and the sentiments he expressed were reciprocated by Lord Knutsford on behalf of the Government. The union of the various Australian colonies, of which there has been much talk of late years, seems now to be fairly in the way of accomplishment. The Federation Conference, which had been sitting at Melbourne for some days, closed in the end of last week, and at its final meeting passed a number of important resolutions. It was unanimously agreed that the time has come for the union of the Australian colonies under one Government, and various motions were passed with this end in view. Provision was made for admitting into the federation the more remote colonies, and arranging for the appointment and regulating the number of delegates to a National Australasian Convention which is to be held early next year. This Convention is empowered to consider and report upon an adequate scheme for federal constitution. The advantages of inter-union amongst the Australian colonies are manifest. By this means a community of interest will be established, internal free trade will be secured, and the subject of national defence will receive much needed attention. The federation of the Australian colonies is an indispensable preliminary to the plan of Imperial Federation, or union of the whole Empire, which Lord Roseberry has so much at heart. When the lesser scheme has been successfully carried through, the greater question will demand that attention from politicians which it has not yet received. It is a perennial complaint amongst our colonists that their affairs do not interest the people at home as they should do. From the fussy meddling which led to the American Rebellion the Colonial Office has passed to the opposite extreme, and now in general our possessions are left severely alone. They are allowed to manage themselves, and do in effect as they please. This is right enough were the mother country to show some interest in the wellbeing and progress of her daughters, and lend her influence to what is for the advantage of Greater Britain. Sir Gavan Duffy, in a bitter article in one of the month's magazines, declares that, instead of leaving this question of federation to the colonists themselves, the two Houses of Parliament ought to have invited the local Legislatures to consider the subject, and that men such as Lord Roseberry and Lord Carnarvon should have

Dundee Courier—*continued.*

been appointed to carry the resolution to Australia, and hold conferences with the leading men in the different colonies. "Never since human history began," Sir Gavan remarks, "was so noble a patrimony treated with such ignorant and perilous insensibility. There are six great states which possess more natural wealth, wider territory, a better climate, and richer mineral deposits than the six greatest kingdoms in Europe, where a new England, a new Italy, a new France, a new Spain, and a new Austria are in rapid process of growth, and are already occupied by a picked population. These prosperous states are ready and willing to unite for ever with the nation from which they sprang in terms of fair partnership and association; but what cordial hand is stretched out to clasp theirs in affectionate embrace?" There is something, no doubt, in this eloquent appeal, although the colonists are themselves much to blame for the indifference felt towards them. By the protectionist policy they have adopted and in other ways, they have encouraged a certain school of politicians to contend that our colonies are no benefit, but a loss, to Britain, and that we would be better without them. This view, however, is a mistake. Trade undoubtedly follows the flag, and our commerce has always had a preponderating influence in the colonies. A scheme of Imperial federation, should it ever come to pass, will serve to knit our great Empire together in firmer bonds, and prove very much to the advantage of the United Kingdom as well as the colonies.

Chronicle—

February 18*th*, 1890.

Lord Belmore asked the Secretary of State for the Colonies last night whether there is any correspondence in the Colonial Office on the subject of Australian federation which could be made public without inconvenience, and he took the opportunity of expressing his sympathy with the object which Sir Henry Parkes and his coadjutors have in view. The interests of Australia are, we may be sure, near to Lord Belmore's heart, for he spent some years at the antipodes as Governor of New South Wales, and learnt to love the land and to respect the people. Lord Belmore suggested last night that when the Federal Parliament and Federal Executive have been created it will be necessary to

Chronicle—*continued.*

find a federal capital. Afterwards, such questions as the common defence of the Dominion and a uniform tariff will have to be discussed. All these questions will present difficulties to the statesmen of Australia; but we have no fear regarding the ultimate success of those statesmen in triumphing over such difficulties. Lord Granville expresses the opinion that the same success will attend the Australian colonies in uniting as the North American colonies have experienced. We may confidently assume that the Australians will not find greater difficulties or obstacles in their way than were found by the Canadians; and they may be encouraged by the growth of Canadian greatness and prosperity to follow the example which must be ever present to their minds. The Canadians found the same difficulty about the federal capital as Lord Belmore suggests in regard to Australia. Quebec, Montreal, and Toronto asserted their respective claims; but the compromise suggested by the Imperial Government conferred the distinction on Ottawa. Whether the rival claims of Sydney, Melbourne, and Adelaide will in like manner be adjusted by the selection of Albany remains to be seen; but, at all events, this question is not likely to interfere with the realization of national aspirations in Australia. So far as we can judge, the chief difficulty will be found in the fiscal question, though it is not improbable that the various colonies will soon recognize the absolute necessity of at least having free trade between themselves. The Secretary of State for the Colonies expressed his satisfaction last night with the results of the Melbourne Conference, but he did not think that any good purpose would be gained by debating the questions which are now under consideration by the statesmen of Australia. This view commended itself to Lord Granville's experienced judgment. But we are glad that Lord Belmore's question served to elicit from the Secretary of State and his predecessor those expressions of sympathetic interest which will necessarily give much satisfaction in our Australian colonies. This in itself is a substantial advantage.

Warm approval has been expressed by many Australians in England, including the Agents-General of the Australian colonies, of Sir George Baden Powell's resolution expressing sympathy with the Australian Confederation movement. Several members of the Cabinet have also declared themselves cordial supporters of the resolution, and there appears, therefore, good hope that the House of Commons may have the opportunity of discussing it on an early day.

Chronicle—*continued.*

It was somewhat of a triumph for Victoria to have the Conference on Australasian Federation assembled in Melbourne; but it was really a victory for Sir Henry Parkes, who was determined not to recognize the Federal Council to the extent of selecting its normal meeting-place as the locale for the new departure in Australian history which his genius had initiated.

Daily Graphic—
February 18th, 1890.

In the House of Lords last night, the leaders of both political parties concurred in pronouncing a benediction on the project of a federation of the Australasian colonies, which has lately been resolved upon by an enthusiastic Conference at Melbourne. We are gratified that an early opportunity has been seized by statesmen at home to assure the great dependencies of the Crown in the southern hemisphere that their legitimate aspirations have the sympathy of public opinion in the mother country. It is with pride that Englishmen of all classes and parties watch the growth of the colonies which were founded by the wisdom and enterprise of their fathers. No small feelings of jealousy, no suspicious fears of disloyalty, mar the serenity of this parental satisfaction. The expansion of Britain could wish for no more splendid monument than this consolidation of a new Empire, which will add enormously to the strength of the old.

The Weekly Budget—
February 18th, 1890.

THE Conference of the Representatives of the Australian colonies, convened to consider the question of Australian Federation, has met at Melbourne. By a unanimous vote, Mr. Duncan Gillies, the Premier of Victoria, was elected president, and Mr. George H. Jenkins, Clerk to the Legislative Assembly of Victoria, was appointed secretary. At a dinner given by Mr. Duncan Gillies to the delegates, Sir Henry Parkes, the Premier of New South Wales, by whose efforts chiefly the Conference has been convened, made an important speech, which was loudly applauded. "They were," said Sir Henry, "four millions of people, all of

The Weekly Budget—*continued.*

British origin, united to the soil by the ties of birth, parentage, friendship and love. If they were incapable of making a nation, they were hardly fit to occupy their bounteous country. The time had arrived when they were no longer isolated. The crimson thread of kinship ran through all. No sane man would say that it would be an advantage to the whole to remain separated. If this were so, no advantage, but much evil, might arise from delay. Federation implied no separation from the Empire, nor the separation of a separate political organization. The question of a common tariff was a mere trifle compared with that of a national existence." New South Wales, he declared, was prepared to go into the National Union without making any bargain, and without stipulating for any advantage whatever, and trusting to the justice and good faith of a Federal Parliament. Sir Henry, although a staunch free-trader, is thus prepared to sacrifice free-trade in New South Wales to federation. But, on the other hand, it is a matter of course that this measure would secure free-trade between all the colonies within the federation, in which case there would be a real gain for free-trade, and not a loss.

Manchester Examiner—

February 18*th*, 1890.

The Ministerial statement on the subject of Australian Federation, which was made in Parliament yesterday, ought to contribute to the success of that cause, and to ensure that its promotion shall follow the lines of loyalty to the Empire and affection for the mother country as closely in the future as it has done hitherto. Lord Knutsford had little to add in the way of facts to what had previously been made known through the ordinary channels of information regarding the recent Federation Conference in Australia. That Conference has served its purpose of uniting all the Australian colonies in a frank discussion of the arguments for and against federation. The ground has been broken, and must now be cultivated. Federation has been advanced to the first line of practical public questions in Australia. It now occupies attention to the comparative exclusion of even the much-vexed labour question, as well as that of Chinese immigration. The next step will be for the several Colonial Legislatures in Australia to agree to a second

Manchester Examiner—*continued.*

Conference for the purpose of deciding upon the precise form of federation. This will no doubt be summoned during the present year. Meantime our kindred under the Southern Cross receive the assurance that the sympathies of the Home Government are heartily with the movement, and that the Queen's Ministers " believe that the prosperity, the welfare, and the strength of these great colonies would be materially increased and secured by a closer union under some form of federation." It is possible to conceive circumstances in which federation of the Australian colonies among themselves might prove an obstacle to closer union with the mother country, and might tend to create an independent centre of unity ten thousand miles away from England; but these circumstances do not exist now, and there is no prospect of their being called into existence within a measurable period of time. The actual circumstances are such, that the formation of an Australian federation would greatly simplify and facilitate the work of Imperial federation. Of course there are difficulties in the way. Each of the Australian colonies has a commercial policy of its own, independent both of its neighbours and of the mother country. New South Wales is jealous of Victoria, and there are many points of difference between the stirring genius of Queensland and the plodding temper of South Australia. It is, however, the business of statesmen to solve such difficulties, and the very nature and existence of the latter should deepen in the colonial mind the sense of dependence on England, even if it were not the fact that their public property is mortgaged, to a very large proportion of its value, to the wealth of the mother country.

Edinburgh Scotsman –

February 18th, 1890.

Australian federation has, within the last few days, risen auspiciously above the horizon of practical politics. The expressions of interest and satisfaction with which the result of the Conference lately held at Melbourne was hailed yesterday in the Lords by Lord Knutsford and Lord Granville will, no doubt, be echoed on both sides of the other House, and by the country at large. Sir Henry Parkes has scored a success, upon which that veteran statesman, the colony he represents, and the Australian colonies generally,

Edinburgh Scotsman—*continued.*

have good cause to congratulate themselves. It is true that our Australian kin have as yet only arrived at mutual agreement upon the opinion that federation in some form is desirable, and that steps should be taken without delay to ascertain what that form should be. A large diversity of view was expressed by the delegates present respecting the shape, the extent, the process, and the objects of constituting a union among the family of young Australian States. An infinite number of difficulties have been brought into the foreground, or lie waiting in the background; but the rate of progress made, and the degree of unanimity already revealed, have been unexpectedly large and gratifying. Men who have a right to speak for their respective colonies, and for Australian opinion generally, have declared, without a dissenting voice, that " the time has come " for their union under some form of federal government. Recognizing the special obstacles lying in the way of incorporating the more distant colonies, the proposal for union is for the present limited to what may be spoken of as the future provinces of the continent of Australia, with Tasmania and New Zealand; but the resolutions contemplate an extension of the scheme at some later period to the more outlying British possessions in the antipodes. A Convention is to be called to draw up the plan and constitution of an Australasian Dominion; and finally, and not least satisfactory among the fruits of the Melbourne Conference, an address has been adopted, assuring Her Majesty of the warm feelings of loyalty to her Throne and person that animate her Australian subjects.

These are but the preliminaries to what will probably be prolonged, and may possibly be futile, negotiations for bringing about Australian union. Such as they are, however, they would scarcely have been deemed attainable seven years or even seven months ago. Australian opinion has ripened rapidly since the formation of the Federal Council, as the outcome of the colonial deliberations in 1883, and more especially since the publication of Sir Henry Parkes' letter to Mr. Service, giving voice, on behalf of New South Wales, to the view which has now been endorsed by the delegates of the other colonies, that " the time has come " for union on a larger plan and of a more intimate kind. The New South Wales Premier is himself the most remarkable monument of the development of Australian sentiment and conviction upon this question. In 1883 it was greatly due to his influence and arguments that New South Wales declined to join with Victoria and other colonies in adopting

Edinburgh Scotsman—*continued.*

the Federal Council Act, enabling them to deal collectively with questions of civil and criminal procedure and other matters of common interest. The reason, it has now been explained, was that he did not see in the Federal Council scheme a sufficiently broad and solid basis for co-operation. This certainly was not understood at the time; and at a later period, on being sounded on the subject, his "suspicious fears and difficulties were endless." This must have meant that, as an experienced statesman, he was indisposed to open his mind in public or to let himself be "drawn" in private, until his own mind and the mind of Australia were ripe. At all events, there can no longer be any question of the earnestness and enthusiasm with which he has taken up the work of Intercolonial Federation. He is no longer disposed to let any minor considerations or questions stand in the way of his own wish and that of the Australian colonies for union; and the suddenness of his conversion, and the ardour with which he has advocated integration, has raised in his case, as in that of a veteran politician nearer home, whose labours are in another direction, the suspicion that he is in a hurry to see the fulfilment of his own desires, and enjoy the political credit and rewards attached thereto.

Such a work as Australian federation, however, cannot be usefully hastened out of regard for any personal or sectional ends. One of the first matters brought before the Conference, as it probably will be the first that the coming Convention will have to settle, was whether the proposed Australian Government and Legislature is to be evolved out of the Federal Councils, or is to be a new creation. The genius of the mother country has usually manifested itself by making use, as far as possible, of old materials in the carrying out of constitutional changes; but this slow method may not be suitable or practical upon fresh ground, and under conditions of such rapid social and commercial development as we find existing in Australia. The settlement rests as much on the predilections or prejudices of different colonies and colonial statesmen as on principle. Victoria and Mr. Gillies prefer development of the Federal Council, because they have the credit of having approved of it as a basis of federation. Sir Henry Parkes and New South Wales object to it, because they have already rejected this corner stone. If there is any reality and strength in the Australian movement for union, the obstacles presented by the rival methods will soon be removed. A much more serious impediment is that offered in the colonial tariffs. A

Edinburgh Scotsman— *continued.*

Federal Parliament and Executive, representing states which are waging a commercial war, not only against outside countries, but against each other, would be something new in the history of constitution-making. Although it has been urged that the colonies should lose no time in uniting for the purposes, such as defence and criminal and civil jurisdiction, upon which their interests are already recognized as identical, and should wait for time and the force of events to settle whether Australia is to be a free-trade or a protective country, it seems necessary that an agreement on the subject of their common fiscal policy should be arrived at before they join in federal bonds. This is almost the solitary cause which the mother country has for feeling disquiet at the spectacle of these young communities seeking to develop and complete their powers of self-government. The eagerness with which New South Wales is pressing for federation is interpreted in some quarters to mean a readiness to sacrifice the policy of free-trade, to which it has clung so firmly and with such excellent results to its own trade and prosperity, for the sake of "the main question" of union. This view may be mistaken; but it is evident that, if the subject of the tariff comes up before the Convention, Sir Henry Parkes will have an uphill battle to fight against the combined strength of the colonies, headed by Victoria, that have given themselves over to protectionist devices. Another battle will have to be fought upon the question of the future seat of government—the respective weight that should be given to the seniority of Sydney, and the size and commercial importance of Melbourne. The proportionate share of representation to be assigned to the different colonies, the terms upon which admission could be given to colonies so specially circumstanced as New Zealand and Western Australia, and the arrangements for the consolidation of the colonial debts, will also be fertile themes of dispute. Difficulties as formidable have already been faced and overcome by their kin in Canada, and the benefits to be reaped from an incorporating union are at least as great. The difficulties and the advantages are already pretty well realized by the Australians themselves, and most of them were touched upon in the course of last week's discussions at Melbourne. The obstacles tend to disappear, while the gains, to the colonies and to the Empire at large, increase. One significant fact which we are called upon to observe is that, in seeking to draw their fortunes more closely together, the colonists, so far as their mind can be interpreted by the

Edinburgh Scotsman—*continued.*

voices of their leading men, desire also to draw more closely to the British connection. The "scarlet thread" of blood that Sir Henry Parkes speaks of as running through the length and breadth of Australia, begins and ends at the heart of the empire ; and its symbol is the "golden link" of the Crown.

Commonwealth—

February 19th, 1890.

THE Australian colonies will be pleased to hear of the very favourable reception which was accorded to the subject of the federation of the Australian colonies in the House of Lords on Monday, and doubtless the feelings expressed there will be shared by the great majority of the people of this country. Lord Knutsford, in replying to a question, said that there were no public despatches in the Colonial Office which could be laid on the table; but he understood that a second Conference would shortly be held in Australia, which would be attended by seven delegates from each government colony, and four delegates from each Crown colony. We are glad that our statesmen are thus early showing their interest in the question which is the foremost question in the colonies at the present time. The recent Conference at Melbourne was enthusiastically in favour of federation, and while there are difficulties in the way, which will require great tact and thorough discussion to remove, yet the sympathy of public opinion in the mother country will do much to bring about a result which is so desirable. At home we are not jealous of the progress of our colonies. Rather it is with natural pride that we watch the growth of the countries founded by our fathers, and which are a growing monument to the wisdom and enterprise of our sturdy nature. The consolidation of a new Empire in the southern hemisphere, which shall by the strongest ties be bound to the old, cannot but add enormously to the strength and prosperity of the latter.

Guardian—

February 20th, 1890.

AUSTRALIAN federation has made an important step forward. The Conference which has been sitting at Melbourne came to an end on Friday, and the representatives of the several

Guardian—*continued.*

colonies have unanimously resolved that the time has come for the union of the Australian colonies into one Government. They have further undertaken to induce the Legislatures of their respective colonies to send delegates to a National Australian Convention which shall consider and report upon a Federal Constitution. It seems likely, therefore, that the difficulties which have hitherto prevented Australian federation are in a fair way to be removed, and that Australia will no longer lag behind Canada on the road to become a nation. Whatever may be the ultimate relations between the colonies and the mother country, the extension of local federation is a decided advantage to both. Whether as an equal member of the same Empire or as an independent ally, the co-operation of Australia will be better worth having and better worth giving.

Brighton Gazette—

February 20th, 1890.

THE Conference recently held at Melbourne, with a view to the Federal Union of all the Australian colonies, is a matter of the very highest moment, as much for them as for the mother country. So great has been the progress of these colonies, so vast the extent of territory included therein, and so rapid the increase of population, that the question of their union into one great national body, virtually independent, is inevitable, and cannot be long delayed. It is a happy and a fortunate circumstance that there really may be said to exist but one feeling in regard to this important matter, alike in Britain and Australia. Concerning both it may be with truth averred that whilst there is no desire for absolute separation, but, on the contrary, a desire to uphold the union long existing between the mother country and her offshoots, yet, at the same time, it is recognized on all hands that the time has come when there must be an expansion of the old bonds of intercourse. The feeling now is vastly different from that which preceded the separation of the United States from the mother country. A wiser and more mutual feeling now exists, and on all hands the truth is recognized that the formation of the Colonial Federation may prove to be mutually beneficial alike to Britain and Australia, so that while the colonies may unite for the better conduct of their own affairs, the union that

Brighton Gazette—*continued.*

still upheld may be such as shall prove of the great advantage to all, whether in times of peace or war. There are, of course, great difficulties in the path of a consummation of the end desired, but the way in which the work has been begun in Melbourne gives great hope that those difficulties will be met and overcome. The Conference has unanimously passed a series of resolutions for the formation of a Home Union under one Government, and for the necessary steps being taken to induce the Legislatures of the several colonies to appoint delegates to a National Australasian Convention, to be held next year, when all the difficulties will have to be fought, and, we trust, overcome. An address has also been passed to the Queen, expressing the colonist's loyalty to the Throne, and informing her Majesty of the steps that have been taken for uniting the English-speaking colonies of Australia under a single Government. When the Convention meets, the great obstacle will be the existence of hostile tariffs, affecting not merely the relations of the colonies with other countries, but also the commercial intercourse between themselves. This will involve a certain amount of accommodation and compromise. Another question, though one more easy of settlement, will be the choice of a capital, as neither of the great colonies would like to see either of the others formed into the seat of a Central Government. Sir Henry Parkes has suggested Albury as a most suitable spot, and occupying a central position. It stands on the Murray River, at the point where the railway connecting Sydney and Melbourne passes the boundary of the two colonies, and it is thought that a district of some hundred square miles on either side of the river could be marked out and made subject only to the Federal Government. In this way neither of the two great rival colonies could claim to own the capital. Another subject into which we need not enter is the question whether the new Federation should be constructed upon the model of the United States or of Canada. This, however, is a fair question for debate, and no serious difficulties need be anticipated with regard thereto. A few facts may be stated as serving to show that the present condition of the colonies is suitable for the great change contemplated. Australia, with its three millions of people, is in just about the same position numerically as were the United States at the time of their declaration of independence. By adding New Zealand, Tasmania, and other smaller colonies, another million of people would be brought within the federation. The wealth

Brighton Gazette—*continued.*

of Australia is also very considerable, seeing that since 1851 the gold produced has been equal to one-third of our National Debt, whilst its imports are worth fifty millions a year, and its exports nearly as much. It should also be noticed that the fact of the colonies being nearly all upon the coast, and the vast interior being unexplored, points to the necessity of Australia becoming a great naval power.

John Bull—
February 21st, 1890.

LAST week constituted a memorable era in the history of our South Sea colonies. The representatives of the several Australasian communities, assembled in Conference at Melbourne, under the presidency of the Prime Minister of Victoria, adopted a loyal and dutiful address to the Queen, conveying to Her Majesty a series of resolutions expressive of the unanimous desire of all the colonies concerned to enter into federal union with each other. In the opinion of our fellow subjects at the antipodes, the time has come for combining together in a close federal bond the various Governments under which a British-born population numbering four millions is now living. It is keenly felt that the colonies united have a great future before them, but that disunited they must fail to realize that future. Seven years ago the first step in the direction of federation was taken by the constitution of the Federal Council, from which, however, New South Wales and New Zealand have held aloof, the latter owing chiefly to the great distance that separates her from the Australian Continent; the former for reasons which is difficult not to trace to a not very worthy jealousy of the lead taken by Victoria in promoting the Council scheme. The bearings of the various discussions that have for some years past taken place with regard to the Federal Council are fully and clearly explained by Sir Charles Dilke in the second part of his *Problems of Greater Britain,* reviewed in another column of our issue to-day. As Sir Charles Dilke observes, the Federal Council has been little more than a periodical conference of some of the leading statesmen of six out of the eight South Sea colonies. Both the colonies represented, and those unrepresented, on the Council are now, however, agreed in desiring to enter into a closer Federal Union. Whether that end is to be brought about upon the basis of

John Bull—*continued.*

the existing Council—as some colonies desire—or upon a wholly fresh basis—as New South demands—is, perhaps, not a matter of great moment. Sir Henry Parkes, the New South Wales Premier, though still unwilling to join the Council, is apparently quite prepared to co-operate with the other colonies in the matter of military defence, as well as on certain other points, pending the establishment of a Federal Constitution. The really serious difficulty is, of course, that of the tariff. The veteran Victorian statesman, Mr. Service, insists that hostile tariffs between sister colonies are inconsistent with any real unity between them; and the South Australian Premier, Mr. Playford, holds that the fiscal question is even more important than that of defence. Sir Henry Parkes, on the other hand, seems to think the tariff difficulty a mere minor point, which ought not seriously to hinder federation; and Sir Samuel Griffith, on behalf of Queensland, declares that any federation, even without fiscal union, would be better than none. Probably Sir Charles Dilke is right in anticipating that the difficulty will ultimately be settled on the twofold basis of intercolonial freetrade, and of protection against the world, including the mother country. As he further adds, it is rather hard on us that in Australia, as in Canada, we should retain our Empire only by facilitating the imposition of increased taxes on our goods.

Sir Henry Parkes' resolution to the effect that the colonies should be united under one Legislative and Executive Government, hardly deserves the epithets "vague" and "abstract" which some of the speakers at the Conference applied to it. To us it seems sufficiently precise, though it omits to enter into details best settled at the Convention which it has been agreed to hold next year. As it is, the adoption of the principle of a Federal Executive and Legislature represents a very considerable advance on the existing Council. It may now be taken for granted that the union will be a close and intimate one. Opinions at the Conference differed a good deal as to the best model on which to construct the new federation. Mr. Gillies—wisely, as we venture to think—favours the Canadian Constitution, between which and that of the United States the main difference is that in the Dominion the central authority is far stronger, as compared with the Provincial Legislatures and Executives. The representatives of South and of Western Australia strongly object, however, to this limitation of the powers of the local Legislatures; while Mr. Clarke, one of the Tasmanian delegates, declared in favour of a local autonomy on

John Bull—*continued.*

the model of that which obtains in the United States. It must be admitted that one strong argument in favour of adopting the United States' federal system is furnished by the unique position of New Zealand as compared with the other colonies. New Zealand is not only, as Sir Charles Dilke points out, jealous of federal legislation affecting her internal affairs—a feeling which has long induced her to contend for a power being reserved to each colony to retire from federation after joining—but her immense distance from Australia makes it difficult for her to come into any very close union with Australia proper. If New Zealand is to be included at all in the confederation, it must, in Sir Charles Dilke's opinion, be a federal union of a loose character. On the other hand, the view is strongly held—as by Dr. Cockburn, of South Australia—that anything short of complete federation is undesirable.

We cannot but welcome Sir Henry Parkes' declaration that, in his opinion, Australasian federation does not in the least imply separation from the British Empire. As far as we can judge, it will be a distinct advantage to this country that our Colonial Office should have to deal with a single Australian Federal Government rather than, as at present, with a number of separate Governments not always united in opinion on any given subject. The new arrangement will tend to reduce the friction between the mother-country and her daughter States. As Sir Charles Dilke observes, many difficulties will probably be settled before they come to discussion with the Imperial Government, while others will be presented in a simpler form. The federal power will speak to us with an authority more representative of Australasian opinion as a whole on such questions as those of Western Australia, of the presence in the South Pacific of France and Germany, and of united military and naval defence; while federation will also provide an efficient method of dealing with trans-continental telegraphs, ocean mails, telegraph cables, the subdivision of existing colonies, the influx of "servile" races, and intercolonial questions generally. No doubt the Convention that is to assemble next year will have some hard nuts to crack; but public opinion in Australia itself will have received from the Conference which has just closed an impetus in the direction of federation which will help the delegates a twelvemonth hence to tide over difficulties; while the discussion that will take place in the interval will still further assist them in satisfactorily solving the questions now at issue. The Australians hardly need to be

John Bull—*continued.*

assured of the cordial sympathy and goodwill of their countrymen at home, who entirely share the sentiments recently expressed on the subject of federation in Her Majesty's most gracious speech from the Throne, and echoed this week in the House of Lords by the Secretary of State.

The Richmond Herald—
February 21st, 1890.

THERE would seem to be every probability of Australian Federation shortly becoming *au fait accompli.* Reference to the subject was made in the House of Lords on Monday, when the Earl of Belmore asked whether there was any correspondence that could be laid before the House. Lord Knutsford, in answering the question in the negative, said that his colleagues, as well as himself, believed that the prosperity, the welfare, the strength, and the importance of the Australian colonies would be materially increased by a closer union amongst themselves under some form of Federal Government. A second Conference is to be held, and it is gratifying to hear from Lord Knutsford that there is every reason for hoping that the difficulties in the way will be successfully overcome. That there are considerable difficulties in the way goes without saying; but, as Earl Granville remarked on Monday, they are difficulties that ought to, and which certainly will, be solved. The statesmen of Australia, in dealing with this question, have knowledge which was not possessed by the United States and the Dominion of Canada; consequently they are not obliged to start *ab initio.* Sir Henry Parkes, one of the most astute of Australasian politicians, is in favour of a Federal Parliament after the Canadian plan—a Federal Ministry, with a Parliament consisting of an Upper and Lower House. There is, of course, difference of opinion on this point, some favouring a makeshift Federal Government. We believe, however, that the better course will be to have a complete and final Federal Government, though at the cost of working with some amount of friction at the start. All those who have the welfare of Australasia at heart must see the advisability of uniting the different colonies under one governing body; and we believe that the time is now ripe for a federation. The tariff difficulty is, no doubt, one of the most formidable that will have to be dealt with, while the question

The Richmond Herald—*continued.*

of the habitation of the Federal Government is sure to give rise to a good deal of discussion. Doubtless it will be found advisable to fix upon some small town, which, from its geographical and neutral position, will commend itself to the various colonies as the most suitable place for the seat of government. Whatever town be chosen, it is certain to grow apace once the government offices are located there. The question of defence will also have to be dealt with, so that altogether there are plenty of nuts for the statesmen of Australasia to crack. The progress of the movement is sure to be watched with the keenest interest in this country; for, thanks to steam and electricity, the ignorance that formerly prevailed in our midst with regard to the doings of our Australasian cousins is being rapidly dissipated.

Tablet—

February 22*nd,* 1890.

THE most important event of the week has taken place in the Pacific. A Conference of all the Australian Colonies has been held and a resolution adopted, which means the beginning of Australian unity. Seven years ago a Federal Council was formed, but as the mother-colony, New South Wales, declined to be represented, its chief service has been to accustom the people to federal ideas. The present Conference, though held in Melbourne, was convened at the instance of Sir Henry Parkes, the Prime Minister of New South Wales. The great difficulty that lies in the way is the question of the intercolonial tariff. No system of federation can be anything but a makeshift which does not include absolute free-trade between the colonies on the Australian continent, even if that involves protection as against the mother-country. Unfortunately, it is precisely the tariff against the sister colonies which it will cost most to part with. Victoria is ready to make large sacrifices for the sake of federation, and will accept union with a common fiscal system, or without it. Mr. Deakin, speaking in her name, said he looked forward to the near future to having a united Parliament and a single Executive. It needed a united voice to impress the views of Australia as to the future of the lands in the Southern Pacific upon the Colonial Office. Even if the various tariffs had to be maintained for a period of years after federation was established, the various officers of the Federal Government might collect the Customs

Tablet—*continued.*

and control all Australian ports. The general feeling seemed to be that a common system of defence might be adopted at once, and that discussion and mutual concession were all that is needed to secure what all, with the partial exception of New Zealand, which does not intend to be a dependency of Australia, strongly desire. The practical result of the Conference was a resolution pledging the members to try to induce their respective Legislatures to appoint delegates to a national Australasian Convention to consider an adequate plan for a Federal Constitution. The Conference closed with a loyal address to the Queen.

The Statist—

February 22nd, 1890

The representatives at the Melbourne Conference have unanimously agreed that a Convention is to be held at the earliest possible moment, at which all the Australasian colonies shall be represented, for the purpose of promoting a federal union between them. Sir H. Parkes and some other speakers expressed a strong preference for the United States over the Canadian model, while others seemed to prefer the Canadian to the American; but all were agreed that the hands of the delegates to the proposed Convention should not be tied beforehand. It is reasonable to expect, however, that the United States model will be the one adopted, firstly, because the self-governing colonies will not voluntarily part with more of their sovereignty than is absolutely required for union; and secondly, because it seems to us desirable that the several colonies should retain as much independence as is consistent with federation. Our reason for saying this is that although at present the colonists may roughly be said to be all of British and Irish origin, it is impossible to foresee how the population may in the future be affected by immigration from other countries. Secondly, it is to be borne in mind that the differences of climate, soil, natural productions, and so on, are very great between the several colonies. Thus it is probable that laws which may suit one part of Australia may be entirely unsuited to another, and it will be desirable, therefore, that each part of the continent may have the greatest practical power to adapt its legislation to its special conditions. One Federal Parliament having very great powers might desire

The Statist—*continued.*

to assimilate the colonies too much, and might in that way stir up a very antagonistic, if not an actually discontented feeling; whereas, if the Federal Parliament is to have only such powers as are specifically delegated to it, the separate colonies retaining all other powers, it will be unable to stretch its jurisdiction unduly, and the colonies will be able on their side to work out their desires unfettered.

The immediate object for which federation is desired is defence. The spirit of colonization has reawakened in the Continental countries, and they are all endeavouring to get possession of what unsettled parts of the world remain. The French and the Germans, more particularly, are showing an activity in the Southern Seas that is disquieting to our Australasian kinsmen, and they desire, therefore, very naturally to be in a position in which they can assert their own supremacy in those seas. Besides, if a great war were to break out and we were to be dragged into it, the Australasians might find themselves exposed to attack from the sea, and they are wise, therefore, in making such preparations as will ward off attack. Practically, they are now as numerous as the inhabitants of the thirteen American colonies were when they asserted independence; and if they federate and organize their military resources they are certainly strong enough to repel any possible invasion. The second object is the prevention of wars of tariff. The majority of our colonist fellow-subjects are unfortunately protectionists; but they are not all so, and they are not all equally so. If the present drift of feeling continues, and there is no federation, each colony will hedge itself round with a barrier of Custom-houses, and communication between them will be hampered at every step. There is a danger, too, that tariff wars might degenerate into dangerous political disputes; but if federation can be established, and control of the Customs tariffs of all the colonies given to the Federal Parliament, then whatever policy the Australasians may adopt as regards the rest of the world, they will have complete free-trade amongst themselves. The advantage of this in the case of the United States is visible even to the most obstinate protectionists; and as the Australasian Colonies grow it will become more and more evident to them in their case. There are minor points of considerable importance—such, for example, as railway extension, the post office, the telegraph, and a host of other questions. In the United States, as our readers know, the several States have retained up to the present the right to legislate for the railways. It

The Statist—*continued.*

is only quite recently that Congress has ventured to assert a jurisdiction even where railways run through two or more States—to regulate, that is to say, inter-State communication. The States-right feeling was so strong that at one time interference by Congress would not have been tolerated, and though the centralizing spirit has increased very much since the Civil War, it is only three or four years ago that Congress ventured to proceed to actual legislation. Even now Congress does not interfere with the telegraph; and there are many other matters which the States retain in their own hands. If the Australasians are wise they will at once, in framing their Federal Constitution, vest in the Federal Parliament jurisdiction over all matters that concern more than one colony.

There is no doubt, then, that federation is in the highest degree desirable for the sake of the colonies themselves, but whether, as is generally supposed, Colonial Federation would further Imperial Federation, is not quite so clear. Sir H. Parkes, and many other colonial statesmen, say that it is useless to talk of Imperial Federation until there are such Colonial Federations as will be able to negotiate on somewhat equal terms with the mother-country. There is much force in the argument, and no doubt if the colonists are really anxious for Imperial Federation, Colonial Federation will bring that end nearer. But it is impossible not to ask oneself whether the colonists are so very eager for Imperial Federation. Imperial Federation of a kind, no doubt, they would gladly adopt; but Imperial Federation, involving also a Customs union, would not be quite so acceptable to them. Would, for example, Victoria and the other protectionist colonies of Australia be willing to enter into an Imperial Federation, one condition of which should be that between all parts of the British Empire there should be absolute free trade? We venture to think that the Australians do not very much fear Continental competition. The real competition they fear—that which they have erected a protectionist tariff to keep out—is British competition; and it therefore does not seem to us quite as certain as it does to many of our contemporaries that a great Australasian Federal Union, if it were established, and had arranged for free trade within its own borders, but high tariff against all the rest of the world, would be so ready to further Imperial Federation. At all events, we fear that if Australasian Federation is accomplished, the first result will be that the protectionist feeling will prevail, that New South Wales

The Statist—*continued.*

will be dragged into the general vortex, and a tariff will be enforced which will rather injure our own trade with the colonies. That is not a reason, of course, why we should in any way discourage or interpose obstacles against federation. It would be so advantageous for the colonies that the mother-country is bound to promote it if the colonies themselves are in favour of it; but while, for political reasons and out of the feeling which the mother-country must entertain for her colonies, we are all in favour of an Australasian Federation, we must not, if we are wise men, shut our eyes to the very great probability that federation will injure rather than benefit British trade in the colonies in the long run. It may, no doubt, help on Imperial Federation, and that may either involve or lead up to free trade throughout the Empire; but Imperial Federation, though we may hope for it, is yet a long way off, and in the meantime our trade is not likely to be improved by the federation of the colonies.

Edinburgh Scots Observer—

February 22nd, 1890.

THE Conference, whose meetings have just concluded at Melbourne, will be memorable in the history of the Empire. Even if nothing very practical were to be the immediate outcome of its deliberations, it must remain a significant act in the drama of Imperialism, for this reason, if for no other, that the deliberate and unanimous opinions of representatives of the Australasian colonies have been formulated and placed on record. A step has been taken which cannot be retraced unless the colonies desire to make fools of themselves and their representatives.

It is not too much to say that the British people is at present witnessing the practical beginning of a series of events of almost unexampled importance in the modern history of the race; and if the conduct of the march of affairs is characterized in future by the same statesmanship, loyalty, and lofty spirit of compromise which have but now been displayed at Melbourne, there can be little fear that the future is not big with events as satisfactory as important. The Conference unanimously resolved, on the motion of Sir Henry Parkes, whose speeches seem to have been remarkable for even more than his usual vigour and eloquence, that "the time has now come for the union of the Australasian

Edinburgh Scots Observer—*continued.*

Colonies under one Government." This resolution was followed by one which shows that the Australians mean business, and have no stomach for abstract resolutions without practical application. It was resolved, on the motion of Mr. Deakin —it is interesting to remember that Australasian Federation was only recently called "Mr. Deakin's Dream"— that a National Australasian Convention should be held to consider and report on an adequate scheme for the Federal Constitution. This Convention, which is to consist of delegates from each Government colony and four from each Crown colony, will meet in the course of the present year, or at latest early next year. Then the second act—and it will be no light one—will be played. In the meantime the whole scheme, principle and details, will be canvassed by every Australasian politician and in every Australasian journal; public opinion will be educated and developed, ideas will be crystallised, the irrelevant will be eliminated, and the contentious will be set aside. We may thus hope to see before the spring of another year a definite Federal Constitution on paper which, even if it be not entirely workable, will form at any rate a basis for discussion and for compromise.

That there are lions in the path is indisputable. It will not be all easy going. Such matters as the organization of defence and the institution of a supreme federal court of law will doubtless be easy of adjustment. Nor does finance offer any insuperable difficulty. The colonies are solvent. Direct taxation is objected to in all of them (everybody objects to taxation); but sounder fiscal views will be thrust upon them soon, and in the meantime it will not pass the wit of the fathers of the Constitution to devise some scheme for defraying the expenses of the new *régime.* The greatest of all the difficulties that will have to be faced is that caused by the fact that New South Wales has adopted free-trade, while her sister colonies are all resolutely protectionist. New South Wales, it has been asserted, desires federation in order to compel the others to adopt her economic reform ; while they for their part support federation with the latent hope that New South Wales will see the error of her ways and follow the majority in the paths of protection. It may safely be assumed that as long as Sir Henry Parkes conducts the affairs of New South Wales no retrograde step will be taken in her fiscal policy; and in the inevitable struggle which ensues there will undoubtedly be room for the exercise of high statesmanship on both sides.

Edinburgh Scots Observer—*continued.*

The part borne in the movement by men of the influence and ability of Sir Henry Parkes, Mr. Gillies, and Mr. Deakin has undoubtedly been the cause of its rapid progress. But it must not be forgotten that the question of the defence of Australia has had much to do in bringing the problem from the region of pious opinion to that of practical politics. The loyalty conspicuous in the address to the Queen and in all the speeches at the Conference is gratifying in the extreme. As long as Australasian statesmen hold and express such sentiments, and the Colonial Office refrains from being actively stupid, there is no fear for the future relations between the colonies and Britain, even if Imperial Federation remain a name and nothing more.

Chronicle—

February 22nd, 1890.

A COMPLIMENTARY banquet was given last night at the St. George's Club, Hanover-square, to Sir William C. F. Robinson, Governor-elect of Western Australia; Sir F. Napier Broome, Governor of Western Australia; and the Hon. S. H. Parker, delegate of Western Australia. The chair was occupied by the Right Hon. Lord Bateman, and among the large and influential company present were Lord Gifford, V.C. formerly Secretary for the Colony; Sir Robert G. W. Herbert, Under Secretary for the Colonies; Sir Saul Samuel, Agent General for New South Wales; Mr. T. Archer, Agent General for Queensland; Mr. H. C. Beeton, Agent General for British Columbia; Sir Frederick A. Weld, who was Governor of the Colony 1869-74; Hon. J. Mitchell, Sir William Vincent, Colonel Garnet, Colonel G. V. Boyd, Major Doherty, Captain Broome, Captain Lund, Captain Barrett, Captain Ellis, Dr. Cardozo, Dr. Alex. Reid, Dr. R. L. Verley, Dr. Willikin, Dr. T. Stretch Dowse, Dr. Gibson, Messrs. T. M. C. Vigors, S. Du Croz, Jno. Waddington, Jas. Newham, A. Castle, H. Lyne, Lister, Dillroy-Parish, Craven, Mullens, F. Hovenden, O. J. Trinden, Charles Bethell, F. H. Cheesewright, F. Burt, M. F. A. Canning, R. Waddington, Mattei R. Doggett, Ea. Bullock, W. Blyth, &c. The loyal toasts having been duly honoured, the Chairman proposed "The Guests of the Evening." He said that one of the characteristics of St. George's Club

Chronicle—*continued.*

was profuse hospitality to strangers and colonists. They received visitors and guests from all parts of the world, and they were always glad to welcome them. They had that night amongst them several gentlemen from the large and important Colony of Australia, who had come on a mission which was vital. Western Australia was the only province governed as a Crown colony, and they had come to ask the Queen to grant such a constitution as the other colonies enjoyed, and they wished them every success. (Cheers.) If they obtained what they had set their hearts upon, no doubt the missing link of Australian Federation would thereby be formed, and they might live to see, before very many years, such a federation as would perfectly astonish them all, and would create in this country such a feeling of amity and consanguinity as could not fail to produce the most excellent results.—The toast having been drunk with great enthusiasm, Sir William Robinson, in reply, said that the whole air was full of questions of public interest, and first and foremost was the great subject of Australian federation. He was delighted that this question had come to the front, and that it promised better success in the future than it had ever yet attained. The council recently held in Melbourne was the outcome of statesmanlike concession of reforms on all sides. Federation of all the colonies was the object in view, and that was the emphatic wish of the whole of the Continent. (Cheers.) Australia was entirely in favour of union, and it must be accomplished. Federation would not lead to separation from the mother-country, but would strengthen the bonds which already existed, and would make the two countries more united; but complete federation could not be without Western Australia was included.— Sir F. Napier Broome also responded, and explained in detail the object of the mission. He thanked the present Government for their action and support, and believed that all had the best interests of the colony at heart.—The Hon. S. H. Parker also spoke, and said that their mission was to ask for self-government for Western Australia. They had not the slightest idea of separation—in fact all the colonies of Australia desired to be federated. They wanted a strong union and a powerful Australia, and as long as Great Britain did not unnecessarily interfere with the internal affairs of Australia the tie with the mother-country would grow stronger. The federation of Australia would be a step in the direction of that great Imperial Federation which they all anxiously awaited, and which would produce an empire

Chronicle—*continued.*

such as the world had never seen. (Cheers.)—Sir F. Broome proposed " St. George's Club," which was acknowledged by Sir Robert Herbert.—The Hon. S. H. Parker gave " The Reception Committee," and the health of the Chairman concluded the toast list.

Chronicle—

February 22nd, 1890.

It is no use disguising the fact, that whilst pretty general unanimity prevails as to the durability of Intercolonial Federation, some of the strongest advocates of the latter are anything but favourably disposed towards that somewhat indefinite quantity known as Imperial Federation. The *Daily Telegraph*, of Sydney, the well-known organ of free-trade and nationalism, writes:—" Neither in England nor in the colonies is it (Imperial Federation) talked of or even thought of among the general body of the people. The English voter has no thought of allowing emissaries from India or Australia to interfere in his legislation, and he has no desire to saddle his own taxes on to anybody else's shoulders. Nor are our voters likely to tolerate any attempt to legislate for Australia from Capetown or Montreal, or to saddle us with a share of burdensome taxes in which we have no interest and care to have no voice." This is a somewhat crude and callous way of regarding the question, but those who desire to accurately gauge colonial public opinion cannot afford to ignore the fact that there are two ways of looking at the matter.

Spectator—

February 23rd, 1890.

Since the summoning in 1787 of a Convention to devise a " Federal Constitution adequate to the exigencies of government and the preservation of the Union " of the States of America, no more important event has taken place in the history of the English race than the decision in favour of Sir Henry Parkes' resolution declaring that " the time has come for uniting the Australian Colonies under one Government." And when we say this, we are not forgetting the federation of the provinces of British North America, or failing to appreciate the splendid future that lies before the

Spectator—*continued.*

Dominion. Though it was of great moment that Canada should be united under one executive Government, it is still more essential that Australia should be preserved from the danger of containing at some future time a collection of possibly hostile States. No new country has ever enjoyed such initial advantages as the island continent. While Canada has a rigorous climate suitable only to a limited number of crops, the greater part of Australia possesses all the advantages of warmth without the drawbacks that usually accompany semi-tropical heat. Again, while in Canada only half the population is English, the rest being composed of persons of French blood, Indians, and half-breeds, Australia has, practically speaking, a perfectly homogeneous English population. When Canada has sixty millions of people, thirty millions at least will be French-speaking Roman Catholics. Australia, when she has reached the same point in population, will show a large majority of Protestant Englishmen, most of whom will be two generations removed from any ancestor who knew what it was to be in want of good food and clothing. Even more than the United States is Australia destined to be the vantage-ground of the English race. The great Republic, no doubt, will some day have a hundred and fifty million citizens; but by that time a third are not unlikely to be negroes or mulattos. Every sign, then, points to the fact that Australia is fated in the future to take the lead among the lands peopled by the Anglo-Saxons. She will beat the mother-country, because she is capable of holding twenty times as great a population; and the United States, Canada, and South Africa, because she contains a race undiluted by foreign intermixture, and occupies a continent of which not a hand's breadth is held by any foreign power. But to be worthy of their high fate, the Australians must be a united people, not a mere geographical expression. Hence the adoption by the Pacific Colonies of the federal principle, and the summoning of a Convention, to meet early next year, to draft a Constitution, is an occurrence which, without exaggeration, may be described as of world-wide import.

When the Convention meets next January at Melbourne, we trust that the first resolution passed will be the same as that adopted by the body which one hundred and four years before entered upon its sittings in the State House of Philadelphia. In obedience to a happy inspiration, that famous assembly decided from the beginning that they would sit with closed doors, and that not even a transcript of their

Spectator—*continued.*

minutes should be made public, and this decision in favour of secrecy was rigidly and faithfully maintained. It may at first sight seem as if the free air of public criticism would be as beneficial to a Constituent Convention as to an ordinary deliberative assembly. As a matter of fact, any such notion is a fallacy. Just as a Cabinet could not last a week if the words used and the policies favoured by its individual members were published to the world, so any body of men engaged in drafting a Constitution must maintain complete secrecy. The reason is this. A Parliament acts by and through a majority, and this fact is universally recognized. A Convention such as that which is to meet at Melbourne, like a Cabinet, acts, on the other hand, in a corporate capacity and as one man. It must act unanimously, or its decisions carry no weight. If the people of the various States of America had known the clauses over which their own special representatives had been beaten, and the exact manner in which the various compromises effected had been arrived at, they could never have been brought to accept the Constitution as a whole. And apart from this, secrecy is essential if a constituent body is to do its work well. In such an undertaking as Constitution-making, men learn as they go, and do not fully realize the advantages or disadvantages of a proposal at first sight. Hence, without any inconsistency, or lack of prudence and stability, a delegate may often find himself constrained to argue against a proposition which the day before he firmly supported, or constrained to advocate a compromise previously declared by him to be utterly impracticable. But to act thus would be utterly impossible if every time a man saw that his original views were wrong or were hopelessly unacceptable to his colleagues, and decided to change them, he were liable to be greeted with shouts of "turncoat" and "traitor" from the outside public. Public debate is perfectly right in the case of ordinary legislatures, where two opposing parties are drawn up in battle array, and harangues are made, not to convert the enemy, but to damage them with the electors, or as mere rhetorical preliminaries to the vote. No constitution, however, could, we feel convinced, be founded on set speeches addressed to the reporters, nor the nice discrimination required for constitutional legislation be fostered by smart partisan articles in the daily Press. The Australians have always shown a strong political instinct, and it will not, we are sure, desert them here. They will so order it, we expect, that the delegates at the Convention shall not take the public into

Spectator—*continued.*

their confidence till their scheme is drawn up and ready for acceptance or refusal; nor will they permit the web woven each day with care and anxious forethought, to be torn to pieces next morning by the dire ingenuity of a hundred active newspapers in every quarter of the Australian continent. The leading journals of the English communities of the Pacific deservedly enjoy a high reputation, and may compare with any newspapers in our language. Still, they must obey the law of their being, and if the doors of the Convention are open, they will be obliged every morning to provide their readers with reports of and comments upon each day's proceedings, which are certain to be mischievous rather than helpful.

Though we have no space to discuss here in detail the various constitutional problems which will be encountered by the Convention, we must express the hope that its members will favour the Constitution of Canada rather than that of the United States of America. In several very important points the former Constitution is the superior. In the first place, the provinces of the Dominion have no power over any military force, the control of the militia resting solely with the central Executive, whereas in the Republic each State has its own militia. Still more important is the fact that the Dominion Government has the sole power of legislation in regard to the criminal law and the procedure of the Criminal Courts, and as to all questions of marriage and divorce. The fact that a man may be guilty of a criminal offence in one State of the Union and be an innocent man in another, and that a marriage may be valid in one State, and invalid over the border, is a grave source of difficulty, and prevents that national homogenity which it should be the chief aim of legislation to secure. Again, the Dominion Government appoints and pays the Judges of the Superior, District, and County Courts. Lastly, the central Government has the power of vetoing provincial laws hostile to the interests of the whole community, a far more effective arrangement than that under which the Supreme Court of the United States when put in motion by a private suitor, declares certain State laws unconstitutional. In one point, however, the United States Constitution is better than that of the Dominion. The Canadian Senate is a mere nominated body, and therefore has no vitality, while that of the great Republic, owing to the fact that it represents the States in their corporate capacity, is one of the most flourishing and respected institutions of the Union. Possibly, however, the Australians

Spectator—*continued.*

may prefer a single Chamber, though this does not seem likely, to judge from the fact that almost all the present Colonies have two Houses. If, then, they decide on an Upper House, we trust that they will give it a firm and democratic basis,—that is the real thing that matters.

Reynold's Newspaper—

February 23rd, 1890.

WHAT will the movement now going on in the Australian colonies for federation lead to, and what federation do the Australians desire? are questions which will ere long become two of the most important within the sphere of imperial politics. Fourteen or fifteen years ago those who proposed and advocated a closer union of the colonies were regarded as visionaries. The majority of the population of Australia opposed it bitterly, because intercolonial jealousy was so great. What one colony advocated was sure to be opposed by the others. Consequently each went its own way, made its own laws, and directed its tariffs against its neighbours in particular and the outside world in general. Still, the Federationists, as they were called, did not rest from their labours, and had the satisfaction of seeing the people gradually but surely come round to their way of thinking, until now there are not perhaps five per cent. of the population of Australia and Tasmania who are not ardent supporters of Australian federation. In New Zealand the number of opponents is much greater, because there is much more difficulty, so far as it is concerned, in arriving at a satisfactory consummation.

The supporters of the scheme were far-sighted enough to see that when the time was ripe Australians and Tasmanians, and possibly New Zealanders also, would forget their jealousies and combine for their mutual benefit. Conferences have been held from which New South Wales held aloof because the initiative came from another quarter. Then the other colonies—Victoria, South Australia, Queensland, and Tasmania—sent delegates to another conference, and the Federal Council was formed. Now, however, that New South Wales has abandoned its former position, and the question of intercolonial land defence has been practically settled, the main points to be surmounted are tariff differences and the question of free-trade or protection. Most of the

Reynold's Newspaper—*continued.*

colonies are thoroughly protectionist, and intercolonial free-trade and protection against all the rest of the world is the theory that at present finds the greatest number of advocates. Two important conditions in the growth of this feeling, that cannot be ignored, are the steady progress of the Australian natives associations and the great increase in the Australian Nationalist party. The former, which comprises a very influential section of the working classes, who are the rulers in the colonies, is confined to those born there. Their motto practically amounts to "Australia for the Australians," and their aim is the development of the colonies commercially and socially, and from within, if possible. Almost to a member they are Federationists. The Nationalist party have also this end in view, but they go a step farther, and urge on the platform and in the press that Australian Federation can only be, and must only be, a means to the establishment of a republic modelled on the lines of the great North American commonwealth and recognized by the world as an independent nation—the United States of Australia. They point out that Australia has its greatest wealth at the coast, and, being comparatively defenceless except at a few important points, would thus be an easy prey to a squadron of any European nation that England is sure, sooner or later, to go to war with. England would want nearly all her fleet in other waters, and could spare neither many nor powerful ships of war to protect her possessions thirteen thousand miles away—possessions fully as large as the whole of the United States of America. If, however, Australia were independent, she would not be drawn into international European quarrels, but could mind her own business, develop her own resources, work out her own destiny, and trade peacefully with the rest of the world. The fear of war is not by any means the only reason that prompts a desire of independence. The population of Australia is not exclusively of British origin. There is a sprinkling of various European nations, and they and their descendants, and the descendants of nearly all settlers, regard Australia as their land. Thus a feeling of Australian patriotism is, as it were, bred in them that cannot be eradicated, and must find expression.

The opponents of this national and patriotic feeling are numerous and powerful. They include a large proportion of those of British birth and a sprinkling of Australians born, and among their leaders are some who have done good service in days gone by and, for some reason or other, have had their backs hit with a sword by the Queen, and them-

Reynold's Newspaper —*continued.*

selves dubbed "Sir." The Australian "sirs," or nine out of ten of them, when they are knighted study "Debrett's Peerage," go back to the colonies, conduct themselves as snobs in the presence of other snobs, talk glibly of English titled families whom they never knew, and do their level best to create a landed gentry in the land of the Southern Cross. The law lets them go on with their foolishness as long as they do not interfere with the workers; but the acquisition of large entailed estates is not allowed, and when once these pretenders make themselves troublesome or obnoxious the working classes will make their power felt at the polls, and wipe the whole lot out. This is the class that favours the will-o'-the-wisp Imperial Federation, for no one else looks upon it as other than sheer nonsense.

Australia is the working man's country. He holds his destiny in his hands. He recognizes that the struggle must come between Capital and Labour, and he is determined that in the issue victory shall rest with him. All means will be employed, and none rejected, to gain this end. The working men throughout all the colonies will sink their differences, and in helping themselves and increasing their strength they will help the downtrodden working masses of England, and increase their strength and better their condition also. If the working men of Australia find it to their advantage to raise the flag of national independence, by all means let them do it. It were better that England should lose a portion of her distant possessions—hers in name only—than that the toilers who make the wealth of the classes, should in Australia lose their influence and control, or in England should exist in their present condition of semi-starvation. It is to this that the Australian Federation movement will lead, and this is the federation desired, if not expressed, throughout the colonies.

Scottish Leader—

February 24th, 1890.

THE letter in which Lord Derby has just set forth his views on the subject of Australian Federation reveals the prosaic, common sense way of looking at public questions which is characteristic of the writer, and which, when based on due appreciation of all the factors in the case, is generally to be trusted. Lord Derby sees in the proposed federation several great benefits for the colonies, and no drawbacks either for

Scottish Leader—*continued.*

them or for the mother colony. He perceives that union would extinguish their mutual jealousies, would sooner or later secure intercolonial free-trade, would enable them to borrow for public works on easier terms than are open to them at present, and would give them a status among the great powers of the world. It need not, on the other hand, do anything to weaken their ties with Great Britain, so long as we are content to leave them to manage their own affairs as they think best. It is a pity that Lord Derby cannot see the force of this latter principle when applied nearer home. He and the other so-called Unionists persist, in the face of reason, that if we were to leave the people of Ireland to manage their own local affairs as they think best their ties with Great Britain would be weakened—nay, destroyed. That is because he leaves the solid ground of fact and common sense for the region of sentiment, and very hollow and artificial sentiment too. Lord Derby evidently does not believe that the connection of the Australian colonies with the Empire could continue if they wished it to cease, but he points out that they have nothing to gain and something to lose by separation. That, again, is precisely the case with Ireland. Give her local Parliamentary self-government and she also would have nothing to gain and everything to lose by separation, as her people are perfectly well aware. It would seem, however, that arguments which Lord Derby thinks quite valid in the Pacific Ocean are worthless when it is sought to apply them in the neighbourhood of our own shores. Talk of Mr. Gladstone's inconsistency—taking his most rancorous critic's version of it—it is as nothing when compared with the utter mental confusion of the sham Unionists.

Nottingham Express—

February 25th, 1890.

THE federation of Australia and the federation of the Empire are two distinct subjects which are run into one by loose thinkers. They are caught by the common term, federation, and jump to the conclusion that it is only a little bigger bundle of wood which they are faggoting in the case of the whole Empire than in that of a certain group of colonies which are adjacent, and have a common origin and common interests; but a faggot and a forest are not more different things from each other than an old and composite

Nottingham Express—*continued.*

Empire such as ours, and the cluster of new settlements in the Southern Seas which we call Australasia. They are coming together as much by natural affinity as by the artificial tie which we call federation. Even with regard to the Australian colonies, the difficulties are not so easily overcome as seems to us who look on from a distance. The remark of several of the delegates to the Federal Council met to discuss the question at Melbourne was to the effect that the idea of the federation had scarcely yet taken root. They had sown the seed from which the tree of federation was to grow; but the seed is in itself as yet in the husk, and with a separate life. By-and-bye—how soon, none can say—when it is in the ground, as it is now in the air, it will strike and grow, and then we shall be able to judge what kind of tree springs from so small a seed. All honour, at least, to Sir Henry Parkes for taking the seed off the shelf and casting it on the earth, there to germinate. As far as the colonies, then, are concerned, we may leave them to strike out a federation scheme at their own time and in their own way.

But, turning to the larger scheme of Imperial Federation, if the one is only a seed just sown, what can be said of the other? Has it even reached the seed stage of a germ having life in itself, and waiting only the congenial soil to take root downward and bear fruit upward? We fear not. It is only sentimental politicians of the school of Lord Carnarvon and Lord Dunraven who see anything practical in proposals to link together an ancient monarchy like the United Kingdom, a dominion called Canada, a continent loosely called the Indian Empire, and a cluster of rising settlements in what is called sometimes Oceana and sometimes Australasia. The factors are too diverse, the ties between them too loose and shifting, and the general state of ignorance and indifference on the subject too rooted everywhere for it to make any impression at present. In a word, like a bone badly set, it must be broken to set it again properly. The United States, vast as the area is, make up a homogeneous whole. As in the similar case of Switzerland, it is a federation of Sovereign States, which, whatever their internal jars and jealousies, are all democratic, and swayed by no traditions which are not purely popular. There is no monarchy, with its two chief props, a hereditary Upper House and a State Church, to disturb the problem. When we have absorbed these three feudal relics of the past, it will be time enough to talk of federating on anything like equal terms with

Nottingham Express—*continued.*

Canada and our Australian colonies. Sentimentalists like Lord Carnarvon do not and will not see this. But it is fatal to federation. Meanwhile, there is a safe and simple policy of sweeping before our own door, and doing what we can in our own day and generation.

There is one way—and only one—of preparing for the larger federation of the Greater Britain of the future. We must have federated groups before we go on to a grand confederation of the whole. Canada is already such a group; so, in a sense, is India; and so, in another sense, our Australian colonies are taking the first step towards a federation of their own, not unlike the Dominion of Canada. But what steps are we taking in that direction? There are four quarterings in the Royal shield, with leopards for England and Wales in two quarters, right and left, with a lion for Scotland and a harp for Ireland. Does this heraldic device not suggest something—a hint as to four local legislatures under one general executive and central and supreme Parliament? The case of Ireland has been argued too much as if it were a thing apart, a concession to turbulence, given as a kind of reward for obstruction and disloyalty. Let us hope that now we have heard the last of "Parnellism and Crime," and the paper Unionists are thoroughly ashamed of their case, an effort will be made at a round table, and some scheme struck out for localizing legislatures. A federation of provinces, as in Canada, would make a Dominion of Great Britain with which the Dominions of Canada, India, and Australasia would readily confederate in a future neither dim nor distant.

Home News—

February 28th, 1890.

There is no English statesman whose utterances now-a-days on Imperial and Colonial affairs command more attention than Lord Derby's. In a letter to Mr. A. Patchett Martin he expresses himself as altogether in favour of Australian federation. A union of the great antipodean colonies is eminently desirable in their own interest, and can be, in Lord Derby's opinion, in no way opposed to the interest of England. The jealousies at present prevailing among the different colonial communities would disappear if Australia were consolidated into one State, and the patriotism and public spirit already so abundant in the country would be still further stimulated. Neither, looking

Home News—*continued.*

to the example of the Dominion of Canada, does it appear to Lord Derby that Australian Federation would increase the feeling in favour of separation from the mother land. Then, again, federation would save the Colonial Office an infinity of labour, and much friction would be removed if the Secretaries of State had to deal with a single Government rather than with several. The exercise of the veto by the home authorities on purely colonial measures is, to say the least, impolitic. Whenever adopted by the Crown, it has tended to the loosening of the ties which should exist between Great Britain and her colonies. On this head, Lord Derby counsels moderation. He relies on the good sense of Parliament and the people to veto any arbitrary or unreasonable decision emanating from the Colonial Office.

Railway Journal—
March 1st. 1890.

THERE has of late been a certain amount of talk about the federation of the Australasian Colonies; but, to our mind, the views current upon the subject are vague and indefinite. We first began to hear of Australasian federation five years ago under the feeble colonial *régime* of the Earl of Derby. Public attention had been called by the Earl of Roseberry to the important question of Imperial federation, and the Earl of Derby appears to have thought that he could help on the work of Imperial federation by inaugurating a scheme for Australasian federation. In our judgment, no greater mistake was ever made by a public man. If anything can retard the progress of Imperial federation it is the creation of a practically independent system of States at the Antipodes. The Australasian Colonies are now very much in the position of the revolting American Colonies in 1776. The Australasian Colonies have now a white population of between 3,000,000 and 4,000,000, and so had the revolting American Colonies in 1776. If it were possible for the North American Colonies to achieve their independence under such conditions as these 100 years ago, the conclusion is rather tempting that the Australasian Colonies might do the same if they chose. To assist or hasten on Australasian federation is thus not only not a step in the direction of Imperial federation, but a distinct weakening of the already fragile tie which binds the Antipodean settlements to the mother-country. It must be remembered that the

Railway Journal—*continued.*

Australasian Colonies are the most remote of the dependencies of Great Britain; and if it were difficult to maintain the authority of the mother-country in the North American Colonies 100 years since, it would probably be found still more difficult to enforce it now in the Australasian Colonies under any circumstances which brought the Imperial Government into unpopularity or disrepute. It may be objected that the position of the Australasian Colonies differs radically at present from that of the North American Colonies in 1776, in as much as the Australasian Colonies have been conceded that very right of representation accompanying taxation which George III so obstinately refused to his troublesome American subjects in 1776. But the concession of self-government made to the Australasian Colonies by Lord John Russell in 1851 may be fairly said to have two sides to it. While, on the one hand, the creation of Australasian legislatures undoubtedly had a tendency to remove or minimise discontent among the colonists, it also accustomed them to think and act for themselves; and this, it must be admitted, is a great step in the direction of national independence. It is the opinion of many persons - and even of many thoughtful persons—that Imperial federation is little more than an optimistic dream. But if Imperial federation is a dream, what is Australasian federation? Are New South Wales, New Zealand, Queensland, South Australia, Tasmania, Victoria, and Western Australia to retain, under a federation *régime*, an independent existence, or are they to become mere counties or provinces of a great Australasian Empire? Is Victoria, which has a debt of only £30 per head of the population, to make common cause with New Zealand, which owes £60 per capita? *Prima facie*, we should imagine that it would be rather hard lines for Victoria to be called upon to do so. Again, is New Zealand, which is the most fertile and rain-blessed colony of the Australasian group, to be placed on the same level as South Australia and New South Wales, which every now and then suffer cruelly from prolonged droughts? Yet, again, what is to be done in the matter of tariffs? Is New Zealand to be a free-trade province and Victoria a protectionist province? Are the Australasian Colonies to be governed by a central legislature? Where is that legislature to meet, and what are to be its powers and responsibilities? Still further, what is to be the position of the federated colonies towards the mother-country? When such questions as these are satisfactorily answered it will certainly be time enough to talk seriously

Railway Journal—*continued.*

about Australasian federation? For our part, we can but think that while a general system of Imperial federation would immensely strengthen the moral and material power of Great Britain and her dependencies, no additional security would result from the feeble course taken by the Earl of Derby in 1885. To suggest a federation of merely one group of colonies is merely to stave off the question of general union. If the matter ended in simply staving off such a combination, such a result would, no doubt, be unfortunate in itself; but we fear that still more serious ulterior consequences would ensue.

CORRESPONDENCE.

Globe—
February 10th, 1890.

[FROM A CORRESPONDENT.]

THESE are epoch-making days in the annals of Greater Britain, for they witness an historic gathering of representative colonial statesmen in Melbourne to lay duly and well the foundation-stone of the future Australasian Dominion. Every British colony in the Antipodean group—that is to say, six self-governed colonies and two still tied to mother's apron-strings in Downing-street—has its delegates at the Conference. New South Wales, whose unfortunate abstention from the tentative federation of five years ago checked and almost paralyzed the movement for a time, now falls into line with her daughter colonies, and sends, as her chief representative her Premier, Sir Henry Parkes, whose voice and pen have rendered good service to the federal cause for more than a quarter of a century. Sir Henry, in truth, by virtue of age, seniority, intellect, tried ability, and proved statesmanship, is the master-spirit of the Conference. He was a prominent public man before any of his co-delegates around to-day's board were heard of, and before some of them were born. It was feared, of course, that being of a somewhat imperious temperament, Sir Henry might presume a little too much on his unique position, and thereby introduce a disturbing element into the Conference, but his speech at the banquet to Lord Hopetoun on Thursday reflected the conciliatory attitude which he has shown of late, combined with a keen and earnest desire to see Australian Federation fully and effectively accomplished without further delay.

Globe—*continued.*

The best and most substantial guarantee that the Conference will be productive of permanently fruitful results, lies in the fact that all the colonies have been profoundly impressed by the report of Major-General Edwards pointing out the absolute necessity of federal organization of their military resources if they really mean to place themselves in a condition of effective defence. The German occupation of New Guinea and the French descent on the New Hebrides had opened the eyes of the Australians to the possibilities of a disturbed future in their waters, but it was the expert testimony of General Edwards—an Imperial officer delegated directly from the War Office—that impelled them to action, and led to the summoning of to-day's Conference. Immense sums of money have been spent in fortifying the approaches to the Australian capitals, and when the colonies learnt on the highest authority that all this vast expenditure may be unavailing if there is not combined action at the critical moment, if there is no central governing authority to focus the military strength of the Continent at the right place and at the right moment, as shrewd business men they clearly perceive that any further postponement of complete federal union will be distinctly dangerous to the common weal, and that all petty intercolonial jealousies must be sunk in the presence of a common peril.

The tariff question is believed by many to be an insuperable obstacle to the federal union of the Australian colonies. I do not think so. Sir Henry Parkes and his colleague from New South Wales are the only militant free-traders at the Conference, and not only will they be in a hopeless minority on this question in the Conference itself but the colony they represent is also divided in opinion as to the respective merits of free-trade and protection. At the last general election in New South Wales the protectionists captured a considerable number of seats from the free-traders, though the latter succeeded in securing a working parliamentary majority. The recollection of this growth and development of the protectionist party, combined with the uncertainty as to what will be the result of the next appeal to the country, may moderate the zeal of Sir Henry Parkes in preaching free-trade to the economic heretics associated with him. "Intercolonial free-trade and protection against the world" will undoubtedly be the key-note of the fiscal policy of Federated Australia for a time. I say for a time, because in none of the colonies where

Globe—*continued.*

protection is now the law of the land is the system regarded as perpetual. It is viewed in the light of a temporary expedient to enable young colonies to foster and build up their industries. This consideration is often lost sight of in the mother-country. The colonies may be pursuing a very selfish policy, but it is at least an enlightened and far-seeing selfishness.

Some difference of opinion has been generally anticipated on the question of the selection of the federal capital. Taking the theory that "to allay jealousy it must be selected for its remoteness or insignificance," three towns have been suggested from time to time as specially qualified for this high honour. Albury, on the north bank of the Murray—the dividing line between New South Wales and Victoria—has enjoyed in anticipation the title of "The Federal City" ever since Sir Hercules Robinson made his famous federation speech there a dozen years ago. Wentworth, some hundreds of miles lower down the Murray, is strongly advocated on the ground of its centrality, being not far from the point where three of the leading colonies—New South Wales, Victoria, and South Australia—meet. This rising town has also sentimental reasons in its favour, for it has been named after the greatest of Antipodean statesmen and orators, William Charles Wentworth, the "Australian Patriot" *par excellence.* Thirdly, Hobart, the capital of Tasmania, is understood to be a candidate for federal honours on the strength of its having been the meeting-place of the academic Federal Council of the past five years. But no small number of thoughtful Australians are beginning to think that it is not altogether desirable to follow American or Canadian precedent in this respect by choosing a fourth-rate provincial town as the Australasian Federal Capital. Many of us would like to see the choice fall on one of the two Australian cities of world-wide repute—Sydney and Melbourne. As a matter of personal liking, I would rejoice to see Melbourne so honoured; but not all my love of Melbourne and its friendly associations of years can blind me to the superior advantages that Sydney presents in this connection. It is the mother-city of the Australias, the site of the parent settlement, the one Antipodean centre that represents the growth of a century. It was there that Wentworth fought and won the battle of trial by jury and the liberty of the press. It was the birthplace of Parliamentary Government on the south of the Equator. It is central, easily accessible from all quarters, and possesses the

Globe—*continued.*

finest and loveliest harbour in the wide range of the British dominions. It is the residence of the Roman Cardinal and the Anglican Primate. Most important of all, it is the official headquarters of the Admiral commanding Her Majesty's fleet in Australian waters, and, in view of the supreme importance of close inter-communication between the heads of the two services, it will assuredly be also the headquarters of the future General commanding the Federated land forces of Australia. For all these reasons Sydney seems to me to be the ideal Federal metropolis of the Southern colonies.

It may be said that, however devoutly this consummation is to be wished, the jealousy of the other Australian capitals will inevitably prevent such a selection. It will be pitiable if it should be so, but for my part I am disposed to believe that this alleged intercolonial jealousy is not, after all, such a potent factor in public affairs as is too freely and too generally assumed.

Manchester Guardian—

February 11th, 1890.

To the Editor of the *Manchester Guardian.*

SIR,—What has come over the British colonial governors? Shortly before leaving the Cape, Sir Hercules Robinson almost urged South Africa to become independent; last November, Lord Carrington, Governor of New South Wales, in opening Parliament, said that "federation was in the air," and counselled the several colonies to rise and unite "in the formation of one powerful Australian nation"; and in his speech at the close of last year at Glenelg, where some 40,000 people had assembled to celebrate the anniversary of the formation of the colony, Lord Kintore, Governor of South Australia, wished the colonial federation movement God-speed, and looked hopefully forward to the time when South Australia would become "a bright portion of a strong, united, and free Australian nation." He also assured them of the hearty sympathy of the Colonial Secretary, and indeed of the entire Home Government. Therefore England's attitude towards the movement leaves nothing to be wished. Here, however, the only colony vividly interested is New South Wales, and even there the excitement is ebbing.

Manchester Guardian—*continued.*

Why? Are Australians indifferent to federation? Do they not realize the importance and daily-increasing necessity of being able to speak with a united voice on all questions of common concern? Are they not aware that there is danger in delay, that it is their duty to both understand and act in this movement and bring it to a successful issue? The great masses have yet to be aroused, and this can only be done by inducing them to express themselves on the question. Hitherto such federative efforts as have been made have sprung either from the General Government at Home—bent on securing Imperial Federation—or else have originated with and been engineered by one or other of the Colonial Governments, evidently in the expectation that, as a matter of course, legislatures and constituencies must endorse and accept their decisions.

Some retrospect is necessary to a right understanding of the present movement. As long ago as 1850, Earl Grey suggested that the various Colonial Agents-General in London, together with special appointees by the Privy Council, should form an Executive Government "competent to act for all the colonies in matters of common concern." It fell through, but it served to show the desirability of an Intercolonial Federation, and the Committee entrusted with drafting the Constitution of New South Wales (granted December 19, 1855) suggested in its report the establishment of a General Assembly "to make laws in relation to those intercolonial questions that have arisen or may hereafter arise among the colonies." Among such questions were enumerated (1) intercolonial tariffs and the coasting trade; (2) railways, roads, canals, and other such works running through any two of the colonies; (3) beacons and lighthouses on the coast; (4) intercolonial gold regulations; (5) postage between the said colonies; (6) a general court of appeal from the courts of such colonies; (7) a power to legislate on all other subjects which may be submitted to them by addresses from the Legislative Councils and Assemblies of the colonies, and to appropriate to the objects named the necessary sums of money, to be raised by a percentage on the revenues of all the colonies interested. This proposition was opposed by the Home Government, and the next conspicuous step in the agitation was the report of the Royal Commission at Melbourne in 1870 to devise a plan of Imperial Federation. The colonies were favourable to the scheme generally, and were willing to contribute their share for securing adequate protection on both land and sea. It

Manchester Guardian—*continued.*

was not, however, until 1883 that any actual initiative was taken in the colonies for Intercolonial Federation. Queensland had, single-handed—though also in the name of the other colonies—annexed New Guinea. To this the Home Government refused its sanction; and Queensland, as a protest against the Home Government's action, invited the other Colonial Governments to a Convention for the purpose of founding a Federal Government. This Convention met at Sydney. It was found, however, that the divergence on essential issues was great; New Zealand became thoroughly disaffected, and New South Wales and South Australia were hardly better satisfied. The outcome of the Convention was the formation of the so-called Federal Council. The Governments of Queensland, Victoria, and Tasmania, the representatives from Western Australia and Fiji, by pressure and manœuvring, induced their respective Parliaments to accept the Federal Council as a temporary expedient, as a stepping-stone to something better; but the Legislatures of New South Wales and South Australia would have nothing to do with it. Later on, however, South Australia joined the coalition. This Council has since met annually at Hobart, Tasmania. At first, under the energetic leadership of Mr. Service, it did something to justify its existence; but since he left, in 1886, it has shown little or no *raison d'être*. In the present agitation, however, the Federal Council plays an important part, and is likely to cause great trouble, and be, for some time at least, a most formidable obstacle to true federation. Therefore it is important that the English as well as the Australian public should know something of its character. Though it has nominally jurisdiction over a vast number of questions—political, judicial, and economic, such as (1) the protection of Australasian interests in the Pacific, (2) the prevention of criminal immigration, (3) fisheries, (4) service of civil or enforcement of criminal process, &c.,—yet it is expressly provided that bills relating to the first three items must be reserved for the signification of Her Majesty's pleasure; other bills might be assented to by the Governor of the colony in which the Council was held, subject, however, to possible disallowance by Her Majesty. In the next place, the Federal Council can only make laws, enforcement depending on the sanction of the respective colonies, and naturally the Council, being jealous of its own dignity and prerogatives, takes care to recommend only what is certain to be accepted by the allied colonies. Although it has been so cautious, yet at the last session one of its

Manchester Guardian—*continued.*

propositions for an enlargement of the Council was rejected by the Legislative Council in South Australia. Lastly, the Council has no revenue. All the same, it obstinately refuses to be displaced by any federal body, and owing to this persistence Sir Henry Parkes' original plan to secure an authoritative expression of colonial sentiment on the subject of federation has been modified into a mere informal consultation between the members of the Federal Council and representatives from New South Wales, and possibly New Zealand, as to what steps should be taken to establish federation between the Australasian Colonies.

The next step in the federation movement was the great Imperial Federation Conference held in London (April-May, 1887). Its discussions turned largely upon Australasian affairs, as is seen from the programme:—(1) Naval defences of Australasia, (2) defence of coaling stations, (3) condition of colonial land forces and defence precautions. (4) position of the New Hebrides, (5) future government of British New Guinea. Its decisions resulted in the despatch of naval and military men of high standing to Australasia to personally inspect and report upon affairs and recommend measures jointly to be taken by the Imperial and Colonial Governments. In consequence of their reports it was agreed to strengthen the naval squadron in Australasian waters, and last year Major-General Edwards, after making thorough investigation of the resources for land defence in the colonies, submitted an elaborate report and plan advocating the establishment of a federal colonial army. In response to this suggestion it was proposed to refer the matter to the Federal Council; but New South Wales, not being represented thereon, opposed the proposition. Sir Henry Parkes, the Premier of New South Wales, argued that as the conditions were ripe for federation, the Federal Council should be set aside and a Convention completely representative of the public sentiment of Australasia be convened for the purpose of founding a great and complete Federal Government for the whole of the colonies. No doubt Sir Henry Parkes went too far in suggesting the drawing up of a permanent Australasian Constitution—at a moment's notice, so to speak; on the other hand, the allied Governments were equally unreasonable in proposing that New South Wales, though utterly opposed to the Federal Council, should make it arbiter of the obligations of New South Wales in regard to general defence. The compromise that has been entered into—namely, that New South Wales

Manchester Guardian—*continued.*

delegates should meet the members of the Federal Council as representatives of their respective Governments on the federation question—was therefore but a natural consequence. All the same, this has materially changed the character of the Convention from a representative expression of the views of the colonies upon the federation question to a mere consultation between the Federal Council and the New South Wales delegates.

It is settled that the Conference shall meet in the first week of February next. Although but little can be expected from the Conference, constituted as it is, it must serve to rouse the public mind upon the question. The most that can be expected from the Conference itself is the establishment of some *modus vivendi* between New South Wales and the coalition, and an outline of a possible plan for united action in the future tending towards federation. Should, however, the same spirit prevail in the Conference which has marked the negotiations for convening it, it will certainly discredit the Governments, in which case, probably, the popular verdict will be "A plague on both your houses!" and the people will take the matter into their own hands, in which case Sir Henry Parkes is not unlikely to become their leader. Throughout these negotiations he has insisted that it was a question for the people to decide. In one of his last letters to Mr. Gillies (Premier of Victoria), Sir Henry Parkes says: "It is more than probable that a question so intimately concerning the whole of the Australian people, and on which the wishes of the people ought to be kept constantly in view, will not be decided without appeals to the electoral voice; and there can be no truer wisdom in democracy than that a movement so momentous in its consequences, when its foundation and principles have once been clearly stated, should throughout receive the support of a national majority." Federation of the Australian Colonies is but a question of time, and for England and Australia the when and how are matters of infinite importance. I purpose to deal in my next letter with the chief issues involved in an Australian Federation and their bearing upon the destinies of Great Britain and Australasia alike.

I am, &c.,
AXEL GUSTAFSON.

Melbourne, January 3, 1890.

Manchester Guardian—

February 2nd, 1890.

To the Editor of the *Manchester Guardian*.

Sir,—My purpose in the present letter is to deal with the chief issues involved in an Australasian federation, and their relative bearing upon the destinies of Great Britain and Australasia. In the first place, as great political issues cannot be solved either on the lines of gush and sentiment or of bluster and brag, so, in judging of the prospects and results of Australasian federation, it is well not to base too much faith upon what we may hear of the love and deference of Australians for the mother-country, of the enthusiasm with which the Queen's health is responded to, or "God save the Queen" is sung. These are at most signs of kindly sentiment towards England, and this feeling may no doubt be maintained and strengthened, but only on condition of England's non-interference with Australasian affairs. The historic trend unmistakably shows that Australasia will—indeed must—at some time become independent. Loop by loop she has forced England to loosen the motherly apron-string, and in yielding at the right moment England has shown a discretion from which it is to be hoped that she will not be led to stray by the clamourers who urge "shot and shell," "forcible intervention," &c. Australasia is essentially democratic; it does not believe in empire. "Deciding on a plan of Imperial Federation means deciding for or against a monarchy, and we do not want to raise that question," said the ex-Premier of Victoria, Mr. Service, when interviewed by the *Daily Telegraph* (Melbourne) a short time ago; and the most widely-read and politically influential paper of Victoria, the *Melbourne Age*, in a leader on the resolution recently passed by the Imperial Federation League at London, says:—"These gentlemen would surely do well to consider that the revolution which cost England her dominion over the United States was provoked by the contention of English statesmen that Massachusetts and New York were not to be governed by their own Parliaments, under the Crown, but by the Parliament at Westminster." And when in this connection it is borne in mind that Victoria is an easy first in loyal sentiments towards England, it seems improbable that English statesmen at least will not very gravely consider any policy for attempting to force the Australian colonies into an Imperial federation. The fact that New South Wales volunteered assistance in the last Egyptian war does not change the fact—of weighty signifi-

Manchester Guardian —*continued.*

cance in the present consideration—that she is pervaded by a strong let-me-alone sentiment. The *Sydney Bulletin*, the most effective weekly in the colonies, has been wrought up to white heat by the Imperial federation speeches recently delivered, and in a long leader (November 30, 1889)—unique for Radicalism and rampant Australianism—it ably compares the social and political conditions of Great Britain and Australia, and concludes:—" We may assume that the only people who are at all likely to profit by the ' judicious system of mutual confidence' are the titled flunkies and Lords of the Bedchamber who from time to time receive tokens of gratitude from their empire-mother by being appointed to fat sinecures as colonial Governors. . . . We do lack a peerage; we do lack a State Church; we have no costly navy, no standing army; our Civil Service is not a refuge for the younger sons of the great! We want no old-world wars and complications; we yearn for no share in Great Britain's boasted responsibilities; we have no quarrel with any State, and our arms are strong enough to protect the country of our adoption or our birth; we refuse to nurse Australia as a stamping-ground for England's overplus, unless that overplus be as Australian and as democratic in heart as we are ourselves; and if to retain our place it is necessary to cut the painter--why, we'll cut it!"

Turning to Queensland. A letter was recently published, written by Sir Charles Lilley, Chief Justice of Queensland, to a friend, which mentions the fact that "at festive gatherings of labour organizations, whilst the toast of the Queen is courteously honoured, the assemblage frequently breaks up with " Three cheers for the Australian Republic." In his advice to England to "let well alone" he says:— " Many of us love the old land; but it by no means follows that we adore modern Englishmen, and Australians desire above all things to work out the principles of freedom in their own way." Non-interference in Australian affairs, therefore, is the essential condition for good-feeling between the two countries. England has everything to gain from friendly intercourse with Australia, while, on the other hand, she has much to lose, more to risk, and nothing whatsoever to gain from hostile or strained relations with this country. Australasian federation is supremely an issue of Australasian concern. Its character and degree must depend on the logical evolution of Australian life and environment, and be based on intercolonial needs and interests. It is, of course, very possible that in working out her destiny Australasia

Manchester Guardian—*continued.*

may come into conflict with English interests, in which case England will no doubt make the fact known. If she does so in a frank and friendly spirit, her complaint will almost certainly receive the friendliest consideration; but she may be sure that the time for either forcing or commanding Australasia has passed. No one conversant with the facts of the case can fail to see that with all her power England could not rule Australasia against her will. She could seriously harass, obstruct, and delay the federation movement, but in the end would have to yield and see Australia achieve independence in spite of her, with the result that in all future complications England would have to reckon with an independent Australasia, made indifferent or hostile at enormous cost in life and treasure, instead of with a naturally friendly Australasia made into a powerful ally by the benevolent neutrality which contributed to the establishment of her independence. The fact cannot be too strongly affirmed that if Australasia is fit for federation, or even independence, and feels that the time is ripe for such steps, she will take them, whatever the cost. And why should she not? If England found that protection of Australasia would overload the ship of State, would she not slip the link, Australasian prayers or protests notwithstanding? Self-preservation is the first law of nature, nationally as well as individually.

Australasian federation is supremely an Australasian concern. It is a consummation devoutly to be wished that British statesmen should recognize the fact and allow Australia full liberty to solve the problem in her own way. On the other hand, it is to be hoped that Australasian statesmen will not go abroad seeking precedents or trying to mould Australasian federation according to the systems of Canada, or the United States, or Switzerland, or Germany, or any other country, in the past or in the present, but that they will go to work in a true Australasian spirit, dealing with Australasian needs, and seeking their solution on the best basis possible for Australasian development and progress. May not the agitation which resulted in the union of the New Zealand provinces under a general Government furnish some suggestions for the solution of the Australian federation question? What should be the relation between federated Australia and the mother-country is the problem whose solution is of paramount importance to both. Great changes are, of course, inevitably involved. For example, federal Australia could ill afford to risk a possible veto of

Manchester Guardian—*continued*.

Australian Bills at Downing-street. Australia must be independent in the management of her internal affairs, but in matters of foreign trade and politics must be free from responsibility for England's foreign policy. But again, so long as Australia continues an English dependency, will she not be subject to such worry and hurt as any Power at variance with England might wreak upon her? It comes to this: Is independence of England more advantageous to Australia than any connection with her? With regard to China especially, it is certain that for many years to come Australia cannot afford to lose the protection of England. Again, on the other hand, the friendship and goodwill of Australia are of great value to England. Both would suffer from separation, and hence it would seem wise that some union should be maintained, and for this a mutually acceptable basis can be found. If the coming Federal Convention should arrive at no other decision except that Australian federation is necessary and urgent, it will have accomplished great good. The building of federation must rest upon the broad and deep basis of popular understanding and consent, and an Australian Constitution, to be a blessing, must be writ in the hearts of the people.

AXEL GUSTAFSON.

The Speaker—

February 22nd, 1890.

Letter from Mr. A. Patchett Martin.

It cannot fail to have attracted the attention of those who are seriously interested in the political future of our kinsmen at the antipodes, that at the recent Federation Conference in Melbourne, the word Australian, and not Australasian, was employed in the wording of the main resolution, which was moved by Sir Henry Parkes, and carried unanimously. Yet New Zealand, which is the most important member of the outer Australasian group of what Sir Charles Dilke terms our South Sea colonies, had two representatives at the Conference. Moreover, one of them, Captain Russell, brought forward a specific motion " providing for the admission into the Union of the more remote Australasian colonies, at such times and under such conditions as might hereafter be agreed upon." It is still more noteworthy that the Hon. Alfred Deakin, of Victoria, in his subsequent motion for the appointment by the various Legislatures of a "National

The Speaker—*continued*.

Convention" to draw up during the present year a scheme for the Federal Constitution, employs the wider term Australasian. As Mr. Deakin's resolution was likewise adopted, it seems to be intended that not only New Zealand, but the Fiji Archipelago and British New Guinea, are to be represented at this "National Australasian Convention." This discrepancy between the wording of the two resolutions may perhaps be accounted for by the fact that Sir Henry Parkes, wishing, at his advanced age, to claim the honour of solving a great political problem, thought it wise to simplify his task as much as possible. It may also have arisen from the fact that he is desirous of maintaining the consistency of his position in standing outside the "Federal Council of Australasia." For that very reason, probably, Mr. Deakin, who, like the majority of Victorians, has been an ardent upholder of the Federal Council, prefers the more comprehensive scheme of an Australasian Federation which should bind the whole of our South Sea colonies into one powerful union.

To many of the more cautious and circumspect of colonial politicians Mr. Deakin's scheme will seem visionary; and yet the arguments that Sir Henry Parkes used on behalf of a mere Australian federation apply *a fortiori* to an Australasian federation.

"Among the great objects requiring central government," he declared "two of the most important related—firstly, to the Asiatic races, because it was impossible to foresee what political or social changes might take place in China, and how they might affect Australia; and secondly, to the Pacific Islands, because Australia should be mistress of the Southern Seas." Surely Sir Henry should here have used the word Australasia.

We must, however, it seems to me, be prepared, if anything of a practical nature is to arise out of these antipodean conferences and conventions, to expect—at all events, at first—an Australian and not an Australasian federation. As Sir Henry Parkes clearly sees, the difficulties in the way of welding the five colonies of the mainland and Tasmania into one State are sufficiently great to tax all the resources of colonial statesmen. Faint echoes have already reached us of grave differences on the all-important fiscal question. Victoria, the parent of protection in Australia, is now all for intercolonial free-trade; while South Australia, which has only recently adopted a protective tariff, is not at all

The Speaker—*continued.*

inclined to remove those barriers against her neighbours' products. On this point one of the representatives at the Conference maintained that the revenue from the Customs was inadequate to pay the interest on the total public debts in all the colonies. It is true Sir Henry Parkes, speaking on behalf of his own colony, declared that "New South Wales was prepared to go into this national union without making any bargain and without stipulating for any advantage whatever, trusting in the good faith and justice of a Federal Parliament." Furthermore, he declared in his somewhat grandiose way, that the "question of a common tariff was a mere trifle."

It is, however, self-evident that to speak of an Australian Dominion in which the provinces are divided by hostile Custom-houses, is simply to play with words, and an idle mockery. Lord Derby, writing to a correspondent on this very subject, in a letter which well deserves publication in full, observes:—"It is absurd as well as mischievous that communities, situated as the Australian colonies are, should exclude one another's productions by Custom-house regulations. The Americans of the United States, though not free-traders in principle, have at least entire free-trade within their own country." Self-evident as the truth of this may be, it may nevertheless appear an act of foolish self-sacrifice to the South Australians to open their ports freely to the more teeming manufactures of Victoria. Yet it is equally evident that time will only increase these intercolonial trade rivalries, and that the only thing for the "National Australasian Convention" to do is to face this fiscal problem at the outset, and by an overwhelming majority decide in favour of intercolonial free-trade. No doubt, as a concomitant of this, the Convention will insist on a uniform protective tariff against the rest of the world, including the mother-country. Sir Henry Parkes, sturdy old Cobdenite as he is, clearly foresees this eventuality, and is prepared to sacrifice free-trade on the altar of Australian Federation.

Another thorny question which the Convention will have to face is the selection of the metropolis. So far, nothing seems to be decided, except that the Sydney folks will never consent to Melbourne, nor the people of Melbourne recognize Sydney, as the seat of Government of "United Australia." Sir Henry Parkes has already declared in favour of Albany, the border-town on the Murray. The suggestion of Sir Charles Tupper, who speaks from his Canadian experience, that the names of a select number of cities and towns

The Speaker—*continued.*

should be submitted to the Queen for her final decision, is a timely one.

It remains to say something on the possible change of relations between England and Australia when the latter is welded into one compact State. There are not wanting those who believe that this federation will intoxicate our kinsmen with a sense of their own strength, and a consequent desire to free themselves from the trammels of the Empire. Read between the lines, this was the moral of a somewhat remarkable article in the *Nineteenth Century* by Sir Julius Vogel on the fancied right of a colony to secede, if it chooses, from the Empire. According to Sir Julius, this is an all-prevailing political heresy in Australia; and he seemed to insinuate that some of the Colonial statesmen who are now controlling the Federation movement are doing so in no friendly spirit to England. I remember so cautious and diplomatic an official as Sir Dillon Bell, in a public discussion on a paper read by Lord Carnarvon before the London Chamber of Commerce, on the "Mutual Duties of England and Australasia in time of War," expressing himself very clearly as to the duty of the mother-country, insisting on the fact that the colonies could not, at their own will, be suffered to sever their allegiance. This, he said, should be made quite plain before England rendered any further assistance to them in such matters as their naval and military defence.

All this implies, I venture to think, a distrust of the great self-governing colonies which is based on a fallacy. So far from Australian, still less Australasian, Federation weakening the tie between us, I firmly believe that, if we are wise, it will strengthen it. The predominant loyalty of all the speakers at the Melbourne Conference is one of its salient characteristics. What reason have we to suspect the genuineness of Sir Henry Parkes' splendid tribute to the virtues of the Sovereign, or the well-worded loyal address to Her Majesty which closed the proceedings on Friday last?

At the same time, it is evident that England must be content to permit these aspiring young communities to live in accordance with their own social and political necessities. There is no weightier lesson in the whole of Sir Charles Dilke's admirable work on the "Problems of Greater Britain" than in the chapter on the future relations of the colonies and the mother-country. The interference of the shifting politician, who, from time to time, fills under our system of party government the partially obsolete office of Colonial

The Speaker—*continued.*

Secretary, in the domestic concerns of any great self-governing colony, is too often still a cause of grave annoyance.

In the case of such a self-willed and powerful federated dominion as Australia, it might at any moment imperil the connection with the mother-country. Should we, however, continue to pursue with unfaltering step the broad path of true Liberalism, and suffer our adventurous kinsmen at the Antipodes—who, in the span of a single lifetime, have created a nation—to manage their own affairs, and refrain from all interference in their domestic concerns, then it may be predicted that, through "the crimson thread of kinship," there will be a lasting alliance and an undying affection between the scattered members of our race.

Globe—

March 1st, 1890.

LORD DERBY ON AUSTRALIAN FEDERATION.

Mr. A. Patchett Martin has written to Lord Derby requesting his opinion on Australian federation, and putting a number of specific questions. Lord Derby has sent the following reply:—

" Derby House, February 10, 1890.

"Sir,— In answer to your letter of yesterday I have more than once expressed in public, and am very willing to repeat my conviction, that the federation among themselves of the Australian Colonies is eminently desirable in their interest, and in no way opposed to the interest of England. The mutual jealousies of the various colonies seem to be rather increasing than diminishing, and if not checked they will become a serious inconvenience, possibly a danger. It is absurd, as well as mischievous, that communities situated as they are should exclude one another's productions by Custom House regulations. The Americans of the United States, though not free-traders in principle, have, at least, entire free-trade within their own country.

" Australian credit is already good in the markets of the world; but Australia consolidated for financial purposes would be able to borrow at a cheaper rate than any separate colony. Patriotism and public spirit, already abundant in Australia, cannot fail to be stimulated by the sense of belonging to a State which, if united, is, in point of wealth and population, already more important than many inde-

Globe—*continued.*

pendent Powers. Against these advantages I see nothing to set on the other side. I see no reason why Australian Federation should increase the strength of the feeling in favour of separation from England. Federation has not produced this effect in Canada, and there seems no cause why it should do so in Australia.

"For the Colonial Office it will be much easier and more convenient to deal with a single government than with several. As things now are, if Queensland, New South Wales, and Victoria disagree as to what they want the mother-country to do, the decision must necessarily give offence in some quarter. Once federated they will settle their difficulties among themselves, and the will of the majority will be taken for that of the whole. I do not believe in what is called 'Imperial Federation,' but if we leave Australia and Canada to govern themselves as they think best, they can have nothing to gain by separating from us, and something to lose in the protection which we give them. The only serious risk to the maintenance of the connection which I can foresee is that which would arise in the event of a naval war undertaken for some European object, in which Australians would feel little or no interest, while their trade would necessarily suffer. But whatever separatist tendencies might be displayed in such a contingency, I should expect them to be diminished rather than increased by the federal union of the various colonies. As to the veto on colonial measures, I entirely agree with you that its exercise would be impolitic in the case of such Bills as those by which the marriage laws of New South Wales, Victoria, and South Australia are proposed to be altered. Where local interests only are concerned, the decision of the Colonial Legislature should be respected; but it is not always easy to draw an exact line of distinction between local and Imperial concerns, and I think it better that the power should remain as at present, trusting to the good sense of Parliament and the public at home to guard against it being exercised in an arbitrary and unreasonable manner.—I remain, your obedient servant,—DERBY."

IMPERIAL PARLIAMENT.

HOUSE OF LORDS.

Monday, Feb. 17, 1890.

The LORD CHANCELLOR took his seat upon the woolsack at a quarter past 4 o'clock.

Australian Federation.

The EARL of BELMORE asked the Secretary of State for the Colonies whether there was any correspondence in his department on the subject of Australian federation; and, if so, whether it could be laid before the House without public inconvenience? The noble earl referred in terms of satisfaction to the progress which had been made so far in Australia at the Conference which had in the last week been sitting on this question. It was gratifying to him, both in its results and in the lines on which it had proceeded. Sir Henry Parkes, the Prime Minister of New South Wales, a gentleman with whom he had had the pleasure of working in former days, had gone on the lines not only of a Federal Parliament, but a Federal Executive. He also was strongly of opinion that it was only on those lines that what was desired could be practically carried out. There were certain ulterior questions which would have in due course to be considered in relation to the general subject of federation. The first of these was, supposing a Federal Parliament and Executive to be established, whether they should have a federal capital. His own feeling would be in favour of setting up Albany, a place which he thought had many advantages, as a federal capital. The next question that would have to be considered would be the question of defence—the contribution of the different colonies to the purposes of defence; and he was glad that this great and important question was now in a fair way of settlement. The other remaining point would be the question of a common tariff, as to which he had always had a very strong desire to see established, if possible, a system of colonial free-trade.

LORD KNUTSFORD. My Lords, with respect to the special question which the noble earl has asked me, I have to say that we have no public despatches or information which could be laid before the House. With respect to the general observations of my noble friend, he has expressed a feeling which is shared by the great majority, if not by all people in this country. Her Gracious Majesty, in the Speech from the throne, assured us of the lively interest with which she awaited the result of the Conference which was being held to discuss the important question of the federation of the Australaian colonies; and how warmly and keenly her Majesty's subjects in these great colonies appreciate that interest is shown by the loyal terms of the address, which was unanimously agreed to by the members of the preliminary Conference. The result of the Conference will be regarded as most satisfactory by all who believe, as I hope and as I am sure my colleagues do, that the prosperity, the welfare, the strength, and importance of these great colonies will be materially increased and secured by a closer union amongst themselves under some form of federal government, which will be for them to decide upon, leaving full powers to the local Legislatures. The Conference of the different colonial Legislatures will now be asked to agree to and hold a second Conference, at which no more than seven members will attend from each responsible self-governing colony, and four from each Crown colony. That difficult questions will be raised before that Conference I have no doubt. Some of those questions have been pointed at by the noble earl, who speaks with experience on this subject; but I would not even deal with them so far as he has done, because I think no good purpose would be gained now by our offering any opinion on those questions which are essentially for the members of the Conference to decide. I am quite satisfied that the difficulties of those questions will be overcome by the tact and judgment of the statesmen who are to take part in that Conference. I will conclude by saying that we do in this country most heartily wish success to their work. (Hear, hear.)

EARL GRANVILLE said that, after the very satisfactory statement of the noble lord the Secretary of State for the Colonies, it was unnecessary for him to say any more than he had the opportunity of saying on the motion for the adoption of the Address, that he and his friends entirely concurred with the Government on this subject. In his opinion, the noble lord had followed a judicious course in not going into the details of this matter. No doubt there were great difficulties to be contended with, but they ought to be, and doubtless would be, solved. On behalf of those with whom he acted, he could only say that they concurred very heartily in what had been done, and he hoped that the success of the federation of the great Australian colonies might be as great as that of the North American colonies had been. (Hear, hear.)

www.ingramcontent.com/pod-product-compliance
Lightning Source LLC
Chambersburg PA
CBHW051900300426
44117CB00006B/473